PHOTOGRAPHIC RECOG ☑ W9-CEO-085

The following numbers indicate the page and item number of each individual piece of jewelry: 12-5 (page 12, item 5); Color-6 (entire color page 6)

Loaned by Ares Incorporated, New York, NY - 429-1, 446-102, 449-1.

Courtesy of Ashland, Sarasota, FL - 618-6, 618-7, 619-8, 621-16, 622-17, 623-21, 623-28, 627-45, 630-53, 630-26.

Courtesy of Auktionshaus Peter Ineichen, Zurich, Switzerland - 121-103, 293-15 to 17, 303-41, 312-9, 619-11, 620-12, 622-22, 623-29, 626-40, 626-41.

Courtesy of Lydia S. Cormier, - 207.

Courtesy of N. Bloom & Son (Antiques) Limited, London, England - color 1 to 3 and 6-8, 131-18 to 20, 132-24, 134-33, 140-65, 197-54, 218-1 (bottom), 286-5, 308-2, 317-47, 323-4, 344-16, 393-6, 411-52, 438-58, 442-79, 447-110.

Courtesy of Christie's, 1979 - 90-2 (clasp), 91-3 to 8, 361-13 to 16, 362-17 to 20, 363-21 to 25, 364-26 to 30, 365-31 to 35, 366-36 to 40.

Courtesy of Christie's, 1980 - 100-5, 100-6, 188-22, 229-7, 319-57, 411-56.

Courtesy of Christie's, 1982 - 93-9, 134-34, 136-42, 136-44, 147-82, 163-49, 180-60, 195-35, 314-27, 376-29, 400-18, 404-33, 433-23, 444-92, 462-10, 468-55.

Courtesy of Christie's East, 1979 - 148-42, 168-6, 169-13, 169-15, 180-61, 190-12, 191-18, 399-15, 402-26, 408-44, 463-20, 465-33, 465-34, 501-219, 501-220, 506-256, 585-29.

Courtesy of Christie's East, 1981 - 78-50, 82-74, 84-93, 101-9, 149-44, 205-95, 370-4, 371-7, 372-10, 376-30, 390-6, 403-29, 442-79, 445-103, 625-36, 632-11, 645-47.

Courtesy of Christie's East, 1982 - 159-36, 199-62, 347-36, 377-37, 413-64, 420-10, 432-18, 445-105.

Courtesy of Christie's East, 1983 - 99-4, 101-11, 102-15, 106-31, 109-46, 109-47, 109-50, 111-58, 118-90, 120-98, 120-100-102, 128-3, 129-6, 129-7, 136-46, 140-67, 143-8, 145-16, 152-65, 152-1, 154-12, 183-4, 183-7, 185-5, 192-27, 196-47, 196-48, 200-70, 205-103, 218-3, 220-9, 225-6, 225-7, 226-10, 235-8, 239-24, 255-11, 255-13, 255-14, 285-2, 286-9, 286-10, 286-12, 287-3, 310-11, 313-13, 318-51, 318-54, 321-74, 323-8, 325-26, 340-4, 341-8, 343-13, 343-14, 344-18, 344-20, 345-24, 355-1, 355-4, 360-10, 367-41, 367-42, 367-44, 367-45, 369-54, 377-34 to 36, 378-39, 381-55, 393-4, 396-1, 398-11, 400-16, 400-17, 402-23, 403-27, 414-67, 414-68, 415-71, 417-80, 418-1, 418-3, 419-5, 426-20, 439-2, 439-62, 443-84, 443-87, 444-90, 444-94, 445-98, 448-122, 449-4 to 7, 457-6, 457-11, 467-46 to 48, 474-106, 480-32, 489-122, 489-124, 496-185, 509-285, 510-7, 511-11, 523-14, 523-18, 527-40, 529-51, 535-19, 540-21, 545-53, 546-55, 547-64, 555-1, 556-6, 556-9, 556-10, 557-13 to 16, 557-19, 559-27, 598-56, 599-59.

Courtesy of Christie, Manson & Woods, Ltd., London, England - 90-2, 102-16, 136-49, 138-53, 399-13, 557-10, 557-17, 571-31, 587-30.

Courtesy of Peter Delfino, Jr. - 346-29.

Courtesy of Facere, Seattle, WA - 75-28, 85-104, 119-95, 153-6, 205-97, 205-98, 229-13, 391-8, 404-32, 432-16, 434-32, 440-67, 443-85, 590-35, 591-41, 592-42.

Courtesy of G amd M Antiques, Washington, D.C. - 432-17.

Courtesy of Mr. and Mrs. R. Galey, Cheektowaga, NY - 159-37.

Copyright Hart Publishing Company, Inc. - 74-15 to 22, 75-23 to 27, 76-33, 77-45, 79-53, 80-58, 81-70, 81-71, 82-73, 83-86, 89-8, 90-1 (bracelet), 97-1, 98-6, 99-2, 103-19, 106-29, 106-30, 114-70, 114-72, 115-73, 115-74, 116-79, 232-31, 233-34, 242-4, 247-26, 270-6, 271-8, 275-31, 277-47, 280-63, 298-28, 302-37, 303-39, 305-9, 307-19, 316-38, 316-39, 316-41, 316-42, 319-56, 321-71, 322-1, 322-2, 323-5, 323-6, 324-19 to 21, 325-22, 325-23, 325-25, 328-1, 329-9, 337-20, 337-21, 378-40, 378-41.

Courtesy of Heirloom Jewels Ltd., Baltimore, MD - 76-37, 77-42, 80-61, 84-97, 101-14, 128-5, 138-57, 158-28, 159-38, 165-7, 205-99, 378-38, 381-57, 412-59, 415-70, 433-27, 579-14, 624-33, 649-67.

Courtesy of Heirloom's Ltd., Cincinnati, OH - 111-59, 155-13, 187-16 to 18, 594-44.

Reproduced by permission of the Director, Institute of Geological Sciences, Crown Copyright reserved, London, England - color 4 and 5.

Courtesy of Barbara B. Jackson - 162-45, 226-13, 227-14, 450-13, 558-23.

Courtesy of Jacqueline, London, England - 130-17, 132-26, 136-47, 155-14, 283-17, 371-5, 375-24, 379-43.

Courtesy of Carmelita Johnson - 121-22, 215-25, 458-16.

Courtesy of Trina Kearney - 188-25, 375-21, 413-66.

Courtesy of Ceceile Klein - 273-21, 273-22, 278-50, 311-17, 315-37, 486-94.

Used with permission 1896 Marshall Field Jewelry and Fashion Catalogue, Copyright by DBI Books, Inc. - 98-3, 141-9, 142-15, 143-3, 145-19, 149-45, 228-1, 228-5, 228-6, 230-17 to 22, 231-23, 231-25 to 27, 231-29, 232-30, 233-38 to 40, 234-3, 235-11, 236-12, 236-13, 238-22, 239-23, 240-29, 240-30, 250-3 to 6, 251-7 to 10, 252-11 to 14, 281-1 to 6, 282-7 to 12, 283-13 to 16, 283-18, 284-19 to 24, 285-25, 285-26, 287-1, 287-2, 291-10, 304-2, 309-10, 313-11, 313-12, 315-30, 321-80, 328-2 to 5, 329-6 to 8, 330-10 to 15, 338-22 to 27, 339-28, 339-29, 340-1, 340-2, 340-5, 340-6, 341-1 to 3, 341-6 to 7 (top), 342-4 to 6, 343-14, 343-15, 345-25, 350-49, 350-52, 351-54 to 58, 352-59, 352-60, 352-62 to 64, 353-68 to 70, 354-71, 354-72, 354-75, 354-76, 370-2, 381-55, 382-1, 383-2, 449-125, 451-1 to 3 (top), 451-8, 352-9 to 21, 453-22 to 28, 453-2, 453-3, 455-15 to 17, 456-25, 476-1 to 4, 476-7, 476-10, 482-53 to 57, 484-76, 487-98, 487-104, 487-105, 488-108 to 113, 489-122 to 124, 490-125 to 129, 493-152 to 157, 493-159, 496-184 to 186, 497-187 to 195, 498-196 to 202, 502-226 to 233, 503-234 to 236, 506-260, 507-267 to 269, 513-1, 515-8, 521-1, 526-31, 528-45, 531-61 to 67, 532-1 to 3, 533-9, 534-17, 535-23, 536-24, 536-28, 539-14, 539-15, 540-18, 540-20, 540-22, 544-48, 545-49, 546-57, 547-65 to 67, 548-68 to 72, 549-75 to 77, 560-1, 560-2, 562-13, 562-15 to 17, 563-19 to 24, 564-28 to 31, 565-2 to 4, 565-6, 565-7, 567-15 to 17, 568-19, 568-22, 570-28, 572-32 to 35, 617-1, 617-4, 620-15, 621-19, 621-20, 622-24, 623-25, 623-27, 624-30, 625-37, 626-38, 629-51, 630-54, 635-7, 635-9, 637-17, 638-20, 639-24, 639-26, 640-34, 642-36, 644-45, 647-55, 647-58, 648-62, 648-63, 649-66.

Used with permission 1894-95 Montgomery Ward & Co., Catalogue, Copyright by DBI Books, Inc. - 97-2, 141-1 to 8, 142-10 to 14, 142-16, 142-1, 143-5, 143-6, 144-12, 145-18, 146-28, 146-29, 147-30, 148-38, 148-39, 151-60, 152-66, 193-28, 193-29, 202-83, 203-84, 207-107, 207-108, 228-2, 228-3, 229-14, 230-16, 231-24, 232-32, 233-35, 233-36, 253-2, 253-3, 254-4 to 8, 256-15, 256-17, 257-18 to 20, 258-1 to 6, 259-7 to 12, 260-13 to 18, 261-19 to 24, 262-25 to 30, 263-31 to 36, 264-37 to 43, 265-44 to 46, 266-49 to 54, 267-55 to 60, 268-61 to 65, 270-1, 270-4, 270-5, 271-7, 271-9 to 12, 272-13, 272-14, 273-18, 273-20, 274-24, 274-27 to 29, 275-30, 276-37, 276-38, 276-40, 276-41, 277-48, 277-49, 278-54, 279-56, 279-57, 280-65 to 67, 280-71, 312-3 to 5, 313-15 to 18, 314-21, 314-23, 314-24, 315-28, 315-29, 315-31 to 36, 316-44, 319-59, 319-60, 320-62 to 69, 321-72, 321-73, 321-75 to 79, 323-10 to 13, 324-14 to 17, 429-4, 435-35, 435-37, 437-48, 437-53, 446-108, 447-111, 451-1 to 6 (top), 451-4 to 7 (bottom), 453-29, 453-1, 453-4, 454-6, 454-8 to 10, 454-12, 454-13, 455-18, 455-19, 455-21, 456-24, 456-26, 470-68 to 75, 471-76 to 82, 472-83 to 90, 476-8, 476-9, 482-58 to 60, 483-61 to 66, 484-77 to 81, 487-99 to 102, 488-114, 488-115, 490-129 to 136, 493-158, 493-160 to 162, 494-163, 494-164, 494-167 to 171, 498-203, 499-204, 503-237 to 240, 506-261, 507-270, 507-271, 514-2, 515-7, 522-7 to 9, 523-13, 523-14, 525-28, 526-33, 526-34, 527-40, 529-50, 530-57, 532-4 to 6, 533-8, 533-12, 535-18, 535-22, 536-25 to 27, 536-29 to 33, 539-13,

539-16, 540-23, 541-24 to 27, 543-38, 544-42 to 45, 545-51, 545-52, 546-54, 546-60, 547-61, 550-80 to 85, 555-1 to 5, 556-8, 566-12, 567-13, 567-14.

Courtesy of Munderly Antique Shows, Salisbury, MD – 406-37, 409-50, 647-54.

Courtesy of M. McAleer, London, England – 224-1, 225-4, 225-5, 225-9, 226-11, 226-12, 227-15, 316-40, 316-43.

Courtesy of James Robinson, Inc., New York, NY – 135-40, 410-51, 582-19, 585-23.

Courtesy of E. A. Shaw Antiques – 119-91, 186-10, 249-32, 253-15, 306-14, 347-34, 360-11, 360-12, 445-100, 478-20, 478-22, 480-31, 489-118, 515-3 to 5, 525-29, 526-32, 529-49, 538-9, 549-73, 549-74, 557-11, 574-2, 603-12, 617-2.

Courtesy of Robert W. Skinner, Inc. – 72-7, 85-105, 87-114, 89-10, 100-8, 101-13, 103-20, 104-23, 105-26, 105-28, 110-51, 110-52, 112-66, 120·96, 128-4, 133-28, 134-36, 161-41, 163-2, 167-3, 169-14, 172-27, 181-65, 186-11, 186-12, 192-26, 198-58, 201-77, 204-92, 218-2, 234-2, 255-10, 285-27, 300-31, 323-7, 337-16, 355-3, 356-9, 356-12, 357-5, 371-6, 376-27, 377-33, 381-55, 382-60, 389-4, 390-7, 393-5, 398-7, 398-8, 400-19, 400-22, 402-25, 403-28, 403-30, 403-31, 408-46, 412-58, 412-63, 415-72, 417-79, 418-2, 419-6, 419-8, 420-9, 421-14, 426-18, 431-11, 432-19, 435-34, 436-45, 437-46, 438-54, 439-58, 439-61, 441-71, 442-78, 443-83, 443-86, 447-116, 450-9, 460-30, 485-87, 530-58, 562-18, 579-12, 580-15, 590-34, 590-37, 596-52, 597-54, 598-57, 604-14, 617-3, 618-5, 619-9, 619-10, 620-13, 620-14, 624-32, 626-39, 627-45, 628-47, 629-52, 630-1, 630-2, 631-2, 633-2, 633-13, 633-14, 633-15, 634-2, 637-16, 638-22, 639-25, 642-35, 643-41, 643-42, 644-43, 647-56, 647-57, 648-60, 649-68.

Courtesy of Simeon, London, England – 144-13, 145-20, 151-58, 159-35, 204-91, 294-93, 358-1.

Copyright Sotheby Parke Bernet, Inc., 1979 – 73-19, 75-29 to 31, 76-35 76-36, 76-38, 77-40, 78-47, 81-66, 82-75, 83-84, 83-85, 83-87, 84-92, 84-93, 85-103, 86-106, 92-1 to 3, 92-5, 93-7, 93-8, 94-10 to 13, 95-15 to 18, 96-19 to 22, 100-7, 103-18, 103-21, 104-23, 108-42, 109-43, 109-44, 113-68, 115-75, 116-78, 116-80, 117-84 to 87, 120-97, 128-1 128-2, 129-8, 129-9, 129-11, 129-11, 130-12 to 16, 132-25, 133-29 to 31, 134-35, 135-38, 135-39, 135-41, 136-43, 136-45, 137-50, 138-54, 138-58, 139-59 to 61, 140-63, 140-64, 143-2, 143-4, 143-9, 144-14, 146-23, 146-26, 146-27, 147-34, 147-35, 148-36, 148-40, 149-47 to 49, 150-50 to 54, 151-56, 151-59, 151-61, 157-21, 157-24, 157-25, 160-33, 161-42, 161-43, 163-1, 163-2, 164-3 to 6, 165-8 to 11, 166-13, 166-14, 167-4, 167-5, 168-7 to 9, 169-10, 169-11, 170-19, 170-20, 171-24, 172-25, 173-30 to 33, 174-35 to 37, 175-38 to 40, 175-42, 176-43, 176-45, 176-45, 176-46, 177-47 to 50, 178-51, 178-53, 178-54, 179-55 to 59, 180-62, 181-64, 181-67, 182-69, 182-70, 183-3 183-5, 185-6 to 8, 186-14, 187-19 187-20, 188-24, 188-25, 189-3 to 189-5, 190-7 to 11, 191-20, 192-24, 192-25, 193-30 to 32, 194-33 to 35, 195-38, 195-41, 196-43, 196-44, 196-46, 198-55, 198-59, 199-61, 199-63, 199-67, 200-69, 200-71, 201-74, 201-75, 203-84, 203-85, 204-89, 204-90, 204-94, 205-96, 206-104, 206-106, 206-107, 207-109, 207-2, 208-4 to 6, 218-1 (top), 218-2, 236-15, 238-20, 239-25, 239-26, 243-7, 243-9, 244-13, 245-15, 245-17, 246-19, 246-23, 247-24, 253-1, 255-9, 278-55, 279-59 to 62, 280-70, 285-3, 304-1, 304-3, 304-4, 305-8, 305-11, 306-12, 306-13, 306-15, 307-18, 309-6 to 9, 310-12, 310-13, 310-14, 311-16, 311-1, 312-8, 314-25, 314-26, 317-45, 317-46, 322-81, 327-2 to 4, 339-30, 342-9, 343-12, 345-25, 345-26, 345-27, 346-28, 346-30, 348-42, 350-48, 353-66, 356-10, 356-11, 359-4, 359-6, 369-49, 370-3, 372-9, 375-25, 375-26, 378-42, 379-45, 379-49, 387-27, 388-28, 389-2, 391-10, 399-12, 400-20, 402-24, 405-34, 405-35, 405-36, 406-38, 407-42, 408-43, 409-48, 412-57, 412-60, 413-61, 417-78, 418-4, 419-7, 420-12, 421-15, 423-1 to 3, 423-6, 424-8, 424-10, 424-11, 425-12 to 15, 426-16 to 19, 426-21, 430-8, 430-9, 434-28, 434-29, 435-38, 435-39, 437-49, 438-57, 441-72, 442-77, 443-88, 443-89, 444-91, 446-104, 447-115, 488-120 448-122, 448-23, 450-10, 454-5, 456-22, 461-1, 461-2, 462-6 to 8, 462-12, 463-14, 463-15, 463-17, 463-19, 464-21, 464-22, 464-26, 465-28, 465-30 to 32, 466-35, 466-36, 466-38 to 43, 467-44, 467-49 to 52, 468-53 to 58, 468-60, 469-61 to 67, 473-91 to 93, 474-103 to 105, 474-107, 475-108 to 110, 475-116, 475-117, 476-6, 477-14 to 17, 478-18, 479-31, 480-33 to 39, 481-41 to 50, 482-51, 482-52, 483-69, 484-72 to 75, 485-88 to 90, 486-91, 489-116, 489-117, 489-120, 489-121, 492-147 to 150, 494-166, 495-174 to 177, 496-179 to 183, 499-206 to 211, 500-212 to 218, 501-223 to 225, 504-241, 506-255, 507-263, 507-264, 509-286, 510-3, 510-5, 511-12 to 15, 512-1, 512-2, 515-9, 518-10, 521-4, 530-54, 535-20, 537-4 to 7, 538-8, 542-35, 543-39, 544-47, 545-50, 546-58, 560-3 to 5, 561-7, 561-9, 561-10, 563-26, 563-27, 564-32, 564-33, 564-35, 569-24, 569-26, 570-27, 575-4, 576-5, 577-9, 579-11, 582-20, 583-21, 588-30, 588-32, 595-47, 595-48, 596-51, 597-54, 597-55, 625-34, 631-1, 631-3 to 6, 632-7 to 10, 633-12, 634-4, 637-18, 638-9, 638-21, 640-28, 641-33, 642-39, 644-44, 645-48, 649-64.

Courtesy Spinning Wheel Magazine, Antique & Early Crafts, September, 1973 – 290-8, 292-13, 294-20, 295-21, 295-22, 297-26, 298-27, 301-34, 301-35, 302-36, 303-40.

Copyright Sotheby Parke Bernet, Inc., 1980 – 72-3, 72-4, 72-5, 73-9, 73-10, 73-12, 77-39, 77-42, 77-44, 78-48, 78-49, 78-51, 79-52, 79-54, 79-56, 79-57, 80-59, 80-62, 80-64, 81-65, 81-67 to 69, 81-72, 82-76, 82-80, 82-81, 83-82, 83-83, 83-88, 83-89, 84-91, 84-95, 84-96, 85-99, 85-100, 85-103, 85-105, 86-107 to 109, 87-110 to 113, 87-115, 90-1 (clasp), 93-6, 95-14, 96-23, 104-24, 106-33, 107-36, 108-40, 108-41, 109-48, 109-49, 110-53 to 57, 111-62, 112-64, 112-65, 113-67, 116-81, 119-92 to 94, 120-99, 132-21 to 23, 137-52, 138-55, 139-62, 140-67, 143-7, 144-10, 144-11, 145-21, 146-24, 147-31, 147-33, 148-37, 148-41, 149-43, 149-46, 150-55, 151-57, 151-62 to 63, 152-67, 153-4, 153-7, 154-8 to 10, 158-26 to 28, 158, 159-31, 159-32, 167-1, 167-2, 170-17, 170-18, 171-21 to 23, 172-28, 172-29, 174-34, 175-41, 176-44, 182-68, 182-1, 182-2, 183-5, 184-1 to 3, 185-4, 186-13, 187-15, 190-9, 191-13, 191-14, 191-6, 191-17, 192-21 to 23, 194-36, 195-40, 195-42, 197-49, 197-50, 197-52, 198-57, 200-72, 200-73, 201-76, 201-78, 202-79 to 81, 203-85, 203-87, 203-88, 205-100, 205-101, 207-3, 228-4, 231-28, 234-5, 235-7, 238-19, 238-21, 242-1 to 3, 242-5, 243-6, 243-8, 244-10, 244-12, 245-14, 245-16, 246-18, 246-21 to 23, 247-25, 247-27, 249-33, 249-34, 249-2, 270-3, 286-7 to 8, 294-19, 304-5, 305-6, 305-7, 305-10, 307-16, 307-17, 307-20 to 22, 308-3, 311-15, 312-6, 314-22, 318-50, 318-52, 318-55, 319-58, 320-61, 327-1, 337-17 to 19, 340-3, 342-8, 342-10, 344-17, 344-21, 347-35, 349-47, 350-50, 355-2-3, 355-5-6, 358-2, 359-3, 359-7, 360-9, 368-47, 369-51, 371-8, 372-12, 374-17, 376-28, 376-30-31, 377-32-33, 379-43, 379-46, 384-11, 387-24 to 26, 388-29, 388-1, 389-3, 390-5, 391-8, 391-11, 392-1, 396-2 to 3, 397-5, 397-6, 399-14, 407-40, 407-41, 409-47, 411-53 to 55, 415-69, 416-73, 416-74, 420-11, 421-13, 423-4, 423-5, 424-7, 424-9, 429-2, 429-3, 431-13, 434-30, 434-31, 436-44, 437-20, 437-21, 437-47, 437-50 to 52, 438-55, 438-56, 439-64, 440-65, 441-73, 441-75, 442-80, 442-82, 444-95 to 99, 445-101, 446-106, 446-108, 447-113, 448-117, 448-122, 449-3, 450-11, 456-23, 456-1, 456-3, 457-4, 458-14, 458-15, 460-26, 461-4, 462-9, 462-11, 462-13, 463-16, 464-24, 465-29, 468-59, 474-101, 475-115, 477-13, 479-26, 479-27, 479-29, 479-30, 483-68, 484-70, 485-83 to 86, 486-95 to 97, 487-107, 489-119, 491-141, 492-143 to 145, 492-151, 499-205, 501-221, 501-222, 504-247, 505-251 to 254, 507-265, 507-266, 508-275, 510-6, 511-17, 517-2, 517-5, 518-8, 519-17, 519-19, 520-23, 524-19, 525-25, 527-37 to 39, 534-13, 538-10, 540-19, 541-28, 542-33, 546-59, 547-62, 555-2, 556-7, 557-18, 560-6, 561-8, 561-11, 561-12, 562-14, 563-25, 564-34, 565-1, 569-23, 570-30, 574-1, 575-3, 578-10, 579-14, 581-16, 583-21, 583-23, 584-25, 594-45, 594-46, 596-49, 596-50, 601-63, 629-50, 627-1, 628-8, 630-10 to 14, 637-15, 639-23, 640-29, 641-30, 641-31, 643-40, 643-46, 645-49, 646-50, 646-52, 648-59, 649-65.

Courtesy of Kathleen Sullivan – 359-5.

Courtesy of Victoria's, Williamsville, NY – 98-7, 152-2, 157-22, 157-23, 163-49, 189-1, 196-45, 197-51, 205-105, 233-37, 290-9, 291-12, 300-32, 323-9, 353-67, 356-8, 367-43, 417-77, 430-10, 431-12, 447-114, 597-53.

Courtesy of Howard Vaughan, F.G.A., Henley-On-Thame, England –73-8, 73-14, 77-41, 88-5, 101-10, 114-71, 135-37, 145-17, 145-22, 154-11, 155-15, 162-46, 166-12, 189-2, 189-6, 191-15, 191-19, 198-56, 199-65, 199-66, 204-92, 218-1, 219-3, 220-7, 220-8, 220-10, 220-11, 272-15, 275-34, 285-1, 308-1, 308-5, 312-7, 314-19, 322-3, 324-18, 325-24, 343-11, 345-22, 349-45, 430-7, 433-25, 435-36, 439-63, 441-74, 441-76, 524-20, 550-78, 582-18, 602-2.

Courtesy of Everna Marguerite Zabell –221-1 to 3, 222-4, 222-5, 223-6, 223-7.

THE OFFICIAL
PRICE GUIDE TO
ANTIQUE JEWELRY

BY
ARTHUR GUY KAPLAN

We have compiled the information contained herein through a *patented computerized process* which relies primarily on a nationwide sampling of information provided by noteworthy collectible experts, auction houses and specialized dealers. This unique retrieval system enables us to provide the reader with the most current and accurate information available.

EDITOR
THOMAS E. HUDGEONS III

FIFTH EDITION
THE HOUSE OF COLLECTIBLES, WESTMINSTER, MARYLAND 21157

DEDICATION

To Robin—my wife, partner and friend.
To Jennifer and Sarah—our daughters.
To My Parents—whose love and teachings have
guided me through the years and whose wisdom
continues to give me strength.
To Gail, Howard, Rachael and Ariel—whose love
is a continued source of support.
To Marcia and Harold—two very
special people.

IMPORTANT NOTICE. The format of **THE OFFICIAL PRICE GUIDE SERIES,** published by **THE HOUSE OF COLLECTIBLES, INC.,** is based on the following proprietary features: **ALL FACTS AND PRICES ARE COMPILED THRU A COMPUTERIZED PROCESS** which relies on a nationwide sampling of information obtained from noteworthy experts, auction houses, and specialized dealers. **DETAILED "INDEXED" FORMAT** enables quick retrieval of information for positive identification. **ENCAPSULATED HISTORIES** precede each category to acquaint the collector with the specific traits that are peculiar to that area of collecting. **VALUABLE COLLECTING INFORMATION** is provided for both the novice as well as the seasoned collector: How to begin a collection; How to buy, sell, and trade; Care and storage techniques; Tips on restoration; Grading guidelines; Lists of periodicals, clubs, museums, auction houses, dealers, etc. **AN AVERAGE PRICE RANGE** takes geographic location and condition into consideration when reporting collector value. **A SPECIAL THIRD PRICE COLUMN** enables the collector to compare the current market values with last year's average selling price indicating which items have increased in value. **INVENTORY CHECKLIST SYSTEM** is provided for cataloging a collection. **EACH TITLE IS ANNUALLY UPDATED** to provide the most accurate information available in the rapidly changing collector's marketplace.

All of the information, including valuations, in this book has been compiled from the most reliable sources, and every effort has been made to eliminate errors and questionable data. Nevertheless the possibility of error, in a work of such immense scope, always exists. The publisher will not be held responsible for losses which may occur in the purchase, sale, or other transaction of items because of information contained herein. Readers who feel they have discovered errors are invited to **WRITE** and inform us, so they may be corrected in subsequent editions. Those seeking further information on the topics covered in this book are advised to refer to the complete line of Official Price Guides published by The House of Collectibles.

©1985 The House of Collectibles
All rights reserved under International and Pan-American Copyright Conventions.

Published by: The House of Collectibles
P.O. Box 149
Westminster, Maryland 21157
Phone: (301) 583-6959

Distributed by Ballantine Books, a division of Random House, Inc., New York and simultaneously in Canada by Random House of Canada Limited, Toronto.

Manufactured in the United States of America

Library of Congress Catalog Card Number: 84-080522

ISBN: 0-87637-289-2

TABLE OF CONTENTS

ACKNOWLEDGEMENTS

This book involved the cooperation and assistance of a countless number of individuals and firms, many of which are mentioned under the Photographic Recognition list. Thanks are due to Howard Vaughan, Jacqueline, Raizel Halpin of Ares Antiques, Ian Harris of N. Bloom & Son (Antiques) Limited, Helen E. Rice and Elizabeth Armstead of Victoria's, Karen Lorene of Facere, Sarah N. Kutas of Christie's East, Susanna J. Fichera of Robert W. Skinner, Incorporated, Mary Feilden of Christie, Manson & Woods, Ltd., Carmelita Johnson, Bernice H. Friedman of Heirlooms Ltd. and Lydia S. Cormier for her fine line drawings. Special thanks to Susan Garten of Heirloom Jewels, Ltd., Baltimore, Maryland and Carolyn Guzski, M. K. Harwood of James Robinson, Inc., Kathy Mitzel, typist, Maggie Nimkin of PB Eighty-Four, Roy Perry, photographer, M. Dougas Schmidt, photographer, The Victorian Society in America, The Surrat Society, Clinton, Maryland, and Duane Suter, photographer. My family also deserves recognition for their sacrifies during the years it took to prepare this book.

Dozens of private individuals have supplied photographs or lent their collection to me to have photographed, with the sole express direction that their name not be included. Without this assistance it would have been impossible to collect the number and range of photographs included in the book. A special thanks to each of you.

The substantial portion of the glossaries and textual material included in this book concerning silver, gold and diamonds have been edited by the author from *The Official Investors Guide, Buying, Selling, Gold, Silver, Diamonds* by Marc Hudgeons.

PHOTOGRAPHIC RECOGNITION

Cover Photograph: Photographer — Bernie Markell, Orlando, FL 32809.

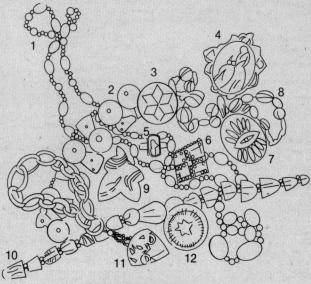

COVER DESCRIPTION

1. Beads, carnelian, crystal rondelles — **$175.00-$225.00**
2. Bracelet, watchcocks, cabochon amethysts, base metal, English, c. late 18th, assembled late 19th — **$300.00-$400.00**
3. Brooch, marble, silver, Scottish, c. mid-19th — **$125.00-$150.00**
4. Brooch, ivory cameo, swivels with hair design on reverse, English, gold, c. mid-19th — **$650.00-$800.00**
5. Ring, cameo of full figure, Etruscan granulation around shank, gold, Victorian — **$350.00-$400.00**
6. Pendant/brooch, natural pearls, diamond in center, gold, c. mid-Victorian — **$1500.00-$1800.00**
7. Locket, diamonds, rubies, gold, c. mid-Victorian — **$1600.00-$1800.00**
8. Necklace, turquoise with matrix, gold, Arts and Crafts — **$450.00-$500.00**
9. Brooch, leaf motif, malachite, silver, Victorian — **$150.00-$200.00**
10. Necklace choker, agates, carnelians, bloodstone, silver ball links, Scottish, c. mid-Victorian — **$300.00-$400.00**
11. Bracelet, heart motif, tortoise shell, silver, c. late Georgian — **$450.00-$550.00**
12. Brooch, fancy-cut cabochon amethysts, seed pearls, Etruscan granulation, gold, c. mid-Victorian — **$650.00-$750.00**

ABOUT THE AUTHOR

Arthur Guy Kaplan, a Maryland attorney, has been actively involved in the antique jewelry field for the past 12 years. In addition to participating in antique shows throughout the United States and lecturing on antique jewelry, items from Mr. Kaplan's collection have been exhibited nationally in several museum exhibitions, including *REMEMBER THE LADIES* co-sponsored by the National Endowment for the Arts, Philip Morris and Clairol, (1976); *A TIME TO MOURN* co-sponsored by the Museum of Stonybrook, N.Y. and the Brandywine Museum, Del. (1980-1981); and *MOURNING BECOMES AMERICA* sponsored by the Harrisburg Historical Society, PA (1976).

He has published numerous articles on various facets of antique jewelry both here and abroad and has recently acted as expert consultant for the article on antique jewelry in *THE ENCYCLOPEDIA OF COLLECTIBLES,* Time-Life Books, Inc., (1979).

The author requests that the reader forward any photographs and descriptions for inclusion in subsequent volumes. Information regarding any errors or other omissions would be welcomed. Send information to:

Arthur Guy Kaplan
P.O. Box 1942
Baltimore, Maryland 21203

PREFACE

The 1986 edition of this book is the 5th edition in the series. As in previous editions, over 300 additional color and black and white photographs have been interspersed throughout. The black and white photographs primarily consist of additions to the brooch and earring sections, though photographs of other types of jewelry have also been included.

The 1985 market for antique jewelry remained relatively steady with few significant price increases or decreases. Watches which were in decline during the past several years, bringing lower prices than anticipated at the major auction houses, seemed to have begun to rally and hold a steady price. The most dramatic rise in prices, however, can be seen in fine signed pieces, large Art Deco items and large single stone rings. The jewelry from the 1940s has also become popular, though the prices have remained relatively low in comparison to jewelry of other eras.

As with all types of antique jewelry, including watches, the price is affected considerably by the condition of the merchandise. It is critical to carefully examine each piece of jewelry to be certain that all of the parts are original. Special attention should be given to the fittings attached to the rear of a brooch, the earring wires and the chains attached to a pendant. These areas, as well as others, have frequently been changed over the course of years and as a result the value of the entire piece of jewelry is not as great as if it was all original. Be sure to view the stones carefully as they are frequently replaced. The cut of the stones can indicate that they are not contemporary with the style of the piece. Frequently, stones have been replaced as well as the replacement of prongs which hold the stone. As an example, during the Georgian period it was customary to have a necklace with a ribbon attached rather than a chain. The ribbon went around the back of the neck and could be adjusted to the desired length. When necklaces such as these were inherited during the Victorian period, individuals frequently had Victorian chains permanently attached to the necklace as was the fashion of the day. Very few of the original necklaces with the loops for the ribbons exist in the marketplace. Other examples were Georgian brooches, known as stomachers. They were extremely large brooches with the ability to come apart to convert into pendants, earrings, hair decorations, etc. As brooches of this type were inherited, from generation to generation, they were divided among several members of the family. Though you might own a beautiful pair of Georgian earrings, the wires may well be Victorian with both earrings originally having hung from a large brooch during the Georgian period. The converted earrings have a definite value on the antique market but as an original stomacher the value would be greatly increased. Reviewing the thousands of illustrations with descriptions in a book of this nature should enable an individual to obtain a feel for the type of jewelry of the different periods and help determine what should be original to a piece.

The color section is of particular interest. In the center of the color section are two gem plates from the Institute of Geological Sciences in London. These have been included to give you a comparison of the various colors of the different gem stones. The color section also has six additional plates with thirty to fifty pieces of jewelry on each plate. Though these photographs are smaller than the photographs reproduced throughout the black and white sections of the book, they are of particular interest because they demonstrate a feel for the color combinations that were used. I have included items from the Georgian period through the 1940s in this section for just this purpose. Also the various types of enamel processes which have been defined at the beginning of the text are pictured in the color section.

To get optimum use of this book the reader should use the price ranges presented as a comparison from one item to another within the book and use the photographs with the descriptions to identify the period and style of jewelry. Exposure to as many photographs as possible is invaluable to the novice as well as the experienced collector. Therefore, there are carved wooden jewelry along with tortoiseshell, ivory, coral, seed pearls and a multitude of lesser known gem stones. The gold craftmanship and the enamel work is a history lesson in itself.

INTRODUCTION

Antique jewelry, as in all fields of antiques, can be found almost anywhere. The major sources for the purchase of antique jewelry consist of organized indoor antique shows, retail stores, auction houses and outdoor flea markets, all of which are located throughout the United States and Europe. Each country has its own particular flavor in the kind of antique show or market available to the person interested in the purchase of antique jewelry. In Madrid, Spain, the Rastro is an area, open every Saturday and Sunday, consisting of block upon block of street vendors who lay down a sheet and set up a small wooden frame table to display and sell their wares. Jewelry and watches are often found among the items for sale. The following photograph illustrates one of the hundreds of booths at the Rastro selling pocket watches.

RASTRO, MADRID, SPAIN

BERMONDSEY, LONDON, ENGLAND

Paris and Rome are both famous for their enormous flea markets. London is in a class by itself. It is possible to spend several weeks in London and visit antique shops or outdoor antique markets from morning to night without going to the same place twice. Every Saturday in London is an outdoor-combination-indoor market at Portobello Road. It has become as much a tourist attraction as a serious selling market. Camden Passage is open every Tuesday, Wednesday and Saturday, Bermondsey every Friday, and scores of indoor markets throughout the City are open the entire week. On almost any Sunday a one-day indoor fair of approximately 50 to 100 dealers can be found in the ballroom of one of the local hotels. The country outside of London is as active as the City of Dickens in its selling of antiques.

Both nationally known and local auction houses in the United States sell a tremendous volume of antique jewelry. As an example, one auction house in New York sold almost ten million dollars in jewelry during the fall of 1980. Indoor antique shows and outdoor flea markets have developed a large devoted following in the United States. Antique shows provide hours of entertainment and free education without the requirement of a single purchase. Most antique jewelry dealers are anxious to share their knowledge and allow the public to examine and handle their stock.

The purpose of this book is to present as many illustrations as possible of jewelry from 1750 to 1930 with the primary emphasis on the 19th century. This book is arranged in chapters according to the type of jewelry, i.e., rings, bracelets, pendants, chains, etc. Each chapter is then sub-divided. After each picture is a brief description and a price range, in order to enable you to compare the described item of jewelry to a similar piece that you own or might acquire. Unfortunately, some of the descriptions are not detailed due to the fact that photographs were supplied from many sources — private collections, museums, auction houses, and other antique dealers. When the jewelry photograph is from an auction catalogue, information from the description in the auction catalogue has been included in the written description in this book. Sometimes the description has been modified by the author. Descriptions were only supplied with some of the photographs, therefore it was impossible to give you specifics such as the length or weight of each item.

The data to calculate the prices listed in this book are from numerous sources, all of which were compiled and adjusted by the author. The photographs of jewelry from auction houses supplied the author both an estimated range that the items would sell for as well as the actual prices realized at the date of the auction. The photographs supplied from antique shops and dealers were also supplied with the current retail price of those items from the respective dealers locality. Individuals that supplied photographs from their private collections often presented the insurance appraisal as a guide. All of the above information was considered, with the ultimate responsibility for the price range falling upon the author. When an item is sold at auction the price can indicate one of many things — it can be a realistic indication of the retail price of that item on the current market or it can be either grossly lower or grossly higher than the actual retail price due to the lack of interest or a frenzy of activity on a particular day. Information has been supplied from several sources in London, England, as well as the United States and the Continent. One English pound has been valued at $1.75 and one Swiss franc has been valued at .48¢ in the price calculations.

The best and simplest advice that we can give to the individual interested in purchasing a piece of antique jewelry is that they should only purchase an expensive piece of jewelry from a dealer or auction house whom they have confidence in or who has a reliable reputation. A receipt should be given listing in detail the description of the item purchased along with the date and a statement that the item can be returned if found not to be accurately described.

INSURANCE TIPS

During the past several years, burglaries have increased substantially due to the dramatic rise in price of gold and silver. Consequently, family heirlooms and recently acquired antique jewelry need to be properly insured. If you are purchasing a piece of antique jewelry solely for investment purposes, then that piece of jewelry should be stored in a safe deposit box for maximum safety. If the piece of antique jewelry is also being purchased to wear and enjoy then the jewelry needs to be accessible and convenient for use. Therefore, it should be hidden in your home. If you do hide the jewelry we strongly suggest that you inform a close relative where the jewelry is hidden. Unfortunately, we have heard too many stories of individuals hiding jewelry and then forgetting where the jewelry was hidden or becoming ill and unable to retrieve the jewelry. Though there are enumerable excellent locations to store jewelry at home, we suggest that the jewelry not be kept in the bedroom, which is the first area explored by burglars. A jewelry box with costume jewelry which is worn on a daily basis should be kept in the bedroom. If a burglar discovers the jewelry box with the insignificant jewelry, it is possible that he feel he has discovered your entire collection. The jewelry should be hidden in a location where there is obviously other metal objects. Sophisticated burglars use metal detectors to explore throughout a house the location of gold and silver. In the kitchen where pots and pans are stored or in bathrooms around piping are excellent locations for the hiding of good antique jewelry. The above locations are not to be taken as the only effective hiding places but rather as two examples. Do not hide antique jewelry in places of extreme temperature such as freezers or behind radiators. Certain gemstones can be detrimentally affected by extremes in temperature.

Regardless of whether or not your jewelry is retained in a safe deposit box or hidden in your home, it should be properly insured. The first step in obtaining full and complete insurance coverage is to obtain a written appraisal of your jewelry. The appraisal should be by an expert in the field who is recognized as an authority. The appraisal should include a detailed description of each item of the jewelry along with a retail insurance replacement cost. Appraisals can be for many purposes. Jewelry can be appraised at a wholesale value to inform the owner of the value of the jewelry if the owner wished to sell the jewelry on a wholesale level. Jewelry can also be appraised on a retail basis to inform the owner of the retail value of the jewelry if the owner wished to sell the jewelry to a private party. The appraisal which you need for insurance purposes is a replacement value. This is the value placed on the jewelry by the appraiser which indicates the cost to replace that piece of jewelry. Since many pieces of antique jewelry are unique and irreplaceable, the replacement value will indicate the value in replacing the lost item with a similar item of comparable quality and workmanship. Appraisals cannot take into account the sentimental attachment that one has to a piece of jewelry.

Once you have a written appraisal, the appraisal should be forwarded to your insurance agent to be listed as a schedule on your homeowners policy. The vast majority of homeowner policies do not cover jewelry or silver unless they are specifically listed on the policy, except for a $500.00 limitation on unscheduled jewelry and silver. The policy owner will pay an additional premium each year on those items which are specifically listed on the policy. If your deductible is $100.00, and your jewelry is not specifically listed as explained above, then regardless of your loss, you would receive from the insurance company $400.00, which would be the $500.00 maximum coverage minus the $100.00 deductible, irrespective of the value of the jewelry. Each insurance policy is unique and the figures can vary. The appraisal on antique jewelry should be re-examined every two to three years so that current market trends and changes can be reflected in a new appraisal.

Though neither the sentiment nor an exact duplicate of a stolen piece of jewelry can be replaced, if you are properly insured, you will be able to purchase a comparable piece of jewelry on the open market at the sources discussed at the beginning of the introduction to this volume.

CLEANING, REPAIRING AND STORING ANTIQUE JEWELRY

Antique jewelry by its very nature is delicate. Gemstones, whether in antique or contemporary mountings, all have different physical characteristics and different degrees of hardness from the hard gemstone, diamond, to the softest, talc. Some gemstones are affected by heat, some by cold. Others absorb moisture. As a result, we do not recommend the amateur to clean or repair any jewelry containing gemstones. The risk of damage and destruction is immense. Any reliable jeweler or antique jewelry dealer will be more than glad to offer to clean your jewelry and to refer you to a source that is capable of repairing your jewelry. Antique jewelry, as contemporary jewelry, should be stored in a soft lined jewelry box divided into sections so that one piece does not rub against another. Do not wrap jewelry in plastic or use rubber bands to hold items together as a chemical reaction can occur which can cause damage to your jewelry. Specific instructions for the cleaning of diamonds are located in the diamond section.

THE HISTORY OF JEWELRY

In discussing antique jewelry, it is first necessary to define what is "antique jewelry." The British Antique Dealers' Association defines "antique jewelry" as that jewelry which was made before 1830, with 1830 signifying the beginning of the Industrial Revolution. Even though some simple machinery was used in the manufacture of jewelry prior to 1830, it was basically a handcraft. In the past ten or fifteen years, jewelry made after 1830, during the Victorian period, has surged in respectability and popularity, both with museum curators and collectors. The purpose of this section is to provide an overall view of the styles and characteristics of Georgian and Victorian jewelry and to guide and develop the abilities of the reader to identiry Georgian and Victorian jewelry.

GEORGIAN JEWELRY

Georgian jewelry is that jewelry which was made during the reign of King George I - IV, from 1714 to 1830:

George I	1714-1727
George II	1727-1760
George III	1760-1820
George IV	1820-1830

Georgian jewelry therefore encompasses the majority of the Eighteenth Century and the first quarter of the Nineteenth Century.

Before reviewing specific popular styles of bracelets, rings, brooches, etc., a feeling for the entire Georgian period, both as to the historical background and influences which affected the type of jewelry worn, as well as general statements as to popular trends through all field of jewelry during this period will be presented.

There are many trends which can be reviewed, but perhaps the most popular or significant are the following:

Faceted gemstones
Engraved goldwork
French influence, especially during the first 25 years
Imitation jewelry

During the Eighteenth Century, British jewelry was largely influenced by foreign fashion, particularly the French and Italian. England increased its political power throughout the world and prospered. Prosperity attracted a migration of craftsmen of all fields of the decorative arts to England. As a result, the background and training of the craftsmen was of a continental flavor. The austere elegant English influence affected their work.

For the first time in history, there was a small but prosperous, growing middle class. The wealthy traveled throughout England, but the roads were unsafe with highwaymen. As a result, imitation jewelry was developed during the Eighteenth Century — paste, cut steel, pinchbeck and marcasite.

The imitation jewelry was of equal craftsmanship and design to jewelry consisting of genuine gemstones and precious metals.

During the early Georgian period, the reign of King George I, 1714-1727, the French influence was predominant in all fields of art. There was a considerable migration of French artisans to England. The opulent French rococo asymmetrical style dominated the arts. There was no real individual British style of jewelry, as compared to the Victorian period, when the British outshone themselves in developing new styles of jewelry, decade after decade.

The jewelry during this early Georgian period consisted almost entirely of designs of nature with a fine sense of color, form and design. Jewelry was delicate and light in appearance. Many articles of jewelry were "en tremblant." The jewelry, set with precious gemstones, was entirely hand-made and consequently, was individualistic in design. There was no mass production of jewelry during the early Georgian period. Fine articles of jewelry would be inherited from generation to generation.

Jewelry with less precious gemstones was produced in greater quantity, though not mass-produced as in the Victorian period. Garnets, turquoise, coral, paste and imitation gemstones were popular for the less expensive jewelry.

The natural theme throughout jewelry consisted of flowers, leaves, insects, birds, feathers and ribbons.

During the early Georgian period, precious stones were more important than the metals, and therefore, the jewelry almost entirely consisted of simple designs encrusted with gemstones. The designers were interested in incorporating as many diamonds or other precious gemstones as possible into a single piece of jewelry. The most popular motifs for diamond jewelry were:

Baskets of flowers
Sprays of foliage
Curving feather plumes

As the Georgian period progressed during the second half of the Eighteenth Century, engraved gemstones and intaglios became popular. James Tassie, a London craftsman, developed a secret paste formula around 1766, in which he produced paste repliicas from wax models of gems. These are available on today's market, and are commonly known as Tassies.

The small but prosperous middle class during the beginning to mid-Georgian period developed a need for secondary or imitation jewelry. Therefore, a great quantity of paste or rhinestones were substituted for diamonds, cut steel or marcasites substituted for silver, and pinchbeck substituted for gold. Christopher Pinchbeck was a London alchemist who developed a metal consisting of copper and zinc around 1732. The end product looked remarkably like gold and wore extremely well. There is still Pinchbeck available on today's market, though the majority of what is called Pinchbeck is simply an old gold-filled material.

During the last quarter of the Eighteenth Century, jewelry became more austere and dignified as a result of a classical art influence. The directorire style, 1795-99, was developed. It consisted of a very classic simplicity of dress, with simple jewelry styles. It was not popular or in vogue for the French to display their wealth, and, as a result, the imitation gemstones and substitutes for precious metals again became popular. Lesser-known gemstones, such as agate, developed great popularity. Cabochon cut gemstones were the rage. As a result of the French political system at the end of the Eighteenth Century, the apprenticeship system for the arts was destroyed. With the destruction of the apprenticeship system, the high standard of craftsmanship also was forsaken. The clients of the jewelers were no longer critical or cultured, but rather semi-educated and the new rich did not require such a high standard of craftsmanship.

With the beginning of the Nineteenth Century, there was no real change in style of jewelry merely because a new century had begun. The French influence was still predominant. Nevertheless, the classic simplicity of Greek dress and style influenced mythological subjects, scrolls, foliage, classical styles and festoon motifs in jewelry.

During the end of the Eighteenth Century and the beginning of the Nineteenth Century, sentimental or classical subjects were popular in France, with the result that jewelry frequently reflected portraits of women writing at a classical pedestal, lovers' knots in hair, flaming hearts, doves, bows and quivers.

Beginning in the Nineteenth Century, cameo brooches and earrings were extremely popular. Empress Josephine was fond of shell cameos, and, as a result, shell cameo brooches and earrings were extremely popular during the beginning of the Nineteenth Century. England contributed Wedgewood cameos, which were frequently exported to France for setting. Garnets, turquoise, amethyst, and particularly pearls, were extremely popular during the beginning of the Nineteenth Century.

The archaeological excavations at Pompeii were under French government control from 1806-1814, when they played a major role in influencing jewelry styles:

Mosaic
Pseudo-classical cameos with gold grandulated borders
Rams heads

Another popular style developed in France during the first quarter of the Nineteenth Century was the "ear of wheat" motif. During this period, the pavé style of setting gemstones reached a height of popularity, not to be exceeded until the 1930's in the United States. In the pave style, gems are set close together, low down, and held by small turned over beads, almost as if they were a paved road. With the popularity of pave mountings, diamond jewelry developed a major revival during the first quarter of the Nineteenth Century.

IMITATIONS OR SUBSTITUTES

It is important to understand the general characteristics of the imitation jewelry that was used, because it is available on today's market.

PASTE: Paste was developed in France, though the English quickly developed a sophistication in the manufacture of paste. Paste is a high-quality lead glass, which is faceted and polished as if the stone were a genuine gemstone. In the middle of the Eighteenth Century, rock crystal was used as a substitute for diamonds, along with paste.

Paste was a substitute not only for diamonds, but colored paste was a substitute for colored gemstones such as pink topaz, rubies, emeralds, sapphire and garnet.

Paste opals were also manufactured with a colored oil backing to imitate the color of an opal. On today's market, you might come across paste set around the bezel of an Eighteenth Century watch or surrounding the frame of a miniature portrait. Both buttons and shoe buckles were also popular motifs for the use of paste. Paste was most frequently set in silver with a gold back.

Paste was important both as a substitute for diamonds but also for its own sake. It is difficult to distinguish early paste from white sapphire, rock crystal and diamonds without sophisticated testing equipment.

The Georgian jeweler often set a large faceted paste stone in a brooch which was surrounded with genuine faceted diamonds. Any Georgian diamond article of jewelry should be closely examined to identify each stone.

IRON: During the late Georgian period, one of the substitutes for precious jewlery was jewelry made from iron. This began in 1804, when the Berlin Iron Foundry was started and reached a peak during the 1814 Prussian War. Precious metal jewelry was turned into the government to show support and substitutes were presented the owners made from a very delicate lacy ironwork. Very little of this jewelry has survived, as it rusted and was very brittle. Due to the fact that it was not made of precious material, it was not regarded as valuable.

CUT STEEL: Cut steel was developed in the second half of the Eighteenth Century as a substitute for silver jewelry. It was primarily manufactured in Birmingham and Sheffield, both of which became jewelry manufacturing centers. The earlier pieces of cut steel are more valuable than the later pieces, partially due to the fact that the earlier pieces are individually cut, rather than an entire sheet of steel molded and cut. Cut steel is used through the end of the Georgian period and into the Victorian period. The pieces of cut steel are highly polished and riveted to the item of jewelry.

MARCASITE: Marcasite is a piece of iron pyrite which is faceted as if it were a gemstone and set in silver.

ENAMEL: Enamel jewelry played an important role in the Georgian period, though it was a different role than in the Seventeenth-Century jewelry. Seventeenth-Century enamel jewelry was enameled on both the front and the back of the item, whereas Eighteenth-Century jewelry was primarily only enameled on the front with either a plain back or an engraved back. During the first half of the Eighteenth Century, continental enamel work was extremely delicate in nature.

Clothing of gentlemen at the beginning of the Eighteenth Century consisted of very tight pants with cutaway coats. As a result, watch pockets became popular and the watches were an excellent source for the delicate enamel work. Boxes and chatelaines were also prime sources for the enamelers' art.

During the early Georgian period, the favorite color enamel was a deep, rich blue with designs of stars, urns and bows frequently set with small diamonds, pearls, or marcasites.

During the reign of King George II, in 1750, the Battersea Enamel Works opened in England and resulted in brightly-colored enamel over copper boxes. This reinforced the enamelers' art in Britain for jewelry. Around the same time in Bilston, England, a rival enamel factory began producton, but it closed during the last quarter of the Eighteenth Century. Though enamel was delicate and popular, it should be remembered it was only used on the front of an item of jewelry in the Eighteenth Century, and if it was a bracelet, it was only enameled on the clasp and not on all of the links, as would have been popular in the Seventeenth Century.

GEMSTONES: As stated earlier, the Georgian period is known as the age of the faceted gemstone. It should be noted, that Georgian diamonds have 24 facets, rather than the 58 facets of the brilliant-cut diamonds on today's market. You should also note that there are very sophisticated diamond reproductions of Georgian jewelry that are made in Portugal and Spain today. The most obvious way to spot such a reproduction is to watch the marketplace carefully and feel suspect of any jewelry of which you see several identical pieces. The little monkeys hanging from each other on a swing set in silver with gold backs and old mine cut diamonds are generally reproductions. Also the little roosters.

There are several types of jewelry, which, though not unique, are distinct and were extremely popular during the Georgian period. Nutmeg graters, vinaigrettes, chatelaines, shoe buckles, fobs and hair ornaments were all popular during the Georgian period.

As a curiosity, train or hankie holders became popular during the second half of the Eighteenth Century.

The hair comb was popular during the first quarter of the Nineteenth Century. it was arched with mosaic, pearls, ivory, or coral set in the top part of the tortoise hair comb.

One characteristic that spread through many different types of Georgian jewelry is the convertible nature of the jewelry. In other word, a hair comb would be extremely elaborate, but the top jeweled section would be convertible so that it could be removed and worn as a pendant or a brooch.

BROOCHES: At the end of the Seventeenth Century and the beginning of the reign of King George I, women's fashions included very stiff bodices with pinched-in waists and large skirts. As a result, visual attention was focused on the female breasts. The fashion dictated and the style developed that brooches became extremely large and were worn from the neck to the waist. This form of brooch was known as a stomacher. A stomacher was frequently three or more large pieces of jewelry which fit together to basically cover the entire section from the breasts to the waist of the woman. The stomachers most often were an openwork motif in a flower of foliage design set in silver with gold backs. Sometimes the front would be delicately enameled and the entire item would have tassels hanging from it.

Natural themes, such as flowers, foliage and ribbons were the most popular styles, along with single curved feathers completely diamond-set.

NECKLACES: With fashion dictating bare necks and shoulders, delicate necklaces that were fluid in movement with lots of fringes and cascading drops became popular. Again, flower motifs, foliage, feathers, bows and ribbons were the styles. Most of the necklaces consisted of the front section with a loop at either end to be attached to a ribbon so that the length of the necklace could be adjusted. Consequently, the Georgian necklaces that are on the market today frequently have a gold chain attached to the remainder of the necklace rather than the ribbon. This was most frequently done during the Victorian period when the necklaces were inherited. It is rare to find an original Georgian necklace without the converted chain attached.

Necklaces were all very light and delicate in nature. The design was paramount and the gemstones were secondary. Paste was frequently used, though the wealthy used quantities of small diamonds in a delicate, flowing design. Along with the designs described above, the snake motif became popular with enameled heads and gem-set bodies. Cameos linked in panels by gold chains were employed and heart-shaped lockets with enamel fronts and hair under crystal backs became popular. The gems set in necklaces frequently had backs which were totally closed in metal settings with foil behind the stone. If genuine diamonds or gemstones were employed, the metal setting might have a small opening in the back.

The following are the major characteristics of Georgian necklaces: flowing lines, naturalistic design, adaptible, convertible, graduated motifs and tassels.

EARRINGS: Georgian earrings were similar in style to the necklaces in that they were long, dangling, free-swinging and encrusted with gemstones. The earrings generally used larger diamonds or paste stones than the brooches or necklaces. The motifs were the same — flowers, foliage, ribbons, knots and feathers.

BRACELETS: Bracelets were popular and most frequently consisted of wide bands set with jewels or a wide velvet band with a clasp consisting of a medallion, portrait miniature, or cameo. Rows of pearls or gold-link chains with an important clasp consisting of diamonds, paste, or a miniature were also popular. When the clasp was significant, it frequently detached so that it could also be worn as a pendant or a brooch.

Flower themes were the predominant theme in reference to the bracelets. During the classical revival at the end of the Eighteenth Century, cameos became popular. The serpent theme was also a motif employed, often in blue enamel with rows of diamonds.

RINGS: Rings were perhaps the most popular form of Georgian jewelry. The stones were set in silver with gold backings and gold shanks. Cameos were popular, as were diamond cluster rings, which were pavé set with paste in the center surrounded by genuine diamonds. Emeralds, rubies, garnets, amethysts, and topaz were extremely popular for rings during this period.

Motifs: Love motifs — engraved messages and mottos
       Hearts and flowers
       Crowned heart with hands

During the second half of the Eighteenth Century, enamel and gold band rings were worn by those in mourning with the enameled names of their loved ones and the date of death. The classical style of a drooping classical figure painted in a sepia paint on a navette shaped piece of ivory as the focal point of a memorial ring was popular during the second half of the Eighteenth Century. The designs frequently included Grecian funeral urns and inscriptions. Enamel was used as background in earlier Georgian pieces, rather than in the later Georgian pieces.

The Georgian period ended in 1830, and the Victorian period began with the reign of Queen Victoria in 1837. Victoria loved jewelry. Her influence was controlling in the development of many styles of jewelry peculiar to the Victorian period. It should be remembered that the general characteristics of the Georgian period were an imaginative, delicate use of colored stones, and an aesthetically pleasing and light-hearted approach to jewelry, whereas the Victorian jewelry was heavy-handed with an overexuberant use of colored stones. The flower theme was predominant throughout all fields of Georgian jewelry.

VICTORIAN JEWELRY

Perhaps because of a feeling of nostalgia for the security of the last century, the arts of our Victorian ancestors are increasing in popularity.

Prior to the Nineteenth Century and during the first few years of the Nineteenth Century, jewelry was only for the very wealthy, and correspondingly, each piece was individualistic in design and executed to the highest standards.

If any two words can be characteristic of a period — QUANTITY and VARIETY would stand for the Nineteenth Century. The Industrial Revolution created a growing middle class, and the successful businessmen loaded their wives with jewels to display their new found wealth. The ladies were decorative, but not active members of society. Mechanical processes were developed to mass produce jewelry, such as the stamping-out of gold settings by 1835.

France had been the leader of jewelry design during the Georgian Period, but with the reign of Queen Victoria, Britain became a major jewelry center. Victoria ruled from 1837-1901. She was fond of jewelry and wore it profusely. Her reign is divided into three periods, the first being the Early Victorian or Romantic Period — 1837-1860. The jewelry during this time was imaginative, delicate, and reflected a nostalgia for the Middle Ages. Gold was plentiful, especially because of the 1849 California Gold Rush.

The Mid-Victorian or Grand Period ran from 1860-1885. The jewelry became bolder in design as women became bolder. Women began to work, and in 1870 gained the right to keep the money they earned. Jewelry continued to be plentiful. With the growing use of electric light, diamonds began to displace colored gemstones for evening wear.

A greater sense of social responsibility and an even more liberated woman emerged during the Late Victorian or Aesthetic Period — 1885-1901. The universities opened education to women and women began to question the wearing of jewelry. The lesser gemstones became popular — Periodot, Alexandrite, Tourmaline, Garnet, and Opals. With the opening of the South African Diamond mines, and the expanded American tourist trade, large solitaire diamond rings became popular.

With the revolt against tradition during the last quarter of the Nineteenth Century, the Arts and Crafts Movement and Art Nouveau Movement were developed. The Art Nouveau period created a revolutionary style of jewelry. It is characterized by female heads with long flowing hair, delicate enamels, sweeping flowers, and soft-colored stones. The Art Nouveau period ended the Nineteenth Century in a flourish of originality.

SELLING ANTIQUE JEWELRY

The public is frequently baffled as to how to dispose of a piece of antique jewelry. Before selling any antique jewelry the first step that you must take is to obtain an idea of the value of that jewelry. If it is an item which you have recently purchased, then at least you have a conception of the retail value. If the jewelry was given to you by a family member or you purchased it several years ago, then you should obtain a competent appraisal of the jewelry before attempting to sell the jewelry. It is to your benefit to inform the appraiser that you desire to sell the jewelry and that you wish to know both the retail and wholesale value. If the appraiser is aware of the purpose of the appraisal, he will best be able to give you a realistic price according to your needs.

It is highly recommended that you obtain an appraisal from an appraiser that charges you by the hour rather than a fee based on a percentage of the appraised value. The appraiser should be a recognized authority with practical experience in the field of pricing antique jewelry. It is also strongly recommended that you only deal with an appraiser who is not interested in the purchase of the jewelry that is being appraised. Even if the appraiser is highly ethical, the appraisal might have the appearance of impropriety if the appraiser has the ability to purchase the jewelry being appraised.

Once you have an idea of the value, there are several sources to investigate before disposing of the jewelry. The major auction houses conduct periodic auctions. We suggest that you avoid the summer months as the auction prices are frequently lower during those periods. Before consigning the jewelry for auction, it is critical that you obtain a written statement as to the terms of the auction. It is necessary that you understand all of the costs for which you will be responsible. Each auction house has their own procedure. You must be informed as to the insurance costs while the jewelry is in the possession of the auction house, the cost of photographs of the jewelry in a catalog, the reserve and the buy-back procedures. If an important piece of jewelry is photographed in the catalog, additional interest is sparked on a national level. The fee to the auction house is usually based on a percentage of the price realized for the jewelry at auction. This percentage can be negotiated depending on the importance of the jewelry being sold. The percentage figures range from 10% up to 20% of the price realized.

The reserve procedure is critical to understand. The reserve simply means a dollar figure below which the auction house will not sell the jewelry. For example, if the reserve on a diamond ring is $500.00, then the auction house will not be able to sell the diamond ring for less than $500.00. Most auction houses, which prepare printed catalogs, list an estimated price range for which the item will sell. Sometimes these figures are realistic and other times they are not. The estimated price range has no relationship to the reserve figure which is confidential between the seller and the auction house. If the jewelry does not bring a price equal to or more than the reserve figure, it is customary for the consignor, the individual selling the jewelry, to pay a percentage of the highest bid received at the auction as a fee. For example, if our diamond ring, which was reserved at $500.00, received a high bid of $400.00, then you will have to pay a percentage of $400.00 to the auction house for their efforts in attempting to sell the jewelry for you. They will return your ring to you and you will pay them the agreed percentage of $400.00 for their troubles.

Another method of disposing of antique jewelry is to sell it to a friend at or below the retail value which you have obtained from an appraisal. If you cannot sell it privately, it can be sold directly to a dealer who will place the jewelry in his stock and resell it in the ordinary course of his business. A dealer obviously must pay less than the retail value. The selling price by the dealer must include all of the overhead expense incurred by the dealer. Even a dealer only participating in antique shows has a considerable overhead including but not limited to booth rent, showcase rent, electricity charges, transportation, motel and food expenses, stationery, continuing education costs, supplies, employee expenses, etc., etc. You should be aware that whether the dealer is an established shop or a dealer who participates solely in antique shows, the operating expenses can be significant and, therefore, the price offered by a dealer will normally be considerably less than the retail value of the item of jewelry. Though there is no magic percentage figure, a dealer will normally purchase an item from 40% to 60% of its retail value depending on the desirability of the item.

If time is not a factor, perhaps the best avenue to dispose of good quality antique jewelry is to locate an antique jeweler in which you have confidence and to place the jewelry on consignment with that dealer. This means that the dealer will take your antique jewelry and attempt to sell it at the highest possible price. When the jewelry is sold, the dealer will take a percentage off of the top of the sale and turn over the balance to you. If you sell your jewelry through a dealer on consignment, you will receive a higher price than if you sell it outright to the dealer. Prior to giving the jewelry on consignment, the percentage which the dealer will retain for his efforts should be agreed upon in writing. The written statement indicating the percentage to be paid to the dealer for selling the jewelry should also include a statement that the dealer will be responsible for insuring the jewelry while it is in his possession. Antique jewelry, as all commercial fields, is affected by the economy. It can frequently take several months or up to a year or more before a special piece of antique jewelry can be sold. Therefore, you should have patience when placing an item on consignment.

INVESTING IN ANTIQUE JEWELRY

Though the price of gold, silver and diamonds has drastically fluctuated in the past few years, the value of antique jewelry has either remained constant or steadily increased in value. Contemporary gem quality diamonds at the end of 1982 have decreased in value considerably from their recent record price levels. Gold has decreased from a high of $800.00 to between $350.00 and $400.00 per ounce. Even with these fluctuations, the value of high quality antique jewelry has remained constant. As explained in detail throughout the section on gold, silver and diamonds, the value of a piece of antique jewelry is based on workmanship, style and historical significance as well as the precious materials out of which the piece of jewelry is manufactured. An excellent example is jewelry woven from human hair which is illustrated throughout the book. In the bracelet section are bracelets woven from hair, in the ring section are rings woven from hair, etc. Though most of the hair jewelry has gold fittings, the gold is almost insignificant to the value of the item. A contemporary jeweler will dismiss a piece of hair jewelry as valueless. It is not the type of jewelry, as are many pieces of antique jewelry, which the contemporary jeweler is familiar. Nevertheless, a piece of hair jewelry in mint condition is a wonderful example of jewelry with significant historical value which is highly prized by a select few. A simple ring might be worth hundreds of dollars with factors affecting its value that the contemporary jeweler is unaware. The color of the hair, the form of the weave and the dated inscription within the jewelry adds to its significance.

The data to calculate the prices listed in this book are from numerous sources, all of which were compiled and adjusted by the author. The photographs of jewelry from auction houses supplied the author both an estimated range that the items would sell for as well as the actual prices realized at the date of the auction. The photographs supplied from antique shops and dealers were also supplied with the current retail price of those items from the respective dealers locality. Individuals that supplied photographs from their private collections often presented the insurance appraisal as a guide. All of the above information was considered, with the ultimate responsibility for the price range falling upon the author. When an item is sold at auction the price can indicate one of many things — it can be a realistic indication of the retail price of that item on the current market or it can be either grossly lower or grossly higher than the actual retail price due to the lack of interest or a frenzy of activity on a particular day. Information has been supplied from several sources in London, England, as well as the United States and the Continent. One English pound has been valued at $1.45 and one Swiss franc has been valued at .45¢ in the price calculations.

THE ALLOYING OF METALS

Alloying is the blending together of one metal with one or more of another metal. As all metals can be melted by intense heating, there is virtually no limitation to the variety of alloys that can be produced by varying the recipes. In the case of gold and silver used for jewelry the desire is to give the metal greater durability by introducing a proportion of a stronger metal.

Alloying is accomplished in the refineries. The metals must be measured out in exact proportions and blended thoroughly together. If the blending is not thorough, the resulting product will show streaks, as no two metals have precisely the same color or surface appearance.

DURABILITY

In their pure states, 24K gold and .999 + silver are too soft for use in manufacturing and are hardly ever employed in that state, except in instances where a minute quantity is needed or the metal can be beaten very thin into sheets. An example of the use of 24K gold is in the "Gold Tissue" used by bookbinders, by which the spines of leather bindings are imprinted with the book title, author, etc., and the covers worked with elegant "gold tooled" designs. But for any articles intended to be handled a great deal and withstand use, gold and silver must be alloyed. Sterling silver tableware is softer than most silver coins, containing 92.5% silver against only 7.5% copper. Countries and regions have customarily manufactured jewelry in different purities of gold. For instance, America is known for 14K and 10K, England for 15K and 9K and India and the Far East for as high as 22K.

STRETCHING OR "WATERING DOWN"

Economic and commercial considerations often lead to alloying, so that an article may have the appearance and general quality of bullion. Jewelry makers use gold alloyed down sometimes to less than 50%; such pieces may still be advertised as gold, but they will react positively when tested by nitric acid because of the high copper content.

GOLD

PHYSICAL PROPERTIES OF GOLD

Atomic Number - 79
Atomic weight - 196,967
Boiling point - 2,970F
Crystal system - face-centered cube

Hardness (Mohs) - 2½-3
Melting point - 2,063F
Specific gravity (24K Pure) - 19.32
Symbol - Au
Tensil strength, psi - 19,000

WHITE GOLD

White gold is made by taking yellow gold and alloying it with one of the white metals, in sufficient quantity to change its color and at the same time provide stability and toughness. Nickel or palladium are generally chosen, sometimes a combination of the two. White gold can, just like yellow, be of high or low grade, depending upon the degrees of alloying. This can only be determined via testing.

In antique jewelry diamonds are frequently set in silver with yellow gold on the reverse for strength or in white gold. Diamonds set in yellow gold reflect a yellowish tint.

GOLD PURITY BY KARAT

When used in the manufacture of jewelry and decorative objects, the fineness or grade of gold is stated upon the item by a karat mark. These karat marks should not be taken at face value in some cases, because

(1) in the jewelry trade it is legal to mark gold one full karat higher than it actually is, if solder has been used in making the article. Recent legislation in the United States requires jewelry gold articles to be accurately marked in reference to their karat content, which is known as "plumb gold."

(2) The mark could refer merely to an outer covering or plating, which would have to be determined by chemical test or specific gravity.

KARAT	CONTAINS % PURE GOLD	
24K		This is the highest degree of purity. It denotes gold unalloyed with any other material. However, when expressed in decimal terms, 24K is not indicated as 1.000 — which would be absolute purity — but as .999 fine, because it is not possible to refine out every trace of adhering metal. Gold of 24K is extremely soft and weak. It cannot be used in the making of jewelry. Nor is it suitable for coinage. 24K gold is generally seen only in the form of bars and ingots or as gold plating. For plating it is quite useful as strength is supplied by the core metal.
23½K 97.92		The very small proportion of alloying still does not permit use in manufacturing.
23K 95.83		
22½K 93.75		
22K 92.67		Some coin gold and jewelry, though not that of the U.S., is 22K.
21½K 89.58		Here the alloy becomes greater than 10%. U.S. coins are approximately 21½K.
21K 87.50		
20½K 85.42		
20K 83.33		Still too soft for most jewelry, despite the addition of nearly 17% alloy.
19½K 81.25		
19K 79.17		Will still show negative with nitric acid — that is, that proportion of copper, though more than 20%, is not high enough to react with the acid.
18½K 77.08		
18K 75		The highest grade of gold used regularly in the jewelry industry, consisting of three parts bullion to one part copper. Will not react to nitric acid, whether applied on the surface or to a filed notch.
17½K 72.92		
17K 70.83		
16½K 68.75		The gold now contains more than 30% base metal (copper), but even at this level will react the same to nitric acid as pure 24K.
16K 66.67		Exactly two parts of gold to one part copper. No reaction when tested by nitric acid. Usually most dental gold is 16K.

KARAT	CONTAINS % PURE GOLD	
15½ K	64.58	
15K	62.50	Widely used grade of gold for jewelry in England.
14½ K	60.42	
14K	58.33	The composition is more than 40% copper, but still will not react to acid testing. One of the most widely used grades of gold for jewelry in the medium price range in the United States.
13½ K	56.25	
13K	54.17	
12½ K	52.08	The proportion of copper is now almost as high as the proportion of gold. Nevertheless, nitric acid will show the same reaction as with higher grades.
12K	50	Exactly one-half gold and one-half copper. Very extensively used in the manufacture of low-priced jewelry in the United States. Will show brownish tinge when tested with nitric acid.
11½ K	47.92	Now the percentage of copper exceeds that of gold.
11K	45.83	
10½ K	43.75	
10K	41.67	Sometimes used in jewelry. Shows a more marked reaction to nitric acid than 12K. Almost all class rings are 10K in the United States.
9½ K	39.58	
9K	37.50	Not much more than one-third gold. Widely used grade of gold for jewelry in England.

TESTING METHODS FOR GOLD

There are two matters to be determined in testing objects believed to be made of gold:

1. Whether the item is gold or something of similar appearance.
2. The fineness, because gold ranges from pure (24K) to heavily alloyed, such as 9K.

Determination that the exterior is gold means little, as the article could be any metal with a gold plating. Even if the plating is very high quality bullion, it will be of only minimal value.

Nitric acid is the standard test for gold. It has no effect on gold but reacts to the basemetal alloys. It will not react to gold of 10K or higher. Therefore, nitric acid is useless in determining the karat fineness of gold between 14K and 24K. For this, the touchstone method is used.

NITRIC ACID TEST. A notch is filed on the object, in an inconspicuous place. This is done because of the possibility of plating. It need not be very deep — about ⅟₃₂nd of an inch will do on most items. A drop of nitric acid is placed on the file mark. If no change in color is noted, this item is 10K gold or higher. If a very brownish tinge appears, it is lower than 10K. When the acid turns green, this indicates that the object contains no gold whatsoever.

The acid should be wiped away as soon as results are obtained.

TOUCHSTONE TESTING. If the article has not reacted to nitric acid, we know it to be 10K or better. To determine the exact karat, a "streak" is made by rubbing it firmly across a touchstone (these are available from dealers in jewelry supplies). Streaks are then made on either side of the test streak, using gold-testing needles of different karats. These needles are sold in sets with gold tips. Each needle is marked by karat. Normally you would begin by streaking 10K and 18K alongside the test streak. A drop or two of aqua regia is then spread across the streaks. If the test streak is either 10K or 18K, its reaction will be the same as that of the 10K or 18K needle streak. If the test streak dissolves faster than the 10K needle streak but slower than the 18K, it is most likely 14K. This can be proved by making a new test and streaking the item plus the 14K needle side by side. Their reactions to aqua regia should be identical or very close. A slight variation could mean that the test object is an odd karat, such as 15K or 17K, or that the streaks were not made with equal pressure.

Aqua regia can be made by combining 8 drops of water with 2 drops of hydrochloric acid. Ten drops of nitric acid is then added. Do not inhale the fumes and keep the stopper in the bottle when not in use.

Nitric acid has long been the chief chemical for testing precious metal. It is volatile and should be handled and stored with caution. It is, as the name denotes, an acid, which will seriously burn human skin.

A sensible precaution is to wear a long-sleeved shirt and heavy gloves while using nitric acid. Rubber gloves are not recommended because this acid can burn through them very rapidly. Canvas laborers' gloves, or gloves of good heavy leather, are better. Do not attempt to store a sizable quantity of nitric acid in the home, because of the hazard it presents in case of fire or other accident. When using it, take care not to inhale its fumes at close range. Nitric acid should be used in a well ventilated room, not in cellars or attics. Pets and children should be removed from the area. Do not smoke while using it. Always use the glass "dipper rod" attached to the bottle stopper, rather than attempting to use brushes or other devices. Brushes are not safe for working with nitric acid as they can cause tiny droplets of the liquid to fly about.

SPECIFIC GRAVITY. As the specific gravity method is a highly reliable test for determining the nature of metals and mineral substances, everyone who buys or intends to buy gold, silver, jewels, etc. ought to become familiar with it.

This is an extremely delicate test which, if not performed to precise standards, will not yield correct results. On the other hand its accuracy when properly carried out is far about that of almost all other methods of testing, including those employing more costly apparatus.

If one plans on trading commercially or handling a great deal of valuables, it would be wise to purchase a specific gravity testing device. Otherwise, a "homemade" substitute can be used, whose reliability will be fairly close to that of professional models.

Specific gravity is the ratio at which a material displaces water in relation to its bulk. We all know that lead sinks while cork floats on water. This tells us nothing beyond the fact that some materials are heavier than others, which could as easily be learned by weighing on an ordinary scale. Specific gravity goes much deeper than the mere difference between sink-or-float. It give the weight of an object in relation to its exact size, as water fully encompasses whatever is submerged in it and therefore measures far better than rulers or calipers. As every object of the same material gives the same specific gravity reading regardless of size, the specific gravity reading easily distinguishes between gold and copper, silver and copper, or alloys of these metals, as well as helping to identify precious gems.

A specific gravity scale may be concocted from an ordinary pan scale calibrated in grams. Remove the pan and tie a length of string (thin nylon is good) from the pan holder, at the extreme southeast edge as the scale faces you. The string should not be long enough to touch the desk on which the scale rests. A glass tumbler about ¾ths filled with water is then positioned beneath the string. It may be necessary to rest the tumbler upon a low platform to arrive at the proper height. It will need to be positioned so that the article to be tested, when tied to the string and dropped into the glass, is fully submerged but does not touch the bottom of the glass.

As the object dangles in the glass, a reading is taken of the weight indicated on the scale. This is called the "weight in water." It does not determine the specific gravity but is the chief step in arriving at that figure. To get the specific gravity reading, the object must then be weighed on the scale in the ordinary manner, or "in air." Subtract the weight in water from the weight in air (the latter will always be a higher number), then divide the weight in air by the loss of weight in water. The answer will be the item's specific gravity.

Example A:
Weight in water, 55.5 grams
Weight in air, 60 grams
Loss of weight in water, 4.5 grams
4.5 divided into 60 = 13.33 (specific gravity of the item)

The item tested in this sampling, with a specific gravity reading of 13.33 was 14K yellow gold.

Depending on the accuracy of your scale you will probably only be able to obtain very close approximations rather than precise readings. In the previous example we got a specific gravity of 13.33 and called it 14K gold. This is because 13.33 is the closest in the following table to 14K gold. As in all of these tests and formulas there is always "visual inspection" involved and in this case the item appeared to be 14K gold, so the conclusion reached after testing was obvious.

Example B:
Weight in water, 27.10 grams
Weight in air, 30 grams
Loss of weight in water, 2.9 grams
2.9 divided into 30 (weight in air) = 10.34 (specific gravity of the item)

The item tested in this sample, with a specific gravity reading of 10.34 was .925 sterling silver.

In this example we got a specific gravity of 10.34 and called it .925 sterling silver. This is because it is the closest on the following table to sterling silver. The "visual inspection" in this case indicated the item to be .925 sterling silver, so the conclusion reached after testing was obvious. It also must be kept in mind that, even using advanced equipment, specific gravity readings can vary minutely on the same grade of silver or gold. This is because the alloy material is not always exactly the same. If bronze or brass is used as an alloy instead of pure copper, .925 sterling (or any other grade of silver) made from it will not have the exact same specific gravity reading as .925 alloyed with pure copper.

SPECIFIC GRAVITIES OF METALS

Brass	8.52
Bronze	8.82
Copper	8.93
24K gold	19.32
22K gold	17.72
18K gold	15.47
14K gold	13.55
10K gold	11.75
Iron	7.81
German silver	8.74
.999 silver	10.50
.925 sterling silver	10.31
Stainless steel	7.8
Platinum	21.45
Tin	7.31

METHODS OF WEIGHING GOLD

You don't put gold ingots or silver earrings on a bathroom scale. Techniques employed for weighing precious metals are highly sophisticated, because a slight difference in weight can mean great difference in value. Unfortunately there isn't as yet any single universally agreed-upon method, though several are reliable if performed correctly.

The weight of gold may be given in troy ounces, pennyweight, or by metric division. Troy is the most common and most universally understood by jewelers and bullion dealers. Pennyweight, an invention of the British and later adopted in the United States, is somewhat archaic but widely followed. It has convenience on its side. The metric system, now becoming international, has not yet penetrated into the bullion market to a very major extent and probably will not do so for a number of years.

As statements of weight are likely to be given in grains by one dealer, grams by another, and dwt (pennyweight) by a third, it is important that anyone buying or selling gold become familiar with the different weight systems.

It may be of interest to note that equipment used for weighing precious metal is today indentical in design and function to that of the ancient world, as the balance principle is relied upon rather than scales with springs.

AVOIRDUPOIS WEIGHT. Like troy weight, the avoirdupois system also uses pounds and ounces, but these are not equal. Avoirdupois is the common method by which just about everything — except precious metals — is weighed. Your bathroom scale is an avoirdupois scale. Unlike troy scales, avoirdupois scales may be equipped with springs.

PENNYWEIGHT. Abbreviated as DWT. ("D" stands for penny, in British coinage, and "WT" for weight). The system of weighing by pennyweight was an innovation of English merchants of the distant past, who used pennies as counterweights on their scales. The American penny weighs two pennyweight, which equals 48 grains. The important point is that a pennyweight, used as a measure of weight, is 24 grains. So it is readily apparent that pennyweight is an extremely small proportion of a precious metal. A Pennyweight is considerably less than one full ounce. But this is a very useful method of measuring, as gold is frequently bought and sold in quantities well below a full ounce. When the price of gold is $500 per troy ounce, you should divide it by 20 (because there are 20 dwt per troy ounce) to get the price per dwt, which is $25.

TROY WEIGHT. This is a standard system by which the weights of precious metals are figured all over the world. Its basic unit is the grain. Scales (using balances, not springs) for weighing items in troy measure are available and are usually referred to as jewelers' or gemologists' scales.

WEIGHTS AND MEASURES
APOTHECARIES' WEIGHT

one grain	=	.01666 dram
20 grains	=	.33 dram
60 grains	=	one dram
480 grains	=	one apothecary ounce (8 drams)

AVOIRDUPOIS WEIGHT

.0625 ounce	=	1.7719 grams
one ounce	=	28.350 grams
16 ounces	=	one pound (453.59 grams)

TROY WEIGHT

one grain	=	.0416666 pennyweight of .648 grams
24 grains	=	one pennyweight
480 grains	=	20 pennyweights, or one troy ounce
5760 grains	=	240 pennyweights, or 12 troy ounces, or one troy pound

FORMULAS OF CONVERSIONS

To change . . .
grams to pennyweights, multiply grams by .643
pennyweights to grams, multiply pennyweights by 1.555
grams to troy ounces, multiply grams by .032
troy ounces to grams, multiply troy ounces by 31.103
pennyweights to troy ounces, divide pennyweights by 20
troy ounces to pennyweights, multiply troy ounces by 20
grains to grams, multiply grains by .0648
grams to grains, multiply grams by 15.432
avoirdupois ounces to troy ounces, multiply avoirdupois ounces by .912
troy ounces to avoirdupois ounces, multiply troy ounces by 1.097
avoirdupois ounces to grams, multiply avoirdupois ounces by 28.35
grams to avoirdupois ounces, multiply grams by .035
avoirdupois pounds to kilograms, multiply avoirdupois pounds by .454
kilograms to avoirdupois pounds, multiply kilograms by 2.205
avoirdupois pounds to grains, multiply avoirdupois pounds by 7000
grains to avoirdupois pounds, multiply grains by .00014

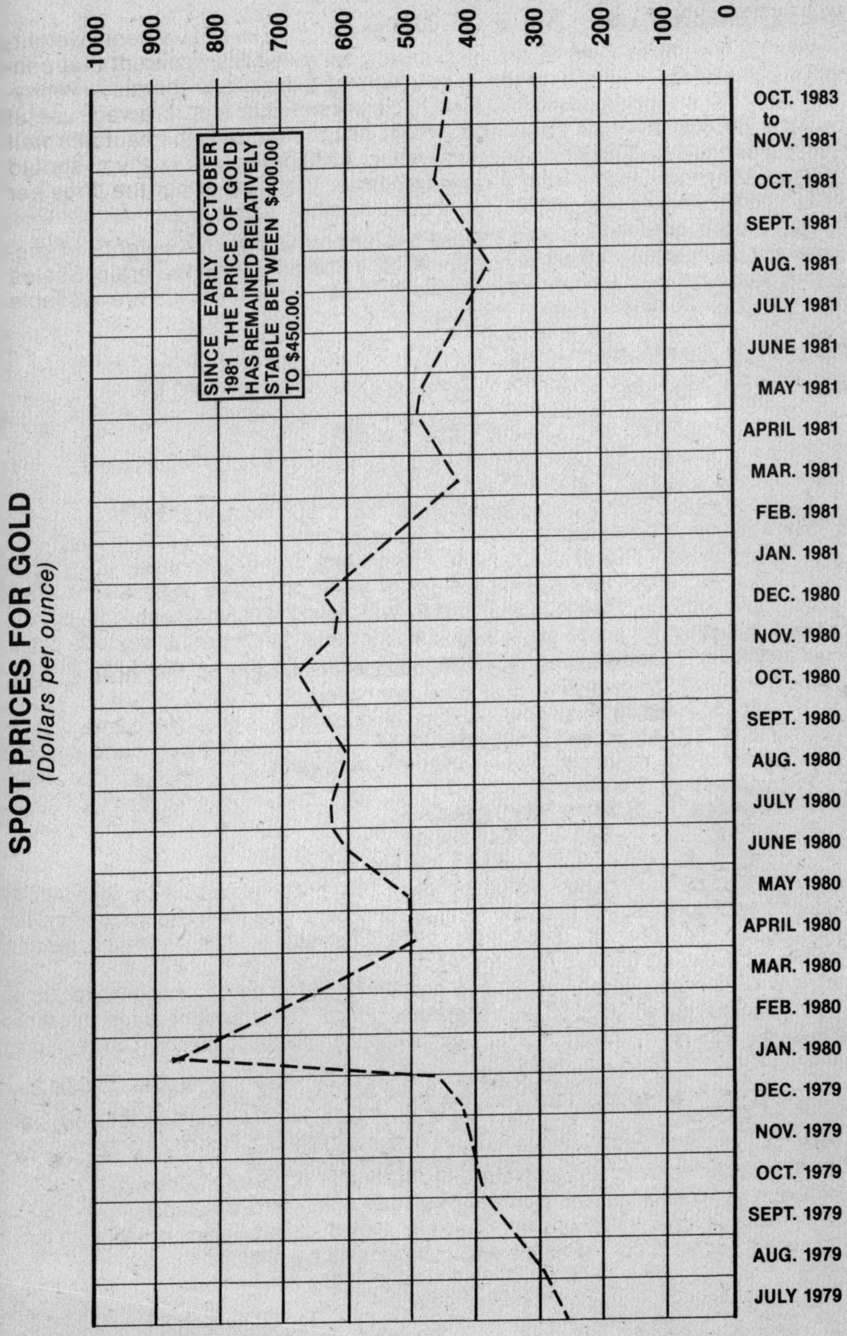

SPOT PRICES FOR GOLD
(Dollars per ounce)

SINCE EARLY OCTOBER 1981 THE PRICE OF GOLD HAS REMAINED RELATIVELY STABLE BETWEEN $400.00 TO $450.00.

1000	900	800	700	600	500	400	300	200	100	0

OCT. 1983 to NOV. 1981
OCT. 1981
SEPT. 1981
AUG. 1981
JULY 1981
JUNE 1981
MAY 1981
APRIL 1981
MAR. 1981
FEB. 1981
JAN. 1981
DEC. 1980
NOV. 1980
OCT. 1980
SEPT. 1980
AUG. 1980
JULY 1980
JUNE 1980
MAY 1980
APRIL 1980
MAR. 1980
FEB. 1980
JAN. 1980
DEC. 1979
NOV. 1979
OCT. 1979
SEPT. 1979
AUG. 1979
JULY 1979

DETERMINING THE VALUE OF GOLD

As the weight of gold is often given in pennyweights rather than grains, grams or ounces, anyone handling gold will face the challenge of translating the daily "spot" price (always stated in troy ounces) into pennyweight values.

After determining the karat and weight of the item, the following formula can be used to find its price per pennyweight at spot value on any given day. If you've determined the item's karat to be 14K, then you will see on the chart that this translates into 58.33% pure gold. In other words, the gold content is 58.33% pure gold and the remainder is nongold alloy. This percentage of fineness is needed in order to calculate price per pennyweight.

Next you have to use the following formula:

Spot ÷ 20 = price per dwt

Price per dwt × fineness = melt value per dwt

Example: Let's assume that we have a 14K item which we now know is 58.33% pure and spot was $600 that day. The figures would be:

$600 ÷ 20 = $30 per dwt

$30 × 58.33 = $17.50 melt value per dwt

This formula can be used whether spot is $100 or $1,000 or anywhere in between. Just use the formula exactly.

Now let's take an example through all the steps we've discussed.

We'll say you have a bracelet and want to determine its value. First you would have used one of the gold test formulas and determined its karat at 14K. Now you must find out its weight. If you don't have access to a gram scale, any regular (avoirdupois) scale will do, if it gives readings by the ounce. A bathroom scale obviously isn't suitable, but a postal scale is satisfactory. If the bracelet weighs 2 ounces, you would then proceed to the following formula:

ounces × 28.35 = grams

grams × .643 = dwt (pennyweights)

dwt × melt value per dwt = market melt value

With this item it would be:

2 ounces × 28.35 = 56.70 grams

56.70 grams × .643 = 36.46 dwts

36.46 dwts × 17.50 = $638.05 market value

In this case the market value of your 14K bracelet would be $638.05. It weighs two ounces, yet the value is just slightly more than the spot price for one ounce. The reason, of course, is the fineness — 14K — which means nearly half the content is basemetal.

Now remember, when you sell to a dealer, for the value of the metal only, he will be buying at 10-25% less than this figure. The discount is fair because he must recover refining costs, pay freight or postage to the refinery and leave himself a reasonable profit.

So, keeping this in mind, you should be able to sell your 14K bracelet to a dealer for roughly $475 to $575. This should be a fair transaction for both parties. If the offer you get varies a great deal from this — on the low side, naturally — you should definitely shop around for another offer.

SILVER

PHYSICAL PROPERTIES OF SILVER

Atomic number - 47
Atomic weight - 107.870
Boiling point - 2,212C
Chemical symbol - Ag
Crystal system - face centered cubic

Melting point - 2,212C
Specific gravities of:
  .999 pure silver - 10.50
  .925 sterling silver - 10.31
German silver - 8.74

PURE SILVER (.999 FINE)

Pure silver is bullion with all, or nearly all, adhering mineral or other matter (generally known as waste matter) removed. This is done by refiners as the raw silver comes from the mines. In its freshly mined state, silver is very far from pure, it is normally fused with miscellaneous "rock junk."

Pure silver is made into bars, ranging in weight from one ounce upward; 30 pound bars are the largest commonly produced. They carry a fineness marking, which will be .999 or .999 +. The fineness is never given as 1.000, which would stand for absolute purity, since it cannot be guaranteed that every last trace of adhering matter has been successfully removed. In addition they should carry the refiner's name and a statement of the weight.

Pure silver is rarely made into anything but bars or ingots (small bars). It isn't study enough for use in manufacturing.

The belief of some beginners that antique silver jewelry is made of pure silver, is incorrect. All of these items, no matter how splendid, old or valuable, are made from alloyed silver.

BRITANNIA SILVER (.9584 FINE)

This is an industry term for a very high grade of silver, the highest used in manufacturing. It is made in Great Britain and carries an impressed figure of Britannia, a goddess-like female who symbolizes the British Empire. Britannia silver is 95.84% pure, meaning it contains less than 4½% alloy. It is very soft — too soft for most uses but satisfactory for tableware.

STERLING SILVER (.925 FINE)

Sterling is the best-known grade of silver in manufacturing. It's purity is slightly less than that of Britannia, which is 95.84% against 92.5% for sterling. This negligible difference cannot be detected by the naked eye, nor can the difference in weight. However, objects made of sterling are slightly less valuable as bullion than those of Britannia. Whether they are less valuable overall depends upon their merits as possible collectors' items.

Sterling is normally hallmarked and/or stamped "sterling," depending on the place of origin and prevailing regulations in that country. Occasionally the marking .925 is used.

Though sterling is identified with Great Britain, mainly because of the term "pound sterling" to denote the British currency, its manufacture is universal. Sterling is made from the Orient to America.

Origin of the word sterling is doubtful. Its use in relation to silver is of great antiquity, going back to the Middle Ages. Apparently, "silver" and "sterling" were interchangeable words at one time. It may have arisen as a means of identifying silver used by smiths in the making of plate, etc., opposed to the slightly inferior grade used by coiners.

COIN SILVER (.900 FINE)

A misleading term, because silver coins exist with varying proportions of silver content. Coin silver is taken to mean .900 or 90% silver against a 10% basemetal alloy, which nearly always is copper. It is thus a slightly lower grade than sterling and an appreciably lower grade than Britannia. Coin silver, when marked (which it frequently isn't), will usually carry the designation "coin silver" or ".900." Antique objects of coin silver are sometimes marked "DOLLAR" or "D," to indicate their manufacture from melted dollars.

GERMAN SILVER

A low grade silver, composed chiefly of nickel and copper and containing a small amount of silver, or an exterior silver wash that accounts for perhaps 3% of the overall weight or less. As German Silver has been manufactured for more than 150 years, the composition has changed many times. It first appeared as a material used in the making of novelties and souvenirs in Bavaria, sold at a very cheap price to tourists and to the import/export trade. The motive was to achieve a substance which could retain a high surface polish and bear the general appearance of silver, or at least sufficiently to be convincing to undiscriminating persons. By 1850 the world market was being innundated with German Silver trinkets of all descriptions. After 1890, when the law was passed in the U.S. requiring all imported merchandise to be stamped, the designation "GERMAN SILVER" showed up on countless numbers of articles. German Silver is produced worldwide. The common reference to it as "low grade" silver is misleading; it should more correctly be called "no grade."

ALLOYS AND SILVER

Like the other precious metals, silver in its pure state (.999 or .999+) is quite soft and unsuitable for use in art or industry, except in instances where ruggedness is not important. The degree to which silver is alloyed for manufacturing depends largely upon the type of items to be made from it. Durability, appearance, and price are the three chief considerations.

Whether used to a small or great degree in any given article, copper is the standard and universal alloy for silver — just as for gold. It alloys silver splendidly. When used in small ratios it does not materially affect the color or brilliance, and just a minimal quantity lends the necessary durability. Of course, the alloying process is important in itself and must be executed correctly to achieve proper results. Since silver and copper are of very different colors in their natural state, silver being white or grey-white and copper being dark brown or red, streaking is inevitable if the blending is not carefully carried out. The silver will show dark streaks or cloudy areas, where the copper has not totally mixed in. Alloying must be done when the ingredients are in absolutely liquid state, and the blending cannot be rushed. Before the modern age, this was done by workers who literally churned the mixture in the manner of cream.

Silver can, of course, be alloyed with metals other than copper. This is done occasionally but is rare in the modern world, as there seems no possibility of improving on the silver/copper combination excepting for an occasional special use. There is nothing to be gained, for example, in alloying silver with brass or bronze, which themselves are largely copper. This was often done in early times, because the foundries used whatever was at hand without really caring one way or another. This is why old coins, especially those of the Romans, are found in the same denomination made from various metals or combinations of metals.

If there is a desire to whiten the color, silver can be alloyed with nickel or zinc; but the resulting product is not as handsome, nor does it consistently polish as well as silver alloyed with copper.

Naturally, the more alloy used, the lower the grade of silver. Britannia silver contains nearly 20 parts of silver for every part of alloy, and is therefore an extremely high grade. So called coin silver is .900, which means nine parts silver to one part alloy. Even though the difference between coin silver and Britannia is just .900 to .958, Britannia is more than twice as pure as coin silver. This is because it contains less than half as much alloy.

The lowest grade of silver to carry a fineness is .800, which contains 80% silver and 20% alloy. At this point the silver begins taking on a darker color, which could, of course, be mistaken for oxidation or failure to polish it regularly. An experienced silver handler can tell the difference in weight, too, when this much alloy is employed, unless the item is very small.

TESTING METHODS FOR SILVER

Most silver is marked, but in marked articles, tests must be performed.

The object in testing silver is to determine one or more of the following:

1. Whether the item contains any silver at all, or is simply an imitation such as German Silver, polished nickel, or some other substance that gives the appearance of silver (there are numerous combinations of metals that look more or less like silver, especially to the untrained eye).

2. If the object is silver plated — that is, coated with silver, but containing a core of basemetal.

3. If solid silver, the grade or quality. The "grade" is the degree to which the silver it contains has been alloyed with basemetal. If heavily alloyed, the item may be worth very little in spite of being solid silver. "Solid silver" simply means that it isn't plated; it makes no representation of the fineness.

As a general rule it can be presumed that most, or nearly all, manufactured items intended for commercial sale are not of high grade silver unless marked. It is obviously to the maker's and seller's advantage to mark high-grade items, as this increases their appeal. The only instances in which markings may not occur on good silver are custom made items, antiques and objects d'art fashioned by persons who are not licensed smiths or guild members.

NITRIC ACID. Nitric acid has traditionally been the popular method of testing silver. It reacts to basemetal differently than to silver. If a positive reaction is obtained, proof is given that the metal is either not silver or silver heavily alloyed. The nitric acid test should be run on any article suspected of being made of low grade silver, or plated in silver. It is important to conduct such testing carefully, as laxness can cause incorrect results.

Applying nitric acid to the surface will determine if the object is made wholly of low-grade silver or non-silver, but it does not provide proof of plating. A plated item tested on its surface will give the same reaction as one made entirely of silver because the acid reacts only on the outer layer. It is therefore logical to make both tests at once, for silver content and the possibility of plating. A notch or groove must be filed into the surface, down to a depth of about 1/32nd of an inch.

Choose an inconspicuous place for filing the notch, such as the inside of a watch case. A drop of nitric acid is placed in the notch and determination of content will be made by the acid's change in color, which will occur very quickly.

If the object is made of high grade silver, such as sterling, the acid will merely turn a greyish color. In other words it will tone down the metal a bit but not change its basic color. Should there be a high proportion of copper alloying, a green color will appear. Whenever green is obtained you are dealing either with low grade silver or an article made chiefly of copper with the addition of enough nickel or other metal to give an appearance of silver (usually 75% copper/25% nickel).

Be certain to remove the acid as soon as possible after obtaining results, by wiping with a clean cloth. It may cause pitting to the surface or permanent discoloration if this is not done.

Dichromate acid can also be used to test silver. This is a more sophisticated approach because the dichromate solution does not merely tell if the item is silver or non-silver, it indicates the presence of several other metals, depending upon the color to which the acid-treated region turns. But dichromate acid is somewhat more difficult to get. If you can't get it from a chemist or jewelry supply house, it can be prepared in the following manner. Use care in handling ingredients. The fumes are quite toxic and serious burns can result from dichromate acid coming into contact with the skin.

Dissolve an eighth of a teaspoon of potassium dichromate into the nitric acid, not the other way around. This should be done in a small bottle, not a dish, to contain fumes as much as possible. Stir it around gently with a glass rod until it achieves a rich burgundy color. It is then ready for use. If not to be used immediately, the bottle ought to be tightly stoppered to keep it fresh. Dichromate acid deteriorates rapidly in contact with air. It will deteriorate in a stoppered container but not as quickly.

The same testing procedure outlined above is used: filing a notch and applying a drop of solution. If the article is solid silver of a high grade, the resulting color will be bright red. When applied to an item containing a large proportion of copper, it turns green — just as does nitric acid alone. If the metal is lead, the color will be yellow. Pewter gives a black color.

WEIGHING METHODS FOR SILVER

Silver bars and Morgan Dollars aren't weighed on a bathroom scale. Methods of weighing precious metals are very sophisticated, as a minute difference in weight can mean a big difference in price.

There isn't, as yet, any universally agreed-upon technique. Several are reliable if performed carefully.

The weight of silver may be stated in troy ounces, pennyweight, or by metric division. Troy is the most common and the most universally understood by jewelers and bullion dealers. The daily spot price of silver is always given by the troy ounce. Pennyweight is much more commonly used for gold than for silver, but is included here in the event you may need to make this calculation. The reason why pennyweight is applied to gold more than silver is that it represents a very small measure of weight. Silver, being much less valuable than gold, has little value by pennyweight.

The metric system, now becoming international, has not yet penetrated into the bullion market to a very major extent and probably will not do so for a number of years.

As statements of weight may be given in grains by one dealer, grams by another, and dwt (pennyweight) by a third, it is important that anyone buying or selling silver become familiar with the equivalents, and methods of changing one to another.

DETERMINING THE VALUE OF SILVER

The value of silver bullion in any given article of silver is somewhat easier to calculate than gold, so long as the fineness is known, since silver prices are nearly always expressed by the troy ounce.

The daily spot price of silver and gold are always stated in troy ounces.

The daily spot price is quoted for one ounce of .999 fine. If you have bars or ingots of .999 or .999 +, their value is obvious. You merely multiply the spot price on that day by the number of ounces in your bars or ingots. Of course, when selling you will not receive that sum, as the broker or dealer deducts a percentage of commission. With silver the percentage margin tends to be larger than with gold.

Spot price of $15 per troy ounce.

six .999 silverbars weighing 1 oz. each = 6 ounces

six × $15 = $490.00 (melt value)

If your silver is not .999 fine, it is naturally worth less than spot, but the difference in value is extremely slight if you have fine quality ware such as Britannia or sterling. Britannia is .956 and sterling .925. Since coin silver is .900 fine, the calculations for it are very simple — you need only deduct 10% from the weight and then multiply the resulting figure by "spot." Technically, the answer will not be precise, since the 10% of alloy (copper, usually) does not comprise exactly 10% of the weight. This is because silver and copper have slightly different weights, it is, nevertheless, accurate enough for buying and selling purposes.

Before any price calculations can be attempted, it is necessary to learn.

1. How much the article weighs in ounces.

2. What the fineness is.

Good quality silver, .800 fine and over, will usually carry a marking, stamped on some inconspicuous part of its surface. If the marking is not in numbers and/or letters, but a decorative symbol, it is probably a foreign hallmark or touchmark. As the variety of markings that can be encountered are numerous, and often very similar but with different meanings, the aid of a book on hallmarks or an expert will be needed. Generally, though not invariably, hallmarked silver that does not state the fineness is .925. Many dealers will buy it at .925 even if further evidence is lacking. This grade is known as "sterling." Unmarked antique jewelry should only be tested by an expert so as not to adversely affect its value.

Once the fineness is known, the weight must be determined to calculate the article's melt value.

This can be done easily by weighing it on any scale that gives readings in troy ounces, or on an avoirdupois scale and then converting the weight into troy ounces. To change avoirdupois ounces to troy ounces, the avoirdupois ounces are multipled by .912.

You now have a fineness reading plus a weight. The next step is to multiply the fineness by the weight, which will tell you the amount of .999 silver the object contains.

For example:

Tray made of coin silver, .900 fine, weighs 5 troy ounces

$5 \times .900 = 4,500$, or 4½ troy ounces of .999 fine

You then multiply the spot price by this figure to arrive at the melt value:

Spot price of $15 per troy ounce

$15 \times 4½ = \$6.70$ melt value

It is important, when contemplating the sale of silver as scrap bullion, that the item's overall value be considered in relation to the "melt" value.

When something is sold for melting, whatever it may be, you will be paid the current spot price on that day (if the buyer is reputable) less a discount for the buyer's commission. This is true whether the object is a coin, a silver ingot, or a chalice made in France in the 14th century. The scrap dealer buys it as scrap — nothing more.

The scrap dealer profits greatly from the simple fact that the public has a hard time distinguishing silver that should be melted from silver that shouldn't. This is especially true of persons who have not personally bought the objects presented, but found them in their attic or acquired them in some other way. In these cases they are likely to have no idea of the value, and may be very happy to get the "spot" price for something worth many, many times more.

If something is an antique or collectors' item or for some special reason is out of the ordinary (if it belonged to a famous person, for example, or is a highly collectible limited edition), it could very possibly have greater than melt value. The difference between melt value and collector value cannot be shown on a chart. It all depends on the specific object, and varies from one to another. The 14th century French chalice might contain $2,000 worth of silver and have a collector value of $50,000 or more. Silver bookbindings (which are rare) contain extremely little silver by weight, but are very valuable because of their scarcity and the artistry that went into them.

Because of silver's immense popularity in manufacturing and craftwork for centuries, antiques made of silver are abundant.

Their surface appearance may be slightly different than that of modern silver of the identical grade, due to the effects of age. If silver is not regularly cleaned and polished, it can lose its luster and become grimy looking. When exposed for ages to the harshness of nature, such as silver articles from shipboard or decorations from the exterior of houses, the condition may truly be poor.

The melt value of these items, appearance notwithstanding, is the same as for modern silver of the same fineness and weight. It is no more and no less. But, unlike modern silver, which may be flashy and very catching to the eye, these antique pieces of silver jewelry frequently have an added collector value which removes them from the melt category.

If you are uncertain as to the value of any pieces of antique gold or silver jewelry, it is important that you obtain a professional appraisal by a reputable antique jewelry dealer. The appraisal should be from a source not interested in the purchase of the appraised item. The cost of the appraisal should be based on an hourly rate and not on a percentage of the appraised value.

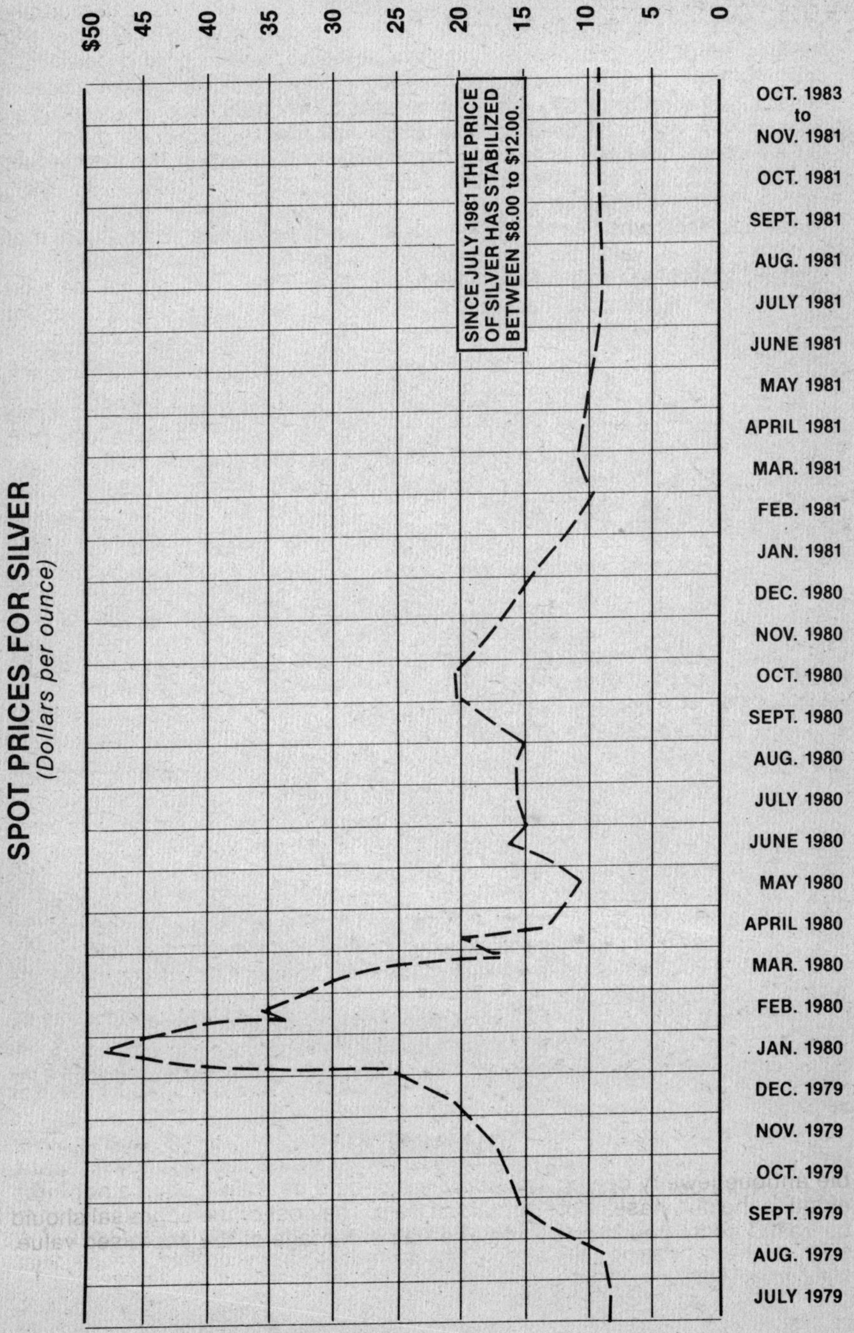

SPOT PRICES FOR SILVER
(Dollars per ounce)

SINCE JULY 1981 THE PRICE OF SILVER HAS STABILIZED BETWEEN $8.00 to $12.00.

$50	
45	
40	
35	
30	
25	
20	
15	
10	
5	
0	

OCT. 1983 to NOV. 1981
OCT. 1981
SEPT. 1981
AUG. 1981
JULY 1981
JUNE 1981
MAY 1981
APRIL 1981
MAR. 1981
FEB. 1981
JAN. 1981
DEC. 1980
NOV. 1980
OCT. 1980
SEPT. 1980
AUG. 1980
JULY 1980
JUNE 1980
MAY 1980
APRIL 1980
MAR. 1980
FEB. 1980
JAN. 1980
DEC. 1979
NOV. 1979
OCT. 1979
SEPT. 1979
AUG. 1979
JULY 1979

HOW TO SELL GOLD AND SILVER

"Scrap gold" or "scrap silver" are the terms applied to gold or silver objects that have no value over and above their value as bullion. They're weighed on a scale and paid for by weight, then sent to a refinery for smelting. Anything which might come under the heading of a collector's item should not be sold for scrap, because a higher price could be obtained for it elsewhere.

SCRAP GOLD OR SILVER DO NOT INCLUDE ANTIQUE JEWELRY, THOUGH SOME CONTEMPORARY JEWELRY MIGHT BE APPROPRIATE TO SELL AS SCRAP.

COLLECTORS' ITEMS IN GENERAL

When gold or silver has been fashioned into a work of art, whether very old or comparatively modern, the possibility exists that it could be of collector value. This is true regardless of the grade of gold or silver and even, sometimes, the state of preservation. The advice of an authority on collectors' items should be sought before selling, preferably one whose opinion can be expressed without regard to personal gain.

The word "antique" has been much misused. As far as U.S. customs is concerned, an antique (to escape import duty) must be 100 years old or more. As far as the British Antique Dealers Association is concerned, an antique, with certain exceptions, must be made before 1830, the start of the Industrial Revolution. However, there are many gold and silver objects of a much more recent date whose artistry or other appeal lends value over and above their metallic worth. Moreover, the value of antique gold or silver does not depend on age. It is a matter of scarcity, skill in designing, preservation, place or origin and historical significance. The value as a collectors' item can sometimes vastly exceed bullion value.

A good example is ancient goldware. Goldwork of ancient Rome is not common on the antique market but it can be found, particularly at the large auction sales in New York, London and Paris. A hairpin containing perhaps $200 worth of gold may sell for $750-$1,000. Gold finger rings of the 1st-3rd centuries B.C., which rarely contain more than an ounce of gold, are not easily purchasable under $2,000. Here the origin is of more importance to buyers than the material. There are collectors specializing in ancient jewelry who will compete vigorously for whatever comes on the market. They couldn't care less about the daily "spot." Where gold has been used as an adjunct or decorative touch in items made largely of other materials this situation can also prevail, such as antique jewelry made from human hair with gold fittings illustrated throughout this book.

If you have gold or silver items which appear, on strength of their age or design or unusualness, to have the potential of appealing to collectors, do not sell them to scrap merchants. Take them instead to antique dealers.

DIAMONDS

CELEBRATED DIAMONDS

History has demonstrated that diamonds are not only a girl's best friend, but they have been equally admired by sultans, princes, nobles, sheiks, shipping magnates and royalty.

Nature occasionally produces diamonds of prodigious size. Stones so big that, even after cutting, they almost fill the palm of the hand. Naturally, such specimens have always attracted great attention, not to mention great prices. They have been given names to identify them (Hope Diamond, Orloff, Cullinan, etc.) and treated with an almost divine reverence. Their histories have been closely chronicled, from the moment of discovery down through various changes of ownership. Some have led swashbuckling lives, getting lost or stolen or disappearing from sight for ages and then turning up with a different cut.

One of the best-known diamonds to come from India was the Mughal, variously known as the Grand Mughal or Great Mughal. An early commentator reported seeing the Grand Mughal at Delhi in 1665. He described it as having the appearance of an egg cut in half and recorded its weight as 280 carats, against a rough weight of 793 carats. Apparently it was a fairly new discovery at the time; it was said to have been found around 1650. The Grand Mughal was then in the possession of the Shah of Delhi, who proudly displayed it among the baubles of his treasury. It was not to remain there long. Another Shah, named Nadir, took it upon himself to relieve the Delhi treasury of most of its higher-grade valuables and carry them away to Persia. Its subsequent fate is not known. The Grand Mughal never appeared again. Or, it might be better to say, it never again appeared with the same cut and a 280 carat weight. Very likely, it was recut, to better escape the prying eyes of those seeking its return to India. The opinion of some authorities is that the Grand Mughal was reincarnated into one of the other celebrated diamonds of the world, possibly the Orloff.

The Koh-i-nor, not quite as big, went through a no less harrowing existence but remains safe and sound today — extremely safe as one of the British crown jewels in the Tower of London.

The Koh-i-nor's history has been traced back as far as 1304 — the earliest date, by the way, at which the whereabouts of any famous diamond has been established beyond reasonable argument. It was then in possession of an Indian potentate in the neighborhood of Delhi. Later it was handed down through several generations of the Mughal emperors. In 1850, after the colonization of India by Great Britain, it was presented by the East India Company to Queen Victoria. The queen, born of the manor royal and having a temperament typical to queens, was not overly enthralled by the glittering goliath. Impressed by its physical proportions, its manner of cut left something to the royal desire. It was not shimmering enough for her taste. So the queen decided to sacrifice a bit of its bulk and shipped off the Koh-i-nor to her diamond cutter. After he was done with it, it weighed 108.93 carats — barely half as much as before. Queen Victoria was now satisfied. No futher cutting was done and the Koh-i-nor still carries a weight of 108.93 carats, plus nearly 700 years of colorful history behind it. Technically, it may be worn by the present queen, Elizabeth II, on state occasions. But this isn't done due to a huge security problem.

Small compared to most other historic diamonds, the Hope has something going for it in addition to size: a rare rich blue color. It is without question the most famous diamond currently on U.S. soil. Its story begins in 1668 and takes us across several continents. In that year Tavernier, a well-known diamond agent, brought it back to France from India. It weighed 112.50 carats and was purchased by Louis XIV. At this time its popular designation was "The French Blue." Louis decided to have the shape changed and in 1673 it was recut into a heart pattern, reducing the weight to 67⅛ carats. For many years it was hailed as the finest diamond in France, if not all of Europe, and served as an object of adoration not only for Louis XIV but his successors, Louis XV and Louis XVI. At the outbreak of France's revolution in 1792 the stronghouse in which it was stored was broken into, and the French Blue disappeared. The revolutionaries were known to be in need of money and general opinion was that the French Blue, along with anything else of value on which they succeeded in laying hands, was probably smuggled out of the country for sale. Officially, it was never heard from again. But unofficially, there is little doubt that the gem now displayed in Washington, D.C., is the French Blue.

In 1830, more than three decades after the French revolution had faded into memory, a diamond weighing 44½ carats appeared for sale in London. It was bought by Henry Hope and thereafter identified as the Hope Diamond. The experts are convinced that this was the French Blue, after a bit of additional recutting and reshaping.

From England the Hope Diamond found its way to America, where it was purchased by Evalyn Walsh McClean of Washington, D.C., a prominent socialite, in 1911. Following her death in 1947 it was acquired by a New York diamond dealer, Harry Winston. After holding it for nine years, Winston gave it to the Smithsonian: the largest gift of a precious stone, in terms of its current value at the time of presentation, ever made to a public institution.

The Regent diamond also came from India. It was dug in 1701 and had an in-the-rough weight of 410 carats. William Pitt, an English politician, purchased it for an undisclosed sum the following year. It was still uncut. Pitt had it cut down to 140½ carats. A number of years later it was sold to Phillippe d'Orleans, Regent of France, and it acquired the title of Regent diamond. Like the French Blue/Hope the Regent was also stolen during the French revolution. But was recovered and deposited in the Louvre museum. It remains there today, and has the distinction of being the largest diamond on public exhibition in France. The Regent has a yellowish tint.

THE GEMOLOGICAL INSTITUTE OF AMERICA

This organization, with offices in New York, Los Angeles and Santa Monica offers courses in gemology and provides graduates with accreditation as gemologists. Perhaps, more importantly, it provides a gemstone certification service. Diamonds submitted for its opinion are subjected to a variety of laboratory procedures and are issued a diamond grading report, known commonly in the trade as "G.I.A. Certificate," stating whether or not the stone is a true diamond, its weight, color grading and clarity grading as well as all measurements. The G.I.A. certificate has come to be regarded as the "Standard of the Industry," as stones accompanied by it can be traded in confidence, without suspicions or differences of viewpoint that frequently occur over matters of grading. Many gem dealers automatically submit every stone they acquire to the G.I.A., if it does not already possess a certificate, as the presence of one adds greatly to its sales appeal. It acts as a kind of pedigree and is universally relied upon, representing as it does the findings of an impartial body that stands to gain nothing by sale or ownership of the material.

DIAMOND GRADING TERMINOLOGY

The grading terminology of diamonds as developed by the Gemological Institute of America (G.I.A.) employs letters and letter/number combinations to refer to clarity and color. This terminology, though frequently a cause of debate, is almost universally used by diamond traders, sometimes with local additions or amendments. No system can please everyone. The G.I.A. has at least removed much of the confusion from describing and grading diamonds.

COLOR RATINGS. The letters used in the G.I.A.'s system of reference to diamond colors is a descending scale, just like the clarity scale except a bit lengthier. It begins with D, which refers to the best color (completely colorless) quality of a brilliant blue-white diamond (the most desirable color for investment diamonds). There is no A, B or C in the scale. The letters toward the beginning of the alphabet represent the more desirable colors; toward the end the less desirable.

D, E, F - These are all crystal clear or completely colorless diamonds. They represent the most attractive investments, assuming their other qualities are comparable.

G - Nearly colorless, fine white
H - Nearly colorless, white
I - Nearly colorless, commercial white
J - Nearly colorless, top silver cape
K - Slightly tinted, ranging from top silver cape (better) to silver cape (not quite to desirable)
L - Slightly tinted, silver cape
M - Slightly tinted, light cape
N - Slightly tinted, light cape, but not as high a grade as M
O - Pale Yellow, cape
P - Pale Yellow, cape, lower grade
Q - Pale Yellow, cape, third lowest grade of this classification
R - Light Yellow (stronger yellow than above), cape
S - Light Yellow, dark cape
T - Light Yellow, dark cape, more heavily colored
U - Yellow, dark cape
V - Yellow, dark cape, strong coloration, very little light refraction, not a gem quality stone
X, Y, Z - Very heavily colored
Z+ - Extremely heavily colored and are considered "Fancy Colored." These are very rare and considered the most valuable of diamonds, more so than say a "D" flawless.

TERMINOLOGY AND DETERMINATION OF DIAMOND CLARITY. The most complicated terminology refers to gem clarity. This is a series of grades ranging from Flawless — expressed as FL — down to badly defective or "1-3." The point to be kept in mind, so far as clarity grading is concerned, is that the quality of a diamond is measured in relation to perfect examples of that shape of cut. Because not everyone had equally keen vision, what appears flawless to one individual could very easily look otherwise to a sharper sighted person. Therefore, the grading criteria are based upon examinations made not only with the unaided and reliable eye but the use of various equipment, such as the jeweler's or diamond appraiser's 10K loupe. (NOTE: 10X magnification is the standard maximum limit for inspecting and grading diamonds throughout the world.) Examination of diamonds for clarity should first be undertaken with the naked eye, then with a 10X jeweler's loupe and finally with a 10X stereo microscope.

Use a bench or table that permits examination while seated. There should be maximum overhead light. Natural light may have to be supplemented by artificial lighting. Be sure that all surfaces of magnification devices are clean. Diamonds should be handled with tongs or tweezers only by the girdle

Do not be in a hurry. Study the diamond from all angles. Move it closer and further from your eye. Take notes as you work. Compare your findings with the descriptions of various grades of clarity given below.

FLAWLESS (FL). Stones in this grade do not reveal imperfections of any kind when magnified with 10X magnification.

The highest grade. It is presumed by beginners or uninformed persons that to qualify as FL a diamond must be so crystal clear that no degree of magnification reveals even the slightest blemish or imperfection. This is not true. Minor deviations from perfection exist; it is an extremely rare stone which magnified to 10X, exhibits no flaws whatever. There may be slight imperfections that are visible only with a magnification greater than 10X, nevertheless, if an imperfection or blemish is not visible at 10X, for evaluation purposes it is insignificant.

INTERNALLY FLAWLESS (IF). Slight surface imperfections but internally the stone is as perfect as an FL.

As with FL, the blemishes or departures from absolute perfection on an IF stone can be observed with 10X magnification but only with extreme effort. There are perhaps more of them, but they are not in any way serious or distorting. In addition to those mentioned above, and IF stone may reveal such blemishes as minor pitting, but this cannot occur in the table — the diamond's most vital area — or else a lower grading is certain to result. There can be infinitesimal facet abrasions but not a network of scratches. A good grading rule to keep in mind: any surface fault or blemish not readily eradicated by simple polishing, in other words blemishes which must be ground out or are impossible to remove without recutting, disqualify the specimen from an IF or FL ranking.

VERY VERY SLIGHT IMPERFECTIONS (VVS). VVS stones are blemished. There will be somewhat more faults than an IF stone, or the faults are slightly easier to observe with 10X magnification. Typical characteristics of VVS stones are minute spots outside the table. There can be a tiny colorless crystal, more than overshadowed by light refraction. When examined from the underside a minute "feather" could be observed. The girdle or outer circumference may reveal minor natural irregularities. These should not be the result of a bad cutting job. The facet edges could be slightly rough. In short, the negative features of a VVS stone should be largely, though not entirely, remedied by simple polishing. VVS stones are broken down into two categories: VVS-1 and VVS-2.

VVS-1. Has very tiny inclusions which can be distinguished with extreme difficulty using 10X magnification.

VVS-2. Like VVS-1, but inclusions are not quite so difficult to see under 10X magnification.

VERY SLIGHT IMPERFECTION (VS). This grade is broken down into VS-1 and VS-2. Here we are sill using 10X magnification, under good strong light. We are looking for any internal or external markings that are not consistent with absolute perfection. The VS stone reveals such markings to a slightly more pronounced degree than the VVS. However, they do not appear obvious as soon as we place the stone under 10X magnification. At first, we are perhaps confident that the stone grades higher. But with investigation, we locate internal growth lines which exhibit pale color from the front. Once we have encountered such lines we have no alternative but to grade the stone below VVS. Upon further inspection it may be necessary to reduce the grading even more. The VS diamond may show small colorless crystals or groupings of pinpoints. There could be insignificant cracks, as well as minor scratching to the surface caused by contact with other diamonds in storage or errors of the cutter. The girdle may show indented naturals not related to cutting. There will be general abrasion and possibly a slightly larger extra facet than would not be allowable on stones of higher grade. The VS stone is, despite this lengthy catalogue of possible shortcomings, an extremely worthy specimen. Its faults, while many, are all of the minor variety and cannot be observed without 10X magnification.

VS-1. Minor inclusions slightly more pronounced than VVS-2, but still difficult to see with 10X magnification.

VS-2. Minor inclusions more noticeable than in a VS-1, fairly easy to see with 10X magnification.

SLIGHT IMPERFECTION (SI). This grade is broken down into SI-1 and SI-2. We are using a 10X jeweler's loupe and the blemishes are relatively easy to see. There will usually be groupings of pinpoints, but not glaring. There are likely to be colorless crystals — not just one but several. One or more of these may be a dark color. There could be minor cracks, cleavages or cloudy areas. There may be a roughness to the culet (the tip of the stone's base) or a nick in the girdle. SL stones are not generally regarded as investment pieces, regardless of color or carat. But as diamonds continue to become scarcer, even SI's should prove to be investment worthy.

Their imperfections are too glaring — despite the fact that they can be noticed only with the 10X loupe — for these diamonds to carry a high resale potential. It might be possible to purchase them cheaply, but they will not advance in value as steadily or rapidly as higher graded stones and very likely the margin of profit on their resale will be slightly lower.

SI-1. Inclusions can be seen without difficulty under 10X magnification.

SI-2. 10X magnification readily reveals inclusions, which may possibly be noticeable with the naked eye looking through the pavilion.

IMPERFECT FIRST DEGREE (I-1). We are now abandoning artificial aids to vision and are examining with the naked eye. Of course, examinations carried out in this fashion do not bear quite such reliable results, being dependent on the individual's keenness of vision. I-1 stones have flaws that can be seen, but just barely, by persons with approximately 20/20 vision at close range. There will be minor cloudiness or fluorescent beneath the table. The crystal exhibits darkness. There is a colorless reflecting crystal located beneath the table. Cleavage may be observed from the front. The girdle is likely to show minor cracking radiating outward, either in one restricted region or across most of its circumference. At the surface there will be small waves or indentations on the table. Additional facets are larger than on more highly graded stones.

I-1. Inclusions very apparent with 10X magnification and can be seen with the naked eye.

IMPERFECT SECOND DEGREE (I-2). Blemishes of the above nature, but somewhat more pronounced.

IMPERFECT THIRD DEGREE (I-3). The extra facets are larger, there are collections of dark colored spots beneath the table which can be seen with the unaided eye, as well as cloudiness, and possible feathering below the table.

The surface shows scratches observed without magnification, and usually shows large dark included crystals. Generally speaking, this grade should never have been cut into a finished stone.

NOTE: The European market generally refers to imperfect stones as "pique" stones, with various degrees of included crystals. They will be graded as I-1 = P-1; I-2 = P-2; and I-3 = P-3.

Many stones fall into a borderline category, between one grade and the next. They could be placed into the higher grade by one appraiser and the lower by another. In such instances the opinion of the G.I.A. serves to resolve argument.

A piece of antique diamond jewelry is not solely valued for the grade of the diamonds, but consideration of overall workmanship, historical significance, origin, age and quality must be taken into account.

DIAMOND GRADING

Correct grading of a diamond is essential in establishing its value. The chief factors in grading a diamond are:

Carat weight	Clarity
Color	Cut

These are known collectively as the "Four C's." An accurate determination of the Four C's of a diamond will establish its value. The key word here is accurate. Misinterpretation of any of the four characteristics will result in an incorrect value. Some experience in handling diamonds is necessary before reliable estimates of value can be made. Grading diamonds is a science, at which the beginner cannot expect to become expert overnight.

CLARITY. Clarity is perhaps a misleading term. Purity would be more descriptive, as the clarity of a diamond is just that: the degree to which it is pure and unadulterated internally and externally. The purer the diamond, the greater its value, compared to other stones of the same color, cut and weight. Absolute purity is an elusive quality in diamonds. Therefore, the occasional specimen that reveals no major blemishes or imperfections of any kind, even under 10X magnification, is extremely desirable and rates as a good investment piece.

Internal flaws are the fault of nature and have been carried by the diamond for millions of years.

Just like a fly in amber, traces of foreign minerals became entrapped within the crystal. It is sometimes possible by judicious cutting to remove the flaws and achieve a stone of good clarity. Frequently, the stone after cutting still bears some evidence of the jailed-in element.

There are other kinds of internal flaws. During the early states of formation, the elements comprising the soon-to-be diamond may have begun to cool and harden, when suddenly another explosion or shifting about of earth took place. No foreign substances were imparted into the stone, but it was squeezed or contorted. Hence it showed, when dry and hard, internal lines or "creases," which have the resemblance of ice cracks.

Cloudiness is another variety of internal imperfection.

External flaws are generally the fault of misuse or accident, either in cutting, mounting or handling. The stone may have a surface scratch or nick.

External flaws also encompass imperfections of shape. The perfect diamond, after cutting, is symmetrically proportioned. If imaginarily divided in half vertically or horizontally, these two halves would be exact duplications of each other. If the two halves would not perfectly match, the stone is not regarded as flawless.

COLOR. The public believes that all diamonds are as colorless as window glass just as it believes all jade is green and all wood is brown. Such is not the case. Diamonds may be found in a variety of colors, or rather color tints, but the degree of coloring is never so intense as to destroy their transparency. Color tints have the same origins as internal flaws. Certain chemicals or substances became mixed with the basic elements at the time of formation and the diamond today bears the color of these substances. Rarity is not an important factor so far as color is concerned, as some colorings or shadings of them fare quite uncommon but are nevertheless not desirable. Preferences of color were long-ago established by purchasers of jewelry and have remained fairly constant. Most highly rated are crystal clear examples with icy whiteness, which under careful inspection reveals highlights of blue.

The Gemological Institute of America (G.I.A.) ranks the blue-white color grades as D, E and F. Stones rated in any of the categories are, if their remaining characteristics are satisfactory, regarded as investment quality.

Also considered as suitable investments are stones falling in the descending categories of classification, H, I and J.

The ranking "G" is applied to stones whose official designation is "fine white." Fine whites have a long and noble heritage in jewelry, especially in Europe among the old aristocratic families.

The letter "H" is applied to ordinary white a cut beneath fine white, white "I" refers to "commercial white," a grade of coloration commonly employed in jewelry.

The lesser classifications, all the way down to "Z", may also be used in jewelry but their values are lower.

Of course, whenever color is discussed, whatever the color or grade may be, the diamond's desirability and value are influenced by distribution of color. Stones are sometimes encountered in which the coloring is not even. These are called occluded stones.

CUT. Cut and weight are both human influenced, unlike color or internal purity. A mediocre diamond can be turned desirable by skilled cutting, and an essentially good quality stone may be reduced in value, or not brought up to its full value potential, by inartistic cutting.

Cut must be considered from two points of view: the shape, which will be obvious at sight, and the excellence with which each individual cut was executed. The term "proportioning" is sometimes applied. The stone must be cut so exactly that each facet and cleavage line on one side agrees perfectly with its counterpart on the opposite side. Also, the cutting must have produced a well-proportioned stone. Perfect proportioning requires that the cut be ideal for that particular stone, allowing light to enter at the correct angles, to be reflected and to exit upward toward the observer. This is how a diamond achieves its "sparkle." When ill-proportioned, the light may enter properly but is incorrectly refracted upon reaching the sides or base, and is expelled along the lower portion of the diamond. When this occurs, the brilliance of even an exceptionally fine stone is diminished, as it cannot attain the gentle play of light and nuance of tone imparted by that play of light, which is so essential to a good diamond.

Some expertise is necessary to judge proportioning. The chief errors of proportioning are cutting too deep or not cutting deep enough. When a diamond is cut too deep, light will exit through the sides. When cut too shallow, it will exit through the bottom. Both these situations are undesirable. Proportioning must be mathematically exact to achieve proper refraction of light.

No matter what shape of cut is used, the various surfaces on a diamond are classified into five basic divisions.

TABLE. This is the uppermost surface, which will be flat, uncut and unmarked in any way.

CROWN. The sloping sides, extending down from the table to the girdle.

GIRDLE. The wides or mid-portion of a diamond. Though called the midsection, its location is not necessarily at the center of gravity.

PAVILION. The inward-sloping sides, leading down from the girdle.

CULET. The point of the base.

When considering a diamond from an investment point of view, stones with a depth percentage in the region of 58% to about 64% are most desirable. The table diameter percentage should be from 55% to 65%. These percentage ratings will be given on the G.I.A. certificate, if the diamond is accompanied by one. The girdle or middle section should ideally be thin or of medium thickness, and evenly proportioned around the stone's circumference.

Correctly cut diamonds, of the standard popular shapes, have 58 facets, regardless of the size of the stone. Their placement and the angle of cleavage is performed according to an established system, which allows light to enter at certain critical angles and thereby be refracted within the diamond to best advantage. If these facets are misplaced, or not sized correctly, or if the angles are off, light will not be properly refracted. Very slight miscalculations can ruin the refractive quality of a diamond, or impair it to such extent that its value is considerably diminished.

The shape of cutting has really nothing to do with any of the points covered above, as diamonds of any standard shape have the required 58 facets, the physical characteristics noted, and the capability of refracting light if properly cut.

The choice of shape into which a rough stone will be cut is influenced in many instances, especially in the case of large or exceptional diamonds, by its natural shape in the raw state. In shaping an attempt is made to take at least partial advantage of the contours provided by nature, thereby losing less in carat weight than would be the case if choosing a shape opposed to the rough or raw shape. This will not be done, however, in instances where a rough stone has a "good" side and a "bad" side. It is then more important to sacrifice carat weight and remove the offending portion, which can be put to industrial use.

There are six basic shapes or styles into which diamonds are cut:

Round Brilliant	Marquise
Oval	Pear
Heart	Emerald

Round is the so-called classic or traditional cut and accounts for the majority of better-quality diamonds. Well over 75% of all diamonds in the market, for use in jewelry and of investment quality, carry the round shape. It results usually in the greatest possible light refraction and hence the most pure brilliance. In the other five shapes listed above, the stone's width does not perfectly match its vertical measurement. Only the round cut measures the same from North to South as it does from West to East across its top.

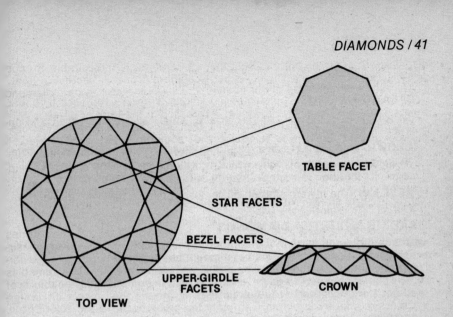

TABLE FACET

STAR FACETS

BEZEL FACETS

UPPER-GIRDLE
FACETS

CROWN

TOP VIEW

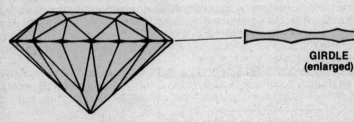

SIDE VIEW

GIRDLE
(enlarged)

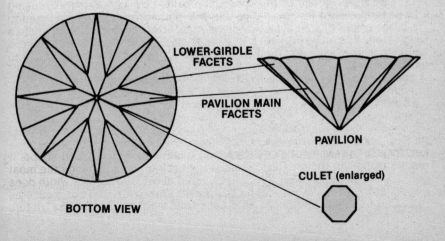

LOWER-GIRDLE
FACETS

PAVILION MAIN
FACETS

PAVILION

CULET (enlarged)

BOTTOM VIEW

Therefore, light as it enters through the facets meets at more precise junctions, and is thrown out a bit more powerfully.

CARAT OR WEIGHT. The size of a diamond is never expressed by linear measurment but rather by its weight, expressed in the form of carats.

One carat equals a fifth of a gram or 1/42 of an ounce. To achieve more precise communication of weight, "points" are sometimes employed instead of carats. A point equals 1/100 of a carat. Therefore, a 25-point diamond is the equivalent of ¼ carat, 50-point would be half a carat and so forth.

Loss of carat weight is inevitable in cutting. For a rough diamond to be properly cut, with introduction of all 58 facets and correct shaping, at least half of the original weight must be sacrificed.

GRADING MOUNTED DIAMONDS

Mounted diamonds cannot be graded as accurately as loose stones. The best that can be hoped for is an approximation of grading.

Mounted stones present grading problems both in terms of clarity and color. The clarity cannot be read as reliably as on unmounted gems because certain areas are obscured by the mounting.

Color grading is a problem with mounted stone because the color of the mounting is reflected into the diamond. If the mount is yellow gold, it will inevitably tinge the stone yellow. There is less color reflection when the mounting is platinum or white gold. A mounted diamond in a setting with colored stones is even more troublesome to grade. When the surrounding stones are blue, this tends to artificially improve the diamond's color, as their reflection imparts a suggestion of "blue-whiteness."

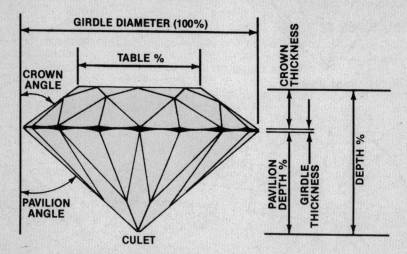

GRADING DIAMONDS FOR CUT

An important step in grading cut diamonds is carefully examining the quality of cut. This includes overall proportioning as well as the cutting of each individual facet and the girdle. Grading for cut is difficult for the inexperienced person, as the ability to distinguish between qualities of cutting is mainly acquired by handling and inspection of many diamonds.

Some diamonds are intentionally misproportioned for the sake of saving carat weight.

THE MAKE. This is the trade term for the diamond's proportioning, generally referred to either as a "good make" or "bad make;" the word "perfect" is seldom used. Essentially the stone should have been cut so that it reflects light to its maximum potential, which is somewhat greater with a Round Brilliant than the other shapes.

Differences between a good and bad make may be so slight as to be indistinguishable with the naked eye, or even with magnification. Actual measuring is often resorted to, in the case of stones large enough to submit to measuring.

The diameter at the girdle is measured, using a Leveridge gauge (these are available at most jewelry supply houses). The diamonds other proportions are then matched against this reading, including table diameter, crown height, and pavilion depth. According to the much-respected Tolkowsky scale the table diameter should be 53% of girdle diameter. Crown thickness should be 16.2% of the girdle diameter. The pavilion should have a thickness of 43.1% of the girdle diameter. Depth from table to culet should be 59.3% of girdle diameter. The crown angles should be 34.5° and the pavilion angle should be 40.75°. The crown and pavilion facets must also be cut at precise angles. Some variation is possible, but only if planned in advance, using a different set of percentages that will yield predictable results.

When the table is larger than it should be, crown thickness is reduced. Consequently the crown facets will be too small. This is more common than cuts with too-small tables.

DIAMOND SHAPES

There are six traditional or popular shapes into which diamonds are cut — Round, Marquise, Pear, Emerald, Heart and Oval. Many variations in shaping and/or faceting of these shapes are possible and will be encountered on the market. You will also find diamonds of other shapes — usually referred to as fancy or miscellaneous shapes. Diamonds with shapes other than these six are normally but not invariably European Cuts and many are antique: For example, the Mazarin cut, named after Cardinal Mazarin (17th century), is a French version of today's Round Brilliant. It is almost but not perfectly circular.

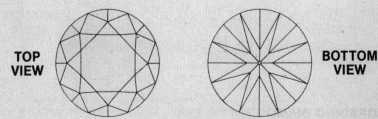

TOP VIEW   BOTTOM VIEW

ROUND OR "ROUND BRILLIANT." This has come to be the most popular cut. The name is self-explanatory: the stone is cut circular (viewed from above) and faceted to achieve maximum refraction of light. If properly executed, this style of cutting affords the greatest "sparkle." An early forerunner of the modern Round Brilliant was the European or English Square Cut which was not truly square but featured bowed sides. Through experimentation and evolution, the sides became more bowed and gradually the shape was altered from roughly square to roughly circular, until the point was reached of shaping the stone perfectly circular. The so-called Old Single Cut was an intermediate step between square and round. It was rounded but squared off into an octagon, either with a large table and short crown or virtually no table at all and high crown. The Rounded Single Cut, also now obsolete, was similar but with a more rounded girdle. Single facets only were cut into the crowns of these stones. They were attractive but the single faceting did not make full use of a diamond's ability to refract light. These cuts were admired in their time because buyers were not exposed to anything better. None are being produced today except in limited quantities of reproductions of antique jewelry.

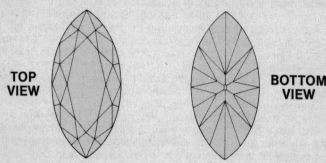

MARQUISE. The marquise is a variation of the brilliant cut, in which the stone is shaped ovally and comes to a point at either end. It may be cut into the classic Marquise, featuring a long table squared at either end and bowing out slightly into a semi-triangle at the sides, or the less-common Navette Marquise, which has a star pattern. The Navette has not been popular in the U.S.

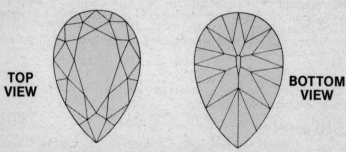

PEAR. The Pear cut is also sometimes referred to as Teardrop. It is actually egg-shaped, coming to a point at the small end. The table is roughly rectangular, intersected with both straight and curving cuts.

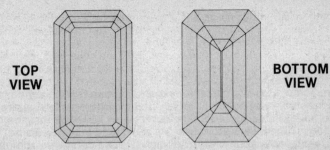

EMERALD. This is what the name suggests; a shape following that into which emeralds are normally cut. It is rectangular with the corners removed and features a very large rectangular table, also with the corners removed.

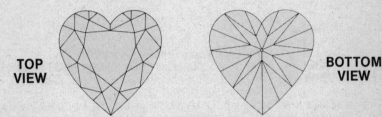

HEART. Heart shapes were at first rated among the novelty cuts. There are several variations of faceting but all stones have the diamond itself cut into a heart shape.

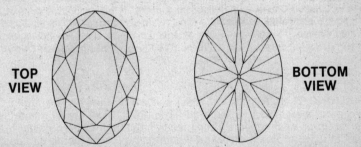

OVAL. The Oval shape is just what the name implies. The table is of modest size and all cuts are curved.

THE OLD MINE CUT

The "old mine cut" is generally found in jewelry made before 1900. This is a crudely cut round shape. Proportions are very inaccurate. They are frequently found in fine pieces of antique jewelry.

Though a modern well-executed Round Brilliant is valued from 300% to 500% of an Old Mine Cut of the same size on today's market, recutting should be avoided to preserve the historical significance and overall workmanship of the piece of jewelry.

The term "old mine cut" originated from the belief that in the 1800's diamonds were cut at the mines before wholesaling. This was seldom the case. These cuts simply reflected the standards and state-of-the-art of diamond cutting prior to the development of the Modern Round Brilliant Cut.

DETERMINING THE CARAT WEIGHT

Where carats alone are used for expression of weight, fractions of a carat are normally given by decimal. A full carat is written as 1.00. A stone weighing one and 1/10th carats would be recorded as 1.10. When two digits appear behind the decimal, the weight is being expressed in hundredths of a carat. If there is just one digit, such as 1.1, the weight is being given in tenths. In this case the weight is one and one-tenth carats.

The following may simplify this:

1.00 = one carat
1.10 = 1 1/10
1.20 = 1 1/5
1.50 = 1 1/2
1.75 = 1 3/4ths
2.00 = two carats
2.34 = two and 34/100ths, or approximately 2 1/3rd carats.

When the weight is lower than a full carat it will be expressed in terms of a zero followed by a decimal, with digits behind the decimal, such as:

0.72

This indicates a stone weighing 72/100ths of a carat, or about 3/4ths of a carat. 0.50 would be half a carat, 0.25 one-quarter of a carat.

Diamonds are also weighed by the point system. In the point system, 100 points is the equivalent of one full carat. 200 points stand for two carats and so forth. A stone weighing 0.81 of a carat would be indicated merely as 81 points.

Equivalents are as follows:

Carat system	Points		
0.10	10	=	1/10 of a carat
0.50	50	=	1/2 carat
1.00	100	=	1 carat
1.50	150	=	1 1/2 carat

DIAMOND ESTIMATION. The most popular method of determining approximate carat weight is the diamond estimator. These are of many types, the most common of which is a plain piece of aluminum with holes of graduated sizes cut in it. Approximate carat weight is indicated by the circles below. It is thereby possible to roughly gauge the carat weight for stones of these diameters.

NOTE: These are approximate sizes and should be regarded as such. Before you buy or sell any diamond its carat weight should be determined by a professional using accurate equipment.

ROUND BRILLIANTS

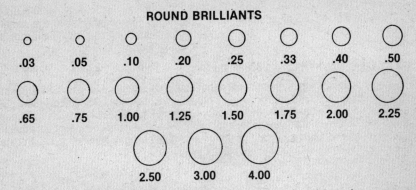

NOTE: With ROUND BRILLIANT cuts you may also estimate by measurement. If you have a ruler or calipers that measure in millimeters, the following table can be used for round cuts.

CARAT WEIGHT	DIAMETER IN MM.	HEIGHT IN MM.
0.01	1.38	0.78
0.05	2.37	1.33
0.10	2.98	1.67
0.25	4.04	2.26
0.50	5.09	2.85
1.00	6.42	3.60
1.50	7.35	4.12
2.00	8.09	4.54
3.00	9.25	5.19
4.00	10.19	5.72
5.00	10.98	6.16

BALANCE SCALES OR PANS. This is the old method of weighing, still employed to some extent today for diamonds because of the ease with which such scales are transported, their resistance to damage, their ability to be used where electrical current is unavailable, and their extremely low price in relation to the modern devices. The principle of the balance scale is that if an object is placed in one pan, and another object in the other, the pan holding the heavier object will fall while the other rises. The extent of fall-and-rise determines the difference in weight. To arrive at a reliable reading it is necessary to use counterbalances whose weights are established beyond doubt. The balance can only give readings in relation to the counterbalance's weight.

Balance scales do not give the most accurate obtainable readings for fractional weights. They weigh a tenth of a carat very well, but their reliability on hundredths of a carat is not accurate.

Among the more sophisticated weighing machines on the current market is the Oertling diamond balance, used extensively in Europe and to some extent in this country. Based on the principle of the pan balance, it offers extreme sensitivity and accuracy of readings impossible with simple balances. It is supplied with counterbalance "rings," each of a stated weight, and by the use of these rings singly or in combination the weight of virtually any diamond in the world can be determined down to 0.01. Fairly advanced portable scales are also on the market, usable without electric power.

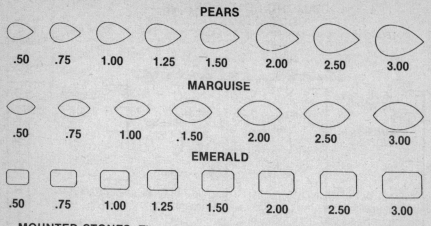

PEARS

.50 .75 1.00 1.25 1.50 2.00 2.50 3.00

MARQUISE

.50 .75 1.00 1.50 2.00 2.50 3.00

EMERALD

.50 .75 1.00 1.25 1.50 2.00 2.50 3.00

MOUNTED STONES. There is far greater difficulty in weighing mounted stones, a problem that has long vexed the industry. Owners of jewelry given over for appraisal will seldom agree to having the stone removed for weighing. Therefore it must be weighed while mounted, which technically, is an impossibility. The best that can be done in such circumstance is for a close estimate of the weight to be made, generally within a tenth of a carat.

Round brilliant cut mounted diamonds can be weight-estimated by use of the diamond estimator illustrated earlier in this section.

More advanced investors may wish to use the Leveridge gauge named after A. D. Leveridge, an American inventor who developed it in 1937. This is a compass-like instrument, of small size, with an encased dial covered by a crystal. Attached to it is a set of calipers, which are placed upon the diamond to be measured. The dial spins and gives the reading in millimeters, which is then translated into carat weight. The Leveridge gauge has an accuracy degree of 98% for larger stones. The readings are of course less reliable for stones of shapes other than circular.

Gauges are also available in which a series of "mold" sizes are furnished, attached to sticks. The mold which most perfectly fits atop the stone being weighed indicates the approximate carat of the latter.

These are all uncertain operations but nothing so far has been developed to make more accurate estimations of the weights of mounted stones.

DETERMINING THE COLOR OF THE DIAMOND

Reaching correct or reliable conclusions about the color of a diamond is somewhat more challenging than grading for clarity, as a number of variables enter the picture. It is not only a matter of differences in the human eye to perceive color, but interference from color reflection of other objects. This is an extremely delicate operation. If conditions are not ideal, the results obtained are likely to be unreliable and will be challenged when the stone is subsequently examined by a person using more sophisticated techniques.

It should also be pointed out that color grading is not an absolute science and that many stones, of both high and low ranking, could easily be placed into different grades by persons of equal expertise.

Sophisticated equipment is now available on the market to assist in color grading.

DIAMOND COLOR GRADING
COMPARISON TABLE

NOTE: Color grading is generally based on increased amounts of yellow tint. This color may also appear in brown tints and grey tints. Any other tint should be considered fancy colors no matter to what degree they are saturated. (Examples: blue, pink, orange etc.)

COMPARATIVE AND OLD WORLD TERMS

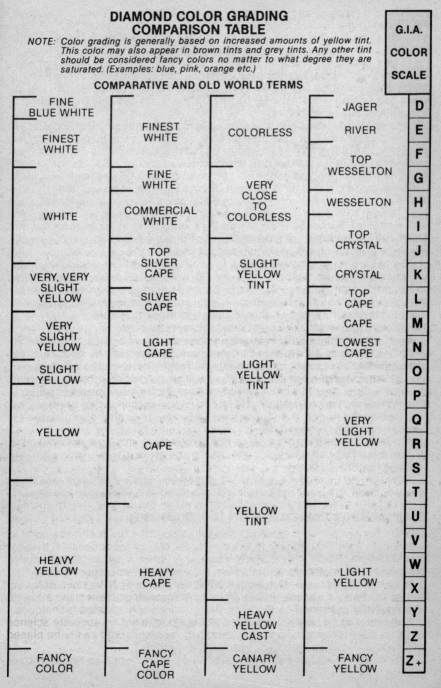

G.I.A. COLOR SCALE

Comparative & Old World Terms				G.I.A.
FINE BLUE WHITE			JAGER	D
FINEST WHITE	FINEST WHITE	COLORLESS	RIVER	E
			TOP WESSELTON	F
	FINE WHITE	VERY CLOSE TO COLORLESS		G
WHITE	COMMERCIAL WHITE		WESSELTON	H
				I
			TOP CRYSTAL	J
VERY, VERY SLIGHT YELLOW	TOP SILVER CAPE	SLIGHT YELLOW TINT	CRYSTAL	K
	SILVER CAPE		TOP CAPE	L
VERY SLIGHT YELLOW	LIGHT CAPE		CAPE	M
		LIGHT YELLOW TINT	LOWEST CAPE	N
SLIGHT YELLOW				O
				P
YELLOW	CAPE		VERY LIGHT YELLOW	Q
				R
				S
				T
		YELLOW TINT		U
				V
HEAVY YELLOW	HEAVY CAPE		LIGHT YELLOW	W
				X
		HEAVY YELLOW CAST		Y
				Z
FANCY COLOR	FANCY CAPE COLOR	CANARY YELLOW	FANCY YELLOW	Z +

By far the most accurate means of diamond grading is "comparison grading," used by the G.I.A. You must use what the industry refers to as a "master set of diamonds." These are stones that have been graded by the G.I.A. into specific color categories. They are then put in a row under correct lighting and the stone of undetermined color is compared to each, until the closest match is found. Example: if you have a stone that appears lighter or more colorless than a J grade but is definitely a shade darker than an H, then the obvious conclusion is that its color is an I. This is really the only true method of determining diamond colors.

Recently there have been developments in the manufacturing of Cubic Zirconia "master sets" or "CZ master sets." Placed on the market within the past year or so, these have proved to be most accurate. They are fairly inexpensive and can be transported without fear of losing a $30,000 or $40,000 genuine master set. The cost of a 1.00 carat 5-stone CZ set is under $1,000.

When grading a diamond yourself, it is first of all important that the surroundings be ideal. Reflections of color can occur from great distances, even in lighting which is not particularly strong, and will interfere with testing. The very nature of diamonds is such that they amplify nuances of color fed into them by light, and it is not possible for the human eye to distinguish between the natural color of a diamond and introduced or reflected color.

The testing room must be set up to simulate conditions under which diamonds are graded in a laboratory, with white walls, which have been covered in flat rather than gloss paint. There should be no highly reflective objects in the room. Light entering through a window should not pass through curtains, even if filmy and white, nor should the glass itself be tinted.

It is important that the subject diamond be tested against the proper background. The stone must be placed on a sheet of good white non-reflective paper. Do not use typewriting or other similar paper as the surface is too glossy. In the absence of special diamond testing paper, ordinary white blotting papers may be substituted. The paper is folded lengthwise to create lines of fluting, so that when laid on the table it presents a series of ridges of perhaps ½ inch each in height. The stone is now placed in one of the valleys between these ridges and is in correct attitude for examination. Instead of being viewed from the top it will now be examined from the side, which will give a more reliable reading. Tests conducted from looking down at the top, or table, are hampered by the much greater reflection of light from within the diamond in that position.

The lighting should be natural if possible. When diamonds are to be graded under artificial light, it is wise to avoid the standard incandescent bulb in favor of white fluorescent. Do not place the source of light too near the stone, and be certain that it falls centrally overhead rather than at an angle.

CLARITY CHARACTERISTICS

Clarity characteristics of diamonds are really defect characteristics.

It is important to note that BLEMISHES are marks or other characteristics on the surface of a stone. INCLUSIONS are trapped or imbedded within the diamond.

The more commonly encountered BLEMISHES are:

ABRASION. Chip on a facet edge, nearly always caused by two diamonds coming into contact with each other. Sometimes called Paper Marks.

EXTRA FACET. An additional facet or plane surface, beyond the number required in shaping. This generally occurs through accident in the cutting process.

NATURAL. An overlying portion of the crystal covering or skin. Found, if at all near or at the girdle.

PIT. Small nick or cavity. Also known as CHIP.

SCRATCH MARK, WHEEL MARK. Scratches on diamonds may result from contact with other diamonds or defects in the polishing wheel.

SURFACE GRAIN LINE. Evidence (at the surface) of irregular crystal development.

The more commonly encountered INCLUSIONS are:

CLOUD. An area within a diamond that is not perfectly clear but appears opaque.

FEATHER. Break within the structure of a diamond.

FEATHERED GIRDLE. Networks of very fine featherly lines radiating outward from the girdle into the stone's interior.

INCLUDED CRYSTAL. A second crystal within the first or main crystal. It may be clear or colored. When the included crystal is colored or has the appearance of black, it is called a "dark included crystal."

INTERNAL GRAIN LINE. Internal marks of abnormal crystal development.

KNOT. Included crystal (second diamond crystal) which has broken through the surface.

LASER DRILL HOLE. Tiny hole caused by drilling with a laser beam in an effort to launder the stone.

DETERMINING THE VALUE OF A DIAMOND

The following pages detail how to evaluate the investment potential of diamonds. It should be remembered throughout this section that diamonds set in antique jewelry are only one indicator of the value of the antique jewelry. Simply stated, the value of a diamond is determined by its quality and size, "quality" meaning not only its natural characteristics but the cutting and shaping. Many diamonds that score high on one point are deficient in other respects. A stone of exquisite color may have blemishes visible to the naked eye and will therefore rank I-1 or lower. The clarity on the other hand may be fine enough to grade IF or FL, but the stone has a bad "make," the trade term for improper proportioning. Whenever a diamond scores poorly on one of these quality considerations, its value is less than that of a perfect stone of the same size and characteristics. Of course, some shortcomings are more detrimental to value than others. Nor should it be presumed that specimens failing to grade high in all respects are worthless. It is mostly a matter of the individual stone's overall appeal and salability. Some stones can carry a defect better than others. Some have their defects well camouflaged by ingenious cutting.

Diamond appraisal is not an exact sicence. The appraiser operates from the standpoint that certain colors are more valued than others; that strong light refraction is desirable; that prospective buyers will give a premium for a well-executed cut; and so forth. The diamond must be taken into account of as a whole, after careful inspection and consideration of its characteristics, and value estimated by a weighing out of good and bad features.

The experts themselves are often in disagreement over value of a given stone. This is why prices realized at major gem auctions, such as those conducted by Sotheby/Parke-Bernet and Christie's, bear less relation to the pre-sale estimates than prices at most other kinds of auctions.

Even the word "value" is open to interpretation. There are a number of meanings of "value," in the world of diamonds.

RETAIL VALUE. Usually taken to mean the price that the average customer pays at the average jewelry store for a diamond to be used chiefly for personal adornment.

INVESTMENT VALUE. The price that an investor could be expected to pay, with fair prospects for a profitable sale at some future date. This will be considerably beneath the retail value.

WHOLESALE VALUE. The price a wholesaler would charge a jewelry manufacturer or other purchaser for the stone.

APPRAISAL VALUE. This might be even higher than retail value, depending on the appraiser's practices. Appraisal value is often referred to as "insurance value."

CUTTING VALUE. A stone that is large enough for recutting may be purchased on the basis of "cutting value," to correct a poor or obsolete cutting job. This will be a low price as it means reduction of carat weight, along with the inevitable risks taken in cutting.

Therefore, any potential buyer, after determining a stone's quality and weight, thinks in terms of the value to him, based on the purposes to which it will be placed. A very attractive purchase for one class of buyers may be unprofitable for another. A wholesaler cannot pay more than a fraction of the retail value. To a jewelry manufacturer, a diamond is worth anywhere from 10% to 30% of its retail value. And, of course, the ultimate retailer must buy at a good margin, paying around 50-60% of the price at which he sells, or less, if the stone requires mounting.

COLOR. It is debatable to what degree color counts in the value of a diamond. But when a diamond is highly graded in other respects, its color will count very much in fixing sales potential. An IF stone with round brilliant cut is certainly worth much more in D, or the highest grade of colorless/bluewhite, than in G or H or some other grade. The difference may be 50% or more or the difference in color can be of minor significance.

Take two stones for example. One weighs 1½ carats, with a clarity rating of VVS and the color is L (slightly tinted, silver cape). Both have identical shapes and proportioning is equally good. The only difference between them is that diamond #1 ranks a couple of notches lower on the color scale. Their values will be extremely close, perhaps less than 5% apart.

Many diamonds are wonderfully colored — in the D, E and F class — but are otherwise quite ordinary or have characteristics which automatically disqualify them as investments.

ONE CARAT STONES. When a single carat stone has a clarity grading of VS, its color should be generally no less than IF to qualify for investment, regardless of the merit of its other characteristics. Marriage of good color and good clarity grading is necessary to produce an investment diamond. They need not both be of maximum superiority, but perfection of one does not cancel out the shortcomings of the other.

ONE AND A HALF CARAT STONES. A 1½ carat diamond in VS clarity grading may be suitable for investment in the F color class. That extra half carat compensates for the slight deficiency in color.

TWO CARAT STONES. Or 200 points. The larger stones are more in demand and it would be safe to purchase for investment a two carat diamond whose clarity rating is VS with a color of G. With less than G you assume some risk, as the lesser colors are not as scarce or as highly desirable. A two carat stone in H is, however, a good investment when the clarity rating is VVS or better.

THREE CARATS AND MORE. When a stone weighs three carats or better — that is, more than 300 points — it is acceptable for investment in FL to VVS grading all the way down to I coloration (commercial white), though if the grading is VS it is necessary for the color to be G or higher on the scale.

CLARITY. Refer to the section on grading terminology for a detailed explanation of the various gradings. This is a major consideration in determining value. When a stone has an imperfection visible to the naked eye, there is really nothing that can save it. It may be brilliant blue-white, well proportioned, substantial in carat weight, but the imperfectness will reduce its commercial value by 40-70% against the value of the same stone in VS or better condition.

Do not be misled by fancy trappings. It is quite possible that an imperfect stone was, at some time in the past, set into a piece of good jewelry, and the item as a whole may be quite handsome and valuable as a piece of antique jewelry.

SHAPE. All other things being equal, a circular round shape will lend more value to a diamond than any of the other shapes. The other shapes are less common and in less demand. Circular diamonds are highly sought-after.

PROPORTIONING. Also called "make." This is the degree to which the cutting job approaches perfection. An investor would not want to place capital into a stone that is obviously misproportioned: the girdle too wide, the crown too short, etc. Improper proportioning can interfere with light refraction.

CARAT WEIGHT. One hundred points equals one carat. Loose stones can accurately be weighed to obtain the exact number of carats or points, but you can only obtain an estimate of the carats or points of a stone set in a piece of jewelry. Contemporary diamond investors are primarily interested in modern cut loose stones. Diamonds and other gem stones should not be removed from fine pieces of antique jewelry. Antique jewelry investors are interested in the overall workmanship and historical significance of the piece of jewelry.

The following can be used as a rough guide for tabulating percentage advances. We are assuming that we have a selection of stones which are all Round Brilliant and grade FL for clarity and D for color. These prices are not intended to be taken as anything more than an indication of percentage advances.

⅓ carat (0.30), 30 points	$ 6,000 per carat
½ carat (.50), 50 points	16,000 per carat
1 carat (1.00), 100 points	54,000 per carat
2 carats (2.00), 200 carats	60,000 per carat
3 carats (3.00), 300 points	75,000 per carat

Advances for D color VVS-2 are approximately as follows:

⅓ carat	$ 3,000 per carat
½ carat	7,500 per carat
1 carat	22,000 per carat
2 carats	26,000 per carat

Figuring values of uncut stones by carat weight is considerably more difficult. A proportion of weight will be lost in cutting and this portion is never precisely known in advance.

CLEANING DIAMONDS

Despite their non-porous surfaces, diamonds do require cleaning. The frequency of cleaning will depend upon the regularity with which your diamonds are worn or touched, as they acquire a greasy film when handled. Investment stones kept in bank vaults and seldom disturbed will need cleaning only occasionally. The operation is simple and should not be cause for alarm. It can be performed without risk by anyone, observing just a few simple rules.

The chief point to be kept in mind is that diamonds ought to be cleaned individually, as there is danger of scratching if two are allowed to come into contact with each other. If you do not have commercial jewelry cleaner at hand, which is available at most jewelry stores, you can follow the following instructions using simple ingredients.

Into a small bowl introduced a mixture consisting of one cup warm water, two tablespoons liquid dishwashing detergent, and a teaspoon of clear ammonia. Mix this around thoroughly until a frothy lather appears. Now drop one diamond into the bowl and allow it to remain for about 15 minutes. This soaking will sufficiently soften the grease so that it can be wiped away. The wiping operation is performed while the diamond is still submerged, by grasping it with the fingers of one hand and brushing it on all sides with an old toothbrush or artist's brush. The diamond is then rinsed under lukewarm water and patted with a lintless cloth. It is left out to "air" for a while before being returned to the jewel box or wherever it is normally stored.

IMPORTANT: Do not, when rinsing, hold the diamond over a sink drain. As a precaution, be sure to place a stopper over the sink drain.

HOW TO TELL REAL DIAMONDS FROM FAKES

Great advances in technology have given birth to very sophisticated testing apparatus', unknown 50 or even 20 years ago. But this same technology has made possible the production of artificial and imitation diamonds that could not be made with earlier methods.

Diamond substitutes are not illegal in the trade because they have definite uses in industry and jewelry — if properly labeled. Most of these are man-made materials to which various names are given, though it is still possible to encounter "diamonds" faked from one or more natural mineral substances, such as quartz and white topaz. Once these stones have passed from the hands of their original seller, their identification hinges upon the expertise and care of any subsequent potential buyer.

METHODS FOR DETECTING ARTIFICIAL OR SIMULATED DIAMONDS. As each of the materials used in production of artificial diamonds has its own properties and characteristics, methods successful in detecting one will not be useful in testing all.

A number of the available tests require use of high precision equipment. Others can be performed without aid of any tools.

VISUAL INSPECTION. The ratio of success by visual inspection depends mostly upon the individual's experience and expertise. A newcomer will usually be able to distinguish only the more obvious diamond substitutes and imitations, while a gemologist will score much higher. Knowledgeable diamond handlers look for certain characteristics: the surface lustre, straightness and flatness of facets, high light reflectivity, and internally the foreshortening which is peculiar to well-cut diamonds. This foreshortening, which makes the stone appear shallower than it really is, is in the nature of an optical illusion, caused by play of light. It is nevertheless a characteristic that other minerals and most of the synthetics do not possess in quite such a degree and can be taken as good evidence of a diamond's authenticity. To examine for foreshortening, the back facet edges must be inspected while looking through the table or uppermost flat surface, under a good light.

Surface reflectivity is perhaps not a reliable indication of authenticity, but it can at least be said that when this characteristic is not present the odds are good that the stone is not a diamond. Holding the stone near the eye and turning it slowly, it should catch, in mirror fashion, reflections of objects in the room, if the area is well lighted. The less good the lighting, the less that can be expected of a diamond's reflectability.

It is also much more difficult to reach conclusions on the genuineness of mounted than unmounted cut stones, as they pick up reflections from the mounting and cannot be inspected as completely.

TILT TEST. This is a common preliminary test used by all diamond merchants. Despite its simplicity it is very useful. The stone is held close to the eye, table upward, and slowly pointed away from the body. If genuine, the brilliance or sparkle observable through the table will remain even at this angle. Most imitations and fakes lose some measure of brilliance when the table is tilted away.

HEAT CONDUCTIVITY. Diamonds have a high level of thermal conductivity. That is, they acquire the temperature to which they are exposed. They become warm in a warm room and cool if the surroundings are cold. Other minerals do not possess such a high degree of thermal conductivity. Consequently, simple tests may be done, exposing stones to warmth and cold and then touching them to the lips to discover their approximate temperature. Such tests are more conclusive when other gems known not to be diamonds, are tested at the same time.

BREATH TEST. Another simple test is the breath test, which involves nothing more than breathing upon stone. For results to be meaningful, the subject stone and one known to be a diamond should be tested simultaneously. If the coating of moisture clears from both at the same time, it is an indication that the subject stone is likely a diamond. If it clears noticeably sooner from the known diamond, the subject-stone can be presumed to be some other material — but further testing is necessary to reach an irrefutable conclusion. Thermal conductivity is once again the cause. The diamond heats up faster and therefore evaporates the mist quicker.

STICKINESS TEST. If the subject stone can be picked up with the tip of a moistened finger, this points to its likelihood of it being a diamond. The majority of stones cannot be picked up in this way. Of course a large diamond is not suitable for the stickiness test, as its weight will cause it to fall from the finger.

WATER TEST. This test is inexact but worth performing before more complicated procedures are entered into. The diamond table must be perfectly clean. A drop of water is placed on the table. If it begins spreading about, this is an indication that the stone is something other than a diamond. Diamond has the ability to almost "magnetize" water and hold it firmly.

HARDNESS TEST. This old traditional test is still of value; no other gems have the hardness of diamonds. The hardness test is objected to by many persons because it entails risk of injuring the stone, even if it is a real diamond. No attempt should ever be made to test hardness by trying to scratch a possible diamond with another stone or object, but rather using the test stone to make a scratch upon something else. The best material is ruby or sapphire, which cannot be scratched by any mineral except a diamond. Use the diamond girdle — not the culet or one of the facet edges — and draw it with moderate pressure across the ruby or sapphire. If the scratch it leaves cannot be removed by rubbing with a moistened finger, the stone being tested is probably a genuine diamond. Beware of shallow surface scratches that can be easily rubbed away, as these can be created by softer minerals or synthetics. We do not suggest experimentation with this form of testing.

CUTTING ACCURACY. A diamond will generally exhibit more precision of cut than synthetics or gems of lesser value.

SURFACE CHARACTERISTICS. The surface characteristics of true diamonds, while important in identification, are so suitable that a beginner is not apt to learn much from their examination. Straight lines or ridges in the polished surfaces are an indication of authenticity. If examined under 10X magnification, the surface will appear to be slightly rippled or to contain minute hills and valleys. This is called texturing and is peculiar to diamonds. The girdle or central circumference of a cut diamond should display a more waxy appearance than the stone in general, the result of cutting.

INTERNAL CHARACTERISTICS. Internal cleavage is a good indication of authenticity. The only other gemstone to show internal cleavage is topaz, whose brilliance is considerably less than that of diamonds.

SPECIFIC GRAVITY. Diamonds have a specific gravity of 3.51½. The reading must be taken accurately to be of any service. Obviously it is not possible with mounted stones.

We now come to what is probably the most foolproof method in the industry. It is called a "diamond probe." Several models are available on the market. The diamond probe measures reflectivity and gives a specific reading when the tip of the probe is placed perpendicular in the center of the stone's table facet. The indicator will either read "imitation" or "true diamond." To date, this method has been the most successful in detecting even the most sophisticated fakes.

RECOMMENDED READING

Dozens of books have been written on antique jewelry, most of which include glossaries. Since the unique nature of this book is to present thousands of photographs of antique jewelry with accompanying descriptions, space limitations have not permitted a detailed glossary to be included in this edition. The following books offer excellent additional reading material on antique jewelry:

Armstrong, Nancy. *JEWELLERY AN HISTORICAL SURVEY OF BRITISH STYLES & JEWELS,* Luttenworth Press, 1977.

Armstrong, Nancy. *VICTORIA JEWELRY,* Cassell & Collier Macmillan Publishers Ltd., 1976

Baillie, G. H. *WATCHMAKERS AND CLOCKMAKERS, OF THE WORLD,* N.A. G. Press Ltd., 1969.

Baillie, G. H., Clutton, C. and Ilbert, C. A. *OLD CLOCKS AND WATCHES AND THEIR MAKERS,* Bonanza Books, New York, 1956.

Bainbridge, Henry Charles, *PETER CARL FABERGE - GOLDSMITH AND JEWELER TO THE RUSSIAN IMPERIAL COURT,* Spring Books, 1971.

Becker, Vivienne. *ANTIQUE AND 20TH CENTURY JEWELLERY,* N.A.G. Press Ltd., 1980.

Black, J. Anderson. *A HISTORY OF JEWELRY — FIVE THOUSAND YEARS,* Park Lane, 1974.

Bradford, Ernie. *ENGLISH VICTORIAN JEWELLERY,* Spring Books, 1967.

Bradford, Ernie. *FOUR CENTURIES OF EUROPEAN JEWELLERY,* Spring Books, 1967.

Bradbury, Frederick. *GUIDE TO MARKS OF ORIGIN ON BRITISH AND IRISH SILVER PLATE FROM MID-16TH CENTURY TO THE YEAR 1973. OLD SHEFFIELD PLATE MAKERS' MARKS 1743-1860,* J. W. Northend Ltd., 1973.

British Museum Publication. *JEWELLERY THROUGH 700 YEARS,* British Museum Publications Limited, 1976.

Burgess, Fred W. *ANTIQUE JEWELRY & TRINKETS,* Tudor Publishing Company.

Clifford, Anne. *CUT-STEEL & BERLIN IRON JEWELLERY,* Adams & Dart, 1971.

Cooper, Diana and Battershill, Norman. *VICTORIAN SENTIMENTAL JEWELLERY,* A. S. Barnes & Co., Inc., 1973.

Curran, Mona. *COLLECTING ANTIQUE JEWELLERY,* Emerson Books, Inc., 1970.

Delieb, Eric. *SILVER BOXES,* Ferndale Editions, London, 1979.

Evans, Joan. *A HISTORY OF JEWELLERY 1100-1870,* Boston Book and Art, Publisher, Boston, 1970.

Falkiner, Richard. *INVESTING IN ANTIQUE JEWELLERY,* Barrie & Rocklif, The Cressent Press. The Corgi Ed. 1976.

Flower, Margaret. *VICTORIAN JEWELLERY,* A. S. Barnes & Co., Inc., 1967.

Frank, Joan. *THE BEAUTY OF JEWELRY,* Crescent Books, a division of Crown Publishers, Inc., 1979.

Fregnac, Claude. *JEWELRY FROM RENAISSANCE TO ART NOUVEAU,* Octopus Books Limited, 1973.

Garside, Anne. *JEWELRY, ANCIENT TO MODERN,* Viking Press, 1980.

Gere, Charlotte. *AMERICAN & EUROPEAN JEWELRY 1830-1914*, Crown Publishers, Inc., 1975.

Gere, Charlotte; Rudoe, Judy; Tait, Hugh; Wilson, Timothy; *THE ART OF THE JEWELLER A CATALOGUE OF THE HULL GRUNDY GIFT TO THE BRITISH MUSEUM*, British Museum Publications Limited, 1984.

Goldenberg, Rose Leman. *ANTIQUE JEWELRY: A PRACTICAL & PASSIONATE GUIDE*, Crown Publishers, 1976.

Gregorietti, Guido. *JEWELRY THROUGH THE AGES*, American Heritage, New York, 1969.

Kaltenböck/Schwank, *WATCH-KEYS*, Nicolaus Günther, 1983.

Lewis, M. D. S. *ANTIQUE PASTE JEWELLERY*, Boston Book & Art, Publisher, 1973.

Mason, Anita and Packer, Diane. *AN ILLUSTRATED DICTIONARY OF JEWELLERY*, Harper & Row, Publishers, 1974.

Mastai, Marie-Louise d'Otranes. *JEWELRY*, The Smithsonian Illustrated Library of Antiques, 1981.

McNeil, Donald S., editor. *JEWELERS DICTIONARY 3RD EDITION*, Jewelers' Circular-Keystone, Radnor, Pennsylvania, 1979.

Munn, Geoffrey C., *CASTELLANI AND GIULIANO REVIVALIST JEWELLERS OF THE NINETEENTH CENTURY*, Trefoil Books Ltd., London, 1984.

Nadelhoffer, Hans, *CARTIER JEWELERS EXTRAORDINARY*, Thames and Hudson, 1984.

O'Day, Deirdre. *VICTORIAN JEWELLERY*, Charles Letts and Company, Limited, 1974.

Peter, Mary. *COLLECTING VICTORIAN JEWELLERY*, Emerson Books, Inc., 1971.

Poynder, Michael. *THE PRICE GUIDE TO JEWELLERY*, Baron Publishing, 1976.

Sataloff, Joseph and Richards, Alison. *THE PLEASURE OF JEWELRY AND GEMSTONES*, Octopus Books, 1975.

Tait, Hugh and Gere, Charlotte. *THE JEWELLER'S ART*, British Museum Publications Limited, 1978.

Taylor, Gerald and Scarisbrick Diana. *FINGER RINGS FROM ANCIENT EGYPT TO THE PRESENT DAY*, Lund Humphries Publishers Ltd., 1978.

TRADEMARKS OF THE JEWELRY AND KINDRED TRADES, The Jewelers Circular Publishers Co., New York, 1915.

ABBREVIATIONS AND EXPLANATIONS OF TERMS

c. . . . . Circa, approximate period of time when item was made.
ct. . . . . Carat, weight of gemstone, under one carat.
cts. . . . . Carat, weight of gemstone, over one carat.
Gold . . . . Yellow gold at least nine karat pure unless different color or karat stated.
Hair . . . . Human hair of brunette color unless noted otherwise.
HC . . . . Hunting case watch, cover on both sides of case.
MM . . . . Millimeter

OF . . . . Open face watch, cover on one side of case.
Sapphire . . . . Gemstone, blue in color unless noted otherwise.
 9K . . . . Nine karat gold.
10K . . . . Ten karat gold.
14K . . . . Fourteen karat gold.
15K . . . . Fifteen karat gold.
18K . . . . Eighteen karat gold.
22K . . . . Twenty-two karat gold.

BIRTHSTONE LIST

January:	Garnet	July:	Ruby
February:	Amethyst	August:	Peridot, Sardonyx
March:	Aquamarine, Bloodstone	September:	Sapphire
April:	Diamond	October:	Tourmaline, Opal, Rose Zircon
May:	Emerald	November:	Topaz, Citrine
June:	Moonstone, Pearl, Alexandrite	December:	Blue Zircon, Turquoise

BASIC GLOSSARY

The definitions in this glossary are to acquaint the reader with some of the terms used in the descriptions of the pictured jewelry.

AMBER. Light weight fossilized sap, resin or gum from ancient trees which can be cut, etched, faceted or carved. Amber can be translucent or opaque and range in color from shades of yellow, brown, red and even grey or green.

ART DECO. An angular style of jewelry from the 1920's through the 1930's featuring jade, black onyx and pave diamonds.

ART NOUVEAU. A free-flowing curved revolutionary style of jewelry from the 1890's until about 1910. Featuring delicate enamels and non-precious materials in the characteristic motifs of women with flowing long hair, bats, morning glories and dragonflies.

BOG OAK. Natural oak wood which has been darkened and hardened as a result of being immersed in the bogs of Ireland.

CABOCHON. An unfaceted cut stone with a smoothly polished domed top.

CAMEO. A stone or shell cut in relief using the natural colors of the stone or shell to produce the different shadings of the carving. Opposite of an intaglio. See-intaglio.

CANNETILLE. Metal jewelry, usually made from fine wires, often in a pyramid or rosette motif.

CASTELLANI, FORTUNATO PIA. 19th century Italian jeweler noted for his revival of Etruscan and Greek styles in jewelry which were sold as pieces as "Italian Archaological Jewelry."

CHAMPLEVÉ ENAMEL. The sections in which the different color enamel are placed are carved out of the surface of the base, rather than formed by soldering thin strips of metal to the base as in cloisonne enamel.

CHATELAINE. A decorative plaque with a hook attached to its rear to be worn from a belt or sash around the waist from which suspend a series of plaques or chains. Purses, watches, keys, sewing utensils, note pads, pencils, button hooks, etc. were the type of functional implements connected to the ends of the plaques or chains.

CLOISONNÉ ENAMEL. A type of enamel work in which thin strips of metal are soldered to the base to form the outlines of the design. Colored enamel is then placed in each section.

DISSOLVED HAIR. Human hair which has been chopped up and made into a paint or paste to be used for drawing pictures on ivory or porcelain plaques. The result of using dissolved hair is a fuzzy effect.

EGLOMAIZE. Reverse painting on glass.

ENAMEL. Powdered colored glass is fused onto the surface of the piece of jewelry. The following types of enamel work are illustrated and defined in this book: Champlevé, Cloisonné, Guilloché, Jaipur, plique á jour and polychrome.

ETRUSCAN. A 19th century antique revival style of jewelry resembling that which was produced in Tuscany, central Italy, during the 7th to 6th centuries B.C. by the ancient Etruscans. The work is characterized by minute beads of gold soldered onto a gold background forming a pattern. See granulation.

ÉTUIS. A case, hanging from a chatelaine, which contains useful implements, such as scissors, pencil, small spoon, pad, ear cup cleaner, toothpick, etc.

FABERGÉ, PETER CARL (1846-1920). Jeweler to the Russian Czar famous for the gemstone Easter egges made for the Czar's mother and wife.

GRANULATION. Minute metal beads, usually gold, used to decorate jewelry. See Etruscan.

GUILLOCHÉ ENAMEL. A translucent polychrome enamel placed on top of a geometric engraved pattern on the jewelry or watchcase.

GUTTA PERCHA. A plastic or rubber-like substance produced from the natural fluids of certain Malaysian trees. When first introduced in the nineteenth century, all forms of jewelry were produced from gutta percha as a novelty. It is dark brown in color and very brittle.

HAIR. Jewelry woven from human hair which was made either as a romantic token for a loved one or from the hair of a deceased friend or family member as a sentimental remembrance. Jewelry can also be found woven from horsehair and elephant hair.

INDIAN PITCH. A plaque made from pouring green glass onto gold foil, which has been cut out in a mold in hunting scene motifs. After the glass is set, it is polished until the glass is level with the gold foil, forming a silhouette effect. Popular after Queen Victoria became Empress of India in 1876.

INTAGLIO. An engraved stone in which the design is carved into the surface of the stone so that the rim is the highest portion. The opposite of a cameo. See Cameo.

JAIPUR ENAMEL. A region in India named Jaipur which is the center of the jewelry industry. Indian jewelry is characterized by brightly-colored enamels on both the front and back.

JAMES TASSIE. A London jeweler who developed a secret paste from around 1766 with which he produced paste replica intaglio gemstones from wax models. Commonly called "Tassies" on today's market.

JET. Hard coal, mined at Whitby, England, was highly polished and carved and primarily sold as memorial jewelry.

LALIQUE, RENÉ JULES (1860-1845). Leading French jeweler connected with the Art Nouveau movement.

LAVA. Lava found at Pompeii, Italy, was primarily carved as cameos, ranging in color from cream to dark brown and white to charcoal. It is very soft and therefore permits a skilled artisan to carve fine detail with high relief.

MACARONI. A style of chatelaine composed of a series of long chains with a watch on one end and on the other end a series of charms, such as watch keys and seals.

NUTMEG GRATER. A small box made from the 17th century to the middle of the 19th century with a removable grate under the lid for the grating of precious spices such as nutmeg.

PARURE. A matching set of jewelry usually including a necklace, pendant, brooch, earrings and bracelet.

PASTE. Colored or clean glass, often lead or flint glass, which are cut in the same fashion as gemstones. Antique paste jewelry was valued on its own merits and not as an imitation of another piece of jewelry.

PINCHBECK. Christopher Pinchbeck, 1670-1732, was a London jeweler, watchmaker and alchemist who invented a substitute for gold made from an alloy of copper and zinc.

PIQUÉ. Tortoise shell or ivory which has been inlaid with gold, silver or mother-of-pearl.

PLIQUE A´ JOUR ENAMEL. Transparent enamel which is placed between thin strips of metal which are soldered together to form the design, the end result of which is similar to stained glass. Plique a jour is distinguished from cloisonne in that there is no base to which the strips of metal and enamel rest.

POLYCHROME ENAMEL. Enamel in various colors.

"REGARD". A sentimental piece of jewelry containing six gemstones, in which the first letter of each gemstone spells the world "regard":

    R - ruby
    E - emerald
    G - garnet
    A - amethyst
    R - ruby
    D - diamond

SATSUMA. A Japanese ceramic overlaid with a glaze that forms hairline cracks. Over the glaze are figures, flowers and decorations painted in polychrome enamel.

SCARAB. A representation of the ancient Egyptian Scaraboeus bettle carved in either glazed pottery or in gemstones such as amethyst, corneilian, and lapis lazuli. Scarabs were customarily in swivel mountings so that the intaglio carved on the reverse side could be viewed.

SCARF RING. An oval ring to hold a scarf at the neck. The most common style available is one which opens on a hinge and has a pointed spike in the inside center to hold the scarf together. Hollow oval and pressure clip oval scarf rings can also be found in todays' marketplace.

TIGER CLAW. Tiger claws from India were imported to England, mounted in precious metals, and worn as jewelry. Popular in the 1870's, particularly after Queen Victoria became Empress of India in 1876.

TORTOISE SHELL. Jewelry carved, molded, inlaid, polished, welded and cut from the hard protective outer covering of the Hawksbill turtle and the Loggerhead turtle in a blond, translucent amber or dark opaque reddish amber color.

VICTORIAN. Referring to that period of time encompassing the reign of England's Queen Victoria 1837-1901. The Victorian era is generally broken down into three phases, Early Victorian 1837-1850, Mid-Victorian 1850-1875 and Late Victorian 1875-1901.

VINAIGRETTE. A small box with a removable pierced grill under the lid in which a sponge or cotton was saturated with spirits of ammonia or Aromatic vinegar. Circa: late 18th century through 19th century.

WATCHCOCK. The escapement covers in watches made in the late 18th century were highly engraved and cutout in animal, flower and circular swirl motifs. During the 1870's these watches were junked and jewelry was made from combining the watchcocks.

THE GOLD AND SILVER GLOSSARY

ALLOY. (a) To alloy a precious metal is to introduce a quantity of another metal into it. Gold may be alloyed with base metal or with silver.
(b) The metal used for alloying is referred to as "alloy."

ASSAY. The official determination, by a licensed assayer, of the bullion content in an object. The assaying of metal requires testing that includes a measurement of its weight by specific gravity.

AQUA REGIA. A chemical widely used in the jewelry industry, especially for testing the fineness of gold. Aqua regia is made of three parts hydrochloric acid and one part nitric acid.

DICHROMATE. A chemical solution used for testing the composition of metal articles. Dichromate is composed of postassium dichromate and nitric acid.

FINENESS. The degree of purity in an object of precious metal, usually expressed by hundredths in decimal form (such as .995, which means 99½ parts pure and ½ part of alloy). It may also be written in terms of a percentage; in the case of the example given, the percentage equivalent would be 99½%. The highest degree of obtainable fineness in gold or silver is expressed as .999 + , rather than 1.000, because of the impossibility of guaranteeing that all minor traces of incidental metallic substances have been removed.

GERMAN SILVER. A high proportion of nickel alloy with almost no silver. See Nickel Silver.

GOLDBEATERS' SKIN. 24K gold hammered or rolled into extremely thin sheets, used for various kinds of artistic decoration (such as leather tooling). Dates to the time when laborers who hammered gold were called "goldbeaters." One of the remarkable properties of gold is that it can be flattened to extraordinary thinness without becoming overly fragile.

GOLD FILLED. Gold filled articles are similar to plated: they have an exterior of gold and a core of base metal, usually copper. The difference is in the method of application. Plated objects are shaped and then bullion-coated by electroplating, in which the soft gold takes the object's form. Gold filled merchandise is made from sheets of metal to which the outer covering of gold has been applied before the object is shaped.

G.P. When found on an article that appears made of gold, these letters indicate that the gold is merely surface plating (G.P. = gold plated).

HALLMARK. A decorative marking found on gold and silver articles, frequently indicating the maker, country of origin, date and fineness of the metal. The origin of the word hallmark dates to the later Middle Ages of England, when silversmiths were members of the Guildhall.

KARAT. The method by which fineness of gold is expressed. Pure unalloyed gold is 24 karat. As alloy metal is added (usually copper, for strength or to reduce the price), the karat value declines: 22K, 20K, 18K and so on. The lowest grade of gold to carry a karat marking is 10K, or, in Great Britain, 9K. Most gold coins are 20K or 21K. Jewelry is commonly made of 9K to 18K. The word "karat" derives from the carob bean, used as a measure of weight in the ancient world. When spelled "carat" it refers to the weight of a precious gem and has nothing to do with the fineness of a metal in the United States.

MELT VALUE. The bullion value of any object containing precious metal. When sold for melting, the full price of an item's bullion content is not received but only a percentage. Antique jewelry has a higher retail or "intact" value than melt value and obviously should not be melted.

NICKEL SILVER. An alloy of copper, nickel and zinc also known as German Silver first gaining popularity in the 1830's.

PLATING. The covering of base metal articles with a layer of gold or silver, which may be of various thicknesses and grades. Presence of plating may be discovered by filing and using nitric acid, or subjecting the item to specific gravity testing.

PLUMB GOLD. A gold alloy which is the same fineness that it is marked with little or no tolerance. See tolerance.

PRECIOUS METAL. The three primary precious metals are gold, silver and platinum. All others (except derivitives of these three) are known technically as "base metal." Of course, the preciousness of precious metals varies, as does the baseness of base metals.

PURITY. The proportion of precious metal vs. base metal in an object. A purity of .900 would mean a content of 90% precious metal and 10% base metal alloy, or a ratio of 9-to-1.

SCRAP. Material made of or containing precious metal, which has no value beyond that of its bullion content and is suitable only for melting. Almost all antique jewelry and associated fashion accessories have a value exceeding their bullion content.

SOLID. When an object is referred to as solid bullion, this means it is not plated or filled but that its interior composition is identical to its exterior. Bullion can be either heavily or lightly alloyed. "Solid gold" is not necessarily 24K.

SPECIFIC GRAVITY. A method of testing the composition of metallic objects, which measures their displacement of water in relation to their bulk. Each metal element has an established specific gravity.

SPOT PRICE. "Spot Price" is the price at which precious metal is being traded at any given time. Spot prices are always calculated on the basis of one full troy ounce and must be multiplied or divided to arrive at prices for larger or smaller quantities. The spot price is achieved in day to day trading in gold markets, just as are prices for stocks and other commodities. Generally, the London spot is used as the world barometer, after conversion from pounds to dollars.

TOLERANCE. The amount of difference permitted by law between the karat marking on a gold article and the actual fineness of gold it contains. Tolerances up to one full karat are allowable, depending on circumstances (such as whether solder has been used in manufacture). Tolerances are permitted only on craft or other manufactured items, not on bars or ingots.

TOUCHTONE. A stone, of basalt or slate, used in testing gold to determine its karat. Touchstones are used in combination with testing needles and aqua regia.

DIAMOND GLOSSARY

ABRADED CULET. If the culet facet is chipped or otherwise damaged, as the result of harsh contact with another diamond, this is known as an abraded culet.

ABRASION. This is generally taken to mean an injury to a cut diamond. Also used in reference to the natural action of water, and other elements, in shaping or smoothing gems still in the earth.

AMERICAN BRILLIANT CUT. The American Brilliant Cut is a method of cutting diamonds to mathematical perfection to yield greatest brilliancy and fire. This is today the most popular cut for fine stones. It is employed in Europe as well as the U.S. Sometimes shortened to "American Cut."

BAGUETTE. French for "rod." A step-cut used for rectangular stones, chiefly those of small size.

BEARDED GIRDLE. Diamond girdle which is not smooth but instead displays networks of imperfections in the form of hairline fractures. Bearded girdles result from rushing the process of rounding up or shaping the stone. Sometimes called "fuzzy girdle."

BEZEL FACET. The large facets surrounding the table on the crown of a Round Brilliant cut. They are always 8 in number.

BLOCKING. Cutting the first 18 facets into a diamond — known as the "main facets" — is called blocking. The word is borrowed from the art world, where blocking in sculpture means to reduce a block of marble, wood, etc., to roughly the shape of the intended design.

BOURSE. An assembly of dealers, set up to buy and/or sell. There are regularly established, continuous diamond bourses sponsored by trade organizations in various parts of the world (but chiefly in Europe).

BRILLIANTEERER. An artisan who cuts and polishes the "brilliant facets," on Brilliant Cut diamonds. These are a total of 40, and are added after cutting the main bezel and pavilion facets (which is done by the blocker).

BRUTER. Workman in a diamond factory who shapes stones against a high-speed lathe. Though only "dust" is lost in this operation, it reduces carat weight more than might be imagined.

CANARY DIAMOND. Deeply colored yellow diamond, possibly with hues of green or orange. Pale yellow coloration — far more common — is detrimental to value.

CARAT. A unit of weight, by which the size of both uncut and cut diamonds is stated. A carat is equal to .200 grams. The newcomer to diamond buying should be careful not to become overly influenced by carat size that he ignores, or fails to recognize the importance of, such points as clarity, color and cut.

CARBON SPOTS. Dark particles or inclusions in a diamond, which may or may not be visible to the unaided eye. An all-purpose term; the material could be of any nature. It is frequently graphite. "Carbon" spots normally appear black to the unaided eye or under low magnification, but may prove to be another color when magnified further and examined by an individual with keen color perception. Classified as blemishes.

CENTRAL SELLING ORGANIZATION. Collective term referring to the three organizations which place freshly mined diamonds into the world wholesale market. These are: Industrial Distributors Ltd., Diamond Trading Co. Ltd., and Diamond Corporation Ltd., the last two of which are incorporated in South Africa. All were established by the DeBeers firm.

CLARITY GRADE. The quality of a diamond in terms of its clearness or absence/presence of imperfections, expressed according to a standard scale.

CLEAVAGE. Word with many meanings in relation to diamonds, but chiefly used in reference to the dependability of crystals to divide in established directions when properly cleaved (set in a holder, marked, and divided by means of a sharp blade tapped with a mallet or other heavy instrument).

COLORED DIAMONDS. Diamonds are found in a variety of colors, generally very pale, including brown, green, pink, blue, red and yellow. When these colors are intense and well balanced throughout the stone, premium value is likely to be attached. But a diamond of pastel color is not as desirable as a colorless or "white."

COLOR GRADE. The color quality of a diamond, expressed according to a scale of letters representing different grades of color (see Grading Section). Crystal clear, or absolute lack of coloration, is the most desirable; these are often referred to as "white" diamonds.

COLORLESS. A diamond in which no trace of coloration can be detected. The ideal state for stones intended for the Round Brilliant cut. Truly colorless diamonds are worth a premium over others, assuming they are not severely flawed.

CONCHOIDAL FRACTURE. A cut (made by a sharp blow upon a knife blade resting on a diamond) in which the initial pressure of impact radiates outward in a prescribed pattern, something like ripples created by tossing pebbles in a lake.

CRITICAL ANGLE. The greatest angle in a diamond, running from the normal surface to a surface that a ray of light may form when passing from density to lesser density. Of importance in determining the degree of light refraction and, therefore, the ultimate fire of the stone.

CROWN. The upper part of a cut diamond, above the girdle.

CROWN JEWEL. A jewel belonging to the crown or state, as well as gems set in royal crowns.

CRYSTAL LATTICE. The network of structure of atoms within a diamond crystal. The cleavage break is along the atomic plane of weakness. When cleaving is attempted against the plane of weakness, the break will either be uneven or crushing could result.

CULET. Small facet cut into the bottom or pavilion of a diamond. Without this facet the stone would, thanks to cutting, come to a rather sharp point at the pavilion.

DEPTH PERCENTAGE. The relationship of a diamond's height (table to culet) to its diameter at the widest part (the girdle). Good depth percentage is necessary in achieving a proper "make" or cut.

DIAMOND PAPER. Paper folded in a special manner to contain loose diamonds in transit. A durable grade of paper must be used, to prevent the stone breaking through and escaping in the event of pressure or possible rough handling. Revelant information — such as weight, lot number or price — may be penciled on the outside of this packet.

DIAMOND SETTER. A skilled workman who places a finished cut diamond into a jewelry mounting. Expertise and care are necessary, to avoid injury.

DIAMOND-WASHING CUP. Bronze cup, punched with numerous holes in the fashion of a sieve, set inside a glass jar. Used in washing diamonds to remove surface grease.

DISPERSION. The ability of diamonds to turn ordinary light entering them into brilliant colors. The principal is similar to that creating rainbows in the sky when sunlight shines after a rainshower.

DODECAHEDRON. Twelve-sided crystal.

DURABILITY. Diamonds are durable in the sense of not being easily scratched, except by other diamonds. They can, however, be crushed or broken without difficulty. Those who own diamonds should be careful not to form the very mistaken notion that, because of their hardness rating, they are impervious to harm.

EUROPEAN CUT. Method of cutting which varies from the American Briliant approach in that proportions are worked out according to light falling directly from above on the crown.

EXTRA FACETS. Additional facets beyond those intended in the planning stage. Generally caused accidentally in one or more of the cutting and shaping processes, extra facets are considered defects if they occur on the crown or can be seen through the crown.

EYE-CLEAN. A diamond in which no internal imperfections can be seen with the naked eye by a person with normal vision.

FACET. Flat surface cut into a diamond. Correct positioning and angling of facets determines whether the stone will have maximum fire.

FACE UP. A diamond set so that the table faces the observer as in most jewelry.

FANCY DIAMOND. A colored diamond, whose color is intense enough to be a plus rather than a minus. Faintly colored stones are invariably worth less than pure colorless ones.

FEATHER. Any break in a diamond. Feathers are blemishes.

FINISH. The overall quality of a diamond in relation to the "finishing steps" in manufacture as well as overall proportioning. Fineness of polishing, girdle smoothness, and adriotness in cutting the culet are among the considerations taken into account.

FLAW. A blemish or imperfection, either on the surface of a diamond or the interior. This may be in the form of a scratch, feathering, carbon spots, etc. Bad color is not technically considered a flaw; nor is anything relating to the proportioning or cut.

FLAWLESS. The highest clarity grade for a diamond. It does not infer that tiny, minor blemishes are not visible with strong magnification. (See Grading section.)

FLUORESCENCE. The action of one kind of energy-induced radiation changing to another, thereby creating the apparently spontaneous appearance of color or hues. Diamonds generally show a blue/flourescence, though this is not invariable.

FOUR C's. Common trade term to collectively describe the major considerations in a diamond's value: clarity, color, carat, and cut.

GEMOLOGICAL INSTITUTE OF AMERICA. A non-profit, chiefly educational organization, with headquarters in New York and Los Angeles. It conducts courses in diamonds (grading, appraising, etc.) and awards certificates of Certified Gemologist to those successfully completing these courses. In addition it operates a diamond certification service. C.G. papers, when current, serve as the "last word" in grading. Investment diamonds should be purchased only when accompanied by C.G. papers. This is the only guarantee that they will be salable at the same grade purchased — assuming they incur no injury in the meantime.

GEMOLOGIST. An authority in the identification, grading, and appraisal of gems. A certified gemologist is one who has successfully completed a study course in the subject and been issued the equivalent of a diploma.

GEMOLOGY. The study of gems and gemstones: their physical properties, origins, methods of recognition, geographical distribution, uses in science and industry, and the gem trade.

GIRDLE FACETS. When used in the sense of "girdle facets," this refers to the triangular or lozenge-shaped facets in a Round Brilliant cut that touch the girdle both above and beneath it — 16 above, 16 below.

GIRDLER. Name sometimes used for employee of a diamond factory who rounds the stone on a lathe.

GIRDLE THICKNESS. Thickness of the outermost edge of a diamond, where the crown is separated from the pavilion. It does not refer to diameter of the stone itself, a common misunderstanding. Girdle height would be more descriptive, but terms that have established a tradition of long use in the industry are not easily supplanted. In small stones, girdle thickness is greater in relation to the stone's size than in large diamonds. Variations are possible in girdle thickness without seriously influencing desirability or value. However, narrow girdles are more in preference today, as a rule.

GIRDLING. The process of rounding a stone, which is accomplished by grinding it in a lathe. The skill of the girdler who holds the stone against the grinding surface determines its degree of success.

GRADUATE GEMOLOGIST. An individual who has received the Graduate in Gemology Diploma from the Gemological Institute of America, by successfully completing one of its instructional courses.

HARDNESS. In gemology, the resistence of a substance to surface scratching. It does not relate in any respect to ability to escape other kinds of injury such as crushing or breaking. Diamond is the hardest mineral substance with a rating of 10 on the Mohs scale, talc the softest with a rating of 1 on the Mohs scale. Diamonds are at least ten times harder than the next hardest mineral, corundum. Diamonds can be scratched only by other diamonds. They can however be cut and cleaved apart with conventional tools.

IMPERFECTION. A flaw or blemish, caused by nature or man, which may be on the outer surface or the stone's interior. Poor color or unskilled cut are not classified as imperfections, though they do, of course, play a role in value determination.

INCLUDED CRYSTAL. A small crystal imbedded or trapped within a larger crystal. Often has the appearance of an air space and is therefore mistakenly referred to as a bubble.

INCLUSION. Any substance, including fragments of diamond itself or tiny crystals, visible within a diamond. These entrapped "prisoners" have influence on value, which may be greater or lesser depending on their number and size. If not too centrally situated it may be possible in cutting to remove them from a rough stone. Cuts designed to rid a stone of inclusions generally involve considerable loss of carat weight.

INTERNALLY FLAWLESS. A diamond in which no internal flaws, or only those of a very insignificant nature, can be observed at 10X magnification; but whose exterior surface displays imperfections. Abbreviated IF. IF stones are normally polished to remove the exterior blemishes, which slightly reduces their carat weight but results in overall increase in desirability and value.

IRREGULAR GIRDLE. An irregular girdle is one whose thickness varies along different parts of its circumference. Ideally there should be little, if any, variation.

KIMBERLITE. The volcanic underground pipes in which diamonds are found in Africa.

LASER DRILLING. Drilling into a diamond by means of a laser beam, which, because of intense heat generated, can sometimes reduce or remove flaws. Used chiefly to bleach out carbon spots, in which a bleaching agent is used as an adjunct. Results are not accurately predictable, but very good success has so far been achieved by skilled operators.

LEVERIDGE GAUGE. Device invented in 1937 by A. D. Leveridge for estimating weight of diamonds, both loose and mounted. It consists of a micrometer with calipers set with a dial, on which a hand swings to indicate the reading. The user then refers to a conversion table, giving the approximate weight for a stone of its measurements. Though not 100% accurate, the Leveridge gauge has proven to be the most reliable instrument of its kind on the market.

LOUPE. A magnifying glass, either of the folding pocket variety or mounted in an eyepiece. Though a magnifier of any strength can be sold as a loupe, "jeweler's loupe" refers to a glass of 10X power.

MACLE. Rough diamond with a twinned crystal, the twin appearing to have been turned around at a 180 degree angle in relation to the other or parent crystal. Macles are normally flattish and lozenge shaped. Because of the enormous carat loss in fashioning a macle into a Round Brilliant, they are often cut to fancy shapes that take advantage of nature's preshaping.

MELLEE. "Small goods." Roughs of less than two carats and cut stones under 17 points (less than 1/5th of a carat).

NATURAL. Small portion of deliberately unpolished surface on a jewel diamond, usually along the girdle, which appears rough in relation to neighboring surfaces. The motive in leaving naturals is to remove as little as possible in carat weight.

OFF-CENTER CULET. A cut stone in which the culet (base) is out of register with the girdle angles. When viewed through the table, the culet should be at equal distance from each opposing girdle angle. Seldom noticed by persons inexperienced in examining diamonds.

OLD EUROPEAN CUT. Style of cutting popular in the 19th century, direct predecessor to the modern Round Brilliant. Old European cuts have a smaller table than the Round Brilliant and heavier crown; overall depth is somewhat greater. Also called "old mine."

OLD MINE CUT. In general, a diamond cut into an early style of round cut, prior to the Modern Round Brilliant cut method of mathematical calculation, is referred to as an "old mine cut." Apparently it was mistakenly believed that diamonds were once cut at the mines before wholesaling.

PAPER MARKS. Surface blemishes, generally tiny scratches or nicks, resulting not from contact with paper but with other diamonds carried with it in the same diamond paper. Obviously, the practice of carrying loose unprotected stones in a manner that allows them to touch each other is to be avoided.

PAPERWORN. Same as Paper Marks (see above).

PAVÉ. Method of mounting small stones in a piece of jewel, to cove. the entire field of the setting without the setting itself showing.

PAVILION. The lower portion of a cut stone, from beneath the girdle to the culet.

PAVILION ANGLE. The angle at which the pavilion facets rise up from the culet to meet the girdle. Pavilion angle greatly influences light refraction.

PAVILION DEPTH. The vertical distance from the culet to the girdle plane.

PAVILION FACETS. Facets in the pavilion or lower part of the diamond, beneath the girdle.

PIQUE. Term in common use in Europe, and to some extent elsewhere, referring to stones with imperfections. Modified as pique-1, pique-2 and pique-3 to indicate seriousness of imperfections, pique-1 being the least flawed. Often written as P1, P2, P3. U.S. equivalents are I-1, I-2, I-3.

PLANNER. Individual in a diamond factory who decides how rough stones will be cut.

PLOTTING. A modern-day practice of recording the exact characteristics of a cut gemstone, by the use of a paper and pen. On a diagram of the stone's shape and cut, markings are made to indicate the presence and precise location of all characteristics. These are in the form of symbols, according to a system devised by the Gemological Institute of America. For simplification, inclusions are marked in red, blemishes green, extra facets and prong mountings in black. Plotting serves not only as an aid in appraisal but identification.

POLISHED GOODS. Finished stones, cut and polished, as opposed to freshly mined roughs.

PROPORTION PERCENTAGES. A system developed by the G.I.A. in which certain percentages of value are deducted from a stone according to the degree from which it deviates from perfect proportioning. The percentages, which go as high as 15% of base value, are applied against the Table, Girdle Thickness, Crown Angles, Pavilion, Culet and Major Symmetry Faults. Table and pavilion account for the sharpest discounts, if severely misproportioned.

REFRACTION. The angling of light as it passes through a cut diamond, bounding from one wall to another. Reflection is the end result of refraction: the light as it exits from the stone and provides brilliance or sparkle.

SHALLOW CUT. A stone whose main pavilion facets have an angle of less than 39 degrees to the girdle plane.

SINGLE CUT. Simple style of cut employed on small stones, usually those intended to be used in mounting in conjunction with a large central stone. Single cuts are circular at the girdle.

SYMMETRY. The placement of facets on a cut stone, as well as shaping. Opposing facets — those facing each other from opposite sides of the stone — must be of the same size and shape, and placed precisely opposite, to achieve good symmetry. Deviation will result in loss of light refraciton and the stone will not be as firey.

SYNTHETIC. An imitation, commerically made gemstone, which may be very like the natural in its properties and cutting potential. Synthetics are produced in a number of grades and vary considerably in price. All are detectable, using proper equipment.

TABLE. The uppermost plane surface of a cut diamond. Like the other plane surfaces, the table is also a facet.

TAPERED BAGUETTE. Baguette shaped cut with one end smaller than the other.

TRIGON. Tiny pit-like markings found on the surface of octahedral crystals. These are "growth markings."

WHITE. Misleading term meaning colorless or clear. Derives probably from the fact that in olden times white was not recognized as a color but as the absence of color. A really white diamond, smoky or cloudy, is not nearly as desirable as clear.

ZIRCONIA, CUBIC. Synthetic material from which imitation diamonds are made. Extremely difficult to distinguish from a natural diamond, except for a very experienced appraiser or through use of special equipment, such as the Diamond Probe. It has a greater hardness than many other synthetics, but its hardness is not equal to a diamond's.

HOW TO USE THIS BOOK

The reader has two avenues of approach for the retrieval of information. The detailed index is of value to pinpoint the page where a particular topic is located. For example, if you wish to see a photograph of an example of Etruscan in the alphabetical index and it will refer you to those pages in the book where that style of workmanship is pictured.

A collector who desires to identify a personal piece of jewelry, should go immediately to the table of contents. The chapters are arranged according to the type of jewelry, i.e. bracelets, rings, watches, stickpins, etc. If a bracelet needs identification, locate the bracelet chapter, and either turn to the sub-division in that chapter, or if the collector is not sure as to which sub-division would be applicable, the collector can simply skim the entire chapter to identify his article of jewelry. The vast majority of books on antique jewelry are arranged in chapters according to either the period of the jewelry or the material out of which the jewelry is made, i.e. coral, hair, mosaic, diamond, etc. This book is divided simply as to the type of jewelry. As an example, if you have a bracelet made out of woven hair it will be located under the sub-division of hair bracelets in the bracelet chapter. Rings made out of hair will be in the ring chapter.

Antique jewelry cannot be sold or valued according to the weight of the gold in the individual piece, for this does not take into account the historical and rarity of a piece of antique jewelry can place a value on an item far in excess of the melt down value of the metal content of the piece of jewelry. Nevertheless, at the time of the calculation of the prices in this book, gold was selling for approximately $350.00 per ounce.

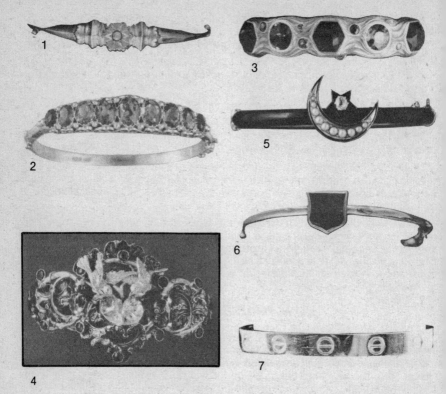

BRACELETS

BANGLE – GOLD

			Price Range	
☐	1	Acid finish center motif, set with single turquoise, hollow triangular tube bangle, American, c. 1830-40	300.00	325.00
☐	2	Amethyst bangle, eight faceted amethysts, ribbon motif, marked: "NBs," 9K gold, English	825.00	925.00
☐	3	Art nouveau motif in a swirl design with faceted amethyst and colored stones, gold, maker: Tiffany & Co., American, c. 1915	5950.00	6500.00
☐	4	Bird and flower motif, green enamel oak leaves, round red cabochon translucent red stones, gold, c. 1870	3300.00	3500.00
☐	5	Black opaque enamel hollow tubular bangle, 11 pearls in crescent, one round diamond in star, gold, c. 1850	1650.00	1850.00
☐	6	Bloodstone intaglio shield motif, hollow tubular bangle, 15K gold, marked: "R° 8228," English	400.00	450.00
☐	7	Button motif, 18K gold, Cartier	450.00	550.00

			Price Range	
☐	8	Cabochon garnets, 18K gold, Edwardian, c. 1900-1910	800.00	1000.00
☐	9	Cameo center, shell cameo of an outdoor market, bangle with black and white enamel in a geometric motif, gold, c. 1880	3000.00	3300.00
☐	10	Chalcedony cameo, seed pearls, black enamel, gold, c. late 19th	2650.00	2850.00
☐	11	Circle motif bangle, rubies in one circle, sapphires in one circle, enamel design, gold	2850.00	3100.00
☐	12	Circular motif center, one round diamond, four round sapphires, 16 pear-shape turquoise, white enamel, gold, c. late 19th	1750.00	2000.00
☐	13	Cultured pearl bangle, modified loveknot motif, three pearls, gold, English, c. 1900	350.00	375.00
☐	14	Cannetille 22K gold work, c. 1830	600.00	750.00

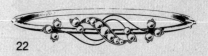

			Price Range	
☐	**15**	*Cultured pearl flat bangle, 18 pearls, engraved scroll motif, gold, English, c. 1903-04*	**475.00**	**500.00**
☐	**16**	*Cultured pearl flat bangle, seven pearls in center, rope motif, engraved, gold, English, c. late 19th* . . .	**350.00**	**375.00**
☐	**17**	*Cultured pearl hollow tubular bangle, 18 pearls in crescent and flower motif, gold, English, c. 1903-04*	**400.00**	**450.00**
☐	**18**	*Cultured pearl hollow tubular bangle, pearls in flower and circle motif, gold, English, c. 1903-04* . .	**350.00**	**375.00**
☐	**19**	*Cultured pearl hollow tubular bangle, nine pearls in circle motif, gold, English, c. 1903-04*	**350.00**	**375.00**
☐	**20**	*Cultured pearl hollow tubular bangle, single pearl in clover, gold, English, c. 1903-04*	**250.00**	**275.00**
☐	**21**	*Cultured pearl hollow tubular bangle, 45 pearls in flower and leaf motif, gold, English, c. 1903-04*	**475.00**	**525.00**
☐	**22**	*Cultured pearl knife-edge bangle, seven turquoise in center swirl, ten pearls in leaf motif, gold, English, c. 1903-04*	**425.00**	**435.00**

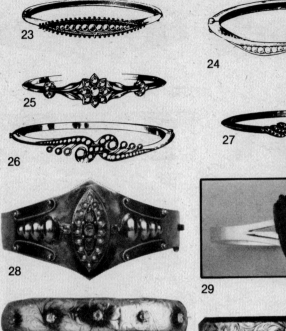

			Price Range	
☐	23	Cultured pearl knife-edge bangle, 14 pearls in straight row in center, gold, English, c. 1903-04 . . .	350.00	375.00
☐	24	Cultured pearl knife-edge bangle, 28 pearls, one cabachon garnet, gold, English, c. 1903-04	375.00	450.00
☐	25	Cultured pearl knife-edge bangle, 19 pearls in flower motif, gold, English, c. 1903-04	425.00	435.00
☐	26	Cultured pearl knife-edge bangle, 40 pearls in scroll motif, gold, English, c. 1903-04	425.00	435.00
☐	27	Cultured pearl knife-edge bangle, 73 pearls pave set in two hearts, bow, and cluster motif, small round diamond in center of each heart, gold, English, c. 1903-04	725.00	775.00
☐	28	Cultured pearls, diamonds, 16K gold, c. 1850	900.00	1300.00
☐	29	Devils head carved from labradorite, rose diamond eyes, plain bangle, 15K gold, English	1750.00	2100.00
☐	30	Diamonds, five old mine diamonds approx. 1.0 ct., engraved bangle, gold	1650.00	1750.00
☐	31	Diamonds, three round diamonds, engraved bangle, gold, inscribed: "A.C.," 1911	1000.00	1200.00

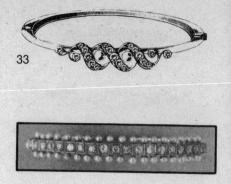

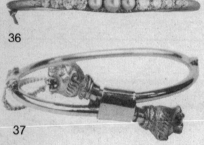

			Price Range	
☐	**32**	Diamond flat bangle, 43 round diamonds in cluster and scrolls, gold, English, c. 1903-04	3750.00	3950.00
☐	**33**	Diamond knife-edge bangle, 19 round diamonds and two pearls in scroll motif, gold, English, c. 1903-04	1450.00	1650.00
☐	**34**	Diamond wide flat bangle, rose diamond approx. 2.5 cts. in elaborate gold on gold motif, designed by Prof. R. Reinhardt, Stuttgart, Germany, c. 1902 .	4600.00	5000.00
☐	**35**	Diamonds and pearls, 20 round diamonds approx. 1.50 cts., two rows of cultured pearls, 14K gold . . .	2650.00	3100.00
☐	**36**	Diamonds and pearls, eight round diamonds approx. 1.50 cts., three cultured pearls, platinum prong setting, plain gold bangle.	3500.00	3950.00
☐	**37**	Dog head motif, hollow tubular bangle, gold	550.00	750.00
☐	**38**	Elephant heads, champlevé enamel round bangle in translucent blue, red, green and opaque white, rose diamonds, gold, Indian, c. 19th	2400.00	2650.00

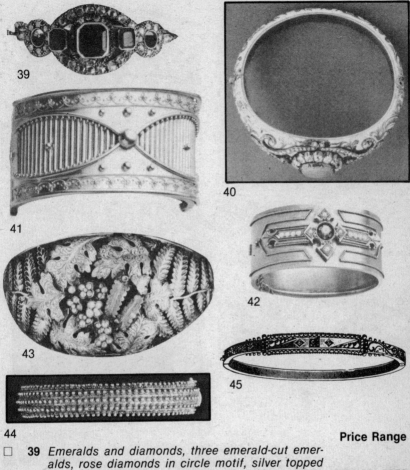

			Price Range	
☐	39	Emeralds and diamonds, three emerald-cut emeralds, rose diamonds in circle motif, silver topped gold, c. late 19th	5250.00	5650.00
☐	40	Enamelled opaque white motif engraved bangle, round blue cabochon stone surrounded by old mine diamonds in center, rose diamond swirl design, gold, c. mid 19th	3850.00	4300.00
☐	41	Etruscan granulation wide bangle, heavy 15K gold, English, c. 1865-75	1400.00	1600.00
☐	42	Etruscan granulation, seed pearls, gold, c. 1860 ..	650.00	900.00
☐	43	Fern and oak leaf motif, cut-out and engraved leaves, seed pearl flowers, gold, c. 1840	1750.00	2000.00
☐	44	Flat bangle, Etruscan granulation, 18K gold, c. late 19th	1550.00	1750.00
☐	45	Flat bangle, two round diamonds and one round ruby in center, Etruscan granulation, engraved, gold, English, c. late 19th	330.00	400.00

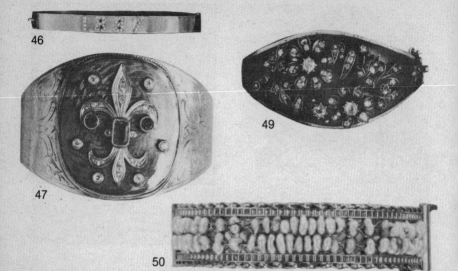

			Price Range	
☐	46	*Flat narrow bangle, the date "1887" is set with oriental seed pearls commemorating the Golden Jubilee (50 years) of the reign of Queen Victoria, gold, English, c. 1887*	400.00	475.00
☐	47	*Fleur-de-lys motif on wide engraved bangle, blue enamel, 22 round diamonds, one emerald-cut and two round emeralds, gold, c. 1820*	2650.00	3100.00
☐	48	*Floral openwork motif, 22 emerald-cut emeralds, one round emerald, seven pearls, rose diamonds, gold, c. early 20th*	1750.00	2000.00
☐	49	*Flower motif, rose diamonds, translucent blue enamel, gold, c. 1860*	2650.00	2850.00
☐	50	*Freshwater pearls, 18K gold, c. 1860*	450.00	550.00
☐	51	*Garnet cluster center, one round pearl, guilloché translucent red enamel, gold, c. 1870*	1300.00	1550.00

52

53

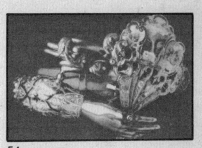

54

55

56   57

		Price Range	
☐	**52** Grape cluster and leaf motif, cutout and engraved, champlevé enamel in translucent green, blue and red enamel with a black border, wide convex shape, gold	1650.00	1850.00
☐	**53** Hand and trellis motif flat bangle, opaque enamel, gold, German, c. 1866	2750.00	2950.00
☐	**54** Hands holding a movable fan over a perfume compartment, damaged blue and white enamel, rose diamond finger ring, gold, c. 1850	3850.00	4300.00
☐	**55** Hardstone cameo, flat engraved band, pinchbeck, c. late 18th	450.00	500.00
☐	**56** Hawk heads with emerald-cut emeralds, oval medallion in center with eight emerald-cut emeralds, seed pearls, one foil-back pink stone in center, gold, c. 1840	4100.00	4500.00
☐	**57** Pair of hollow bangles, flower motif with rose diamonds, one rose diamond flower missing from one bangle, 18K gold, c. 1850	2950.00	3650.00

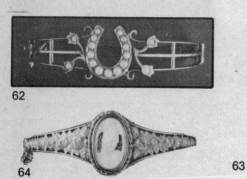

			Price Range	
☐	**58**	*Heart motif hollow bangle, cultured pearl and round diamond in twig on heart, gold, English*	**500.00**	**550.00**
☐	**59**	*Heart motif hollow tubular bangle, scroll and gold ball design, one pearl and one ruby in hearts, gold, c. 1900*	**300.00**	**350.00**
☐	**60**	*Hollow tubular bangle, opal doublet surrounded by round diamonds and pearls, 15K gold, inscribed: "In Memoriam, July 25, 1887, May 19, 1890, Pro Pat 254," English, c. 1880-90*	**2550.00**	**3000.00**
☐	**61**	*Horseshoe and star motif, "Gypsy style," rubies, diamonds, three color gold, American, c. early 20th*	**1100.00**	**1300.00**
☐	**62**	*Horseshoe motif, knife-edge bangle, seed pearls, gold, c. 1900*	**450.00**	**500.00**
☐	**63**	*Horseshoe motif bangle with a hinge, fitted leather box, inscribed: "M.L.M. 1905," maker: The Goldsmiths & Silversmiths Company Ltd., 112 Regent St., London, gold, c. 1905*	**1750.00**	**2000.00**
☐	**64**	*Ivory cameo and floral motif, carved, gold, c. late 19th*	**1450.00**	**1650.00**

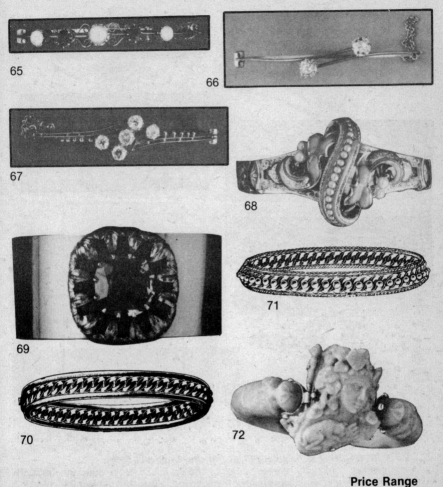

		Price Range	
☐	**65** Knife-edge bangle, two round amethysts, three half pearls, gold, c. 1880	825.00	1050.00
☐	**66** Knife-edge bangle, two old mine diamonds approx. 1.50 cts., gold, c. 1879	4400.00	4600.00
☐	**67** Knife-edge bangle, five old mine diamonds approx. 1.65 cts., gold, c. late 19th	1550.00	1750.00
☐	**68** Leaf motif, pearls, turquoise enamel, gold, c. 1870	1550.00	1800.00
☐	**69** Leaf motif with cushion-cut chrysoberyl center, some enamel on leaves, wide bangle, maker: Cartier, 14K gold, c. early 20th	2950.00	3300.00
☐	**70** Link motif bangle, gold, English, c. 1903-04	375.00	450.00
☐	**71** Link and bead motif bangle, gold, English, c. 1903-04	375.00	450.00
☐	**72** Lion heads, carved lady and small dog in center, coral, gold, c. 1860	2650.00	3000.00

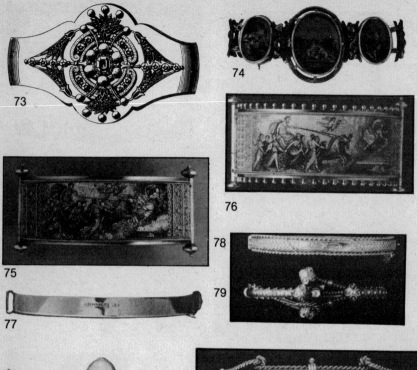

			Price Range	
☐	**73**	*Lotus flower design wide flat bangle, blue and red stones, maker: O. Weber, gold, c. 1868-83*	3500.00	3950.00
☐	**74**	*Miniature scenic panels, gilt mountings, Victorian*	1650.00	1850.00
☐	**75**	*Mosaic of chariot, people and angels, Etruscan granulation borders, gold, Italian, c. 1860*	4850.00	5300.00
☐	**76**	*Mosaic of chariot, people and angels, Etruscan granulation borders, beaded rim, fitted leather box marked: "G. Roccheggiani, Rome," gold, Italian, c. 1860*	4950.00	5400.00
☐	**77**	*Narrow bangle, 9K gold, English*	225.00	250.00
☐	**78**	*Narrow flat bangle, Etruscan granulation, gold, c. 1870*	650.00	700.00
☐	**79**	*Tubular asymmetric bangle, Etruscan granulation, one old mine diamond, gold, c. 1865*	800.00	1000.00
☐	**80**	*Opal, hollow tubular bangle, gold*	375.00	450.00
☐	**81**	*Opal straight row surrounded by rope motif, 9K gold, English*	350.00	400.00

82

83

84

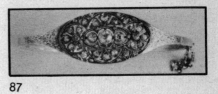

85

86

87

88

89

			Price Range	
☐	**82**	Opals and diamonds, nine oval cabochon opals, 28 round diamonds, gold, c. 1890	2650.00	2850.00
☐	**83**	Openwork motif, 30 round diamonds approx. 2.50 cts., 14K white gold, American, c. 1925	3950.00	4300.00
☐	**84**	Openwork motif, rose diamonds approx. 2.0 cts., gold, platinum	2950.00	3650.00
☐	**85**	Openwork center motif, rose diamonds, three pearls, silver, gold	1750.00	2000.00
☐	**86**	Oriental pearl bangle, pearls in flower and leaf motif, gold, English	750.00	800.00
☐	**87**	Oval openwork center motif, rose and round diamonds, engraved bangle, gold, c. 1845	1650.00	1850.00
☐	**88**	Pair bangles, translucent red, green and blue Jaipur enamel, rose diamonds, gold, Indian, c. 19th ..	2850.00	3200.00
☐	**89**	Pair bangles, platinum, rose and green gold applied flowers and leaves, yellow gold, fitted leather box, maker: Tiffany & Co., American, c. 1890	5400.00	5950.00

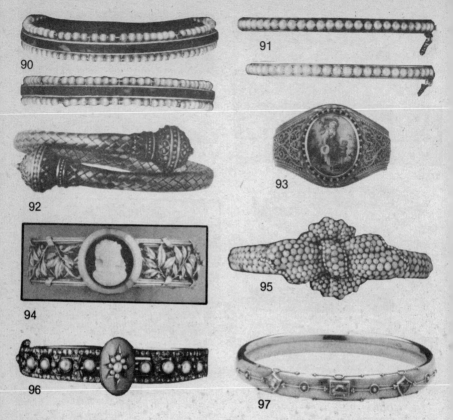

			Price Range	
☐	90	Pair bangles, emerald-cut black onyx in center with a row of genuine oriental seed pearls on either side, c. late 19th	3500.00	3750.00
☐	91	Pair narrow bangles, pavé oriental seed pearls in top half of each bracelet, gold, c. 1860	1550.00	1750.00
☐	92	Plaited bangle, Etruscan granulation ends, gold, c. 1870	1450.00	1550.00
☐	93	Porcelain painted miniature, applied filigree, gold	2650.00	2850.00
☐	94	Renaissance revival motif, hardstone cameo, green gold foliage, yellow gold rims, French owl hallmarks	3950.00	4400.00
☐	95	Ribbon motif, pavé turquoise, seed pearl borders, silver, c. 1820	2650.00	3100.00
☐	96	Rose diamonds in silver, blue enamel oval center with seed pearls, seed pearls collet-set around center of bracelet, gold, c. 1850	2200.00	2750.00
☐	97	Rose diamonds, gold, c. 1880	800.00	1050.00

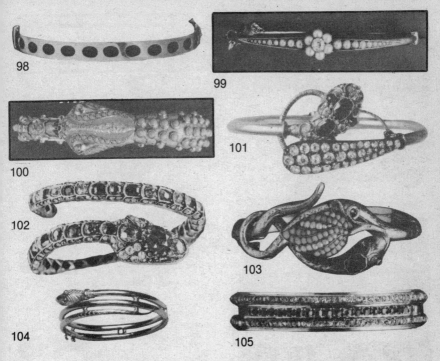

98

99

101

100

102

103

104

105

		Price Range	
☐	**98** Sandwich bangle, inner gold band, woven hair, outer gold band cutout oval designs on front of bangle, 9K gold, English, c. late 19th	450.00	500.00
☐	**99** Seed pearl hollow tubular bangle, one round diamond, gold, c. 1900	950.00	1050.00
☐	**100** Snake, cabochon turquoise in flexible scale links and head, two old mine diamonds in eyes, old mine diamonds in head, 18K gold	2750.00	3200.00
☐	**101** Snake, tubular bangle, 33 old mine diamonds approx. 3.50 cts. pave in tail and head, garnets in head, silver, gold, c. 1820	3750.00	4200.00
☐	**102** Snake, one sapphire, approx. 4.85 cts., old mine diamonds, two champagne diamonds, rubies and sapphires approx. 8 cts., colored diamonds approx. 8.50 cts., rose diamonds in silver approx. 5.50 cts., 18K gold, Tiffany & Co., marked: Peconnet, French, c. 1900.	14700.00	16800.00
☐	**103** Snake and leaf motif, three garnets in snake head, seed pearls and turquoise leaf, 9K gold, English, c. mid 19th	1550.00	1750.00
☐	**104** Snake motif, 18K gold, c. 1840	800.00	1000.00
☐	**105** Straight row motif, one row of round rubies, two rows of rose diamonds, gold, c. 1920	1350.00	1600.00

106

107

108

109

			Price Range	
☐	**106**	Tiger heads, beast, flower and bird motifs, Jaipur champlevé enamel in translucent red, green, blue, yellow and opaque white, rose diamonds, gold, Indian, c. 19th	5000.00	5450.00
☐	**107**	Tubular bangle, carved banded-onyx center medallion, rose diamonds in white gold, bangle in yellow gold, c. mid 19th	1650.00	1750.00
☐	**108**	Wide bangle, three cabachon banded onyx, rope twist borders, engraved flat bangle, gold, c. 1870 .	1300.00	1550.00
☐	**109**	Watch, keywind and separates as pendant, champlevé opaque floral design on movable fan cover, garnets, seed pearls, gold, c. 1840	3300.00	3850.00

110

111

112

113

114

115

		Price Range	
☐	110 Water lily motif, chased, blank initial medallions, gold, Art Nouveau, probable maker: Riker Bros., Newark, NJ, American, c. 1900	2400.00	2650.00
☐	111 Wide bangle set with seed pearls, rose diamonds, fitted leather box marked: "Mackay, Cunningham & Co., Edinburgh, Scotland," gold, c. 1875	2850.00	3200.00
☐	112 Wide bangle, champlevé black enamel geometric motic, center cluster of nine old mine diamonds approx. 2.50 cts., gold, c. 1880	2950.00	3300.00
☐	113 Wide bangle, floral motif, champlevé opaque black enamel, gold, c. 1860	800.00	950.00
☐	114 Wide bangle, opaque black enamel, 14K gold, American, Victorian	600.00	700.00
☐	115 Woven bangle with slide and end with cabochon opals, old mine diamonds, black enamel leaf motif, gold, c. 1850	2550.00	2850.00

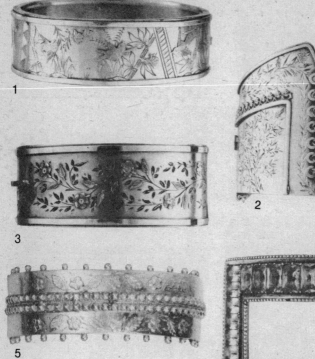

BANGLE - SILVER

			Price Range	
☐	**1**	*Birds in rose and yellow gold applied to bangle, engraved bamboo motif, sterling silver, c. 1900*	225.00	275.00
☐	**2**	*Corset motif, gold wire as lace, applied gold flowers, engraved flower and leaf design, silver, English, c. 1890*	350.00	400.00
☐	**3**	*Flowers and leaves in green, yellow and rose gold applied to wide bangle, engraved leaves, sterling silver, American, c. 1890*	300.00	325.00
☐	**4**	*French paste: emerald-cut, gold bead edges, pair of late 18th shoe buckles attached together as bangle in mid 19th*	450.00	500.00
☐	**5**	*Flat bangle, applied flower and leaf motif, silver, English, c. 1880*	200.00	225.00

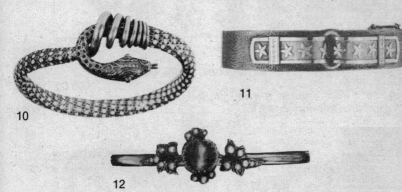

			Price Range	
☐	6	Horseshoe center with leaf engraved motif, maker: J.M.B., Birmingham, England, silver, c. 1882	150.00	175.00
☐	7	Renaissance motif, bangle slides through plain bars to enlarge, sterling silver, c. 1910	200.00	225.00
☐	8	Rope pattern, one plain band, one embossed band, sterling silver, American, c. 1902	125.00	150.00
☐	9	Sandwich bangle, ridges of inner band hold woven hair, engraved edge designs, sterling silver, gold-washed, c. late 19th	250.00	275.00
☐	10	Snake, green and white enamel, silver	400.00	475.00
☐	11	Star design in gold plated silver ribbon attached to lizard engraved narrow bangle, 800 silver, c. 1915 .	125.00	150.00
☐	12	Tubular hinged bangle, cabochon tiger eye center, leaf motif, seed pearls, sterling silver, American, c. mid 20th	150.00	175.00

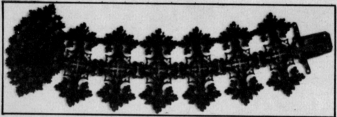

CAST IRON

		Price Range	
☐	**1** *Cast iron, maker: M. Devarannes, Berlin, Germany, c. 1860*	**800.00**	**1050.00**
☐	**2** *Cast iron, approx. 8½ in., signed: A.F. Lehman, Berlin, Germany, c. 19th*	**750.00**	**1000.00**

CLASPS

☐	**1** *Hummingbird and flower motif, rose, yellow and green gold, platinum, American, c. 1875*	**450.00**	**525.00**
☐	**2** *Ivory miniature portrait of officer by Ozias Humphrey, 1742-1810, 1½ in. high, gold, English*	**4000.00**	**4400.00**

		Price Range	
☐	3 *Ivory miniature portrait of Mrs. Hoskins by James Nixon, 1741-1812, 1½ in. high, gold, English*	2200.00	2400.00
☐	4 *Ivory miniature portrait of Lieutenant Henry Hoskins by James Nixon, 1741-1812, 1½ in. high, gold, English.*	1450.00	1750.00
☐	5 *Ivory miniature portrait of a gentleman by J. Jennings, 1763-1793, 1½ in. high, gold, English, dated 1769*	1100.00	1200.00
☐	6 *Ivory miniature portrait of a gentleman by Daniel Dodd, 1752-1780, 1½ in. high, gold, English*	1100.00	1200.00
☐	7 *Ivory miniature portrait of Wilson Gail Broadqill by Richard Crosse, 1742-1810, 1½ in. high, gold, English*	600.00	700.00
☐	8 *Ivory miniature portrait of a gentleman by John Bogle, 1746-1803, Scottish, worked in Scotland and England, 1⅜ in. high, gold*	2650.00	2850.00

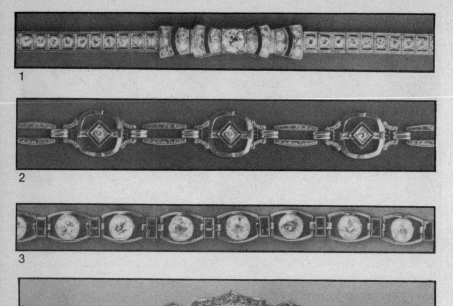

DIAMOND LINK

Price Range

- ☐ **1** *Bow center straight line, French-cut onyx, round diamond approx. .90 ct. in center, 56 round diamonds approx. 5 cts., platinum, c. 1910* **11550.00 12600.00**
- ☐ **2** *Box oval link, round diamonds in alternating links, white gold, American, c. 1915* **950.00 1050.00**
- ☐ **3** *Box oval link, 13 old mine diamonds approx. 9 cts., two square-cut sapphires between each link, platinum, American, c. 1930* **15750.00 18900.00**
- ☐ **4** *Openwork center straight row, one marquise-shape diamond approx. .15 ct. in center, 70 round diamonds approx. 2.85 cts., platinum, c. 1930* **4050.00 4950.00**
- ☐ **5** *Openwork links, round diamonds approx. 5.0 cts., platinum, American, c. 1920* **8100.00 9650.00**

6

7

8

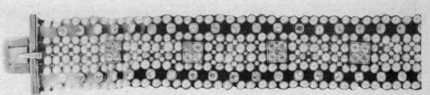

9

			Price Range	
☐	**6**	*Openwork oblong links, 295 round diamonds approx. 22.50 cts., white gold, American, c. 1930*	**31500.00**	**35700.00**
☐	**7**	*Openwork square links, six emerald-cut emeralds, triangular-cut diamonds approx. 2.0 cts., 428 round diamonds approx. 20 cts., platinum, American, c. 1920*	**26200.00**	**28300.00**
☐	**8**	*Oval links, 120 round diamonds approx. 3.75 cts., 32 French-cut sapphires approx. 3.20 cts., platinum, c. 1925.*	**10500.00**	**12600.00**
☐	**9**	*Pearls, one mine diamonds in center square motifs and collet-set, pair of bracelets or necklace, maker: Cartier, Edwardian*	**13650.00**	**15750.00**

10

11

12

13

Price Range

☐ **10** *Pierced center section, one round diamond approx. 1.35 cts., calibre sapphire and 40 round diamonds approx. 1.50 cts. in center panel, 22 round
diamonds approx. 5.25 cts. in remaining panels,
platinum, American, c. 1920* 9450.00 12600.00

☐ **11** *Pierced panels, one round diamond approx. 1.0
cts. surrounded by calibre sapphires in center
panel, round diamonds alternate with diamond-
shape sapphires in remaining panels, platinum,
American, c. 1920*............................. 3900.00 4200.00

☐ **12** *Pierced panels, two round diamonds in center
panel approx. 1.20 cts., calibre black onyx and 78
round diamonds approx. 8.50 cts. in remaining
panels, platinum, American, c. 1910* 12600.00 14700.00

☐ **13** *Scroll links, rose diamonds, gold topped platinum,
French, c. 1890* 1000.00 1200.00

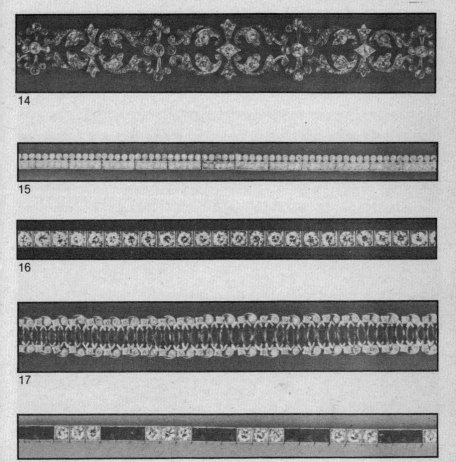

14

15

16

17

18

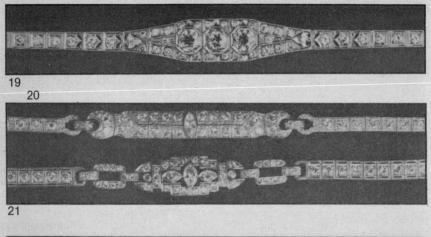

19

20

21

22

23

		Price Range	
☐	**19** Straight line modified, three old mine diamonds approx. 2.60 cts., 54 round diamonds approx. 2.0 cts., platinum, American, c. 1900	3950.00	4100.00
☐	**20** Straight line modified, one marquise-shape and 88 round diamonds approx. 5.50 cts., platinum, American, c. 1930	5250.00	5750.00
☐	**21** Straight line modified, one marquise-shape and 77 round diamonds approx. 3.30 cts., platinum, American, c. 1930	3950.00	4100.00
☐	**22** Straight line modified, round diamond approx. .60 ct. in center, 78 round diamonds approx. 4.70 cts., nine French-cut emeralds in center panels, platinum, c. 1920	6800.00	7850.00
☐	**23** Straight line modified, one marquise-shape diamond in center and 82 round diamonds approx. 3.50 cts., platinum, American, c. 1930	5050.00	5300.00

24

25

			Price Range
☐	**24**	*Straight line modified, one round diamond approx. .85 ct. in center, two round diamonds approx. .25 ct., 30 round diamonds approx. 1.50 cts., eight French-cut sapphires approx. .24 ct., 14K white gold, c. 1920*	3850.00 4050.00
☐	**25**	*Square cluster center, four genuine oriental seed pearls, 11 diamonds, oblong openwork links, platinum topped gold, French, c. 1890-1900*	1200.00 1650.00

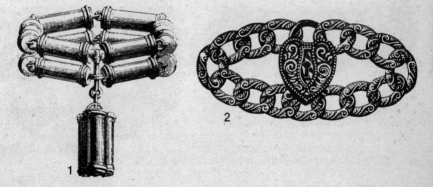

1

2

FLEXIBLE

☐	**1**	*Column motif, granite, silver, maker: Rettie & Sons, Aberdeen, Scotland, c. 1869*	375.00	450.00
☐	**2**	*Curb engraved link, heart motif lock clasp, sterling, American, c. 1894-95*	150.00	175.00
☐		*Same as above but gold filled.*	45.00	65.00
☐		*Same as above but 14K gold.*	400.00	450.00

3

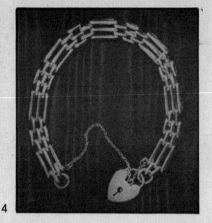

4

5

6

7

			Price Range	
☐	**3**	*Curb link, heart motif, lock clasp, sterling, Ameri-can, c. late 19th*	**125.00**	**150.00**
☐	**4**	*Fancy link, heart motif lock clasp, silver, English, c. early 20th*	**110.00**	**135.00**
☐	**5**	*Flower motif, marcasites, sterling, American, c. 1920*	**125.00**	**175.00**
☐	**6**	*Heart motif, cabochon turquoise and opals, en-graved, sterling, American, c. 1902*	**325.00**	**350.00**
☐	**7**	*Mosaics of Roman buildings, goldstone, gold filled, c. 1850*	**325.00**	**550.00**

1

2

3

4

FLEXIBLE – GEM, GOLD OR PLATINUM

		Price Range	
☐	**1** *Agate, gold, English, c. 1800*	525.00	550.00
☐	**2** *Ancient Architectual motif center panel bordered by two flat plain panels, gold, maker: von Demfelben of Germany, c. 1868-83*	2650.00	3100.00
☐	**3** *Animal gold silhouettes on green glass - Indian Pitch, engraved floral reverse, 22K gold, Indian, c. 19th*	1750.00	2000.00
☐	**4** *Animal motif, jaipur enamel, seed pearls, rose and table-cut diamonds, gold, Indian, Victorian*	1000.00	1300.00

5

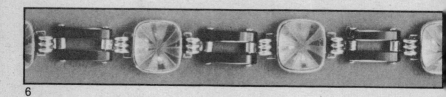

6

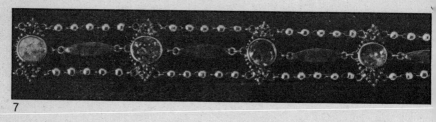

7

8

Price Range

☐ **5** Art Deco motif, two opaline glass squares with a
leaf motif, center rectangle is lapis lazuli carved
and pierced with a bird motif, links are blue and
white enamel, gold, 7½ in. long, c. 1925 . . . . 1550.00 1750.00
☐ **6** Art Deco motif, four rock crystal carved squares,
onyx and gold links, 7 in. long. c. 1925 . . . . 2850.00 3100.00
☐ **7** Black opals, sapphires and demantoid garnets on
either side of seven black opals alternating with
oval enamelled links, bead chains, gold, Arts and
Crafts style, signed: Tiffany & Co., c. late 19th 3500.00 3750.00
☐ **8** Bloodstone, moss agate, gold, Scottish, c. 19th . . 600.00 700.00

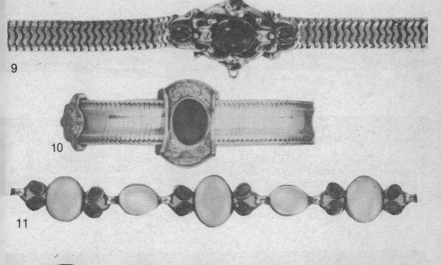

		Price Range	
☐	**9** Cabochon garnets in repoussé plaque, snake chain, 18K gold, c. 1860	**1050.00**	**1350.00**
☐	**10** Cabochon garnet on slide, 15K gold, English, c. 1865	**650.00**	**850.00**
☐	**11** Cabochon moonstones, oval garnets, gold, American, c.19th	**600.00**	**700.00**
☐	**12** Cameos, seven different hued oval lava cameos of classical portraits in gold bezels alternating with gold half-beads, Italian, c. mid 19th	**1100.00**	**1300.00**
☐	**13** Cameo, shell cameo of cupid, engraved link, gold, American, c. 1890.	**400.00**	**500.00**
☐	**14** Cameos, six different hued lava cameos of classical portraits, gold fittings, c. mid 19th	**950.00**	**1100.00**

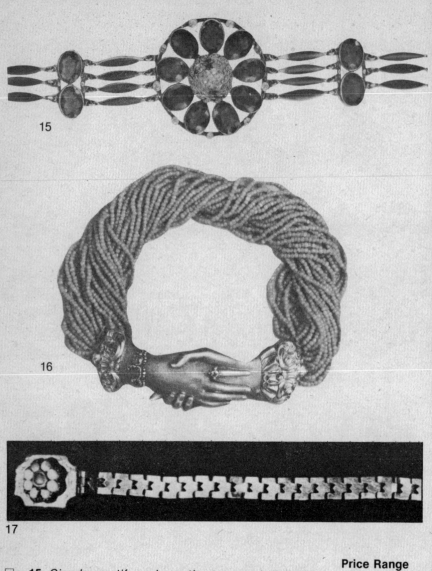

15

16

17

		Price Range	
☐	**15** *Circular motif, oval amethysts, round diamonds, platinum wreath in center, purple enamel baton links, gold*	2000.00	2400.00
☐	**16** *Coral beads, gemset clasp, gold, approx. 7⅜ in.* ..	4400.00	4600.00
☐	**17** *Doll bracelets, hollow book link chains, turquoise, engraved clasps, gold, pair, c. 1840*	400.00	475.00

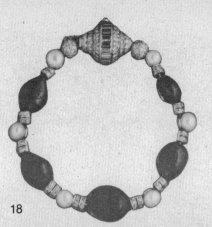

18

19

20

21

		Price Range	
☐	**18** *Emerald beads alternating with round diamonds pavé set in white gold, button pearls, 11 baguette diamonds, 186 round diamonds approx. 2.75 cts., c. 1925*	12600.00	14700.00
☐	**19** *Enamel leaf motif, ribbon hollow links, gold, maker: Martin, Baskett & Martin of Cheltanham, England, c. 1869*	2000.00	2200.00
☐	**20** *Enamel scroll motif, light blue, gold, American, c. 1890*	450.00	550.00
☐	**21** *Enamelled center oval, garnet, four pearls, gold, c. 1840*	2650.00	2850.00

22

23

24

		Price Range	
☐	**22** Escapement covers known as watchcocks from verge watches, c. late 18th, assembled as bracelet c. late 19th, hand-engraved and pierced with animals and designs, cabochon garnets, basemetal, English	400.00	475.00
☐	**23** Family motif, courtship, marriage, parenthood, two color gold, Art Deco, c. 1923	700.00	950.00
☐	**24** Fancy scroll hollow stamped link motif, oval foil-backed amethyst in clasp, French, gold, c. 1840 . .	2750.00	3300.00

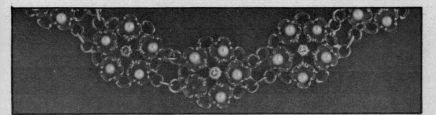

25

26

27

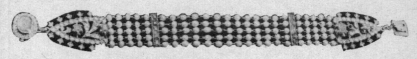

28

		Price Range	
☐	25 Flower motif links, five pearls and one round diamond in each link, gold	2400.00	2650.00
☐	26 Flower motif links, 20 diamonds alternating with 20 rubies, 18K gold...........................	1650.00	1850.00
☐	27 Flower motif links, garnets, gold, c. 1870	1300.00	1750.00
☐	28 Flower motif, oriental pearls, emeralds, rose diamonds, gold	2200.00	2650.00

29

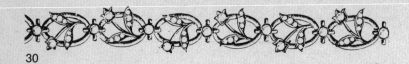

30

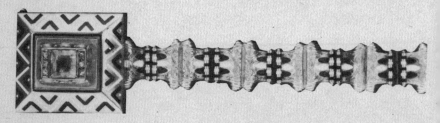

31

32

33

			Price Range	
☐	29	*Flower and leaf motif, seed pearls, five diamonds, twisted trace link chain, gold, English, c. 1903-04. .*	1300.00	1550.00
☐	30	*Flower and leaf motif on oval links, seed pearls, gold, English, c. 1903-04 . . . .*	800.00	1050.00
☐	31	*Geometric motif, engraved, enamel, emeralds, rose diamonds, gold . . . .*	1100.00	1300.00
☐	32	*Geometric motif flat links, one round emerald, one round ruby, one round sapphire, two round diamonds, 14K gold, c. 1930 . . . .*	1550.00	1750.00
☐	33	*Hand motif, cannetille link bracelet, turquoise, rubies, gold, c. 1820 . . . .*	2850.00	3300.00

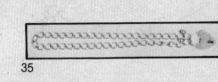

34

35

36

37

38

			Price Range	
☐	**34**	Heart and bow motif, cabochon turquoise, locket on reverse of heart, snake link chain, c. 1860-80 . . .	800.00	1000.00
☐	**35**	Heart lock motif, curb links, 9K gold, English, c. 20th.	175.00	200.00
☐	**36**	Heart locket with one table-cut diamond attached to fancy round link bracelet, gold, c 1860	1000.00	1200.00
☐	**37**	Hollow leaf motif links, gold, c. 1840	450.00	550.00
☐	**38**	Ivory carved flower center motif, ivory squares held together with elastic cord, c. early 20th	350.00	475.00

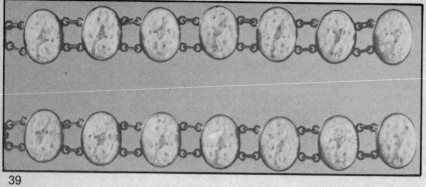

39

40

41

42

			Price Range	
☐	**39**	Ivory carved oval flower plaques, silver bezel, pair of bracelets, c. mid 19th	900.00	1000.00
☐	**40**	Jade carved circular motif, seed pearls, gold, c. 20th	750.00	900.00
☐	**41**	Jade plaques, carved carnelian plaques, gold fittings.	650.00	800.00
☐	**42**	Lady head bracelet, two Georgian chains with eight miniatures of ladies heads, heads in Art Nouveau style, c. 1890-1920	2650.00	3100.00

43

44

45

46

47

48

49

50

			Price Range	
☐	43	Lapis Lazuli oval links alternating with carved donut-shape rock crystal links with lapis lazuli inside borders, embossed white gold links, c. 1925	750.00	1000.00
☐	44	Laurel motif oval links, gold, French, c. 1830	950.00	1050.00
☐	45	Lava beasts surrounding white lava round flower motif, gold mounts, Italian, c. late 18th	1100.00	1300.00
☐	46	Leaf and scroll motif, citrine, black, white and pink enamel, c. mid 19th	1650.00	2000.00
☐	47	Lion head motif, ruby eyes, diamonds, gold, American	900.00	1300.00
☐	48	Malachite plaques in gold frames, c. mid 19th	800.00	1050.00
☐	49	Mesh black enamel on clasp, gold, c. 1880	1300.00	1550.00
☐	50	Mesh link, cannetille, opal pink tourmalines, seed pearls, gold, Georgian, c. 1800 (minor damage) . .	650.00	900.00

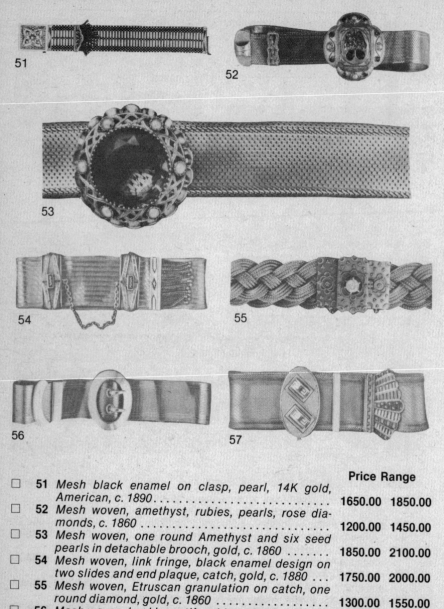

		Price Range	
☐	**51** Mesh black enamel on clasp, pearl, 14K gold, American, c. 1890	1650.00	1850.00
☐	**52** Mesh woven, amethyst, rubies, pearls, rose diamonds, c. 1860	1200.00	1450.00
☐	**53** Mesh woven, one round Amethyst and six seed pearls in detachable brooch, gold, c. 1860	1850.00	2100.00
☐	**54** Mesh woven, link fringe, black enamel design on two slides and end plaque, catch, gold, c. 1880 . . .	1750.00	2000.00
☐	**55** Mesh woven, Etruscan granulation on catch, one round diamond, gold, c. 1860	1300.00	1550.00
☐	**56** Mesh woven, buckle motif, gold, c. 1880	700.00	950.00
☐	**57** Mesh woven, Greek key motif on oval slide, black enamel, gold, c. 1860	1000.00	1100.00

			Price Range	
☐	**58**	*Micro-mosaic of Roman ruins on blue stone plaques, rose gold, c. mid 19th*	1100.00	1550.00
☐	**59**	*Flower motif, mosaic, Etruscan granulation, 18K gold, c. mid 19th*	4400.00	6300.00
☐	**60**	*Mosaic flower motif in center, filigree flower motif link chain, silver, Italian, c. mid 19th*	550.00	650.00
☐	**61**	*Tiger claws, seven, engraved fittings and clasp in shape of tiger claw, gold, English, c. 1870*	1750.00	2000.00

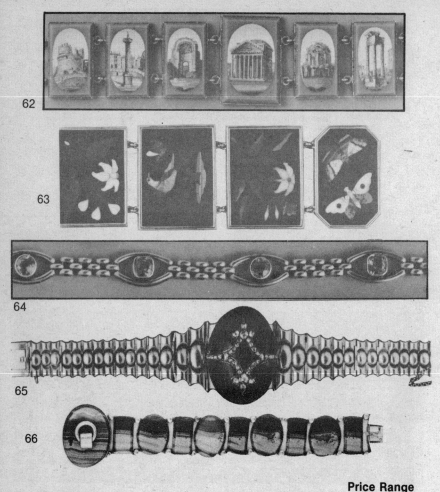

			Price Range	
☐	**62**	Mosaic motifs of the Pantheon, Hadrian's Villa, the Forum and Trajan's column, blue glass plaques, gold, c. 1850	2200.00	2550.00
☐	**63**	Mosaic plaques of flowers, birds and butterflies, gold, Italian....................................	1750.00	2000.00
☐	**64**	Oval link motif, three round peridots and two cushion-cut peridots alternating with chain links, gold, American, c. 1900	650.00	700.00
☐	**65**	Oval motif center, graduated fancy scallop edged-links, oval foil-backed amethyst in center with rose diamonds, gold, c. 1860	4950.00	5800.00
☐	**66**	Oval motif, malachite, gold, Russian	700.00	800.00

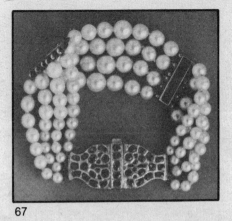

67

68

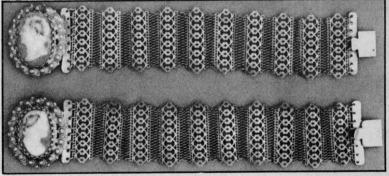

69

			Price Range	
☐	**67**	*Pearls, four strands, cushion-cut rubies in rectangular plaques, cushion-cut foil-back rubies in clasp, gold, Indian, c. 19th*	1550.00	1750.00
☐	**68**	*Pearls bordered by rose diamonds, gold, platinum, French, c. 1890*	800.00	1050.00
☐	**69**	*Pinchbeck fancy link bracelets, sulfide cameo clasps, pair, English, c. 19th*	550.00	650.00

70

71

72

		Price Range	
☐	**70** Portrait miniatures in center plaque of Queen Victoria and the Prince of Wales, hollow half-circle links, diamonds, gold, maker: S.H. & D. Gass of London, England, c. 1851	14700.00	16800.00
☐	**71** Padlock heart motif, cabochon garnet, 15K gold, English, c. 1865	725.00	825.00
☐	**72** Renaissance revival motif, enamelled cabochon garnet in center surrounded by four pair of looped-circles set with rose diamonds, gold, maker: C. Rowlands & Son of London, England, c. 1869	5250.00	5800.00

73

74

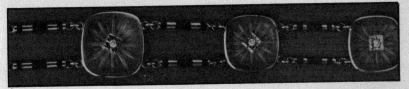

75

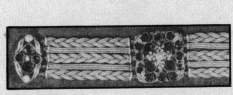

76

77

Price Range

☐ **73** Ribbon and flower motif center panel on wide band, 17 rose diamonds in flowers, gold, maker: G. Ehni, c. 1871 .... 3750.00 3950.00

☐ **74** Ribbon and musical note motif links, alternating with blue and white opaque enamel, gold, maker: Phillips Bros. of London, England, c. 1869 .... 1650.00 1850.00

☐ **75** Rock crystal panels set with one round diamond, etched, alternating with silver and black enamel baton links, platinum, Art Deco, c. 1930 .... 2550.00 2850.00

☐ **76** Rope chains, 20 round amethysts and four pearls in center panel and clasp, silver gold-washed, Italian, c. mid 19th 500.00 600.00

☐ **77** Rope chains, woven gold, black enamel and gold clasp, c. mid 19th 750.00 900.00

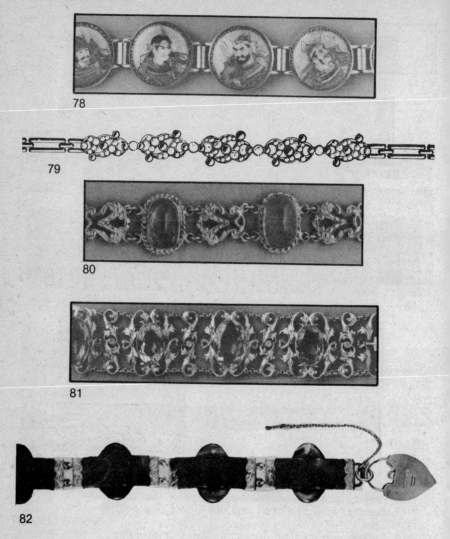

			Price Range	
☐	**78**	*Satsuma buttons of Samurai, five buttons, gold, signed: Cartier*	1600.00	1800.00
☐	**79**	*Scroll motif links, seed pearls, rectangular link chain, gold, English, c. late 19th*	800.00	1050.00
☐	**80**	*Scroll motif links alternating with light green cabochon emeralds, gold*	2950.00	3400.00
☐	**81**	*Scroll motif links and frames, four oval faceted citrines, 14K gold, c. 1860*	1750.00	2000.00
☐	**82**	*Scottish agates, 15K gold mounts, 9K gold heart lock clasp, English, c. 1860*	1100.00	1300.00

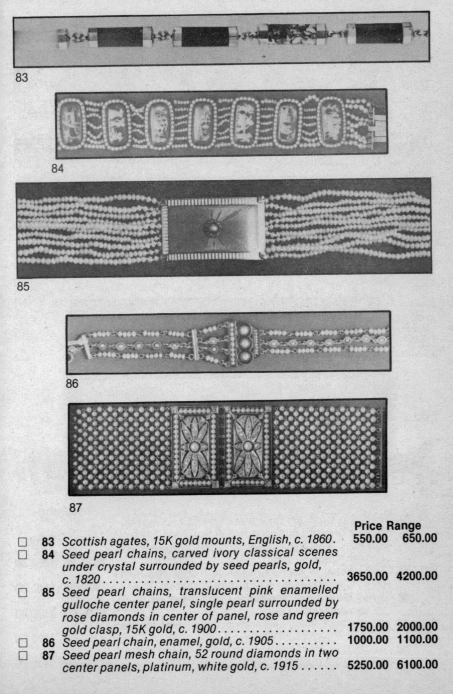

88

89

90

Price Range

☐ **88** *Seed pearls strung on white horsehair on mother-of-pearl templates, fitted velvet-lined leather box marked: J. W. Carr, Goldsmith, 29 Commercial St., Leeds, English, c. 1860* 1750.00 2200.00

☐ **89** *Shell cameo of four heads — one lady, two men, and a ram, flat sandwich link chain, gold, c. 1830* . 1000.00 1100.00

☐ **90** *Shell cameos of three graces, 14K gold* 650.00 750.00

91

95

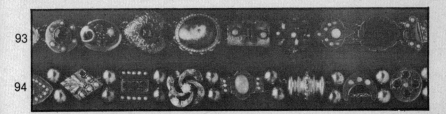

92

93

94

			Price Range	
☐	**91**	*Slide bracelet, ten yellow, green, white and rose gold slides strung on gold wires with gold beads, slides c. late 19th, contemporary assembly*	2750.00	3000.00
☐	**92**	*Slide bracelet of 11 slides of ladies heads, each set with one round diamond, gold, Art Nouveau, c. 1910* . . . . *Reproduction*	2400.00	2750.00
☐	**93**	*Slide bracelet of 13 slides with various gemstones, gold, c. 1860*	2400.00	2650.00
☐	**94**	*Slide bracelet of slides with various gemstones alternating with gold beads, gold, c. 1860*	2200.00	2400.00
☐	**95**	*Slide bracelet of 8 slides with various gemstones, 14K gold, c. 1890*	2850.00	3300.00

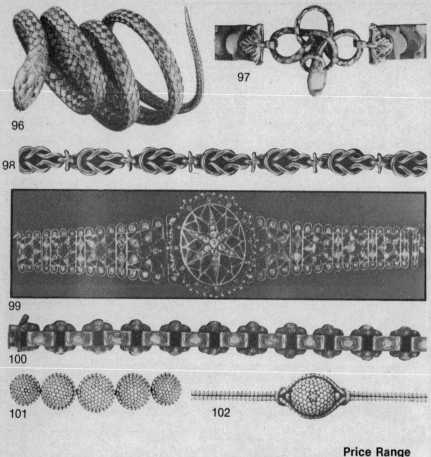

96

97

98

99

100

101

102

			Price Range	
☐	**96**	Snake, woven flexible band, ruby eyes, 18K gold, 100 grams, maker: Tiffany & Co., c. late 19th	2400.00	2650.00
☐	**97**	Snake center, scale motif links, turquoise in snake head, gold, English, c. 1840...................	1200.00	1450.00
☐	**98**	Square knot motif links, gold, approx. 8 divt., American, c. 20th	450.00	550.00
☐	**99**	Star motif, openwork panels, 21 rose diamonds in center oval, plique-á-jour blue enamel background, each link with round sapphires and rose diamonds, silver topped gold, c. 1870	5750.00	6850.00
☐	**100**	Turquoise, clasp with hair locket, gold, Victorian, c. 1840	1300.00	1550.00
☐	**101**	Turquoise, pavé domed discs, gold, c. 1830-50 ...	1200.00	1300.00
☐	**102**	Turquoise, pavé domed oval center, diamonds, gold, English, c. 1830-50	850.00	950.00

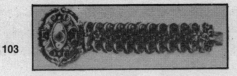

103

Price Range

☐ **103** *Watch motif, watch cover: blue enamel with rubies and diamonds, watch: oval enamel dial, cylinder escapement, gold links, Paris, French, c. 1800* . . . **16800.00 21000.00**

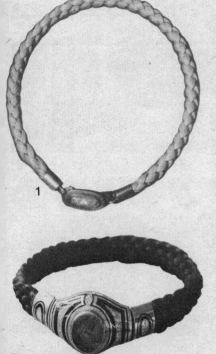

1

2

3

HAIR
All items made from hair referred to throughout this section are of brunette human hair unless stated otherwise.

☐ **1** *Braided white hair, clasp with braided white hair under glass, gold, c. 1880* **175.00** **200.00**

☐ **2** *Clasp, black enamel and gold, woven hair under glass and braided hair* **325.00** **375.00**

☐ **3** *Expandable woven hair, heart and bow motif connector, gold, c. 1860-80* **125.00** **150.00**

			Price Range	
☐	**4**	Expandable woven hair motif, clasps with seed pearl border, woven hair and gold foil under glass, gold, c. 1860-80	**150.00**	**175.00**
☐	**5**	Expandable woven hair motif, scroll motif clasp with three faceted amethyst, gold, c. 1860-80	**175.00**	**225.00**
☐	**6**	Expandable woven hair motif, engraved flower connector, gold, c. 1860-80	**110.00**	**125.00**

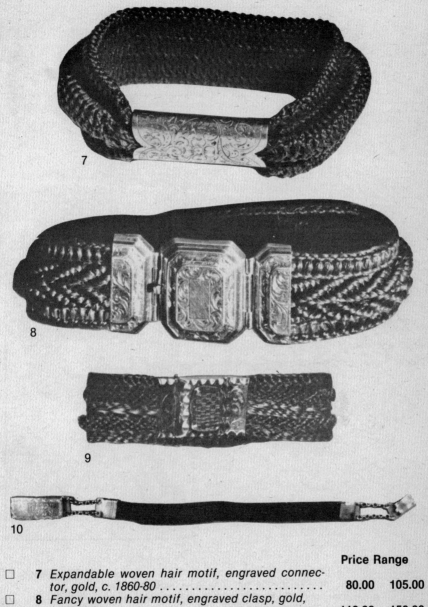

			Price Range	
☐	**7**	Expandable woven hair motif, engraved connector, gold, c. 1860-80	80.00	105.00
☐	**8**	Fancy woven hair motif, engraved clasp, gold, c. 1860-80	110.00	150.00
☐	**9**	Fancy woven hair motif, clasp with woven hair under glass, gold, c. 1860-80	95.00	125.00
☐	**10**	Flat woven hair moif, engraved clasp, gold, c. 1820-40	105.00	125.00

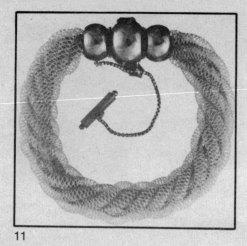

11

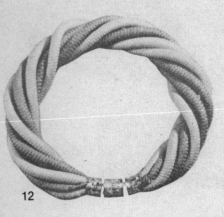

12

13

		Price Range	
☐	**11** *Hollow tube motif of open weave woven white hair, engraved clasp with buckle inlaid with woven brunette hair, c. 1800-30*	500.00	550.00
☐	**12** *Hollow tube motif of tightly woven white and brunette hair, engraved clasp, c. 1800-40*	250.00	275.00
☐	**13** *Hollow tube motif of woven hair with two dangles, three wooden beads covered with hair, c. 1840-65* .	150.00	175.00

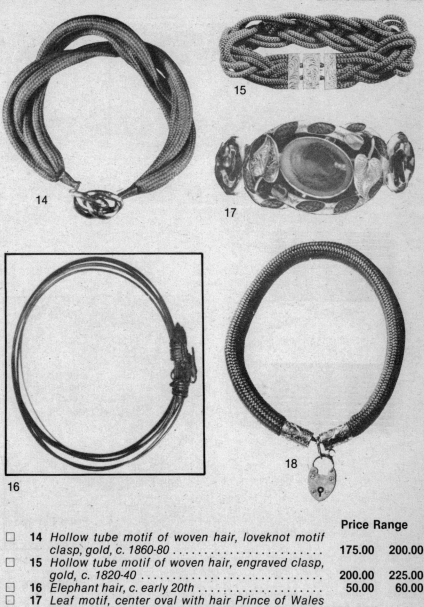

			Price Range	
☐	**14**	Hollow tube motif of woven hair, loveknot motif clasp, gold, c. 1860-80	**175.00**	**200.00**
☐	**15**	Hollow tube motif of woven hair, engraved clasp, gold, c. 1820-40	**200.00**	**225.00**
☐	**16**	Elephant hair, c. early 20th	**50.00**	**60.00**
☐	**17**	Leaf motif, center oval with hair Prince of Wales feather under glass with three seed pearls, hollow tubular bangle filled with woven hair, gold, c. 1860-1880	**1100.00**	**1300.00**
☐	**18**	Padlock clasp motif, tightly woven hair over solid core, gold, English, c. 1732	**300.00**	**325.00**

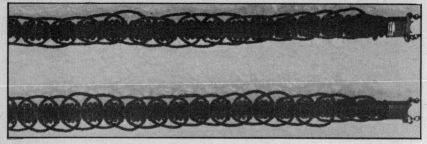

19

20

21

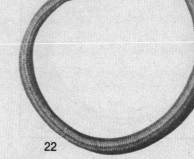

22

		Price Range	
☐ 19	Ribbon woven hair motif, gold clasps, c. 1840-60, pair	350.00	375.00
☐ 20	Sandwich bangle of inner band, woven hair and outer engraved and cutout band, gold, English, c. early 20th	250.00	275.00
☐ 21	Sandwich bangle of inner band, woven hair and outer engraved and cutout band, colored gold flowers applied to outside of reverse of band, silver, English, c. early 20th	350.00	400.00
☐ 22	Snake motif, tightly woven hair over solid core, cabochon garnets in head and eyes, gold, c. 1800 .	900.00	1000.00

**Photograph of a young woman wearing a bar brooch consist-
ing of three hexagonal lava cameos of classical female
heads. The photograph was taken at Walzl's Imperial Portrait Studios in Baltimore, Maryland.**

BROOCHES

ANIMAL and BUG		Price Range	
☐ **1** Bee, rose diamond and silver body, pearl and ruby wings, gold backed, c. 1870		1450.00	1650.00
☐ **2** Bee, emerald and rose diamond body, coral set terminal to bar, c. 1860		1900.00	2150.00
☐ **3** Bee, one pearl, rubies, sapphires, rose and round diamonds, moveable upper wings, silver topped gold, Victorian.		2750.00	3300.00
☐ **4** Bee, rubies, sapphires, pearls, gold, c. 1900		375.00	400.00
☐ **5** Beetle, fancy-shape cabochon garnets in body, carved and pierced jade wings, two seed pearls, gold, c. 19th.		1050.00	1200.00

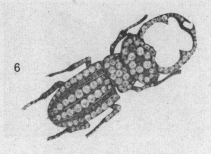

		Price Range	
☐	**6** *Beetle, round diamonds, emeralds, silver topped gold.*	3300.00	4400.00
☐	**7** *Beetle, pavé turquoise, rose diamonds, half seed pearls, Victorian.*	750.00	1000.00
☐	**8** *Bird, ruby bead-set eyes, rose diamond body, briolette diamond silver cap pendant, silver topped-gold, c. 1820*	4850.00	5150.00
☐	**9** *Bird, pavé diamonds, center emerald-cut emerald in closed back mounting, silver, c. 1800-10*	1000.00	1200.00
☐	**10** *Bird, pave turquoise, silver*	550.00	650.00
☐	**11** *Bird-in-Crescent, ruby eyes, 27 old mine diamonds approx. 2.25 cts. in gold double-crescent, rose diamonds in silver bird, c. 1840*	4200.00	4950.00

			Price Range	
☐	**12**	*Butterfly, ruby, diamond, sapphire, silver, gold, c. 1850*	700.00	750.00
☐	**13**	*Butterfly, old mine diamond approx. .45 ct., pavé rose diamond body and wings, gold, c. 1860*	2200.00	2650.00
☐	**14**	*Butterfly, opaque enamel wings on spring hinges, jeweled eyes, gold, c. 1900*	1200.00	1300.00
☐	**15**	*Butterfly, blue and green opaque enamel wings, 62 round diamonds approx. 1.10 cts., platinum, c. 1900*	3000.00	3250.00
☐	**16**	*Butterfly, emerald and ruby wings, old mine diamonds in body, ruby eyes, gold, c. 1860*	3300.00	3750.00
☐	**17**	*Butterfly, opal wings, diamonds, gold*	850.00	900.00

18

20

19

21

		Price Range	
☐	**18** Butterfly, cabochon turquoise, rose diamonds, cabochon ruby eye, gold, c. 1880	1750.00	2000.00
☐	**19** Butterfly, mother-of-pearl wings, 13 round rubies, gold, c. 1915	450.00	550.00
☐	**20** Butterfly, gem set, Etruscan granulation and cannetille, gold, c. 1800	550.00	650.00
☐	**21** Butterfly, two old mine diamonds, rose diamonds, oval rubies, pavé, gold, silver, c. 1830	4500.00	4600.00

22

23

24

25

26

		Price Range	
☐	**22** Butterfly, one seed pearl, rose diamonds, silver, French, c. late 18th	1850.00	2100.00
☐	**23** Butterfly, foil-back faceted stones, Etruscan granulation, gold, c. 1820	1100.00	1300.00
☐	**24** Butterflies, mosaic, gold, c. 1880	450.00	550.00
☐	**25** Cat, pavé rose diamond body, ruby eyes, pearl ball, white gold, French, c. 1935	1300.00	1550.00
☐	**26** Cat, enamel, engraved frame, gold	400.00	600.00

27

28

30

29

31

		Price Range	
☐	27 Deer, carved from single piece of boxwood, English, c. 1870	325.00	375.00
☐	28 Dragon, diamond mouth, ruby eye, gold, Art Nouveau, c. 1880	750.00	950.00
☐	29 Dragons, two pearls, two faceted green stones, one carnelian scarab, gold, c. 19th	4300.00	4500.00
☐	30 Dragonfly, colored stones, silver, c. mid 19th	275.00	300.00
☐	31 Dragonfly, three cabochon emeralds in gold body, nine emerald-cut emeralds in tail, rose diamonds in silver topped gold wings, detachable brooch fitting, c. 1870-80	3300.00	3750.00

32

33

35

34

36

			Price Range	
☐	**32**	*Dragonfly, tortoise shell, sterling, maker: Carl Schon, Baltimore, Maryland, American, c. 1930-50* .	110.00	150.00
☐	**33**	*Dragonfly, one pearl, two emeralds, four rubies, rose diamonds, gold, c. 1870-80*	4850.00	5050.00
☐	**34**	*Eagle, carved, rose cut diamonds, gold, c. late 19th*	950.00	1050.00
☐	**35**	*Eagle, turquoise, 20K gold, c. late 19th*	1000.00	1200.00
☐	**36**	*Eagle, pave diamonds, calibre rubies, platinum, c. 1925.*	1850.00	2100.00

37

38

39

41

40

			Price Range	
☐	**37**	*Elephant, 9K gold, Edwardian, c. 1910*	200.00	225.00
☐	**38**	*Fly, cabochon ruby eyes and body, old mine diamond body and wings, pearl, gold, c. 1860*	2400.00	2650.00
☐	**39**	*Fox head, round emerald eyes, pavé set diamond head and bar brooch, calibre-cut emeralds in bar brooch ends, platinum, gold, c. 1900-20*	4850.00	5050.00
☐	**40**	*Frog, pavé diamond frog and plants, removable tremblant frog, silver, 18K gold, c. 1840*	42000.00	44000.00
☐	**41**	*Frog, carved jasper, rope twist borders, Etruscan granulation, white enamel circlets, maker: Castellani, Italian, c. 1860*	12600.00	14700.00

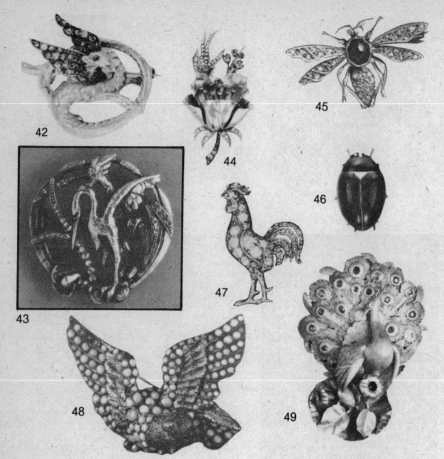

		Price Range	
☐	**42** Griffin, ruby eyes, rose diamond wings, silver wings, gold, c. 1870...............................	750.00	1000.00
☐	**43** Heron, rose diamond branches, demantoid garnet ferns, gold, c. 1890	4050.00	4300.00
☐	**44** Hummingbird and Rose of Sharon, rose diamonds, one oval cut ruby, tremblant bird, gold...........	1550.00	1750.00
☐	**45** Insect, garnet, rose diamonds, silver, gold, c. 1850 ..	1300.00	1550.00
☐	**46** Ladybug, blue guilloché enamel, 18K gold, Victorian.	275.00	1550.00
☐	**47** Rooster, ruby eye, rose diamonds, silver, gold	650.00	800.00
☐	**48** Parrot, pavé cabochon turquoise wings, pave cabochon garnet beak, vermeil, c. 1840............	1000.00	1100.00
☐	**49** Peacock, gemset, gold, approx. 2½ in.	500.00	600.00

50

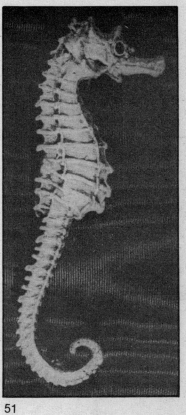

51

52

		Price Range	
☐	**50** *Ram's Head, Etruscan rope motif, gold, maker: Castellani, Italian, c. 1860*	3850.00	4000.00
☐	**51** *Seahorse, cabochon garnet eye, cast silver, maker: Carl Schon, Baltimore, Maryland, American, c. 1930-50*	150.00	175.00
☐	**52** *Shrimp, ruby eye, rose diamond body, gold, silver, c. 1860*	1750.00	1850.00

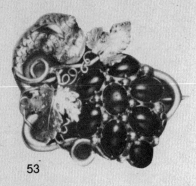

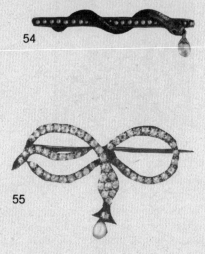

54

53

55

56

57

58

			Price Range	
☐	53	*Snake, garnets, diamond eyes, multi-color gold, approx. 1 3/8 in.*	800.00	1000.00
☐	54	*Snake, green enamel, ruby eyes, briolette diamond pendant, pearls in pin, gold, c. 1875*	4100.00	4300.00
☐	55	*Snake, 62 old mine diamonds approx. 1.25 cts., pavé, pearl pendant, silver, gold, c. late 19th*	2650.00	2850.00
☐	56	*Snake, one cabochon turquoise, gold, English, c. early 20th*	325.00	350.00
☐	57	*Snake and cobalt blue flower motif, rose diamonds, gold, c. 19th.*	1300.00	1750.00
☐	58	*Spider, web and fly, gold, c. 1880*	500.00	550.00

59

60

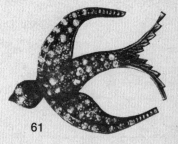

61

62

Price Range

☐ **59** *St. George-and-the-Dragon, enamelled St. George, pearl horse, emerald and green enamel dragon, ruby cartouche, simple link chain to pin, silver, Hungarian, c. 1850* 800.00 950.00

☐ **60** *Swallow, pavé rose diamond wings and body, old mine diamond in crestail, ruby eyes, c. 1810* 3300.00 3500.00

☐ **61** *Swallow, 70 old mine diamonds, ruby in head, silver, c. 1850* 1750.00 2000.00

☐ **62** *Swallow, rose diamonds in feathers, rubies in eyes, blue, black and white enamel, gold, silver, c. 1860* .. 2750.00 3200.00

63

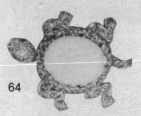

64

65

66

67

		Price Range	
☐	**63** Swallows, rose diamond body and wings in silver topped gold, gold safety pin, c. 1830	950.00	1050.00
☐	**64** Turtle, emerald eyes, cabochon opal body surrounded with diamonds, gold, c. 1935	2000.00	2200.00
☐	**65** Turtle, six rose diamonds, 36 demantoid garnets, gold, c. early 20th	550.00	650.00
☐	**66** Turtle, round diamonds, cushion-cut sapphires, silver topped gold, c. 1860.	1100.00	1650.00
☐	**67** Winged lion, Etruscan granulation, Gothic revival, gold, c. 1860-80	1450.00	1550.00

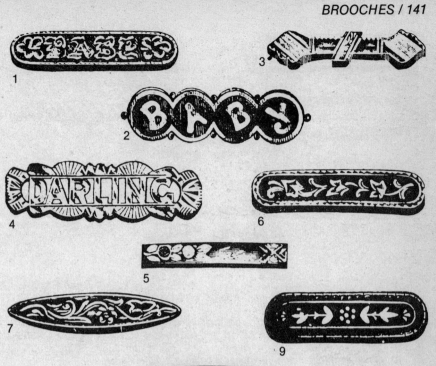

BABY PIN

			Price Range	
☐	1	*"BABY" raised letter motif, gold front, American, c. 1894-95*	**40.00**	**50.00**
☐	2	*"BABY" raised letter motif, gold front, American, c. 1894-95*	**45.00**	**55.00**
☐	3	*Cutout motif, engraved, gold front, American, c. 1894-95*	**45.00**	**50.00**
☐		*Same as above but gold filled*	**25.00**	**30.00**
☐	4	*"DARLING" cutout letter motif, gold front, American, c. 1894-95*	**45.00**	**55.00**
☐	5	*Flower motif, engraved, one round garnet, one seed pearl, gold front, American, c. 1894-95*	**55.00**	**60.00**
☐	6	*Flower motif, blue enamel, 14K gold, American, c. 1894-95*	**60.00**	**65.00**
☐	7	*Flower motif, enamel, 14K gold, American, c. 1894-95*	**60.00**	**75.00**
☐	8	*Flower motif, engraved, 14K gold, American, c. 1894-95*	**60.00**	**65.00**
☐		*Same as above but gold filled*	**30.00**	**35.00**
☐	9	*Flower motif, enamel, sterling silver, American, c. 1896*	**45.00**	**55.00**

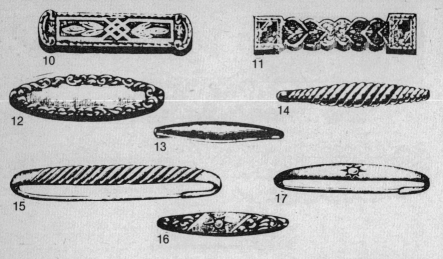

		Price Range	
☐	**10** *Geometric engraved motif, gold plate on sterling silver, American, c. 1894-95*	45.00	55.00
☐	**11** *Heart and square cutout motif, engraved, gold plate on sterling silver, American, c. 1894-95*	45.00	55.00
☐	*Same as above but gold filled*	25.00	30.00
☐	**12** *Oval chased edge motif, 14K gold, American, c. 1894-95*	55.00	65.00
☐	*Same as above but gold filled*	30.00	35.00
☐	**13** *Polished motif, 14K gold, American, c. 1894-95* . . .	45.00	55.00
☐	**14** *Ribbed motif, 14K gold, American, c. 1894-95*	55.00	65.00
☐	**15** *Ribbed motif, sterling silver, American, c. 1896* . . .	45.00	55.00
☐	**16** *Star motif, chased, one seed pearl, 14K gold, American, c. 1894-95*	65.00	70.00
☐	**17** *Star motif, one cabochon turquoise, sterling silver, American, 1896*	40.00	50.00

BAR

☐	**1** *Amethyst, two seed pearls, 15K gold, American, c. 1894-95*	275.00	335.00

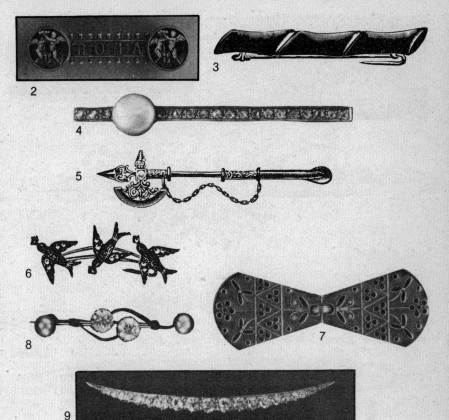

			Price Range	
☐	**2**	*Angel mosaic motif, Etruscan granulation, gold, Italian, c. 1870*	550.00	600.00
☐	**3**	*Bamboo motif, black onyx, 14K gold, American, c. 1896*	125.00	135.00
☐	**4**	*Baroque pearl, rose diamonds, gold topped platinum, French, c. 19th*	575.00	625.00
☐	**5**	*Battle Ax with removable scabbard motif, one seed pearl, 14K gold, American c. 1894-95*	325.00	350.00
☐	**6**	*Bird motif, seed pearls, 14K gold, American, c. 1894-95*	325.00	350.00
☐	**7**	*Bow lace motif, gold, c. 1860*	400.00	475.00
☐	**8**	*Bypass knife-edge motif, two old European-cut diamonds, two rose diamonds, two cultured pearls, silver, gold*	1450.00	1750.00
☐	**9**	*Crescent motif, 21 old mine diamonds approx. 2.0 cts., platinum, gold, c. 1870*	2400.00	2650.00

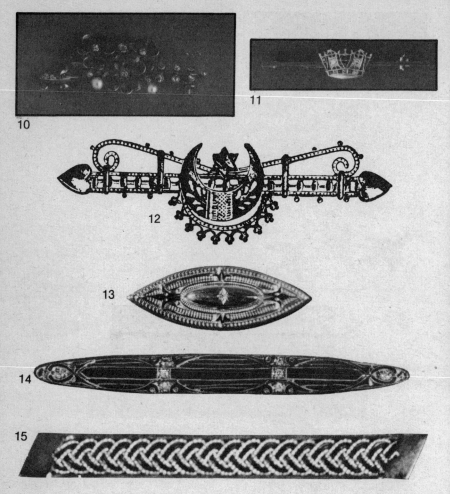

			Price Range	
☐	**10**	*Clover flower motif, guilloche translucent green enamel, two seed pearls, round diamonds, gold, fitted leather box, c. 1880*	**1450.00**	**1650.00**
☐	**11**	*Crown motif, round diamonds, square sapphires, platinum topped gold, c. early 20th*	**550.00**	**600.00**
☐	**12**	*Crescent and star motif, 14K gold, American, c. 1894-95*	**250.00**	**275.00**
☐	**13**	*Diamond, gold, English, c. 1890-1910.*	**225.00**	**275.00**
☐	**14**	*Diamonds, onyx, platinum, c. 1925*	**450.00**	**475.00**
☐	**15**	*Elephant hair, gold, c. early 20th*	**225.00**	**250.00**

			Price Range	
☐	**16**	*Fleur-de-lys motif, blue enamel, round diamond, seed pearls, 14K gold.*	325.00	400.00
☐	**17**	*Flower motif, half-seed pearls, coral, gold, English, mid-Victorian*	375.00	475.00
☐	**18**	*Flower motif, 14K gold, American, c. 1894-95*	175.00	200.00
☐	**19**	*Flower motif, sterling, American, c. 1896*	65.00	80.00
☐	**20**	*Gold, English, c. 1890-1910.*	200.00	250.00
☐	**21**	*Gold, Etruscan granulation, classical Revival motif, c. 1870*	450.00	500.00
☐	**22**	*Gold miner motif of South Africa, gold, Victorian* .	345.00	385.00

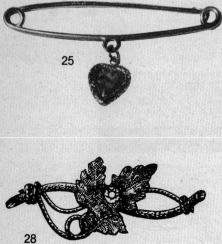

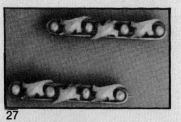

			Price Range	
☐	**23**	*Half pearl, round and rose diamonds, gold, silver, c. mid 19th*	1000.00	1100.00
☐	**24**	*Half pearls, rose diamonds, platinum, c. 1900*	1750.00	2000.00
☐	**25**	*Heart motif, hair under glass, gold, c. late 19th* ...	150.00	175.00
☐	**26**	*Ladies heads motif, carved, Art Nouveau, gold, c. 1900*	175.00	200.00
☐	**27**	*Leaf motif, translucent enamel, seed pearls, gold, Art Nouveau, c. 1900, pair*	550.00	600.00
☐	**28**	*Leaf motif, one round diamond, 14K gold, American, c. 1894-95*	275.00	325.00
☐	**29**	*Leaf motif, three round diamonds, 14K gold, American, c. 1894-95*	375.00	450.00

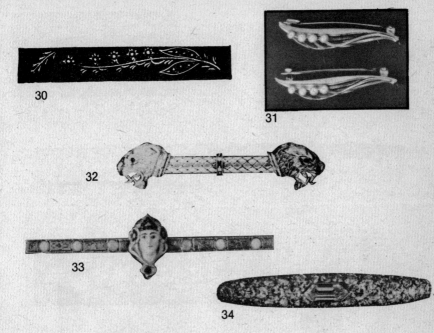

30

31

32

33

34

35

			Price Range	
☐	30	*Lily-of-the-valley flower motif, 11 seed pearls, 14K gold, American, c. 1894-95*	175.00	200.00
☐	31	*Lily-of-the-valley flower motif, seed pearls, translucent green enamel, gold, Art Nouveau, c. 1915, pair.*	500.00	550.00
☐	32	*Lion head motif, red stone eyes, woven gold, c. 1880.*	275.00	375.00
☐	33	*Miniature of a lady, translucent pink and red enamel, emeralds in tiara, six cabochon opals in bar, engraved, gold, Art Nouveau, c. 1900*	1750.00	2000.00
☐	34	*One oblong hexagonal diamond approx. .50 ct., 129 round diamonds approx. 3.0 cts. pave, platinum, French, c. 1925*	4500.00	4600.00
☐	35	*Onyx center, two pearls, one round diamond, rose diamonds, gold, platinum, c. 1920*	1050.00	1100.00

36

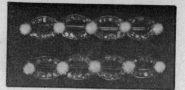

37

38

39

41

40

42

		Price Range	
☐	**36** Onyx: French-cut, one round diamond approx. 1.80 cts., round diamonds approx. 3.25 cts., platinum, c. 1910	5300.00	5450.00
☐	**37** Opals: ten cabochon, rose diamonds, silver, gold, c. 1860, pair..................................	1300.00	1550.00
☐	**38** Pearl, 14K gold, American, c. 1894-95	150.00	170.00
☐	**39** Pearls, knife-edge bar, 14K, American, c. 1894-95 .	160.00	175.00
☐	**40** Pearls: natural baroque, rose diamonds, gold, silver, c. 1840	1200.00	1300.00
☐	**41** Pearls, rose diamonds, gold, c. 1840	1300.00	1550.00
☐	**42** Peridot, seed pearls, 14K gold, Art Nouveau, c. 1890	300.00	325.00

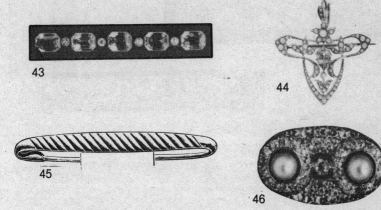

43

44

45

46

47

48

49

		Price Range	
☐	**43** Peridots: five emerald-cut, four round diamonds, platinum, c. 1910	450.00	500.00
☐	**44** Peridot: pear-cut in center, seed pearls, 15K gold, c. 19th.	500.00	700.00
☐	**45** Ribbed motif, sterling, American, c. 1896	125.00	140.00
☐	**46** Rose diamonds, pave, two pearls, platinum topped gold, c. 1880	1750.00	2000.00
☐	**47** Rose diamonds, one pearl, blue enamel, gold, c. 1910	350.00	400.00
☐	**48** Rose diamonds, 12 pearls, silver topped gold, c. 1840	650.00	750.00
☐	**49** Rose diamonds, one natural pearl, silver, c. late 19th	800.00	950.00

50

51

52

53

54

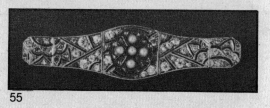

55

			Price Range	
☐	**50**	*Round diamonds: five approx. .50 ct., rose diamonds, four button pearls, white gold, c. 1905*	950.00	1000.00
☐	**51**	*Round diamonds: 59 approx. 4.0 cts., gold, platinum, c. 1870*	2300.00	2750.00
☐	**52**	*Round diamond approx. 1.50 cts., 100 round diamonds approx. 2.0 cts., platinum, c. 1815*	3100.00	3300.00
☐	**53**	*Round ruby, rose diamonds, silver topped gold, c. 19th*	900.00	950.00
☐	**54**	*Round diamonds approx. .75 ct., 14K gold, platinum, c. 1915*	1100.00	1200.00
☐	**55**	*Round diamonds, five seed pearls, platinum, c. 1905*	1650.00	1850.00

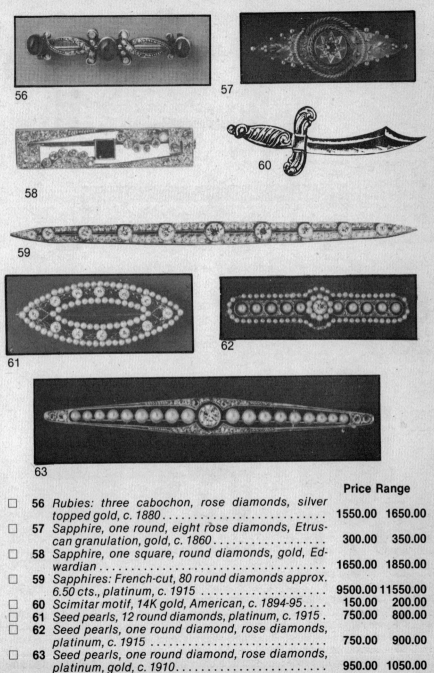

56
57
58
60
59
61
62
63

			Price Range	
☐	**56**	Rubies: three cabochon, rose diamonds, silver topped gold, c. 1880	1550.00	1650.00
☐	**57**	Sapphire, one round, eight rose diamonds, Etruscan granulation, gold, c. 1860	300.00	350.00
☐	**58**	Sapphire, one square, round diamonds, gold, Edwardian	1650.00	1850.00
☐	**59**	Sapphires: French-cut, 80 round diamonds approx. 6.50 cts., platinum, c. 1915	9500.00	11550.00
☐	**60**	Scimitar motif, 14K gold, American, c. 1894-95. . . .	150.00	200.00
☐	**61**	Seed pearls, 12 round diamonds, platinum, c. 1915 .	750.00	800.00
☐	**62**	Seed pearls, one round diamond, rose diamonds, platinum, c. 1915	750.00	900.00
☐	**63**	Seed pearls, one round diamond, rose diamonds, platinum, gold, c. 1910.	950.00	1050.00

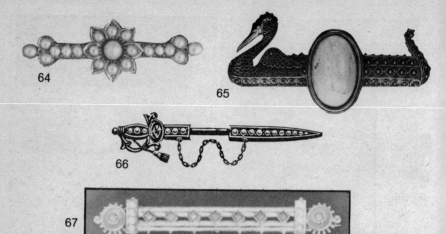

		Price Range	
☐	64 *Seed pearls, gold, fitted leather box marked: Hall & Co., c. mid 19th*	275.00	325.00
☐	65 *Swan barge motif, Etruscan granulation, oval turquoise, gold, signed: Tiffany & Co., American*	95.00	125.00
☐	66 *Sword with removable scabbard, seed pearls, 14K gold, American, c. 1894-95*	350.00	400.00
☐	67 *Turquoise, eight seed pearls, gold, c. 1860*	275.00	325.00

CAMEO

☐	1 *Amethyst cameo of a lady, amethyst teardrops, turquoise, black and white opaque enamel, silver, c. 19th.*	600.00	800.00
☐	2 *Coral cameos of Bacchus, Artimis and Demeter with urns, gold, c. 1860*	1100.00	1300.00
☐	3 *Coral cameo of a lady, coral beads, gold, c. 1860* ..	1200.00	1450.00

4

5

6

7

		Price Range	
☐	**4** *Hardstone onyx portrait cameo of a lady, rose diamonds, pearls, gold, c. 1880.*	1750.00	2000.00
☐	**5** *Green onyx cameo of a Greek Muse, pearls, gold, c. early 20th*	1600.00	1800.00
☐	**6** *Hardstone cameo of a lady, silver gilt, c. 1860.*	650.00	800.00
☐	**7** *Hardstone black and white cameo of a cherub, half pearls, gold, c. 1880.*	1550.00	1850.00

8

9

11

10

12

			Price Range	
☐	**8**	*Hardstone cameo of Athena with chariot, gold, c. 1860*	1350.00	1500.00
☐	**9**	*Hardstone cameo of three gentlemen and a ram, gold, c. 19th*	1200.00	1450.00
☐	**10**	*Hardstone cameo of Angel of Death, pearls, gold, c. 1870*	2000.00	2100.00
☐	**11**	*Hardstone cameo, gold, Victorian*	350.00	450.00
☐	**12**	*Hardstone cameo of a Renaissance lady, seed pearls, gold, c. mid 19th.*	500.00	600.00

13

14

15

16

		Price Range	
☐	**13** *Hardstone cameo of a warrior and a lady, cultured pearls, 18K gold, c. 1885.*	1650.00	2400.00
☐	**14** *Ivory cameo of a lady with grapes, pin back glued-to cameo*	400.00	450.00
☐	**15** *Ivory carving of a cherub, c. 1845*	200.00	250.00
☐	**16** *Ivory scenic cameo with Oriental figures, gold, c. 19th*	550.00	600.00

17

18

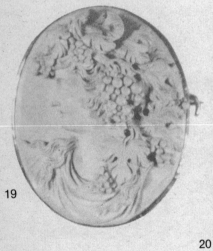

19

20

			Price Range	
☐	**17**	*Lava cameo of a warrior with a dragon on his helmet, gold, c. 1860*	**300.00**	**350.00**
☐	**18**	*Lava cameo of an angel riding a lion, gold, c. 18th*	**950.00**	**1050.00**
☐	**19**	*Lava cameo of a lady with grape vines in her hair, gold, c. 1860*	**375.00**	**450.00**
☐	**20**	*Lava cameo of a mythological figure, three amethyst teardrops, gold, c. late 18th*	**600.00**	**700.00**

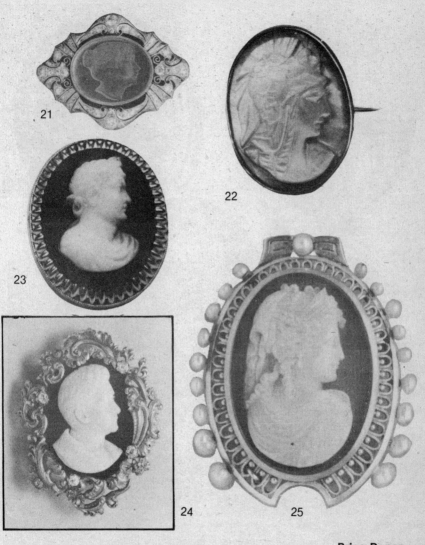

			Price Range	
☐	**26**	*Onyx cameo of a lady, Etruscan granulation frame, gold, c. 1870*	1450.00	1650.00
☐	**27**	*Onyx cameo of a lady, half pearls, black enamel, gold, c. 1870*	1000.00	1100.00
☐	**28**	*Onyx cameo of a gentleman, gold, c. 1850-75*	450.00	500.00
☐	**29**	*Onyx cameo of a lady, brooch or pendant locket, gold, c. 1900.*	800.00	950.00
☐	**30**	*Onyx cameo of a lady, seed pearls, gold, c. 1860* ..	1550.00	1650.00

			Price Range	
☐	**31**	*Onyx cameo of a child, seed pearls, gold, c. mid 19th*	800.00	900.00
☐	**32**	*Opal matrix cameo of the Sphinx, gold, c. 1920* ...	3300.00	3750.00
☐	**33**	*Sardonyx cameo of a Greek warrior, lion motif frame, gold, c. 1870*	2850.00	3100.00
☐	**34**	*Sardonyx cameo of a lady, four round diamonds, eight seed pearls, gold, c. 1880.*	1450.00	1700.00

35   36

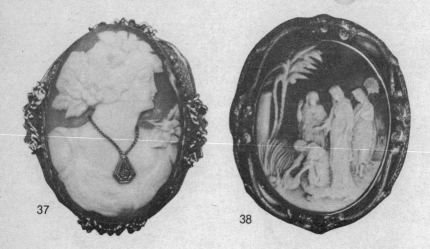

37   38

		Price Range	
☐	**35** Shell cameo of a chariot and rider, Etruscan granulation frame, c. 1880.	**1100.00**	**1300.00**
☐	**36** Shell cameo of a Greek in a Renaissance style frame, opaque enamel, square-cut emeralds, baroque cultured pearls, 14K gold, Victorian.	**650.00**	**750.00**
☐	**37** Shell cameo of a lady, diamond, 18K gold, c. 1890-1900.	**450.00**	**550.00**
☐	**38** Shell cameo of Moses in the bullrushes, Etruscan granulation, gold, c. 1850.	**4200.00**	**4600.00**

39

40

41

42

43

			Price Range	
☐	39	*Shell cameo of three Muses, sterling silver, c. 20th* .	175.00	190.00
☐	40	*Shell scenic cameo with two ladies, gold, c. 19th* .	275.00	300.00
☐	41	*Turquoise cameo of an angel and a woman, 36 seed pearls, 14K gold, c. 1900.*	600.00	700.00
☐	42	*Hardstone cameo of a lady with a bow, Etruscan granulation, gold, c. 18th.*	1300.00	1450.00
☐	43	*Hardstone cameo portrait of a gentleman, gold.* . .	1300.00	1450.00

44

45

46

47

			Price Range	
☐	**44**	*Shell scenic cameo of Rebecca-at-the-Well with two ducks, gold, c. 19th*	275.00	300.00
☐	**45**	*Shell scenic cameo with an Oriental lady, carved flower frame, gold, c. 19th*	350.00	400.00
☐	**46**	*Shell scenic cameo of Jesus with children, cut-out frame, 18K gold, c. 1840*	650.00	750.00
☐	**47**	*Hardstone cameo of a lady, seed pearls, gold, c. 18th.*	1750.00	2000.00

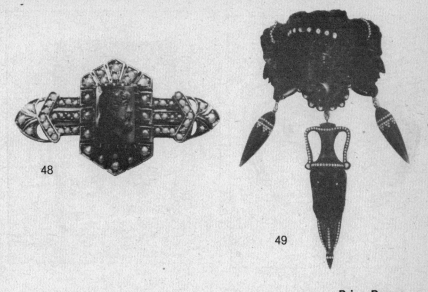

48

49

			Price Range	
☐	**48**	Tiger's eye cameo of a classical man, seed pearls, silver, c. 19th.	300.00	375.00
☐	**49**	Tortoise shell cameo of head of Baccante with two satyrs and urn, gold pique, c. 1860.	750.00	1000.00

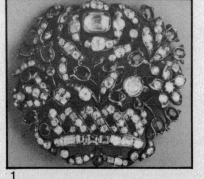

1

2

DIAMOND — PRE 1860

☐	**1**	Basket and flower motif, one old mine diamond approx. .75 ct., 112 old mine diamonds approx. 4.0 cts., four demantoid garnets, emeralds, rubies, sapphires, gold, silver, c. 1860.	10000.00	12000.00
☐	**2**	Feather motif, rose diamonds, white gold topped yellow gold, c 1830.	950.00	1100.00

3

4

5

6

			Price Range	
☐	**3**	*Flower en tremblant with drops, rose diamonds, two natural pearls, gold, silver, c. 1840...........*	2200.00	2400.00
☐	**4**	*Flower motif, eight diamonds approx. 3.50 cts. and one diamond approx. 1.30 cts. in flower, 22 diamonds approx. 2.0 cts. in leaves, silver, gold, c. 1850. ....*	4950.00	5150.00
☐	**5**	*Flower motif, rose diamonds, gold, silver, c. 1840. .*	2200.00	2650.00
☐	**6**	*Flower motif, one round emerald in center, eight pear emeralds, rose diamonds, silver topped, gold, c. 1850. ....*	5050.00	5650.00

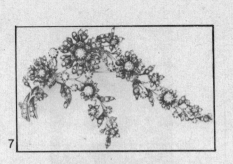

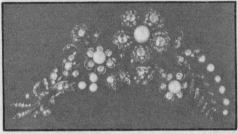

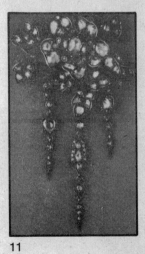

			Price Range	
☐	**7**	*Flower spray motif, rose diamonds, gold topped silver.*	**2650.00**	**2850.00**
☐	**8**	*Flower spray motif, 29 old mine diamonds approx. 4.50 cts., rose diamonds, pearls, gold, silver, c. 1840.*	**3950.00**	**4400.00**
☐	**9**	*Leaf and flower motif, rose diamonds, silver, c. 1830.*	**1200.00**	**1450.00**
☐	**10**	*Pansy motif, one old mine diamond approx. .50 ct., 78 rose diamonds, silver gilt, c. 1840.*	**1650.00**	**1850.00**
☐	**11**	*Rose with tassels motif, Holland-cut diamonds, table-cut heart-shape diamonds, fancy-cut and rose diamonds, silver, c. 1840.*	**1200.00**	**1550.00**

12

13

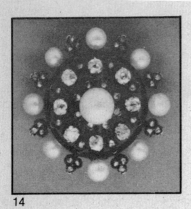

14

		Price Range	
☐	**12** *Rose diamonds, green enamel, floral motif, 2-color gold, French, c. 1845*	2250.00	2500.00
☐	**13** *Shield motif, rose diamonds, round and cabochon emeralds, emerald teardrop, silver topped gold, c. 1850.*	1650.00	2100.00
☐	**14** *Wagon wheel motif, eight old mine diamonds approx. 1.0 ct., rose diamonds, one button natural pearl, eight cultured pearls, gold, silver, c. 1860.* . .	2200.00	2650.00

DIAMOND

<table>
<tr><td></td><td></td><td></td><td>Price Range</td></tr>
<tr><td>☐</td><td>1</td><td>Anchor, crown and leaf motif, rose diamonds, gold, silver, c. 1880. ....</td><td>1300.00 1550.00</td></tr>
<tr><td>☐</td><td>2</td><td>Art Nouveau motif, 11 round diamonds approx. .90 ct., one pearl, lapel watch holder, gold, c. 1890. ....</td><td>2000.00 2400.00</td></tr>
<tr><td>☐</td><td>3</td><td>Art Nouveau tulip motif, rubies, sapphires, diamonds, pink tourmadend, pink sapphires, old mine diamonds, natural pearls, blue green and orange translucent enamel, platinum, gold, c. 1900. ....</td><td>18900.00 21000.00</td></tr>
<tr><td>☐</td><td>4</td><td>Bow motif, round diamonds, platinum topped gold .</td><td>2750.00 2950.00</td></tr>
<tr><td>☐</td><td>5</td><td>Bow with hinged tassels, 208 round diamonds approx. 5.0 cts., two gold European diamonds approx. 2.15 cts., platinum, c. 1900. ....</td><td>16800.00 18900.00</td></tr>
</table>

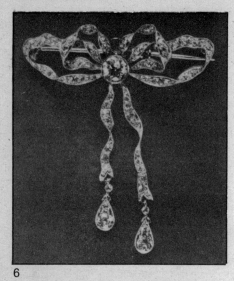

6

7

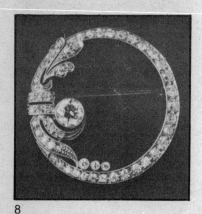

8

9

Price Range

☐	**6** *Bow with hinged tassels, round diamond in center approx. 1.0 cts., ten round diamonds, brooch or pendant, c. 1900.*	3300.00	3750.00
☐	**7** *Bow openwork motif, round diamonds, platinum, c. 1920.*	2850.00	3100.00
☐	**8** *Circle motif, one round diamond approx. .80 ct., 55 round diamonds approx. 1.25 cts., 14K white gold clasp, platinum, c. 1910.*	3100.00	3300.00
☐	**9** *Circle bow motif, round diamonds, calibre sapphires, platinum, c. 1920.*	2100.00	2300.00

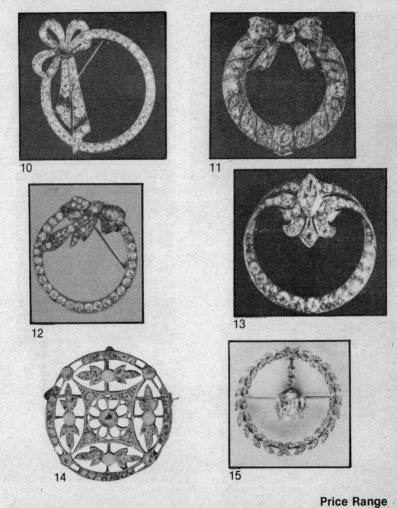

10

11

12

13

14

15

			Price Range	
☐	**10**	*Circle bow motif, 81 round diamonds approx. 3.25 cts., calibre emeralds, platinum, c. 1910.*	**2200.00**	**2650.00**
☐	**11**	*Circle bow motif, 81 round diamonds approx. 3.75 cts., platinum, signed: J.E.C. & Co., c. late 19th.....*	**2750.00**	**3100.00**
☐	**12**	*Circle bow motif, emeralds, 64 round diamonds approx. 2.50 cts., platinum, c. 1910.*	**2000.00**	**2200.00**
☐	**13**	*Circle wreath motif, old mine diamond approx. 2.30 cts., rose diamonds, 14K gold, c. 1890.*	**3850.00**	**4400.00**
☐	**14**	*Circle wreath motif, 68 rose diamonds approx. 1.70 cts., four pearls, silver topped gold.*	**550.00**	**650.00**
☐	**15**	*Circle wreath motif, one marquise-shape diamond approx. 1.25 cts., 32 old mine diamonds approx. 2.75 cts., eight rose diamonds, platinum, c. 1910.* .	**4400.00**	**4950.00**

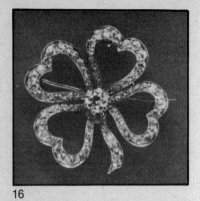

16

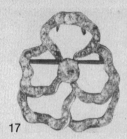

17

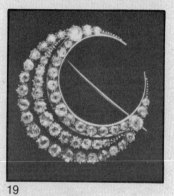

19

18

20

		Price Range	

□ **16** *Clover motif, 70 round diamonds, brooch or pendant, gold, c. 1900.* **2200.00 2850.00**

□ **17** *Clover motif, 64 rose diamonds approx. 2.0 cts., one old mine diamond approx. 1.0 ct. in center, platinum topped gold, c. 1880.* **2750.00 3200.00**

□ **18** *Cluster and bow motif, rose diamonds, gold, pendant or brooch, c. 1860.* **1650.00 1850.00**

□ **19** *Crescent motif, 51 old mine diamonds approx. 5.25 cts., silver, gold, c. 1840.* **3850.00 4200.00**

□ **20** *Crown motif, five old mine diamonds approx. 4.50 cts., 15 old mine diamonds approx. 1.20 cts., gold, c. late 19th.* **5300.00 6100.00**

21

22

23

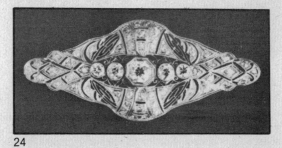

24

		Price Range	
☐	21 Crown, star and septre motif, round diamonds, gold, c. 1900..................................	800.00	950.00
☐	22 Crown motif, one emerald-cut emerald, one round emerald, old mine and rose diamonds, silver, gold, c. 1830.	2750.00	3000.00
☐	23 Crown and flower motif, rose diamonds, red stones, silver, gold, c. 1840.	1200.00	1450.00
☐	24 Cutout motif, five round diamonds approx. 1.75 cts., 50 round diamonds approx. 1.0 cts., platinum, c. 1910.	1850.00	2100.00

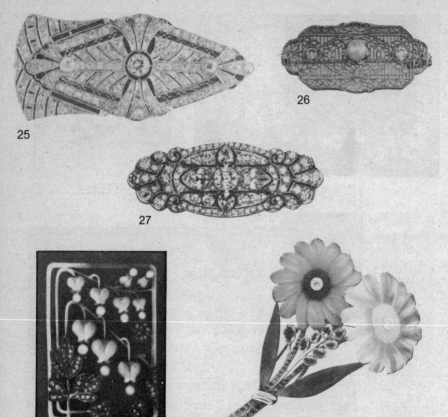

			Price Range	
☐	**25**	*Cutout modified triangular motif, 110 round diamonds approx. 4.0 cts., emeralds, brooch or pendant, platinum, c. 1900.*	3850.00	4300.00
☐	**26**	*Cutout motif, one pearl approx. 6.2MM, two round diamonds approx. .66 ct., platinum, c. 1925.*	1000.00	1300.00
☐	**27**	*Cutout motif, one square diamond, four pear-shaped diamonds, 92 round diamonds, white gold.*	14700.00	16800.00
☐	**28**	*Flower motif, translucent pink and yellow enamel flowers with seed pearls, rose diamond in silver leaves, gold, Art Nouveau, c. 1905.*	2850.00	3300.00
☐	**29**	*Flower motif, carved rock crystal and hardstone flowers, two round diamonds, carved jade leaves, demantoid garnets in stem, topaz flower buds, gold, c. 1900.*	4850.00	5400.00

30

31

32

33

Price Range

☐ **30** *Flower bouquet motif, 12 old mine diamonds approx.
2.50 cts., 141 round diamonds approx. 2.0 cts., rose
diamonds, signed: K. Mikimoto, platinum* 6300.00 6800.00

☐ **31** *Flower bow motif, rose diamonds, platinum
topped gold, c. late 19th.* 1450.00 1550.00

☐ **32** *Flower freeform motif, one round diamond approx.
1.20 cts., 25 round diamonds approx. 1.60 cts.,
platinum topped gold, c. 1920.* 2850.00 3100.00

☐ **33** *Flower and leaf motif, one old mine diamond approx. .70 ct., 73 old mine diamonds and rose dia-
monds approx. 5.75 cts., silver topped gold, c. 1850* 6300.00 6800.00

34

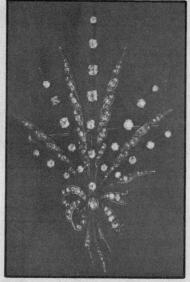

35

36

37

Price Range

☐ **34** *Flower spray motif, two round diamonds approx. 2.0 cts., four round diamonds approx. 2.5 cts., 160 round diamonds approx. 7.0 cts., 128 diamonds approx. 2.0 cts., c. late 19th. . . . .* 27300.00 31500.00

☐ **35** *Flower spray motif, 24 old mine diamonds approx. 2.50 cts., rose diamonds, gold topped silver, c. 1840* 3500.00 3950.00

☐ **36** *Flowing scroll motif, 11 round diamonds approx. 3.75 cts., gold and platinum, Art Nouveau, c. 1900* 3950.00 4400.00

☐ **37** *Freeform motif, six old mine diamonds, rose diamonds, platinum topped gold, French, c. late 19th. .* 1750.00 2000.00

38

39

41

40

42

Price Range

☐ **38** *Greek revival Etruscan motif, old mine diamond letters AEI on enamel center, fitted box, maker: Waterson and Brogden, c. mid 19th.* 1650.00 1850.00

☐ **39** *Geometric motif, 75 round diamonds approx. 3.0 cts., platinum, c. 1920* 2850.00 3300.00

☐ **40** *Geometric motif, one round diamond approx. 1.10 cts., two round diamonds approx.1.50 cts., 114 round diamonds approx. 4.50 cts., platinum, c. 1920* . 7350.00 7850.00

☐ **41** *Hapsburg double-headed eagle motif, rose diamonds, square sapphires, silver, gold, c. 1880* 1200.00 1450.00

☐ **42** *Hexagonal shape openwork, round diamonds, platinum, c. 1900* 3300.00 3750.00

43

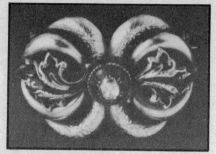

44

45

46

			Price Range	
☐	**43**	Jubilee motif, translucent green enamel, opaque enamel, one old mine diamond, gold, souvenir of Queen Victoria's Diamond Jubilee, English, c. 1897	800.00	1050.00
☐	**44**	Leaf and hollow tube motif, blue enamel on leaves, one rose diamond in silver, gold, c. 1840 ..	950.00	1050.00
☐	**45**	Leaf motif, one round diamond approx. 1.20 cts., 14 round diamonds approx. 5.0 cts., platinum, gold, c. 1910	7100.00	7500.00
☐	**46**	Oblong motif, round diamonds approx. 3.0 cts., platinum, c. 1910	6000.00	7050.00

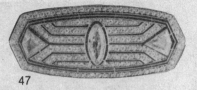

47

48

49

50

Price Range

☐ **47** *Oblong cutout geometric motif, one marquise-shape diamond approx. .75 ct., two fancy triangular diamonds and 175 round diamonds approx. 1.25 cts., platinum, signed: Dreicer & Co., c. 1930 .*   5450.00   6500.00

☐ **48** *Openwork motif, 12 calibre sapphires, one oval diamond approx. 1.35 cts., 65 round diamonds approx. 4.50 cts., platinum, c. 1900 . . . .*   5900.00   6200.00

☐ **49** *Openwork motif, one marquise-shape diamond, round diamonds, calibre diamonds, platinum, c. 1910 . . . .*   3000.00   3500.00

☐ **50** *Openwork motif, 42 round diamonds approx. 2.50 cts., one cushion-shape sapphire in center, platinum, c. 1910 . . . .*   2400.00   2850.00

51

52

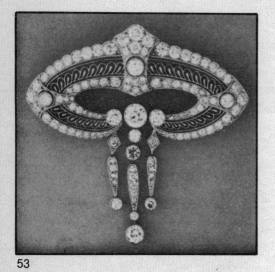

53

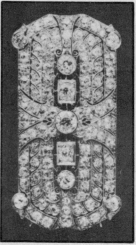

54

			Price Range	
☐	**51**	Openwork modified rectangular motif, 101 old mine diamonds approx. 10.0 cts., platinum, c. 1910	10500.00	12600.00
☐	**52**	Openwork and tassel motif, 110 round diamonds approx. 5.50 cts., one round diamond approx. .50 ct., platinum, c. 1910	7350.00	8400.00
☐	**53**	Oval leaf openwork motif, 79 old mine diamonds approx. 4.75 cts., c. late 19th.	6000.00	7100.00
☐	**54**	Rectangular cutout motif, five old mine diamonds approx. 1.25 cts., 44 old mine diamonds approx. 1.50 cts., marquise and calibre sapphires, brooch or pendant, white gold, c. 1920	1750.00	1850.00

55

58

56

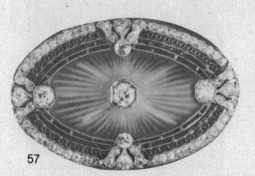

57

59

		Price Range	
☐	**55** Rectangular geometric motif, three round diamonds, rose diamonds, gold topped platinum, c. 1900	2200.00	2650.00
☐	**56** Ribbon motif, one old European diamond approx. .60 ct., round diamonds approx. 1.50 cts., French-cut sapphires, platinum, c. 1900	2850.00	3300.00
☐	**57** Rock crystal center, carved and frosted, surrounded by calibre sapphires, 76 round diamonds approx. 3.50 cts., brooch or pendant, c. 1920	4600.00	4850.00
☐	**58** Round openwork motif, natural fancy color round diamond in center approx. 2.50 cts., four old mine diamonds, gold, signed: Tiffany & Co., c. 1900	6850.00	7250.00
☐	**59** Scroll motif, 11 round diamonds approx. .90 ct., gold, c. 1905	1750.00	2000.00

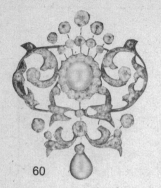

60

61

62

63

			Price Range	
☐	**60**	*Scroll motif, diamonds, natural pearls, platinum, gold, c. 1880*	3500.00	4050.00
☐	**61**	*Scroll freeform motif, 14 old mine diamonds, round and rose diamonds, 18K gold, Art Nouveau, c. 1890-1900*	2850.00	3300.00
☐	**62**	*Shield motif, two round diamonds approx. 2.10 cts., 41 round diamonds approx. 4.0 cts., platinum, c. 1910*	7350.00	8400.00
☐	**63**	*Shield motif, 61 old mine diamonds, .01 ct. to .25 ct. approx. 6.0 cts., gold topped silver, c. 1840*	5050.00	5650.00

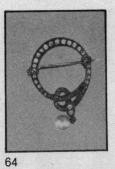

64

65

66

67

68

69

70

Price Range

☐ **68** *Square motif, champlevé black and white opaque enamel, one old mine diamond, marked: C & AG, c. late 19th.* 750.00 1000.00

☐ **69** *Star motif, one old mine diamond approx. 2.50 cts., 162 old mine diamonds approx. 15.50 cts., silver, gold, c. 1750* 21000.00 25200.00

☐ **70** *Thistle motif, round demantoid garnets in body of thistle, rose diamonds, platinum, gold, Scottish, c. 1890* 1650.00 1750.00

1

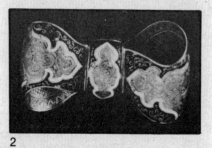

2

ENAMEL – GOLD

☐ **1** *Belt and circle motif, champlevé opaque white and black enamel, rose diamonds and rubies in buckle, gold, c. 1880* 800.00 950.00

☐ **2** *Bow motif, champlevé opaque white, blue and turquoise enamel, gold, c. 1820* 600.00 800.00

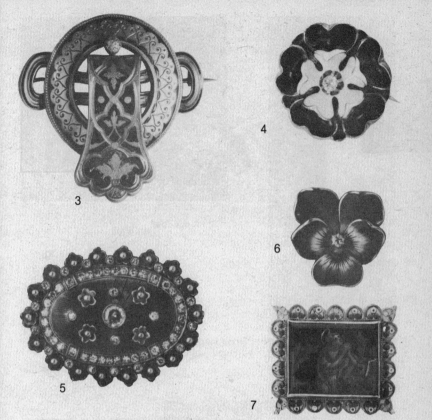

			Price Range	
☐	**3**	*Enamel motif, blue and black, gold, c. 1860*	**550.00**	**650.00**
☐	**4**	*Flower motif, red and green guilloche enamel, opaque white enamel, round diamond, gold*	**600.00**	**700.00**
☐	**5**	*Oval brooch, 54 round diamonds approx. 2.25 cts., guilloché translucent blue enamel, green enamel flowers, c. mid 19th.*	**2200.00**	**2650.00**
☐	**6**	*Pansy motif, purple, black and white opaque enamel, one round diamond, gold, c. 1890*	**650.00**	**900.00**
☐	**7**	*Religious motif, polychrome enamel of Agnus Dei on front and Mary Magdalene on reverse, glass covers, gold, c. 17th.*	**650.00**	**900.00**

1

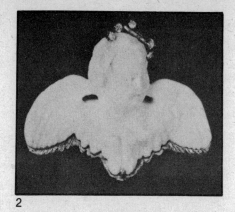

2

3

4

FACE and FIGURE	Price Range	
☐ 1 *Ancient coins with faces, gold frame, c. 1860*	2400.00	2650.00
☐ 2 *Angel, carved coral, five round diamonds, contemporary gold mount, c. 1860*	1550.00	1750.00
☐ 3 *Angel, enamelled on plaque, rose diamond wings, gold, c. 1870*	1100.00	1550.00
☐ 4 *Angel, carved, gold, maker: Wiese, c. late 19th.*	1100.00	1450.00

		Price Range	
☐	**5** Art Nouveau, lady and lily pad motif, blue plique à jour enamel, pearl, detachable pin, gold, French, c. 1890.	900.00	1100.00
☐	**6** Blackamoor, round rubies, one round blue stone, gold, c. 19th.	800.00	950.00
☐	**7** Egyptian motif, rose diamonds, emerald-cut emeralds, round rubies, gold, silver, c. 1925.	5250.00	5750.00
☐	**8** Egyptian motif of God Maáet, emerald-cut emeralds in legs, carnelian torso, mother-of-pearl base, diamonds, Art Deco, c. 1925.	5050.00	5250.00
☐	**9** Egyptian motif of goddess, translucent pink, blue, yellow and red enamel, 44 rose diamonds in border, gold, c. 1925.	1750.00	2000.00

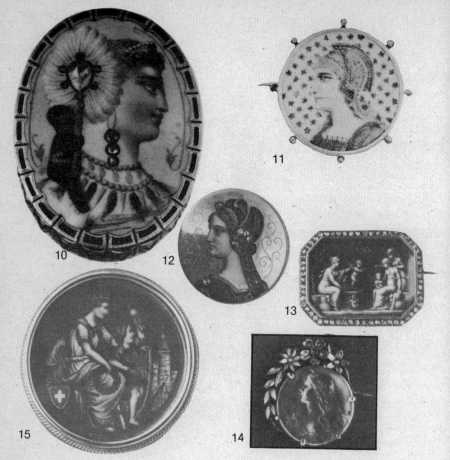

		Price Range	
☐	**10** Enamel portrait of a lady with a Blackamoor, pink, blue, yellow, green, white and black opaque and translucent enamel, four rose diamonds, gold, brooch or pendant, c. 19th.	1750.00	2000.00
☐	**11** Enamel portrait of a lady, eight diamond chips, rose gold	600.00	700.00
☐	**12** Enamel portrait of a lady, polychrome enamel, rose diamonds, c. 1900	1000.00	1300.00
☐	**13** Grisaille enamel scene of three classical ladies with three angels, red background, rose diamond border, gold, French, c. 1810	2200.00	2400.00
☐	**14** Medallion portrait of a lady, rose diamonds in flowers, gold, French, c. late 19th.	1000.00	1200.00
☐	**15** Medieval motif, enamel, gold frame, c. 1840-60 . . .	900.00	1100.00

			Price Range	
☐	**16**	*Micro mosaic of donkey at fountain with peasants, Etruscan granulation, 18K gold, c. 1840*	**3850.00**	**4400.00**
☐	**17**	*Micro mosaic of pastoral motif with lamb and peasants, Etruscan granulation, 18K gold, c. 1840*	**3850.00**	**4400.00**
☐	**18**	*Micro mosaic of peasants and sage, Etruscan granulation, 18K gold, c. 1840*	**3850.00**	**4400.00**
☐	**19**	*Mosaic portrait of the Madonna, Etruscan motif frame, gold, c. 1860*	**3200.00**	**3750.00**
☐	**20**	*Mosaic portrait of St. Joseph, gold, c. mid 19th*....	**1750.00**	**2000.00**

				Price Range	
☐	21	Porcelain miniature portrait of a lady, base metal frame, c. 1920		55.00	75.00
☐	22	Sculptured lady and heart motif, blue and green enamel wings, gold, 1¾ in. high, inscribed: Lalique, Art Nouveau, French, c. 1890		8400.00	10500.00
☐	23	Sculptured lady with bat wings, translucent blue enamel, gold, maker: Lalique, French, c. 1900		6300.00	7350.00
☐	24	Translucent enamel portrait of a lady, diamonds in headband, two pearls, gold, Art Nouveau, c. 1890-1910		1750.00	2000.00
☐	25	Vogue magazine promotional, brass, c. 1926		80.00	105.00

GEMSTONE

		Price Range	
☐	1 Arrow motif, seed pearls, gold, c. 1880	150.00	175.00
☐	2 Amethysts, 18K gold, c. 1865	850.00	1000.00
☐	3 Art Deco motif, carved jade, rose diamonds, gold, c. 1930	450.00	550.00
☐	4 Art Deco motif, carved jade, one diamond approx. .90 ct., black onyx, platinum, c. 1930	1750.00	2000.00
☐	5 Art Deco clip, two cabochon sapphires, old mine diamonds, white gold, platinum, c. 1930	2650.00	2850.00
☐	6 Amethysts, foil-backed, 18K gold, c. 1840	600.00	800.00

7

8

9

10

11

12

			Price Range	
☐	**7**	Art Nouveau motif, rose diamonds, one round pearl, emerald bead, platinum, gold, c. 1890-1900 .	3100.00	3300.00
☐	**8**	Art Nouveau motif, one round ruby, rose diamonds, six pearls, platinum, gold, c. 1890	2000.00	2200.00
☐	**9**	Art Nouveau flower motif, one oval peridot, 14K gold, pendant for lapel watch on reverse, American, c. 1890-1900	700.00	750.00
☐	**10**	Art Nouveau flower motif, translucent green enamel, rose quartz bead, gold, c. 1890	650.00	700.00
☐	**11**	Bar and pendant motif, onyx, round diamonds, one round diamond approx. 1.0 ct., platinum, c. 1925 .	5450.00	5650.00
☐	**12**	Blue synthetic spinel, cultured pearls, 18K gold, pair of clips	450.00	750.00

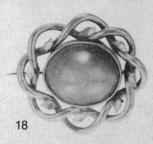

13

14

15

16

17

18

19

20

		Price Range	
☐	**13** Bow motif, table-cut emeralds, gold, Spanish, c. 1750	500.00	600.00
☐	**14** Bow motif, seed pearls alternating with pink coral beads, gold, c. 1840	450.00	550.00
☐	**15** Bow motif, peridots, rubies, gold, English, c. 1840	650.00	850.00
☐	**16** Bow and tassel motif, engraved, fancy link chains, turquoise, gold, c. 1830	1750.00	2000.00
☐	**17** Cartouche motif, five faceted citrines, gold, c. 1840	550.00	650.00
☐	**18** Cat's eye cabochon, hair locket on reverse, gold .	400.00	500.00
☐	**19** Citrines, chased, 19K gold, English, c. 1860	400.00	450.00
☐	**20** Circle motif, eight round demantoid garnets, eight round diamonds, gold, c. 1910	2850.00	3100.00

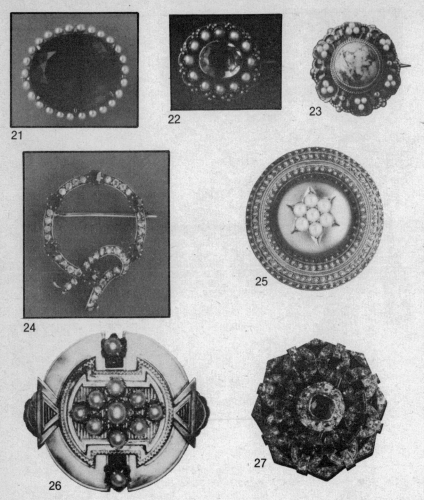

			Price Range	
☐	**21**	Circle motif, amethyst, seed pearls, gold, c. 1910 .	1000.00	1300.00
☐	**22**	Circle motif, amethyst, seed pearls, gold, c. 1860 .	550.00	600.00
☐	**23**	Circle motif, cabochon turquoise, seed pearls, gold, c. 1900	325.00	450.00
☐	**24**	Circle motif, six round sapphires, 37 rose diamonds, silver topped gold, c. mid to late 19th.	1550.00	1750.00
☐	**25**	Circular motif, Etruscan granulation, seven pearls, gold, c. mid 19th.	750.00	850.00
☐	**26**	Circular motif, 11 pearls, black enamel, gold, c.1860	400.00	475.00
☐	**27**	Circular motif, round diamonds, cushion-cut sapphires, brooch or pendant, 14K gold	2200.00	2650.00

		Price Range	
☐	**28** *Clover motif, one round garnet, 14K gold, American, c. 1895*	155.00	200.00
☐	**29** *Crescent motif, one round diamond, 14K gold, American, c. 1895*	175.00	200.00
☐	**30** *Crescent motif, nine round rubies, old mine diamonds, gold, c. 19th.*	3500.00	3950.00
☐	**31** *Crescent motif, one baroque emerald, rose and old mine diamonds, gold, c. 1840*	2850.00	3100.00
☐	**32** *Crescent motif, 23 round diamonds, ten cushion cut rubies, gold, c. 1880*	2000.00	2200.00

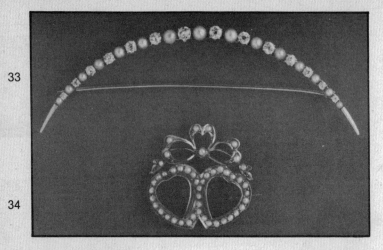

		Price Range	
☐	**33** *Crescent motif, 14 round diamonds approx. 1.20 cts., pearls, gold, c. 19th.*	1550.00	1750.00
☐	**34** *Heart and bow motif, two heart-shape citrines, half pearls, 9K gold, English, c. 1822*	2000.00	2200.00
☐	**35** *Crescent and flower motif, six garnets, ten pearls, gold, c. 1830*	800.00	950.00
☐	**36** *Crescent and star motif, six old mine diamonds, 11 oval rubies, gold, c. 19th.*	800.00	950.00
☐	**37** *Cross: carved wood, engraved circle frame, gold, c. early 20th.*	150.00	175.00

38

40

39

41

42

		Price Range	
☐	**38** Cross motif, hardstone scarab, letters spell "ROMA," gold, c. 1840-60	800.00	900.00
☐	**39** Cross motif, table cut rubies and diamonds, silver, gold, c. early 18th.	4400.00	4600.00
☐	**40** Crown motif, pearls, gold, brooch or pendant, c. mid 19th.	450.00	500.00
☐	**41** Crown motif, seven natural pearls, round diamonds, gold, c. 1880	1000.00	1300.00
☐	**42** Crown motif, six baroque pearls, six diamonds, gold, c. 20th.	1550.00	1750.00

43

44

45

46

47

48

			Price Range	
☐	**43**	Emerald: emerald-cut approx. 3.75 cts., two old mine diamonds approx. 3.75 cts., ten old mine diamonds approx. 1.75 cts., gold topped platinum, c. 1900	21000.00	25200.00
☐	**44**	Emeralds: 11 foil-backed emerald-cut, gold, c. late 18th.	2400.00	2850.00
☐	**45**	Emeralds: cabochon, diamonds, 14K gold, c. 1890	650.00	900.00
☐	**46**	Fire opal, old mine diamonds, gold, Art Nouveau, c. 1890	1650.00	1750.00
☐	**47**	Flower motif, freshwater pearls, 14K gold, Art Nouveau, American	325.00	375.00
☐	**48**	Flower motif, green enamel, one diamond, seed pearls, 10K gold, American, c. early 20th.	225.00	325.00

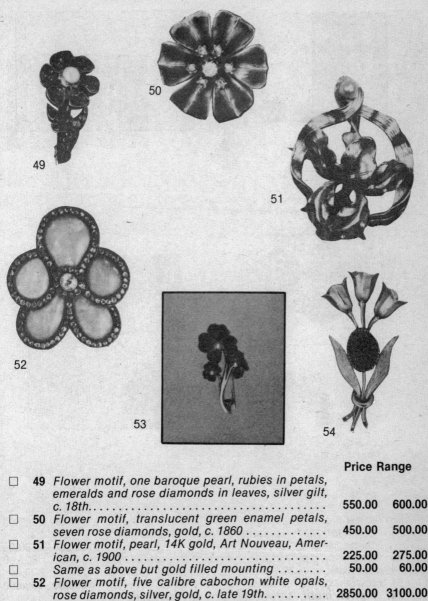

			Price Range	
☐	**49**	*Flower motif, one baroque pearl, rubies in petals, emeralds and rose diamonds in leaves, silver gilt, c. 18th*	550.00	600.00
☐	**50**	*Flower motif, translucent green enamel petals, seven rose diamonds, gold, c. 1860*	450.00	500.00
☐	**51**	*Flower motif, pearl, 14K gold, Art Nouveau, American, c. 1900*	225.00	275.00
☐		*Same as above but gold filled mounting*	50.00	60.00
☐	**52**	*Flower motif, five calibre cabochon white opals, rose diamonds, silver, gold, c. late 19th.*	2850.00	3100.00
☐	**53**	*Flower motif, green enamel, seed pearls, 14K gold, c. 1915*	175.00	225.00
☐	**54**	*Flower motif, one oval sapphire, gold, c. 1890*	1750.00	2000.00

55

56

57

58

60

59

				Price Range	
☐	55	Flower motif, 67 round diamonds approx. 1.25 cts., three pearls, gold, platinum, signed: Tiffany & Co., France, c. 1880		2750.00	2950.00
☐	56	Cross motif, pink topaz, emerald, cannetille 22K gold work, c. 1820		650.00	800.00
☐	57	Flower motif, three faceted citrines, gold, c. 1840 .		450.00	550.00
☐	58	Flower motif, oval tourmaline, rose cut diamonds, silver and gold		400.00	500.00
☐	59	Flower motif, carved black onyx, one seed pearl, gold, c. 1860-80		225.00	250.00
☐	60	Flower basket motif, diamonds, emeralds, sapphires, rubies, gold, c. 1940		550.00	750.00

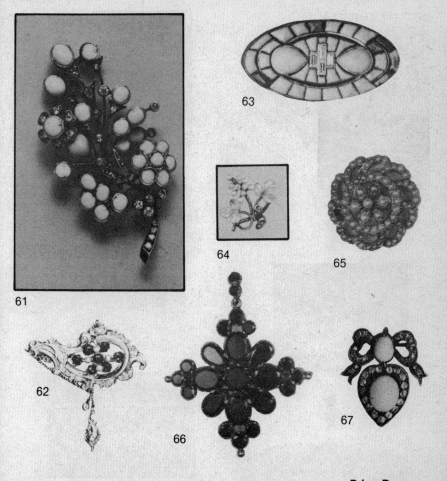

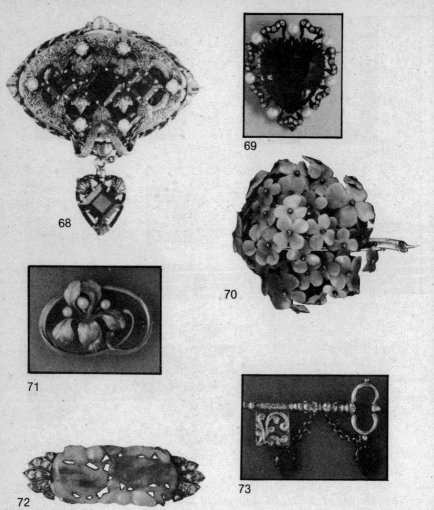

			Price Range	
☐	**68**	*Heart dangle motif, four almandine garnets, six pearls, gold, c. 1860*	500.00	550.00
☐	**69**	*Heart and ribbon motif, amethyst heart, rose diamonds, pearls, gold, silver, c. 1840*	1550.00	1750.00
☐	**70**	*Hyacinth motif, coral, rose diamonds, gold*	650.00	900.00
☐	**71**	*Iris flower motif, translucent enamel, three seed pearls, 14K gold, Art Nouveau, c. 1900.*	700.00	800.00
☐	**72**	*Jade plaque, pierced and carved, rose diamonds, gold, c. 1925*	700.00	800.00
☐	**73**	*Key motif, carved and engraved, two foil-back pear-shape garnets, gold, c. 1820*	750.00	900.00

74

76

75

77

78

			Price Range	
☐	**74**	Lily motif, pink and green translucent enamel, four diamonds, 14K gold, c. 1900	750.00	800.00
☐	**75**	Loveknot motif, four cushion-cut garnets, one cushion-cut diamond, gold, c. 1830	475.00	550.00
☐	**76**	Melon motif, four carved chalcedony beads, gold stems, rose diamonds set in silver, c. 1840	1650.00	1850.00
☐	**77**	Micro mosaic, gold, Italian, c. 1860	375.00	500.00
☐	**78**	Mosaic conch shell motif, flower motif frame, gold, c. 1870	2850.00	3100.00

79

80

82

81

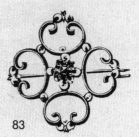

83

			Price Range	
☐	**79**	*Mosaic flower motif, Etruscan granulation frame, gold, c. 1860*	800.00	950.00
☐	**80**	*Mosaic religious motif in white, blue and red, gold, c. 1865*	500.00	550.00
☐	**81**	*Mosaic of St. Peter's Basilica of Rome, malachite background, gold, c. 1870*	1550.00	1750.00
☐	**82**	*Openwork motif, one round white sapphire, 14K gold, American, c. 1895*	175.00	200.00
☐	**83**	*Openwork motif, one emerald-cut garnet, 14K gold, American, c. 1895*	175.00	200.00

		Price Range	
☐	**84** Openwork floral motif, simulated ruby, rose diamonds, platinum, c. 1900	3500.00	3950.00
☐	**85** Oval motif, one oval citrine, half pearls, round rubies, gold, c. 1820	1800.00	1900.00
☐	**86** Oval motif, half pearls, rose diamonds, pavé set, gold, platinum, c. 1850	2850.00	3100.00
☐	**87** Oval motif, engraved, one seed pearl, four dematoid garnets, gold, c. late 19th.	325.00	400.00
☐	**88** Oval and dangle motif, one cabochon and three teardrop-shape banded agates, gold, c. 1850	900.00	1100.00

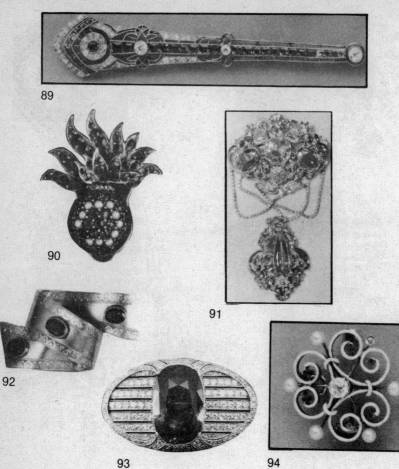

89

90

91

92

93   94

			Price Range	
☐	**89**	Peacock feather motif, square cut sapphires, round diamonds, platinum, gold, c. 1920	2650.00	2850.00
☐	**90**	Pineapple motif clip, rubies, seed pearls, rose diamonds, gold, silver, c. late 19th.	1000.00	1100.00
☐	**91**	Pink topaz, pendant or brooch, gold, c. 1840	2000.00	2200.00
☐	**92**	Ribbon motif, almandine garnets, 15K gold, c. 1890	300.00	350.00
☐	**93**	Sapphire: oval approx. 40 cts., 144 pavé diamonds, approx. 3.50 cts., platinum	16800.00	18900.00
☐	**94**	Scroll motif, one round diamond, pearls, white enamel, gold, c. early 20th.	800.00	950.00

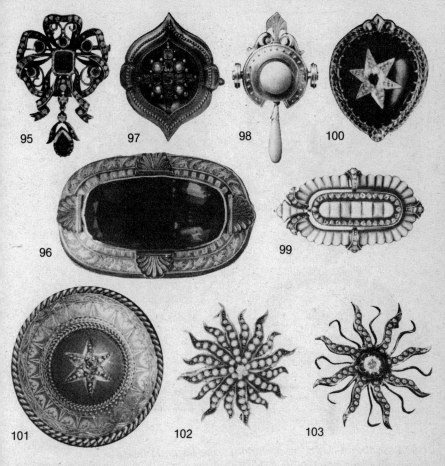

			Price Range	
☐	**95**	Scroll motif, rose cut diamonds, emeralds, silver topped gold, 18K	1100.00	1300.00
☐	**96**	Shell motif, oval faceted citrine, engraved, gold, c. mid 19th.	1550.00	1750.00
☐	**97**	Shield motif, gemstones, 18K gold, c. 1840	750.00	1000.00
☐	**98**	Shield motif, coral, 18K gold, c. 1850	475.00	550.00
☐	**99**	Shield motif, turquoise, rose diamonds, gold, Victorian	750.00	900.00
☐	**100**	Star motif, one old mine diamond, one pear-shape cabochon garnet, 14K gold, c. 1860	1300.00	1550.00
☐	**101**	Star motif, diamonds set in a turquoise enamel circle, engraved, gold, c. 1870	750.00	1000.00
☐	**102**	Sunburst motif, one diamond, seed pearls, gold	325.00	450.00
☐	**103**	Sunburst motif, one round diamond, seed pearls, gold, American	500.00	600.00

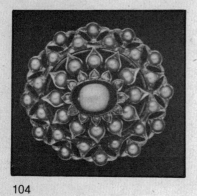

104

105

106

107

		Price Range	
☐ **104**	Sunburst motif, 12 diamonds, one baroque pearl, 36 seed pearls, gold, c. 1870	1000.00	1300.00
☐ **105**	Sunburst motif, opal, 14K gold, c. late 19th.	200.00	225.00
☐ **106**	White opal approx. 11 cts. surrounded by 19 rubies, gold, c. late 19th.	1300.00	1550.00
☐ **107**	Wing motif, rose diamonds, green onyx, white gold, c. 1910	1200.00	1300.00

108   109   110

			Price Range	
☐	**108**	Wreath motif, one opal, 14K gold, American, c. 1895	150.00	175.00
☐	**109**	Wreath motif, green enamel, four seed pearls, 14K gold, American, c. 1895	250.00	285.00
☐	**110**	Wreath motif, six diamonds, oval faceted amethyst, gold, c. mid 19th.	1300.00	1450.00

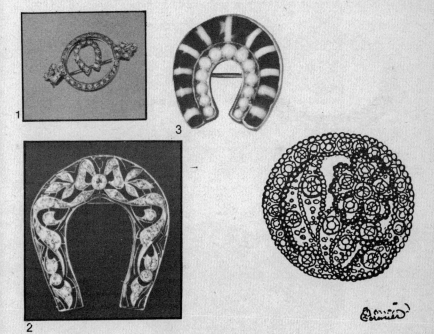

HORSESHOE

☐	**1**	Horseshoe circle motif, 43 round diamonds approx. .50 ct., platinum, c. 1925	750.00	800.00
☐	**2**	Horseshoe motif, openwork, 41 round diamonds approx. 1.75 cts., platinum, c. 1920	1550.00	1750.00
☐	**3**	Horseshoe motif, banded onyx, half pearls, gold, c. 1840	500.00	550.00

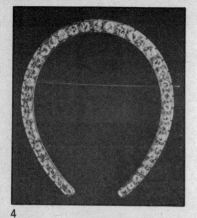

4

5

6

		Price Range	
☐	**4** *Horseshoe motif, 41 round diamonds, platinum topped gold, c. 1910*	2400.00	2850.00
☐	**5** *Horseshoe motif, 23 old European-cut diamonds approx. 1.25 cts., platinum topped gold, c. 1900*	1550.00	1750.00
☐	**6** *Riding crop, horseshoe and clover motif, rose diamonds, turquoise, pearls, gold, c. 1880*	900.00	1100.00

1

HAIR BROOCHES

All items made from hair referred to throughout this section are of brunette human hair unless stated otherwise.

☐	**1** *Acorn and loveknot motif of woven hair, gold, c. 1840-80*	160.00	200.00

2

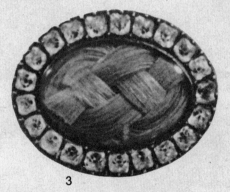

3

			Price Range	
☐	**2**	*Basket weave hair under glass, hollow machine stamped frame, reverse: picture of lady, gold, c. 1860-80*	**175.00**	**200.00**
☐	**3**	*Basket weave hair under glass bordered by pastes, inscribed on reverse: "G. Tomkins She blooms in Life Eternal Ob 23 Oct 1794," bracelet clasp converted to brooch, gold, English, c. 1794* .	**375.00**	**450.00**

		Price Range	
☐	**4** Basket weave hair with cutout urn and name plaque motif under glass, inscribed on reverse: "Thos. Cooking OB 5 July 1787 at 51," gold, English, c. 1787	700.00	750.00
☐	**5** Black enamel flower motif on hollow tube frame for woven hair under oval glass, gold, c. 1880	275.00	300.00
☐	**6** Black enamel border around braided white and brunette hair under glass, chased bezel, outer woven hair border with gold spacers, initial shield, gold, English, c. 1860-80	225.00	275.00
☐	**7** Black enamel motif, "In Memory Of," seed pearls, gold, English, c. mid 19th.	600.00	650.00

8

10

9

11

			Price Range	
☐	**8**	*Bow and chain motif of white woven hair with tassels and heart locket, gold, English, c. 1820-40 . . .*	375.00	450.00
☐	**9**	*Bow and two dangle motif of white woven hair, engraved plaque, safety chain with straight pin, gold, c. 1840-80 . . . .*	155.00	175.00
☐	**10**	*Bow motif of woven hair, engraved plaque, gold, c. 1840-80 . . . .*	90.00	125.00
☐	**11**	*Cage motif, open weave hair, gold, c. 1870-90 . . . .*	130.00	150.00

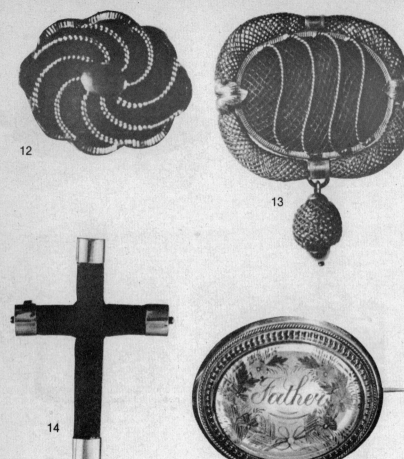

		Price Range	
☐	**12** Cage motif with woven hair, scalloped edges, gold, c. 1870-90	130.00	150.00
☐	**13** Cage motif with woven hair and woven hair tube border and dangle, gold, English, c. 1840-80	135.00	165.00
☐	**14** Cross motif of tightly woven hair over solid core, gold fittings, c. 1860-80	150.00	175.00
☐	**15** "Father" and flower wreath motif of cut and paste hair on an opalescent porcelain plaque, Etruscan granulation frame, gold, c. 1860	375.00	450.00

16

18

17

19

			Price Range	
☐	**16**	Initials of hair on plaque in center with ribbons of hair and seed pearls on pale blue background under glass, gold, c. 1790	475.00	525.00
☐	**17**	Loveknot, acorn and dangle motif of woven hair, black enamel leaves and decorations, gold, c. 1840-80	200.00	250.00
☐	**18**	Loveknot motif of woven hair, gold tips, c. 1840-80 .	95.00	125.00
☐	**19**	Miniature of sheaf-of-wheat of dissolved and cut and paste hair on ivory plaque, Etruscan granulation frame, gold, English, c. 1850	350.00	450.00

21

20

22

			Price Range	
☐	**20**	*Miniature of tree and building beside river painted with dissolved hair on ivory plaque, bordered by pastes, inscribed on reverse: "Mary Chetham Obt 10 October 1818 At 67.H," silver, gold, c. 1818*	450.00	550.00
☐	**21**	*Prince of Wales feathers of hair with gold wires on porcelain plaque, gold frame, c. 1860*	325.00	350.00
☐	**22**	*Prince of Wales feathers of hair with white and blue enamel plaque bordered by seed pearls inscribed: "Not Lost But Gone Before" on porcelain plaque, gold, English, c. 1860-80*	450.00	500.00

23

25

26

24

27

			Price Range	
☐	**23**	Prince of Wales feathers of hair with seed pearl, gold wire and sepia paint on porcelain plaque under glass, gold filled, English, c. 1860-80	65.00	95.00
☐	**24**	Prince of Wales feather of hair with seed pearls and gold wire under glass, fancy cutout frame, gold, English, c. 1860-80	175.00	200.00
☐	**25**	Prince of Wales feather with cut and paste flowers of hair, gold, c. 1860	275.00	325.00
☐	**26**	Prince of Wales feathers of grey hair with gold wire on porcelain plaque under glass, braided grey hair border, engraved shields, gold, c. 1860-80	250.00	275.00
☐	**27**	Seed pearl border, lock of hair and gold inital under glass, gold, c. 1790	300.00	325.00

28

29

30

		Price Range	
☐ **28**	*Seed pearls strung on white horse hair on mother-of-pearl templets, lock of hair under glass in center, gold, c. 1860*	450.00	500.00
☐ **29**	*Swivel motif, black enamel frame "In Memory Of," reverse: picture of deceased, obverse: tree of hair with inscription: "Francis S. Crichton Born 18th May 1840 Died 7 March 1861," gold, English, c. 1861*	1000.00	1050.00
☐ **30**	*Swivel motif, engraved twisted frame, picture of a gentleman on one side, Prince of Wales feathers of hair with seed pearls and gold wire on other side, gold, c. 1890*	350.00	400.00

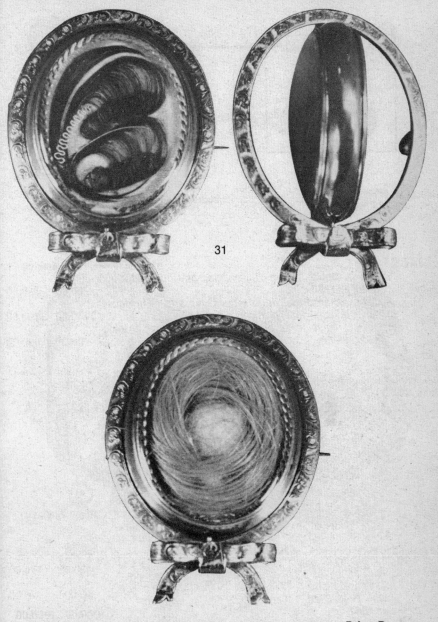

31

☐ **31** *Swivel motif, engraved ribbon frame, lock of hair on one side, Prince of Wales feathers of hair with gold wire on other side, gold, c. 1880* . . . .

Price Range

500.00   550.00

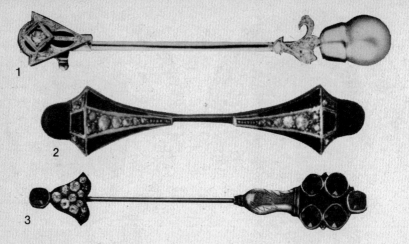

JABOT

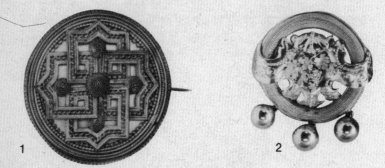

MISCELLANEOUS – GOLD

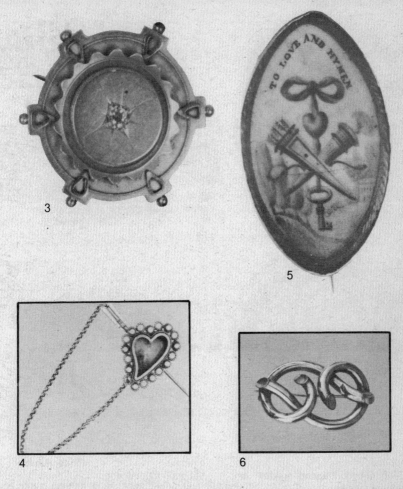

			Price Range	
☐	**3**	Circle motif, diamond, gold, c. 1880	350.00	450.00
☐	**4**	Heart motif, glass front, pin slides through loops on reverse, gold, c. 1790	450.00	525.00
☐	**5**	Ivory miniature depicting chastity of a heart, key, torch, bow and quiver, inscribed: "To Love and Hymen," gold, c. 1790	750.00	1000.00
☐	**6**	Loveknot motif, hollow tubes, gold, c. 1850	150.00	200.00

			Price Range	
☐	**7**	Micro mosaic motif of St. Marks' in Venice, Etruscan granulation, 18K gold, Italian, c. 1865 . . .	550.00	650.00
☐	**8**	Painted porcelain of a young boy, filigree frame, gold, Victorian	600.00	800.00
☐	**9**	Quill motif, oval and cushion-cut pink sapphires, gold, c. 19th.	375.00	450.00
☐	**10**	Pietra Dura floral motif, 15K gold, English, c. 1855	450.00	600.00
☐	**11**	Etruscan granulation, 18K gold, c. 1840s	250.00	350.00

1

2

3

NAME - BROOCHES

		Price Range	
☐	**1** *Flower wreath motif, enamel, gilt metal, New Zealand, c. 20th.*	90.00	100.00
☐	**2** *Oval ivory cutout name brooch, English, c. late 19th.*	90.00	100.00
☐	**3** *"Queen Lizzie" commemorative wire brooch, mother-of-pearl, anchor denotes security, heart denotes love and cross denotes blessings, gold filled, c. early 20th.*	60.00	70.00

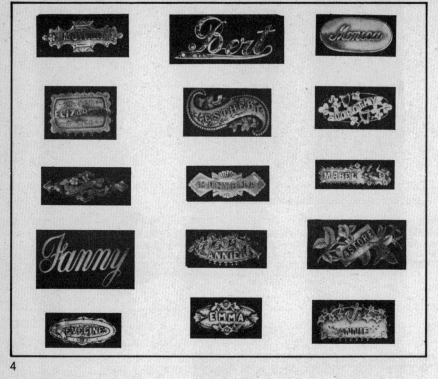

4

5

		Price Range	
☐	**4** *Rectangular and cutout name brooches, silver, English, c. late 19th.*	**60.00**	**70.00**
☐	**5** *Rectangular cutout name brooches, silver, English, c. late 19th.*	**60.00**	**70.00**

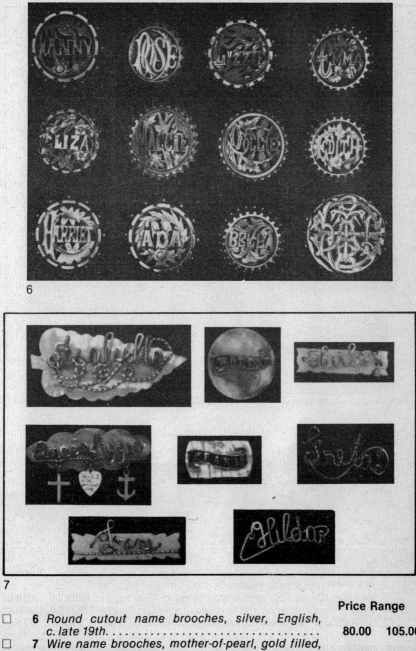

		Price Range	
☐	**6** *Round cutout name brooches, silver, English, c. late 19th.*	80.00	105.00
☐	**7** *Wire name brooches, mother-of-pearl, gold filled, English, c. early 20th.*	40.00	45.00

1

2

3

SCOTTISH AGATE

Price Range

☐ **1** *Anchor motif, engraved, agate, silver, maker: Hilliard and Thomason, Birmingham, England, c. 1848* 250.00 275.00

☐ **2** *Anchor motif, colored agate, silver, English, c. 1850* . 325.00 375.00

☐ **3** *Arrow motif, engraved, agate, silver, English, c. 1850* 250.00 275.00

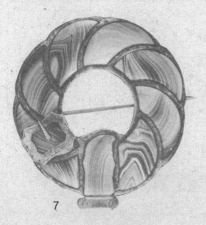

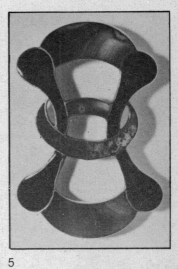

			Price Range	
☐	**4**	*Boat motif, malachite, silver, English, c. 19th.*	325.00	375.00
☐	**5**	*Bow motif, colored agate, silver, c. 1850*	250.00	275.00
☐	**6**	*Bow motif, grey agate, silver, English, c. 19th.*	200.00	225.00
☐	**7**	*Buckle motif, grey agate, silver, English,*		
		c. mid 19th.	200.00	225.00
☐	**8**	*Cross and circle motif, engraved, colored agate,*		
		15K gold, 1 in. diameter, English, c. 1870	450.00	475.00

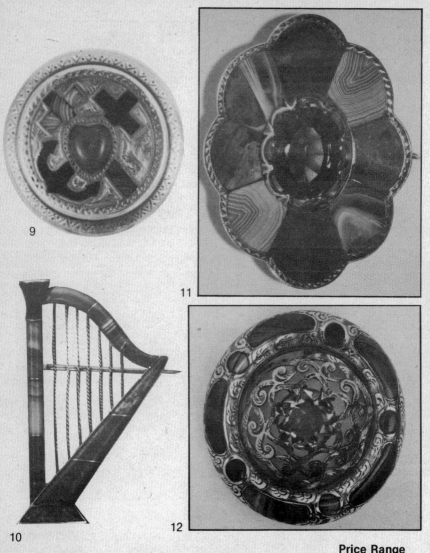

		Price Range	
☐	**9** *Faith, hope and charity motif, pale grey agate cross, bloodstone anchor, carnelian heart, silver, English, c. mid 19th.*	250.00	300.00
☐	**10** *Harp motif, multicolor chalcedony, silver, English, c. mid 19th.*	250.00	275.00
☐	**11** *Round cutout motif, engraved, colored agate, round citrine center, silver, Scottish, c. 1860*	300.00	350.00
☐	**12** *Scalloped oval motif, engraved, colored agate, oval citrene center, gold, c. 1850*	750.00	800.00

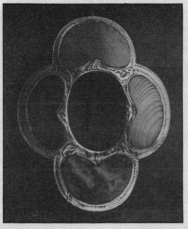

13

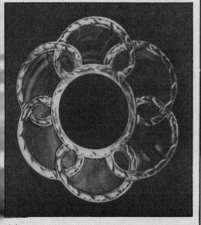

14

15

		Price Range	
☐	**13** *Scalloped oval motif, colored agate, silver, English, c. 1870*	**175.00**	**190.00**
☐	**14** *Scalloped round motif, engraved, malachite, silver, English, c. 1870*	**150.00**	**175.00**
☐	**15** *St. Andrew cross and circle motif, engraved, colored agate, two foilback amethyst, two foilback citrine, English, c. 1850*	**325.00**	**350.00**

1

2

3 /||\

4

5

6

SILVER

			Price Range	
☐	1	*Angel motif, sterling, American, c. 1896*	**175.00**	**200.00**
☐	2	*Berry motif, three simulated pearls, sterling, American, c. 1894-95*	**80.00**	**100.00**
☐	3	*Berry and flower motif, genuine sea shell, three pearls, one rhinestone, sterling, American, c. 1894-95*	**125.00**	**150.00**
☐	4	*Bow motif, one emerald-cut and one round emerald, rose and old mine diamonds, silver, c. late 19th.*	**1750.00**	**2000.00**
☐	5	*Butterfly motif, chased, sterling, American, c. 1896* .	**80.00**	**90.00**
☐	6	*Flower and leaf motif, one seed pearl, sterling, American, c. 1896*	**90.00**	**100.00**

		Price Range	
☐	**7** Flower basket motif, moonstones, silver, 2¼ in. diameter, maker: Georg Jensen, c. 20th.	450.00	525.00
☐	**8** Flower motif, enameled, sterling silver, American, c. 1935	85.00	105.00
☐	**9** Flower motif, marcasites, sterling silver, c. 1920 . .	55.00	75.00
☐	**10** Flower motif, marcasites, sterling silver, clip reverse, c. 1920	45.00	55.00
☐	**11** Flower motif, molded jade-like plastic, marcasites, sterling silver, clip reverse, c. 1925	45.00	55.00
☐	**12** Flower motif, genuine sea shell, two pearls, sterling, American, c. 1894-95	130.00	155.00
☐	**13** Flower motif, sterling, signed: Kerr, Art Nouveau, c. 1890	200.00	250.00
☐	**14** Geometric circle with stationary dangle motif, marcasites, sterling silver, clip reverse, c. 1930 . . .	55.00	65.00

15

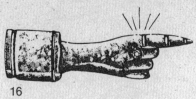

16

17

18

19

20

21

22

			Price Range	
☐	**15**	Geometric motif, black onyx, marcasites, sterling silver, clip reverse, c. 1930. Pair	125.00	150.00
☐	**16**	Hand motif, carved mother-of-pearl, rhinestone in ring, sterling, American, c. 1894-95	65.00	80.00
☐	**17**	Heart motif, enamel, sterling, American, c. 1896 ..	55.00	65.00
☐	**18**	Heart motif, three round red stones, sterling, American, c. 1896	125.00	150.00
☐	**19**	Heart motif, one cabochon turquoise, sterling, American, c. 1896	65.00	80.00
☐	**20**	Heart motif, chased, sterling, American, c. 1896 ..	55.00	65.00
☐	**21**	Heart motif, one opal, sterling, American, c. 1896 .	95.00	125.00
☐	**22**	Heart motif, sterling, American, c. 1896	55.00	65.00

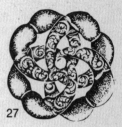

		Price Range	
☐	**23** Heart motif, chased, sterling, American, c. 1896 ..	95.00	125.00
☐	**24** Horsehead motif, carved mother-of-pearl, sterling, American, c. 1894-95	130.00	165.00
☐	**25** Loveknot motif, chased, sterling, American, c. 1896 .	75.00	90.00
☐	**26** Loveknot motif, enamel, sterling, American, c. 1896 .	95.00	125.00
☐	**27** Loveknot motif, chased, one opal, sterling, American, c. 1896	90.00	100.00
☐	**28** Madonna and child motif, bas-relief panel, blue enamel, four half-pearls, silver, c. 1905	250.00	275.00
☐	**29** Miniature painted on porcelain, sterling, American, c. 1896	130.00	165.00

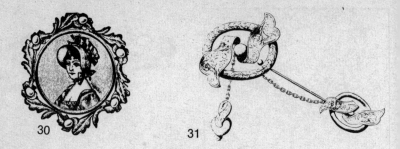

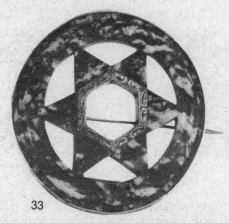

			Price Range	
☐	30	Miniature painted on porcelain, six seed pearls, sterling, American, c. 1896	175.00	200.00
☐	31	Ribbon, circle and dangle motif, engraved, maker: Ellis & Son, Exeter, England, silver, c. 1869	175.00	200.00
☐	32	Ship and oar motif, genuine sea shell, ship is 14K gold, oar is sterling, American, c. 1894-95	175.00	200.00
☐	33	Star of David motif, green marble, silver, English, c. 19th.	200.00	250.00

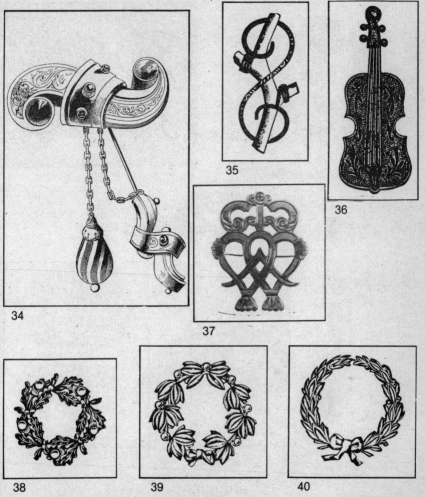

34

35

36

37

38 39 40

			Price Range	
☐	**34**	*Swirl and dangle motif, engraved, maker: Ellis & Son, Exeter, England, silver, c. 1869*	**150.00**	**175.00**
☐	**35**	*Twig motif, carved mother-of-pearl, sterling, American, c. 1894-95*	**50.00**	**60.00**
☐	**36**	*Violin motif, enamel, chased, sterling, American, c. 1894-95*	**125.00**	**150.00**
☐	**37**	*Witch's Heart motif, silver, c. 1850*	**110.00**	**140.00**
☐	**38**	*Wreath motif, five seed pearls, sterling, American, c. 1896*	**80.00**	**90.00**
☐	**39**	*Wreath motif, seven cabochon turquoise, sterling, American, c. 1896*	**90.00**	**100.00**
☐	**40**	*Wreath motif, sterling, American, c. 1896*	**75.00**	**90.00**

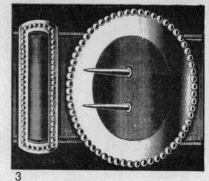

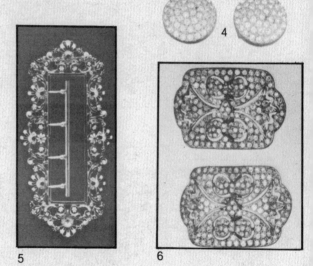

BUCKLES

			Price Range	
☐	**1**	Buckle and button set, translucent apple green enamel, silver, English, c. 1920-30	250.00	275.00
☐	**2**	Cameo motif, carved lava, gold plated, c. late 19th.	250.00	275.00
☐	**3**	Circular motif buckle with beaded edge and slide with beaded edge, sterling silver, American, c. 1896 .	150.00	165.00
☐	**4**	Cluster motif pair of buckles, rhinestone, white metal, c. 1930-40	11.00	16.50
☐	**5**	Fan and scroll motif buckle, champlevé opaque black and white enamel, gold, c. 1870	1300.00	1450.00
☐	**6**	Fancy shape motif pair of buckles, rhinestone, white metal, c. 1930-40	13.00	20.00

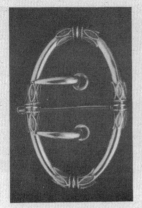

7

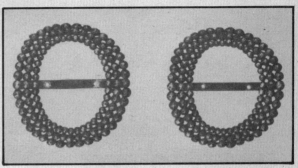

9

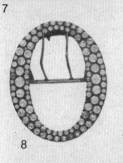

8

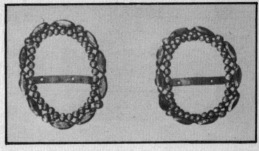

10

11

			Price Range	
☐	**7**	Oval Etruscan granulation motif, buckle pin, gold, c. 1870	275.00	300.00
☐	**8**	Oval motif, paste, silver	450.00	550.00
☐	**9**	Oval motif pair of buckles, cut steel, c. late 19th. . .	40.00	50.00
☐	**10**	Oval wreath motif pair of buckles, cut steel, c. late 19th.	30.00	35.00
☐	**11**	Rectangular buckle and floral motif slide, floral motif belt, sterling silver, American, c. 1896	80.00	95.00

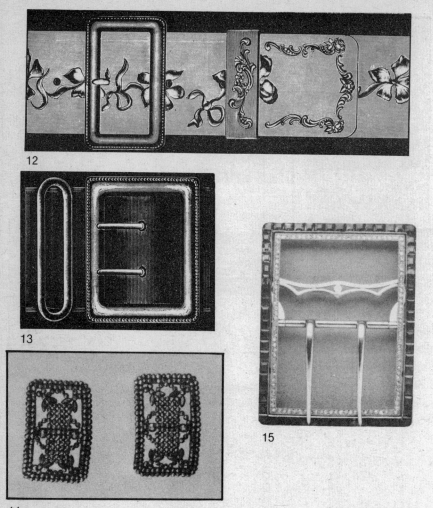

12

13

15

14

		Price Range	
☐	**12** Rectangular buckle and floral motif slide, floral motif belt, sterling silver, American, c. 1896	80.00	95.00
☐	**13** Rectangular buckle with beaded rim and slide, sterling silver, American, c. 1896	95.00	125.00
☐	**14** Rectangular flower motif pair of buckles, cut steel, marked: France, c. late 19th.	45.00	55.00
☐	**15** Rectangular motif buckle, 64 emerald-cut sapphires, 114 round diamonds, platinum, gold, French, c. 1890	3500.00	3750.00

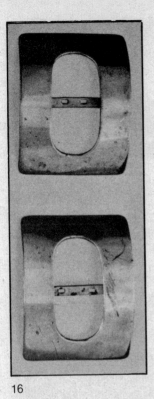

16

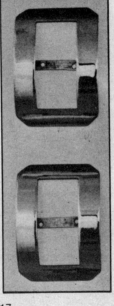

17

18

			Price Range	
☐	**16**	*Rectangular motif pair of buckles, silver plated, c. mid 20th.*	13.00	20.00
☐	**17**	*Rectangular motif pair of buckles, silver plated, c. mid 20th.*	11.00	16.50
☐	**18**	*Rectangular pair of buckles, engraved, sterling silver, c. 1920*	55.00	65.00

19

20

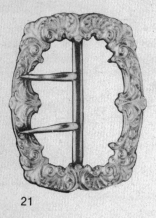

21

22

			Price Range	
☐	**19**	Ribbon and leaf motif, gold, French, c. 1870	1050.00	1200.00
☐	**20**	Scroll motif buckles, gold, c. 1900	750.00	900.00
☐	**21**	Scroll motif buckle, gold, c. 1890	550.00	650.00
☐	**22**	Scroll motif buckle and slide, sterling silver, American, c. 1896	175.00	200.00

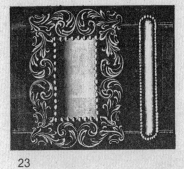

23

24

25

26

			Price Range	
☐	**23**	*Scroll motif buckle and slide with beaded rim, sterling silver, American, c. 1896*	**150.00**	**165.00**
☐	**24**	*Scroll and flower motif, cloisonné and guilloché enamel, Arts and Crafts, c. late 19th.*	**275.00**	**325.00**
☐	**25**	*Shell motif buckle, two round diamonds, six round demantoid garnets, gold, c. 1880*	**1450.00**	**1550.00**
☐	**26**	*Snake motif buckle, enamelled, three round diamonds, gold, c. 19th.*	**1750.00**	**2000.00**

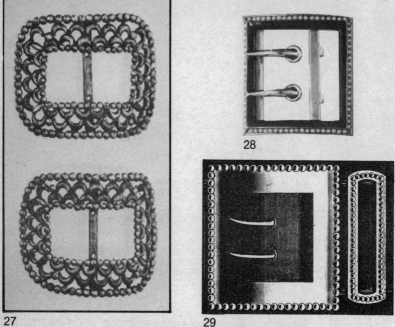

		Price Range	
☐	**27** Square crescent motif pair of buckles, cut steel, c. 19th..	40.00	45.00
☐	**28** Square motif buckle, seed pearl border, cobalt blue enamel, 14K gold, c. 1920	325.00	375.00
☐	**29** Square motif buckle with beaded edge and slide with beaded edge, sterling silver, American, c. 1896	175.00	185.00
☐	**30** Wide rectangular motif buckle and slide, sterling silver, American, c. 1896	95.00	125.00

Photograph taken in Baltimore, Maryland in 1920. The young wife is wearing a pearl cluster bar pin and small gold ball earrings. The husband sports a gold link watch chain from his lapel and a stickpin of a skull and crossbones.

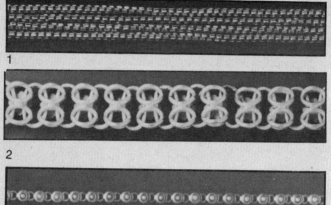

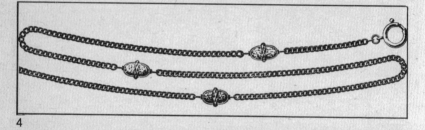

CHAINS

NECK

		Description	Price	Range
☐	1	Box links, gold, 55 in. long, c. 20th.	800.00	1050.00
☐	2	Circular and oblong links, gold, c. 1860	1650.00	1850.00
☐	3	Circular links, seed pearls, gold, c. 1860	1300.00	1550.00
☐	4	Curb links spaced with a crystal rondelle between two cabochon opal beads, gold, English, c. 1900 . . .	1100.00	1300.00
☐	5	Curb ribbed links, gold, c. 1880	2000.00	2200.00

6

7

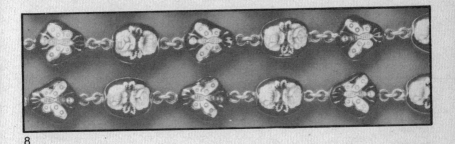

8

9

			Price Range	
☐	6	*Enamel fancy-shape links, opaque black and white flower motif, gold, c. 1870*	4400.00	4850.00
☐	7	*Enamel oval links, black and white flower motif, fancy link chain, gold, 58 in. long, c. 1850*	2400.00	2650.00
☐	8	*Enamel oval and fancy-shape links, black and white flower and butterfly motif, 50 in. long, gold, c. 1860* .	6800.00	7350.00
☐	9	*Enamel rectangular links, opaque and translucent polychrome enamel flower and bird motif, repoussé links, gold, c. 1870*	2800.00	3000.00

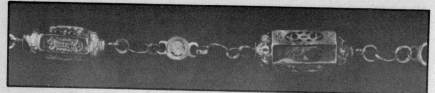

10

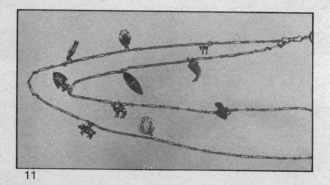

11

12

13

			Price Range	
☐	**10**	*Fancy barrel and circular links, gold, c. 1830*	700.00	800.00
☐	**11**	*Fetter and five links with 11 contemporary and antique charms, gold, 65 in. long, c. 20th.*	1750.00	2000.00
☐	**12**	*Filigree and oblong links, gold, 19 in. long, c. mid 19th.*	1050.00	1200.00
☐	**13**	*Flat circular links, embossed, leaf motif clasp, gold, 41 in. long, c. 1830*	2650.00	2850.00

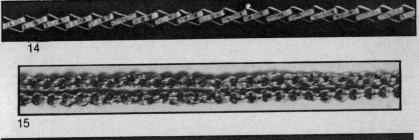

14

15

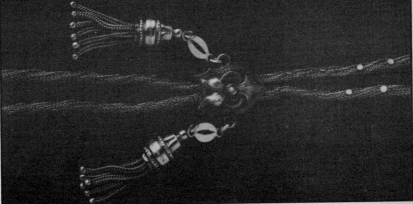

16

17

		Price Range	
☐	**14** *Flat oblong star motif links, gold, 52 in. long, c. 1850*	2400.00	2650.00
☐	**15** *Fluted twisted links, swivel loop, gold, 60 in. long, c. 1860*	800.00	950.00
☐	**16** *Foxtail woven chain, slide with one seed pearl and two tassels, gold, 60 in. long, c. 1860*	1500.00	1800.00
☐	**17** *Garnets: large rose cut and pear-shape clusters, gold, c. mid 19th.*	1300.00	1550.00

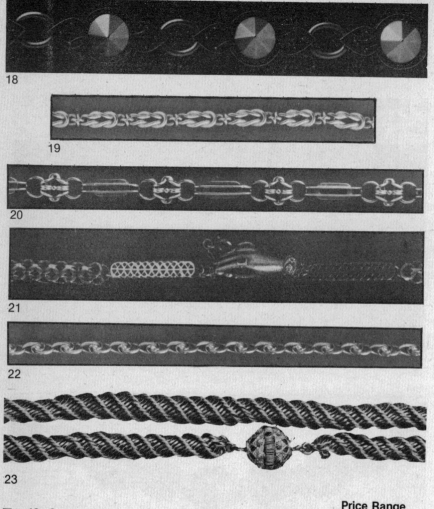

18

19

20

21

22

23

			Price Range	
☐	**18**	Geometric motif link alternating with oval links, gold, c. 1850	1500.00	1700.00
☐	**19**	Loveknot motif links, 18K gold, 60 in. long, French, c. 1910	1700.00	2000.00
☐	**20**	Oblong and fancy links, gold, 52 in. long, c. 1860 . . .	1300.00	1550.00
☐	**21**	Rectangular cutout links spaced with fancy round links, hand motif clasp with blue stone in ring, gold, 45 in. long, c. 1820	4950.00	5250.00
☐	**22**	S-curb links, gold, 60 in. long, c. 1880	2650.00	2850.00
☐	**23**	Spiral woven links, cannetille motif clasp, gold, 38 in. long, c. 1830	2950.00	3200.00

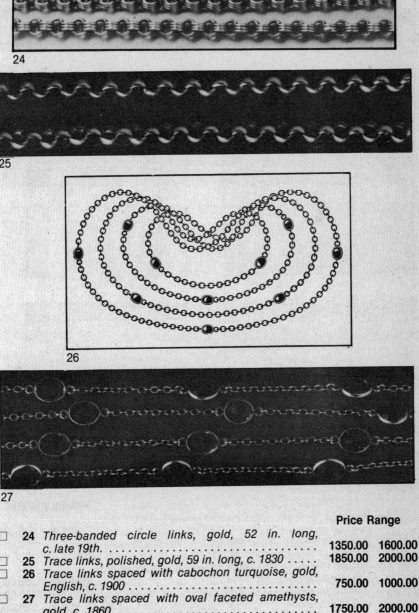

24

25

26

27

			Price Range	
☐	**24**	*Three-banded circle links, gold, 52 in. long, c. late 19th.*	1350.00	1600.00
☐	**25**	*Trace links, polished, gold, 59 in. long, c. 1830*	1850.00	2000.00
☐	**26**	*Trace links spaced with cabochon turquoise, gold, English, c. 1900*	750.00	1000.00
☐	**27**	*Trace links spaced with oval faceted amethysts, gold, c. 1860*	1750.00	2000.00

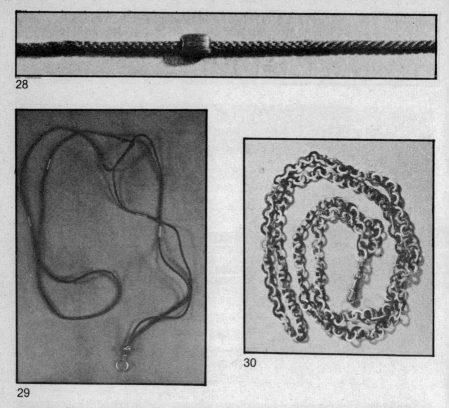

28

29

30

31

			Price Range	
☐	28	Woven hair chain, hair covered wood bead connectors, 65 in. long, c. 1860	175.00	200.00
☐	29	Woven hair chain, tube connectors, repoussé clasp, gold, 68 in. long, c. 1860	175.00	200.00
☐	30	Woven interlocking circular horsehair links, swivel loop, c. 1880	80.00	105.00
☐	31	Woven interlocking hair chains, 24 in. long, gold clasp, c. 1860	130.00	155.00

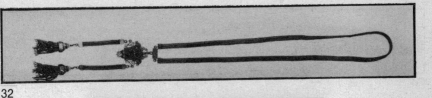

32

33

34

		Price Range	
☐	**32** Woven mesh chain, shield motif clasp with double tassel, seed pearls, 18K gold, 65 in. long, c. 1860	2200.00	2400.00
☐	**33** Woven mesh chain, gold, c. 1860	1100.00	1300.00
☐	**34** Woven mesh braided chain, gold, c. 1860	1550.00	1750.00

1

2

SLIDES and SLIDE CHAINS

☐	**1** Slide, engraved floral motif, gold, c. 1890	175.00	200.00
☐	**2** Slide, oval crystal, woven basket weave hair mat over strands of hair, "MBL" in gold wire, black and white enameled skull and crossbones, insribed: "OB 15 OCT 1684," gold, c. 1684	1550.00	1750.00

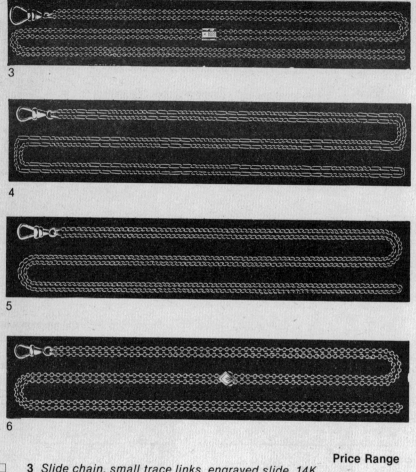

		Price Range	
☐	**3** Slide chain, small trace links, engraved slide, 14K gold, American, c. 1896	450.00	475.00
☐	Same as above but chain and slide gold filled . .	150.00	200.00
☐	Same as above but slide only, 14K gold	55.00	75.00
☐	**4** Slide chain, short and long curb links, 14K, American, c. 1896	275.00	300.00
☐	Same as above but gold filled	135.00	150.00
☐	Same as above but sterling silver	155.00	180.00
☐	**5** Slide chain, curb links, 14K gold, American, c. 1896 .	275.00	300.00
☐	Same as above but gold filled	135.00	150.00
☐	**6** Slide chain, trace links, 14K gold, American, c. 1896	450.00	475.00
☐	Same as above but chain and slide gold filled . .	155.00	200.00
☐	Same as above but slide only, 14K gold	55.00	75.00

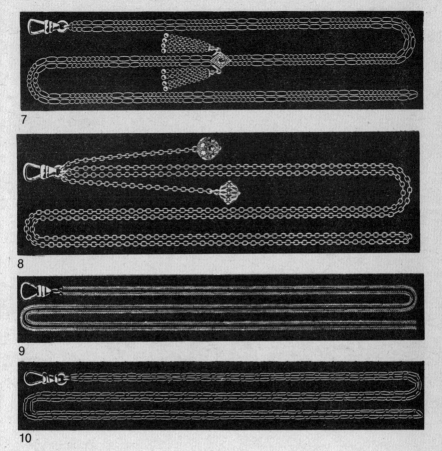

7

8

9

10

			Price Range	
☐	**7**	*Slide chain, short and long curb links, engraved slide with two trace link chain and ball tassels, 14K gold, American, c. 1896*	450.00	500.00
☐		*Same as above but chain and slide gold filled* ..	150.00	175.00
☐		*Same as above but slide only, 14K gold*	85.00	110.00
☐	**8**	*Slide chain, trace links, two trace link extensions with engraved balls, 14K gold, American, c. 1896* .	450.00	500.00
☐		*Same as above but gold filled*	150.00	175.00
☐	**9**	*Slide chain, foxtail links, 14K gold, American, c. 1896*	275.00	300.00
☐		*Same as above but gold filled*	90.00	100.00
☐		*Same as above but sterling silver*	150.00	165.00
☐	**10**	*Slide chain, short and long curb links, 14K gold, American, c. 1896*	275.00	300.00

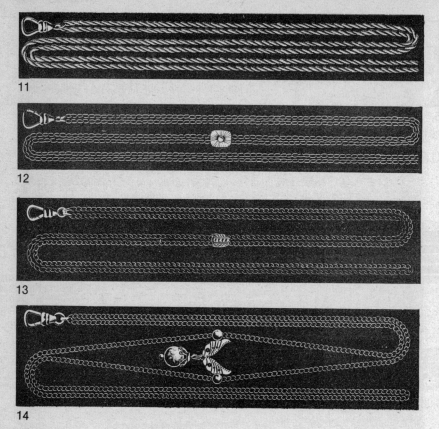

			Price Range	
☐	**11**	Slide chain, rope links, 14K gold, American, c. 1896	325.00	375.00
☐		Same as above but gold filled	85.00	110.00
☐		Same as above but sterling silver	150.00	175.00
☐	**12**	Slide chain, curb links, engraved slide with pearl center, 14K gold, American, c. 1896	450.00	475.00
☐		Same as above but chain and slide gold filled ..	145.00	160.00
☐		Same as above but slide only, 14K gold	65.00	90.00
☐	**13**	Slide chain, curb links, engraved slide with four pearls, 14K gold, American, c. 1896	450.00	550.00
☐		Same as above but chain and slide gold filled ..	145.00	160.00
☐		Same as above but slide only, 14K gold	80.00	110.00
☐	**14**	Slide chain, curb links, fancy shape engraved slide, 14K gold, American, c. 1896	500.00	550.00
☐		Same as above but chain and slide gold filled ..	145.00	175.00
☐		Same as above but slide only, 14K gold	145.00	175.00

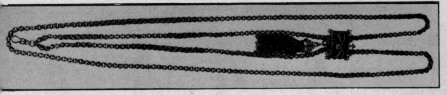

15

		Price Range	

<input disabled="" type="checkbox"> **15** *Slide chain, loop-in-loop links, seed pearls set in fancy shape slide with fox tail tassel, 65 in. long, 14K gold, c. mid 19th* **2000.00 2200.00**

<input disabled="" type="checkbox"> *Same as above but slide only* **400.00 525.00**

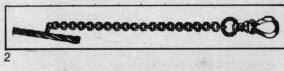

1

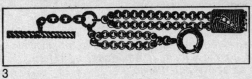

2

3

WATCH – FOB

<input disabled="" type="checkbox"> **1** *Art Nouveau motif, two cabochon sardonyx stones in fob, gold, c. 1890* **750.00 800.00**

<input disabled="" type="checkbox"> **2** *Barleycorn motif links, swivel loop, 14K gold, six in. long, American, , c. 1894-95* **90.00 110.00**

<input disabled="" type="checkbox"> *Same as above but 10K gold* **65.00 75.00**

<input disabled="" type="checkbox"> *Same as above but gold filled* **40.00 45.00**

<input disabled="" type="checkbox"> **3** *Barleycorn motif link double chain with slide, seed pearls in slide, 14K gold, 12 in. long, American, c. 1894-95* **250.00 300.00**

<input disabled="" type="checkbox"> *Same as above but 10K gold* **140.00 175.00**

<input disabled="" type="checkbox"> *Same as above but gold filled* **90.00 110.00**

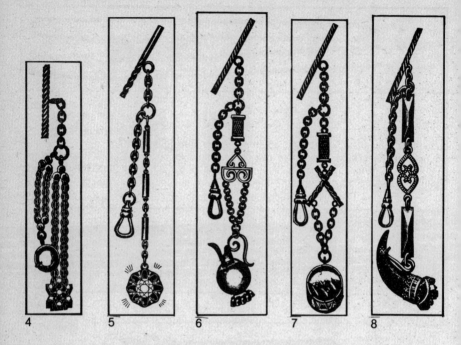

4 5 6 7 8

		Price Range	
4 Fancy motif link double chain with slide, cabochon garnets and seed pearls in slide, 14K gold, 12 in long, American, c. 1894-95		275.00	325.00
Same as above but 10K gold		145.00	200.00
Same as above but gold filled		95.00	125.00
5 Fancy barrel motif links, glass stone in fob, swivel loop, 14K gold, 4½ in. long, American, c. 1894-95 ..		125.00	175.00
Same as above but 10K gold		95.00	125.00
Same as above but gold filled		50.00	55.00
6 Fancy motif links, pitcher fob, swivel loop, 14K gold, 4½ in. long, American, c. 1894-95		175.00	200.00
Same as above but 10K gold		100.00	125.00
Same as above but gold filled		50.00	55.00
7 Fancy motif links, drum fob, swivel loop, 14K gold, 4½ long, American, c. 1894-95		175.00	200.00
Same as above but 10K gold		100.00	125.00
Same as above but gold filled		50.00	55.00
8 Fancy motif links, horn fob, swivel loop, 14K gold, 4½ in. long, American, c. 1894-95		185.00	225.00
Same as above but 10K gold		110.00	135.00
Same as above but gold filled		50.00	55.00

9

10

11

13

14

12

			Price Range	
☐	**9**	*Flower motif, three oval cabochon garnets, gold,*		
		c. 1850	550.00	650.00
☐	**10**	*Greek key motif, 17.5 grams, 14K gold, American,*		
		c. early 20th	325.00	375.00
☐	**11**	*Griffin motif, gold*	650.00	750.00
☐	**12**	*Niello twisted links alternating with gold links,*		
		swivel and round loops, sterling silver, c. 1920 . . .	175.00	200.00
☐	**13**	*Reverse painting under crystal of horse and rider,*		
		gold, leather strap	275.00	325.00
☐	**14**	*Oval and circular cabochon amethyst, gold*	500.00	600.00

15

16

17

			Price Range	
☐	**15**	*S-curb motif links, cube fob, swivel loop, 14K gold,*		
		4½ in. long, American, c. 1894-95	**135.00**	**165.00**
☐		*Same as above but 10K gold*	**95.00**	**115.00**
☐		*Same as above but gold filled*	**50.00**	**55.00**
☐	**16**	*Sardonyx intaglio of a warrior fob, engraved*		
		frame, end fittings and center slide, swivel loop,		
		flat woven hair chain, gold, c. 1890	**140.00**	**165.00**
☐	**17**	*Trace motif links, acorn fob, swivel loop, 14K gold,*		
		4½ in. long, American, c. 1894-95	**125.00**	**165.00**
☐		*Same as above but 10K gold*	**95.00**	**115.00**
☐		*Same as above but gold filled*	**50.00**	**55.00**

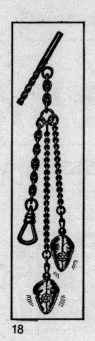

18

19

20

			Price Range	
☐	**18**	*Trace motif links, two genuine sea shell fobs with glass stones, swivel loop, 14K gold, 4½ in. long, American, c. 1894-95*	**135.00**	**175.00**
☐		*Same as above but 10K gold*	100.00	125.00
☐		*Same as above but gold filled*	50.00	55.00
☐	**19**	*Trace motif links, slide and chased ball fob, swivel loop, 14K gold, 6¾ in. long, American, c. 1894-95* . .	**160.00**	**200.00**
☐		*Same as above but 10K gold*	100.00	125.00
☐		*Same as above but gold filled*	50.00	55.00
☐	**20**	*Twisted oval motif links, openwork ball fob, swivel loop, 14K gold, 4½ long, American, c. 1894-95*	**125.00**	**160.00**
☐		*Same as above but 10K gold*	95.00	120.00
☐		*Same as above but gold filled*	50.00	55.00

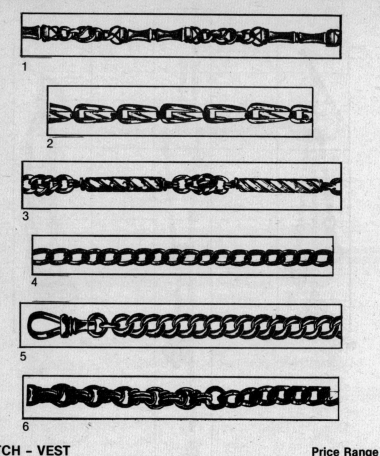

WATCH – VEST

			Price Range	
☐	**1**	*Bamboo motif mother-of-pearl links, fancy links, swivel loop, 14K gold, 12 in. long, American, c. 1894-95*	**325.00**	**350.00**
☐	**2**	*Barleycorn links, swivel loop, 14K gold, 12 in. long, American, c. 1894-95*	**275.00**	**300.00**
☐	**3**	*Barrel carved motif mother-of-pearl links, fancy links, swivel loop, 14K gold, 12 in. long, American, c. 1894-95*	**325.00**	**350.00**
☐	**4**	*Curb links, swivel loop, 14K gold, 12 in. long, American, c. 1894-95*	**200.00**	**225.00**
☐	**5**	*Curb links, swivel loops, 14K gold, 12 in. long, American, c. 1894-95*	**275.00**	**300.00**
☐	**6**	*Curb link center, fancy oval link ends, swivel loop, 14K gold, 12 in. long, American, c. 1894-95*	**300.00**	**350.00**

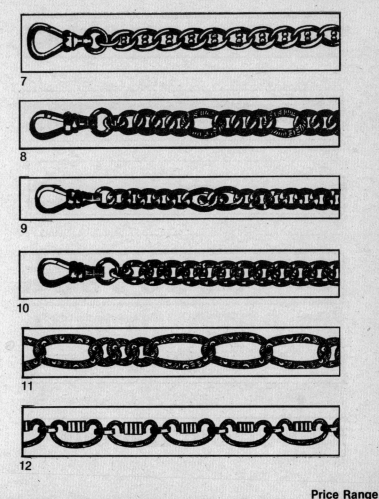

			Price Range	
☐	**7**	*Curb and ball motif links, swivel loop, 14K gold, 12 in. long, American, c. 1894-95*	**275.00**	**325.00**
☐	**8**	*Curb links spaced with oval engraved links, swivel loop, 14K gold, 12 in. long, American, c. 1894-95* ...	**325.00**	**375.00**
☐	**9**	*Curb links spaced with fancy ball links, swivel loop, 14K gold, 12 in. long, American, c. 1894-95* ..	**225.00**	**250.00**
☐	**10**	*Engraved fancy links, swivel loop, 14K gold, 12 in. long, American, c. 1894-95*	**275.00**	**325.00**
☐	**11**	*Engraved fancy links, swivel loop, 14K gold, 12 in. long, American, c. 1894-95*	**300.00**	**350.00**
☐	**12**	*Engraved fancy links, swivel loop, 14K gold, 12 in. long, American, c. 1894-95*	**250.00**	**300.00**

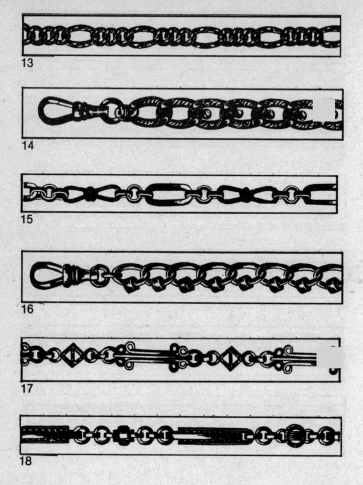

			Price Range	
☐	**13**	*Engraved fancy links, swivel loop, 14K gold, 12 in. long, American, c. 1894-95*	**225.00**	**250.00**
☐	**14**	*Engraved fancy links, swivel loop, 14K gold, 12 in. long, American, c. 1894-95*	**325.00**	**375.00**
☐	**15**	*Fancy links, swivel loop, 14K gold, 12 in. long, American, c. 1894-95*	**250.00**	**300.00**
☐	**16**	*Fancy links, swivel loop, 14K gold, 12 in. long, American, c. 1894-95*	**275.00**	**325.00**
☐	**17**	*Fancy links, swivel loop, 14K gold, 12 in. long, American, c. 1894-95*	**325.00**	**375.00**
☐	**18**	*Fancy links, swivel loop, 14K gold, 12 in. long, American, c. 1894-95*	**250.00**	**300.00**

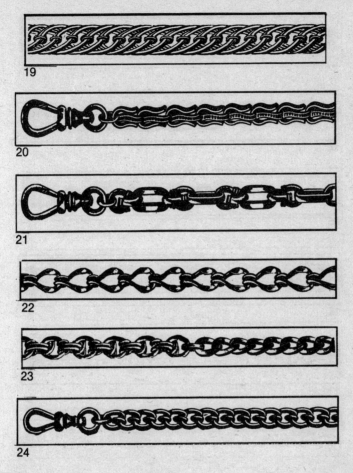

			Price Range	
☐	**19**	*Fancy links, swivel loop, 14K gold, 12 in. long, American, c. 1894-95*	**375.00**	**425.00**
☐	**20**	*Fancy links, swivel loop, 14K gold, 12 in. long, American, c. 1894-95*	**300.00**	**350.00**
☐	**21**	*Fancy links, swivel loop, 14K gold, 12 in. long, American, c. 1894-95*	**275.00**	**325.00**
☐		*Same as any of the above but gold filled*	**60.00**	**125.00**
☐	**22**	*Fancy bell motif links, swivel loop, 14K gold, 12 in. long, American, c. 1894-95*	**250.00**	**300.00**
☐	**23**	*Fancy oval link center, curb link ends, swivel loop, 14K gold, 12 in. long, American, c. 1894-95*	**325.00**	**375.00**
☐	**24**	*Fancy round links, swivel loop, 14K gold, 12 in. long, American, c. 1894-95*	**225.00**	**250.00**

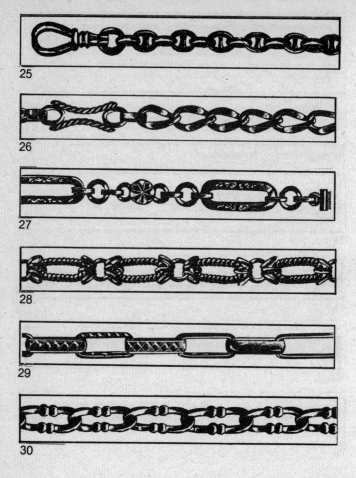

			Price Range	
☐	**25**	Fancy round links, swivel loop, 14K gold, 12 in. long, American, c. 1894-95	300.00	350.00
☐	**26**	Fancy twisted link center, trace link ends, swivel loop, 14K gold, 12 in. long, American, c. 1894-95 . .	300.00	350.00
☐	**27**	Fetter and five modified links, swivel loop, 14K gold, 12 in. long, American, c. 1894-95	325.00	375.00
☐	**28**	Flat fancy twisted links alternating with spiral links, swivel loop, 14K gold, 12 in. long, American, c. 1894-95	350.00	400.00
☐	**29**	Half round plain and engraved square links, swivel loop, 14K gold, 12 in. long, American, c. 1894-95	325.00	375.00
☐	**30**	Horseshoe links, swivel loop, 14K gold, 12 in. long, American, c. 1894-95	350.00	400.00

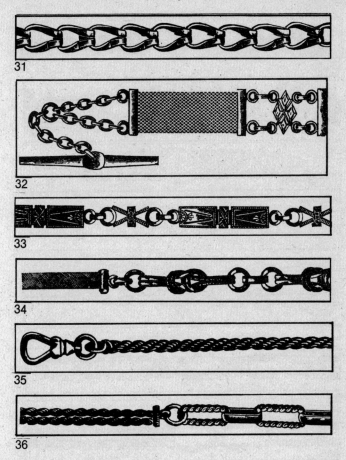

		Price Range	
☐	**31** *Loop-in-loop links, swivel loop, 14K gold, 12 in. long, American, c. 1894-95*	**225.00**	**250.00**
☐	**32** *Mesh woven alternating with fancy diamond-shape motif links, swivel loop, 14K gold, 12 in. long, American, c. 1894-95*	**375.00**	**425.00**
☐	**33** *Plaque and cross motif links, swivel loop, 14K gold, 12 in. long, American, c. 1894-95*	**350.00**	**400.00**
☐	**34** *Roman knot and trace links, mesh woven, swivel loop, 14K gold, 12 in. long, American, c. 1894-95* . .	**300.00**	**350.00**
☐	**35** *Rope links, swivel loop, 14K gold, 12 in. long, American, c. 1894-95*	**200.00**	**225.00**
☐	**36** *Rope link center, trace flat and twisted link ends, swivel loop, 14K gold, 12 in. long, American, c. 1894-95*	**225.00**	**250.00**

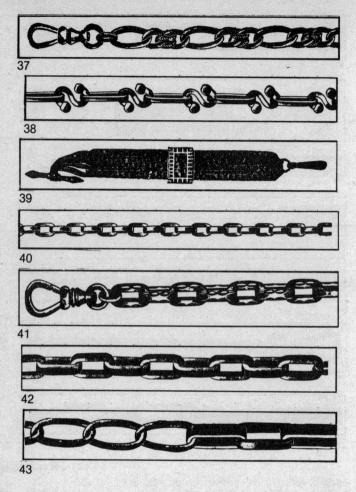

			Price Range	
☐	**37**	*"S" curb links alternting with trace links, swivel loop, 14K gold, 12 in. long, American, c. 1894-95* ..	275.00	325.00
☐	**38**	*"S" links alternating with oblong links, swivel loop, 14K gold, 12 in. long, American, c. 1894-95* ..	325.00	375.00
☐	**39**	*Silk woven, American, c. 1894-95*	60.00	125.00
☐	**40**	*Square links, swivel loop, 14K gold, 12 in. long, American, c. 1894-95*	200.00	225.00
☐	**41**	*Square links, swivel loop, 14K gold, 12 in. long, American, c. 1894-95*	200.00	230.00
☐	**42**	*Square (Boston) links, swivel loop, 14K gold, 12 in. long, American, c. 1894-95*	275.00	325.00
☐	**43**	*Square link center, trace link ends, swivel loop, 14K gold, 12 in. long, American, c. 1894-95*	325.00	375.00

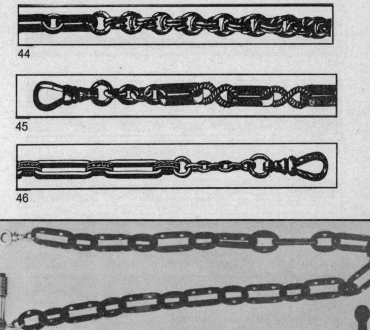

		Price Range	
☐	**44** *Square link center, fancy oval link ends, swivel loop, 14K gold, 12 in. long, American, c. 1894-95* . .	300.00	350.00
☐	**45** *Square links alternating with twisted figure eight links, swivel loop, 14K gold, 12 in. long, American, c. 1894-95*	300.00	350.00
☐	**46** *Square links alternating with engraved oval links, swivel loop, 14K gold, 12 in. long, American, c. 1894-95*	250.00	275.00
☐	**47** *Trace links, pique: tortoise shell inlaid with gold, swivel loop, bar with hidden watch key, gold, c. 1860*	400.00	450.00
☐	**48** *Trace links, gutta percha with gold twisted edges, c. 1840*	200.00	250.00

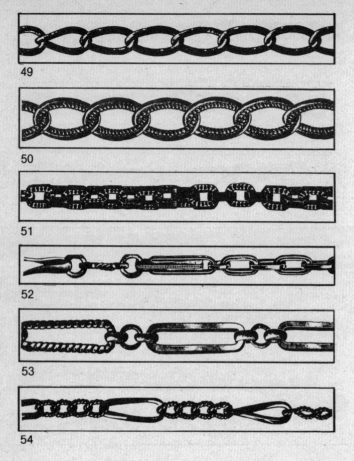

49

50

51

52

53

54

			Price Range	
☐	49	Trace links, swivel loop, 14K gold, 12 in. long, American, c. 1894-95	275.00	325.00
☐	50	Trace fancy links, swivel loop, 14K gold, 12 in. long, American, c. 1894-95	375.00	425.00
☐	51	Trace hexagonal links, engraved, aluminum, swivel loop, 12 in. long, American, c. 1894-95	55.00	70.00
☐	52	Trace and fancy links, swivel loop, 14K gold, 12 in. long, American, c. 1894-95	225.00	250.00
☐	53	Twist and plain alternating links, swivel loop, 14K gold, 12 in. long, American, c. 1894-95	275.00	325.00
☐	54	Trace links alternating with twisted curb links, swivel loop, 14K gold, 12 in. long, American, c. 1894-95	300.00	350.00

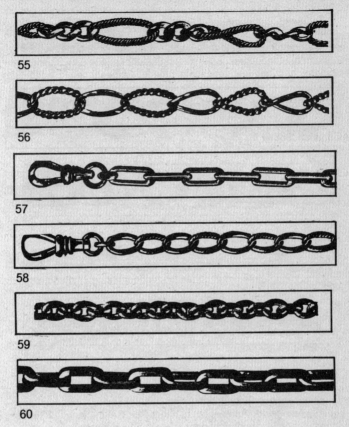

		Price Range	
☐	**55** *Trace twisted links alternating with curb links, swivel loop, 14K gold, 12 in. long, American, c. 1894-95*	300.00	350.00
☐	**56** *Trace polished and twisted alternating links, swivel loop, 14K gold, 12 in. long, American, c. 1894-95*	325.00	375.00
☐	**57** *Trace long links, swivel loop, 14K gold, 12 in. long, American, c. 1894-95*	200.00	225.00
☐	**58** *Trace twisted links, swivel loop, 14K gold, 12 in. long, American, c. 1894-95*	200.00	215.00
☐	**59** *Trace round links, aluminum, swivel loop, 12 in. long, American, c. 1894-95*	50.00	60.00
☐	**60** *Trace square links, aluminum, swivel loop, 12 in. long, American, c. 1894-95*	55.00	65.00

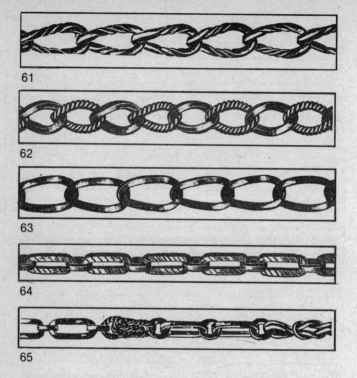

			Price Range	
☐	**61**	Trace square and twisted links, swivel loop, 14K gold, 12 in. long, American, c. 1894-95	325.00	375.00
☐	**62**	Trace square links alternating with trace twisted links, swivel loop, 14K gold, 12 in. long, American, c. 1894-95	375.00	425.00
☐	**63**	Trace square links, swivel loop, 14K gold, 12 in. long, American, c. 1894-95	350.00	400.00
☐	**64**	Trace square and engraved links, swivel loop, 14K gold, 12 in. long, American, c. 1894-95	275.00	325.00
☐	**65**	Twisted knot links alternating with flat and oval trace links and loveknot links, swivel loop, 14K gold, 12 in. long, American, c. 1894-95	300.00	350.00

Photograph taken in Newport, Pennsylvania by Lenney of a young woman wearing a sword motif hatpin through the lace of her blouse at the neckline.

CHARMS, FOBS and SEALS

CHARMS

			Price Range	
	1	Barrel, 14K gold, American, c. 1894-95	105.00	115.00
		Same as above but gold filled	30.00	35.00
		Same as above but sterling silver	55.00	60.00
	2	Barrel, woven hair, gold, c. 1880	125.00	150.00
	3	Barrel, Roman bead, Etruscan granulation on center band, gold, c. 1860	225.00	275.00
	4	Binoculars, 14K gold, American, c. 1894-95	110.00	150.00
		Same as above but gold filled	35.00	45.00
		Same as above but sterling silver	55.00	60.00
	5	Bull, 14K gold, American, c. 1894-95	300.00	325.00
		Same as above but gold filled	40.00	50.00
		Same as above but sterling silver	75.00	90.00
	6	Car, 14K gold, American, c. 1894-95	130.00	175.00

7

8

9

10

11

12

		Price Range	
7 Carriage, 14K gold, American, c. 1894-95		130.00	175.00
Same as above but gold filled		40.00	50.00
Same as above but sterling silver		75.00	90.00
8 Cats in basket, gold, English, c. 1903-04		120.00	160.00
Same as above but gold filled		35.00	45.00
Same as above but sterling silver		60.00	65.00
9 Compass, 14K gold, American, c. 1894-95		150.00	200.00
Same as above but gold filled		40.00	50.00
Same as above but sterling silver		70.00	80.00
10 Compass, 14K gold, American, c. 1894-95		150.00	200.00
Same as above but gold filled		40.00	50.00
Same as above but sterling silver		70.00	80.00
11 Compass, 14K gold, American, c. 1894-95		130.00	160.00
Same as above but gold filled		35.00	45.00
Same as above but sterling silver		60.00	70.00
12 Compass and anchor, 14K gold, American, c. 1894 .		150.00	200.00
Same as above but gold filled		40.00	50.00
Same as above but sterling silver		75.00	90.00

13

14

15

16

			Price Range	
☐	**13**	Compass and ship's wheel, 14K gold, American, c. 1894-95	150.00	200.00
☐		Same as above but gold filled	40.00	50.00
☐		Same as above but sterling silver	70.00	80.00
☐	**14**	Compass and watch motif, 14K gold, American, c. 1894-95	150.00	200.00
☐		Same as above but gold filled	40.00	50.00
☐		Same as above but sterling silver	70.00	80.00
☐	**15**	Boat, 9K gold, English, late Victorian	175.00	200.00
☐	**16**	Cross, anchor and heart symbolizing faith, hope and charity, woven hair, gold, c. 1840	150.00	175.00

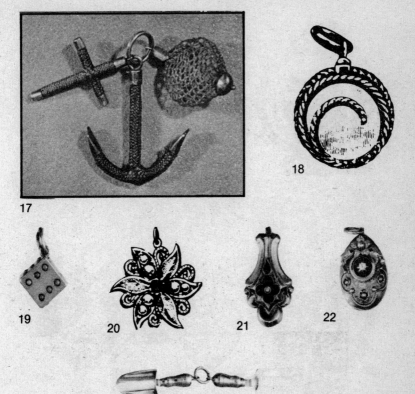

			Price Range	
☐	**17**	Cross, anchor and heart symbolizing faith, hope and charity, woven hair, gold, c. 1860	150.00	175.00
☐	**18**	Crystal ball with rope motif, 14K gold, American, c. 1894-95	75.00	125.00
☐		Same as above but gold filled	30.00	35.00
☐		Same as above but sterling silver	45.00	50.00
☐	**19**	Die, cabochon turquoise marked numbers, 15K gold, one side opens to reveal three miniature sterling silver dice, c. 19th	475.00	500.00
☐	**20**	Flower motif, one garnet, seed pearls, 14K gold, American, c. 1894-95	105.00	120.00
☐	**21**	Flower motif, one seed pearl, garnets, hollow ware, gold, a former earring or dangle from a necklace, c. 1840	105.00	120.00
☐	**22**	Flower oval motif, one round diamond, gold, a former earring or dangle from a necklace, c. 1870 .	225.00	275.00
☐	**23**	Garden tools, 9K gold, English, c. early 20th.	300.00	325.00

		Price Range	
24	Goat with Odd Fellow insignia, 14K gold, American, c. 1894-95	130.00	155.00
☐	Same as above but gold filled	35.00	45.00
☐	Same as above but sterling silver	60.00	70.00
☐ **25**	Hankerchief holder, gold, English, c. 1840	300.00	325.00
☐ **26**	Hardstone scarab, Etruscan granulation on frame, c. 1860	375.00	475.00
☐ **27**	Heart, two garnets, one seed pearl, 14K gold, American, c. 1894-95	75.00	110.00
☐	Same as above but gold filled	30.00	35.00
☐	Same as above but sterling silver	45.00	55.00
☐ **28**	Heart, chased, 14K gold, American, c. 1894-95 . . .	65.00	90.00
☐	Same as above but gold filled	30.00	35.00
☐	Same as above but sterling silver	40.00	50.00
☐ **29**	Heart, one garnet, chased, 14K gold, American, c. 1894-95	75.00	110.00
☐	Same as above but gold filled	30.00	35.00
☐	Same as above but sterling silver	40.00	55.00

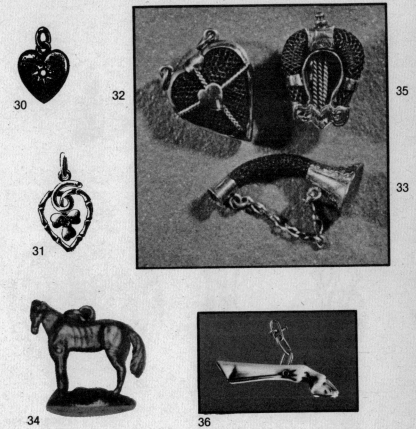

			Price Range	
☐	**30**	*Heart, one seed pearl, 14K gold, American, c. 1894-95*	65.00	90.00
☐		*Same as above but gold filled*	30.00	35.00
☐		*Same as above but sterling silver*	40.00	50.00
☐	**31**	*Heart and clover, one round sapphire, gold, English, c. 1903-04*	110.00	150.00
☐	**32**	*Heart, woven hair, gold, c. 1860*	125.00	150.00
☐	**33**	*Lyre, woven hair, gold, c. 1860*	125.00	150.00
☐	**34**	*Horse, 18K gold, c. 1900*	200.00	250.00
☐	**35**	*Horn, woven hair, gold, c. 1880*	125.00	150.00
☐	**36**	*Horse's leg, carved ivory, gold horseshoe, c. 1870* .	350.00	375.00

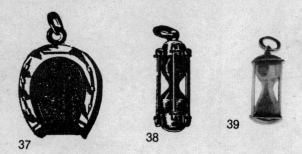

			Price Range	
☐	37	Horseshoe, 14K gold, American, c. 1894-95	110.00	150.00
☐		Same as above but gold filled	35.00	45.00
☐		Same as above but sterling silver	40.00	65.00
☐	38	Hourglass, 14K gold, American, c. 1894-95	130.00	175.00
☐		Same as above but gold filled	40.00	50.00
☐		Same as above but sterling silver	70.00	85.00
☐	39	Hourglass, 9K gold, English, c. 1900	90.00	100.00
☐	40	Initial motif, 14K gold, American, c. 1894-95	65.00	90.00
☐		Same as above but gold filled	30.00	35.00
☐		Same as above but sterling silver	40.00	50.00
☐	41	Ladies shoe, 14K gold, American, c. 1894-95	90.00	125.00
☐		Same as above but gold filled	30.00	35.00
☐		Same as above but sterling silver	45.00	50.00
☐	42	Locket, Prince of Wales feathers of hair under glass, seed pearls, gold, English, c. 1880	150.00	175.00

44

45

46

47

48

49

43

		Price Range	
☐	43 Locket, hair with miniature feather pen under glass, chased case, gold, English, c. 1880	150.00	175.00
☐	44 Locket with photo, gold filled, c. 1900	60.00	70.00
☐	45 Lyre, woven hair, gold, English, c. 1820	375.00	400.00
☐	46 Medallion of Venus and Cupid, sterling silver, American, c. 1920	110.00	125.00
☐	47 Monkey with stick, two seed pearls, gold, English, c. 1894-95	105.00	135.00
☐	48 Mother-of-pearl intaglio, 14K gold, American, c. 1894-95	105.00	135.00
☐	Same as above but gold filled	35.00	40.00
☐	Same as above but sterling silver	60.00	70.00
☐	49 Oval motif, three gemstones, 15K gold, American, c. 1894-95	95.00	125.00

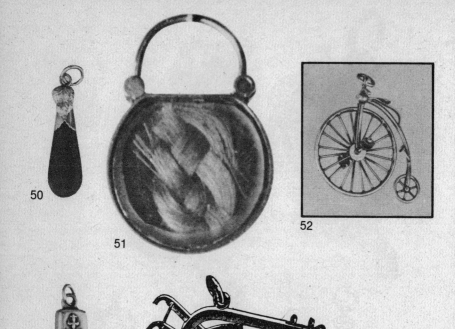

50

51

52

54

53

55

				Price Range	
☐	**50**	Paddle, green jade, gold, c. 20th.		175.00	200.00
☐	**51**	Padlock, braided hair under glass, gold, c. 1880 . .		150.00	175.00
☐	**52**	Penny Farthing bicycle, all movable parts, 15K gold, c. early 20th.		400.00	450.00
☐	**53**	Pin cushion with fleur-de-lys motif, sterling silver, former chatelaine part, c. 20th.		90.00	110.00
☐	**54**	Plow, 14K gold, American, c. 1894-95		110.00	150.00
☐		Same as above but gold filled		35.00	40.00
☐		Same as above but sterling silver . . . :		55.00	60.00
☐	**55**	Pug, diamonds in harness, gold, c. late 19th.		550.00	650.00

			Price Range	
☐	**56**	*Ram, 14K gold, American, c. 1894-95*	300.00	325.00
☐		*Same as above but gold filled*	40.00	50.00
☐		*Same as above but sterling silver*	75.00	90.00
☐	**57**	*Revolver, 14K gold, American, c. 1894-95*	110.00	150.00
☐		*Same as above but gold filled*	35.00	45.00
☐		*Same as above but sterling silver*	60.00	65.00
☐	**58**	*Saw, mallet and plane, gold, English, c. 19th.*	400.00	425.00
☐	**59**	*Scottish Terrier, gold, c. early 20th.*	200.00	250.00
☐	**60**	*Bulldog, gold, c. early 20th.*	250.00	275.00
☐	**61**	*Scottish Terrier, gold, c. early 20th.*	325.00	375.00
☐	**62**	*Mastiff, rose diamonds in collar, gold, c. early 20th* .	275.00	300.00

		Price Range	
□	**63** Shell, one seed pearl, gold, English, c. 1903-04 ...	110.00	150.00
□	Same as above but sterling silver	60.00	70.00
□	**64** Spyglass, rose, yellow and green gold, cabochon turquoise, French, c. 1890	425.00	475.00
□	**65** Square chased motif, 15K gold, American, c. 1894-95	95.00	115.00
□	Same as above but gold filled	35.00	40.00
□	**66** Stanhope with 1893 World's Fair views, 14K gold, American, c. 1894-95	110.00	150.00
□	Same as above but gold filled	45.00	55.00
□	Same as above but sterling silver	60.00	70.00
□	**67** Star motif, seed pearls, 14K gold, American, c. 1894-95	90.00	125.00
□	**68** Watch motif, printed colored paper of scene from Chicago Exposition, gold plated, c. 1893	65.00	90.00
□	**69** Whistle, 14K gold, American, c. 1880	200.00	225.00
□	**70** Wolf's head, ruby eyes, diamonds, silver, gold, c. 1870	425.00	450.00
□	**71** Wreath motif, seed pearl, 14K gold, American, c. 1894-95	90.00	110.00

EMBLEM FOBS

		Price Range	
☐	**1** *A.O.U.W. fob, enamel, gold, American, c. 1896* ...	125.00	175.00
☐	*Same as above but gold filled*	55.00	90.00
☐	**2** *Knights of Maccabees fob, mother-of-pearl center,*		
	enamel, gold, American, c. 1896	125.00	175.00
☐	*Same as above but gold filled*	55.00	90.00
☐	**3** *Knights of Maccabees fob, mother-of-pearl,*		
	enamel, gold, American, c. 1896	110.00	135.00
☐	*Same as above but gold filled*	55.00	90.00
☐	**4** *Knights of Maccabees fob, enamel, gold, Ameri-*		
	can, c. 1896	175.00	200.00
☐	*Same as above but gold filled*	55.00	90.00
☐	**5** *Knights of Maccabees fob, enamel, gold, Ameri-*		
	can, c. 1896	175.00	200.00
☐	*Same as above but gold filled*	55.00	90.00
☐	**6** *Knights of Pythias fob, enamel, gold, American,*		
	c. 1896	185.00	225.00
☐	*Same as above but gold filled*	55.00	65.00

			Price Range	
☐	**7**	*Knights of Pythias fob, mother-of-pearl, enamel, gold, American, c. 1896*	**110.00**	**135.00**
☐		*Same as above but gold filled*	**55.00**	**90.00**
☐	**8**	*Knights of Pythias fob, mother-of-pearl, enamel, gold, American, c. 1896*	**125.00**	**175.00**
☐		*Same as above but gold filled*	**55.00**	**90.00**
☐	**9**	*Knights of Pythias fob, enamel, gold, American, c. 1896*	**180.00**	**225.00**
☐		*Same as above but gold filled*	**90.00**	**110.00**
☐	**10**	*Knights of Pythias fob, enamel, gold, American, c. 1896*	**200.00**	**250.00**
☐		*Same as above but gold filled*	**90.00**	**110.00**
☐	**11**	*Knight Templar fob, enamel, gold, American, c. 1896*	**180.00**	**225.00**
☐		*Same as above but gold filled*	**90.00**	**110.00**
☐	**12**	*Knight Templar fob, 32d degree, enamel, gold, American, c. 1896*	**250.00**	**275.00**
☐		*Same as above but gold filled*	**90.00**	**110.00**

13

14

15

16

17

18

				Price Range	
☐	**13**	*Knight Templar fob, enamel, gold, American,*			
		c. 1896		200.00	250.00
☐		*Same as above but gold filled*		90.00	100.00
☐	**14**	*Knight Templar fob, four rose diamonds, enamel,*			
		gold, American, c. 1896		300.00	400.00
☐		*Same as above but with ten round rubies in*			
		cross		400.00	475.00
☐	**15**	*Masonic fob, enamel, gold, American, c. 1896*		150.00	175.00
☐		*Same as above but gold filled*		55.00	90.00
☐	**16**	*Masonic fob, mother-of-pearl center, enamel, gold,*			
		American, c. 1896		125.00	160.00
☐		*Same as above but gold filled*		55.00	90.00
☐	**17**	*Masonic, polychrome enamel, gold*		300.00	350.00
☐	**18**	*Masonic fob, mother-of-pearl, enamel, gold, Amer-*			
		ican, c. 1896		110.00	135.00
☐		*Same as above but gold filled*		55.00	90.00

19

20

21

22

23

24

			Price Range	
☐	**19**	*Masonic fob, enamel, gold, American, c. 1896 ....*	160.00	200.00
☐		*Same as above but gold filled*	55.00	90.00
☐	**20**	*Modern Woodmen fob, enamel, gold, American,*		
		c. 1896	175.00	225.00
☐		*Same as above but gold filled*	55.00	90.00
☐	**21**	*Modern Woodmen fob, enamel, gold, American,*		
		c. 1896	125.00	160.00
☐		*Same as above but gold filled*	55.00	90.00
☐	**22**	*Modern Woodmen fob, enamel, gold, American,*		
		c. 1896	125.00	160.00
☐		*Same as above but gold filled*	55.00	90.00
☐	**23**	*Odd Fellows fob, enamel, gold, American, c. 1896*	125.00	160.00
☐		*Same as above but gold filled*	55.00	90.00
☐	**24**	*Odd Fellows fob, enamel, gold, American, c. 1896*	200.00	250.00
☐		*Same as above but gold filled*	90.00	110.00

25 26 27

			Price Range	
☐	**25**	*Plain fob, enamel, gold, American, c. 1896*	160.00	200.00
☐		*Same as above but gold filled*	55.00	90.00
☐	**26**	*Royal Arcanum fob, enamel, gold, American,*		
		c. 1896	160.00	200.00
☐		*Same as above but gold filled*	55.00	90.00
☐	**27**	*Polychrome enamel of man and woman in motor-*		
		car, sterling, leather, c. 1920	400.00	475.00

1 2 3 4

SEALS

☐	**1**	*Blackamoor motif, carved agate, gold, c. 1750* ...	900.00	1200.00
☐	**2**	*Cutout motif, agate seal, gold*	250.00	300.00
☐	**3**	*Dog motif, hardstone seal, gold, c. 19th.*	1200.00	1450.00
☐	**4**	*Flower motif, amethyst intaglio inscribed "Though Lost to Sight to Memory Dear" on hidden hinge with glass locket inside, gold, c. 1840*	1200.00	1450.00

5

6

7

8

9

10

12

11

		Price Range	
☐	**5** *Flower motif, chased, hardstone seal, gold, c. 19th. .*	550.00	650.00
☐	**6** *Leaf motif, citrine swivel, gold, c. 1840 . . . .*	750.00	1000.00
☐	**7** *Polished motif, intaglio of a monogram or a car-nelian seal, gold, c. 1850 . . . .*	375.00	450.00
☐	**8** *Ribbed motif, onyx intaglio seal, gold, c. 1850 . . . .*	375.00	450.00
☐	**9** *Rotating wheel motif, six intaglio seals of quartz and hardstone, handle of carved yellow glass, sil-ver gilt, Victorian . . . .*	450.00	550.00
☐	**10** *Scroll motif, faceted and carved crystal seal, gold*	250.00	300.00
☐	**11** *Scroll motif, intaglio hardstone seal, yellow metal, c. 19th. . . . .*	400.00	450.00
☐	**12** *Twisted motif, bloodstone seal, gold . . . .*	225.00	275.00

1

2

3

CHATELAINES

			Price Range	
☐	1	*Angel and wreath plaque with swivel, sterling silver, American, c. 1896*	125.00	150.00
☐	2	*Angel plaque with swivel, sterling silver, American, c. 1896*	105.00	125.00
☐	3	*Bird, wreath and musical instrument motif in black and white enamel, glass perfume flask, gold*	700.00	950.00

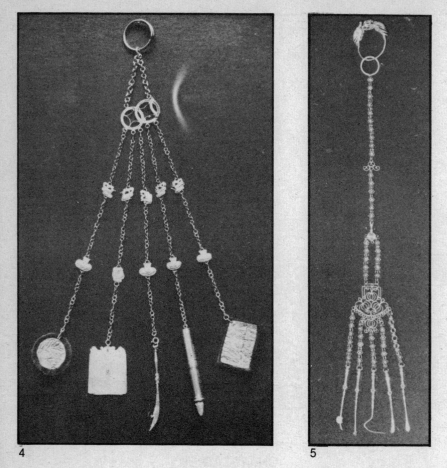

4

5

		Price Range	
☐	**4** Chain motif with round pin cusion, memo pad with mother-of-pearl cover, pick, pencil and square pin cushion, contemporary loop at top, sterling silver, c. 1880	250.00	300.00
☐	**5** Chain motif with implements for cleaning and operating an opium pipe, fancy link chains, silver, Near Eastern, c. 19th	175.00	200.00

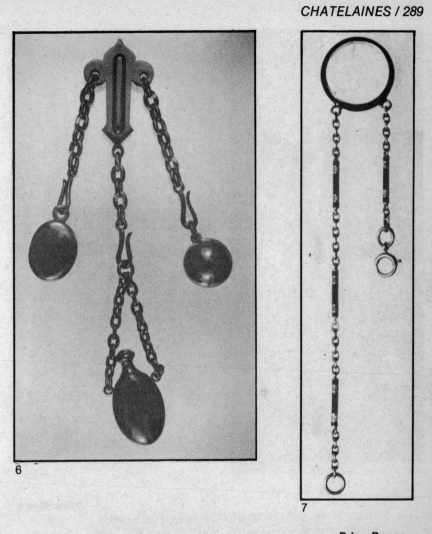

6

7

			Price Range	
☐	**6**	*Cross plaque with locket, scent bottle and vinaigrette, tortoise shell, c. 1860*	750.00	900.00
☐	**7**	*Enamel barrel links and round loop, 14K gold, c. 1930*	375.00	425.00

8

			Price Range
☐	**8**	*Enamel flower and Greek key plaque and chain motif with American 1861 gold dollar, padlock locket with hair, watch, religious locket and heart, rose diamonds in watch, cobalt blue enamel, 7 in. long, gold, c. 1840*	**26250.00 28350.00**
☐	**9**	*Filigree motif, watch, white and yellow gold, c. 1900*	**1100.00 1300.00**

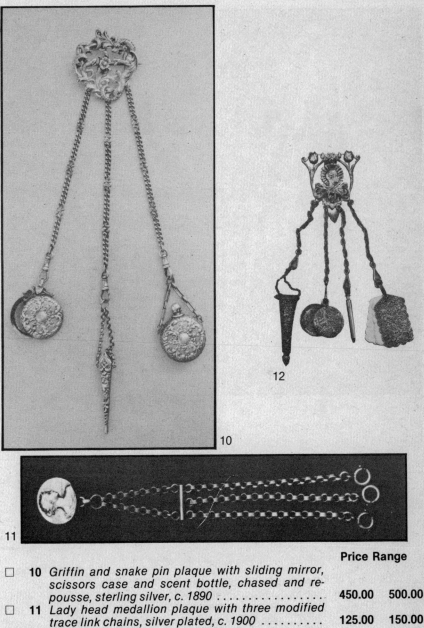

10

12

11

		Price Range	
☐	**10** Griffin and snake pin plaque with sliding mirror, scissors case and scent bottle, chased and repousse, sterling silver, c. 1890	450.00	500.00
☐	**11** Lady head medallion plaque with three modified trace link chains, silver plated, c. 1900	125.00	150.00
☐	**12** Lady head plaque with scissors case, mirror, pencil, memo pad, gold over brass, Art Nouveau, c. 1900	275.00	375.00

13

14

		Price Range	
☐	**13** *Lady head plaque with memo pad, scissors case, thimble case and pencil, yellow metal, c. 1870* ...	225.00	250.00
☐	**14** *Leather motif with purse, memo pad and pencil, scissors with case, mirror and scent bottle, English, c. 1900*	450.00	500.00

15

16

17

Price Range

☐ **15** *Macaroni chatelaine, guilloché red, blue, white, green and yellow enamel, watch: quarter-hour repeater, enamel dial, gold hands, pendant and clasp set with rose diamond, gilt engraved movement, verge escapement, chain and fusee, two translucent red enamel hearts and matching watch key, gold watch and chains, signed: Geo Prior London, c. 1825* **37800.00 44100.00**

☐ **16** *Macaroni chatelaine, guilloché cobalt-blue enamel, seed pearls, rose diamonds, watch: quarter-hour repeater, enamel dial, gold hands, verge escapement, chain and fusee, gold watch and chains, English, c. 1810* **27300.00 33600.00**

☐ **17** *Macaroni chatelaine, guilloché polychrome enamel, two goldstone teardrop charms, watch: quarter-hour repeater, enamel dial, steel hands, pendant set with rose diamond, gilt movement, verge escapement, chain and fusee, gold watch and chains, signed: George Prior London, c. 1825* . **37800.00 44100.00**

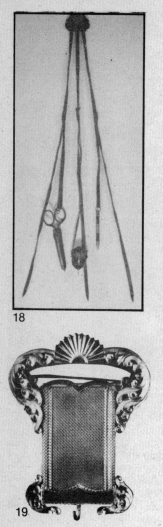

18

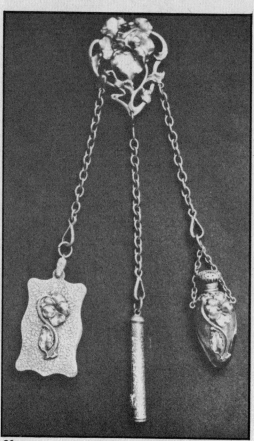

20

19

			Price Range	
☐	**18**	*Leather motif with scissors with case, thimble holder with pencil, English, c. 1900*	225.00	250.00
☐	**19**	*Mesh motif plaque, gold, c. 1860*	300.00	375.00
☐	**20**	*Morning glory plaque with memo pad, pencil and glass scent bottle, white metal, Art Nouveau, c. 1895*	200.00	225.00

21

22

			Price Range	
☐	**21**	*Mourning sewing motif with pencil holder, memo pad, scissors with case, pin cushion and thimble with holder, faceted polished jet, black metal, c. 1865*	475.00	525.00
☐	**22**	*Openwork plaque with pencil, stamp envelope, button hook, cross and memo pad, sterling silver, English, c. 1900*	375.00	425.00

23

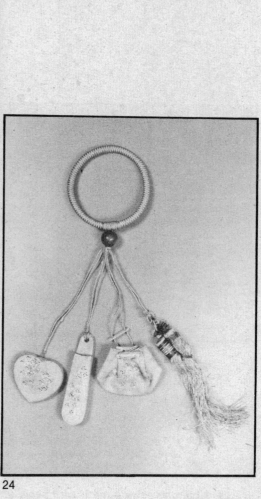

24

		Price Range	
☐	**23** Openwork plaque with pin cushion, needle case in holder and scissors with case, yellow metal, c. 1870	175.00	200.00
☐	**24** Oriental painted silk with heart pin cushion, needle case and purse, c. 19th	200.00	225.00

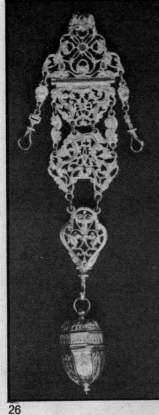

26

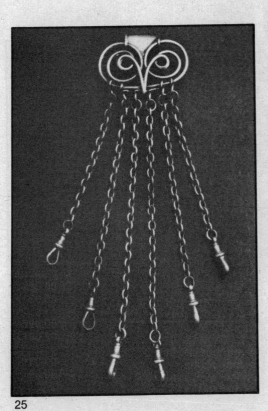

25

		Price Range	
☐	**25** *Owl wire plaque with six trace link chains, silver plated, c. 1900*	150.00	175.00
☐	**26** *Plaque openwork motif with thimble case, pinchbeck, English, c. 1780*	475.00	500.00

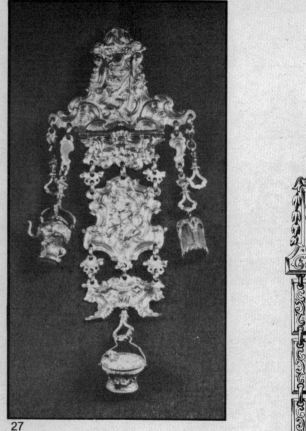

27

28

		Price Range	
☐	**27** Plaque repoussé and chased motif, three hard-stone seal charms, gold, 5¾ in. long, c. 1790	4050.00	4700.00
☐	**28** Plaque repoussé and chased motif, gold, designer: A. Leroy, Paris, France, c. 1868-83	3850.00	4050.00

29

30

		Price Range	
☐ **29**	*Repoussé shield pin with two needle cases and scissors case, pinchbeck, c. 1790*	550.00	575.00
☐ **30**	*Scenic repoussé plaque with four chains, sterling silver, c. 1870*	225.00	275.00

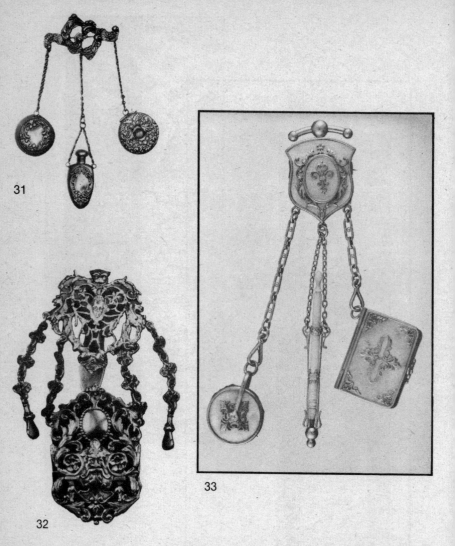

31

32

33

			Price Range	
☐	**31**	*Scroll motif plaque with perfume and two containers, vermiel, Art Nouveau, c. 1890*	250.00	300.00
☐	**32**	*Shield motif, dance card, sterling, c. 1890*	275.00	325.00
☐	**33**	*Shield pin plaque with pin cushion, pencil and memo pad, mother-of-pearl inserts, gold filled, c. 1880*	375.00	425.00

35

34

		Price Range	
☐	**34** *Single purpose eyeglass case motif, openwork flower designs, sterling silver, velvet lined, c. 1880* .	200.00	225.00
☐	**35** *Single purpose folding eyeglass case motif, openwork designs, sterling silver, c. 1880*	175.00	200.00

37

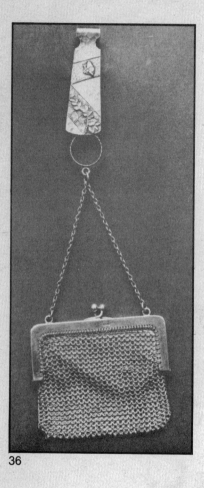

36

38

			Price Range	
☐	**36**	Single purpose mesh purse motif, sterling silver, c. 1900	200.00	225.00
☐	**37**	Single purpose watch motif, family crest plaque, gold, designer: G. Huot, Paris, France, c. 1868-83 ...	4600.00	5450.00
☐	**38**	Single purpose scarf clip motif, white metal, enamel flowers, c. late 19th	125.00	150.00

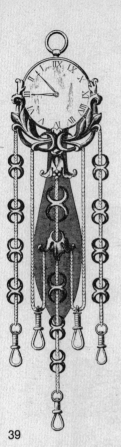

39

40

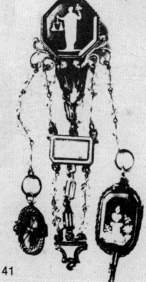

41

		Price Range	
☐	**39** Watch plaque with fancy link chains, gold, designer: Martin, Baskett & Martin, Cheltenham, England, c. 1869	5100.00	5900.00
☐	**40** Wire plaque with button hooks and seal, sterling silver, c. 1890	225.00	250.00
☐	**41** Wedgewood plaque and crystal bead chain motif, gold, English, c. 1800	5750.00	6800.00

1

2

3

4

5

EARRINGS

DIAMOND

Price Range

☐ **1** *Bird motif, rose diamonds, ruby eyes, silver gilt, c. 1820* 750.00 900.00

☐ **2** *Button loveknot motif, round diamonds, gold, American, c. 1895* 250.00 275.00

☐ **3** *Cluster motif, 42 round and rose diamonds, gold, silver, c. mid 19th* 1550.00 1750.00

☐ **4** *Cluster motif, 18 round diamonds approx. 3.50 cts., silver topped gold, c. late 19th* 3950.00 4200.00

☐ **5** *Cluster motif, two center rose diamonds and 22 old mine diamonds approx. 4.50 cts., silver, gold, c. early to mid 19th* 3850.00 4150.00

6

7

8

9

10

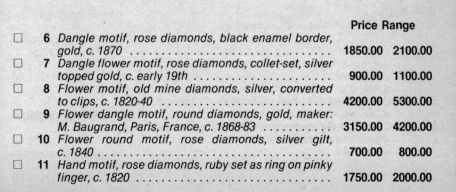

11

			Price Range	
☐	**6**	*Dangle motif, rose diamonds, black enamel border, gold, c. 1870*	1850.00	2100.00
☐	**7**	*Dangle flower motif, rose diamonds, collet-set, silver topped gold, c. early 19th*	900.00	1100.00
☐	**8**	*Flower motif, old mine diamonds, silver, converted to clips, c. 1820-40*	4200.00	5300.00
☐	**9**	*Flower dangle motif, round diamonds, gold, maker: M. Baugrand, Paris, France, c. 1868-83*	3150.00	4200.00
☐	**10**	*Flower round motif, rose diamonds, silver gilt, c. 1840*	700.00	800.00
☐	**11**	*Hand motif, rose diamonds, ruby set as ring on pinky finger, c. 1820*	1750.00	2000.00

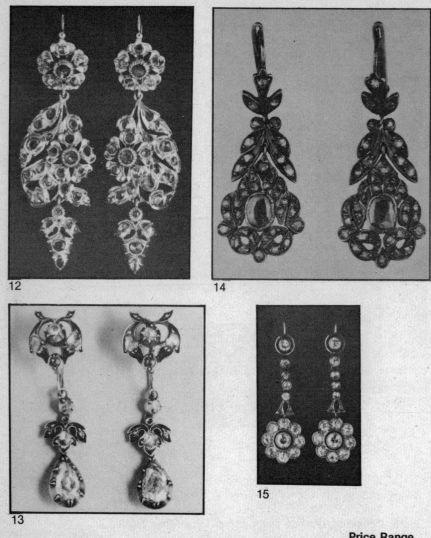

12

14

13

15

		Price Range	
☐	**12** *Leaf and flower dangle motif, rose diamonds, silver, c. 1820-40*	1550.00	1750.00
☐	**13** *Leaf and flower motif, two pear-shape rose diamonds, round rose diamonds, silver back gold, c. 1790*	4200.00	4600.00
☐	**14** *Leaf and flower dangle motif, rose diamonds, gold topped silver, c. 1820-40*	2400.00	2650.00
☐	**15** *Pendants with cluster motif, old mine diamonds and four rose diamonds approx. 2.50 cts., gold, platinum, c. 1900*	2850.00	3100.00

16

19

20

17

21

18

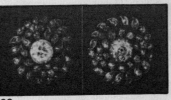

22

		Price Range	
☐ **16** Round Etruscan granulation motif, two old mine diamonds, gold, c. 1860		475.00	575.00
☐ **17** Single stone motif, old mine diamonds, 14K gold, c. 1900		350.00	400.00
☐ **18** Spade motif, 12 round diamonds, 14K gold, c. early 20th.		1200.00	1450.00
☐ **19** Star dangle motif, round diamonds, gold, maker: M. Baugrand, Paris, France, c. 1868-83		6000.00	7050.00
☐ **20** Star motif, blue enamel, rose diamonds, gold, c. 1850		1200.00	1450.00
☐ **21** Straight line dangle motif, rose diamonds, gold, c. 1800		1550.00	1750.00
☐ **22** Wreath motif, two old mine diamonds, rose diamonds, silver, c. 18th.		1550.00	1750.00

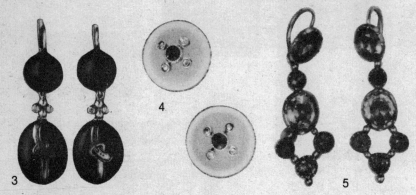

DIAMOND and GEMSTONE

			Price Range	
☐	1	Aquamarines, 15K gold, English, c. 1855	650.00	750.00
☐	2	Bell and bow openwork motif, seed pearls, diamonds, gold, c. early 20th.	3500.00	3950.00
☐	3	Belt motif, enamel, rose diamonds, 18K gold, c. late 19th.	700.00	800.00
☐	4	Button motif, white onyx circle with emeralds, rose diamonds, gold, c. late 19th	550.00	700.00
☐	5	Amethysts, 18K gold, c. 1800	400.00	500.00

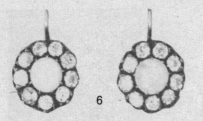

6

7

8

10

9

		Price Range	
☐	**6** Cluster motif, cabochon white opal in center, 18 diamonds approx. 3.0 cts., gold, c. mid 19th.	2800.00	3000.00
☐	**7** Emerald beads, rose diamonds, gold, c. 1920-30 . .	1550.00	1650.00
☐	**8** Flower and berry motif, 14 ruby beads, eight carved emerald leaves, six pearls, diamonds, platinum, c. 1930-40	2300.00	2500.00
☐	**9** Flower motif, baroque natural pearls, round and rose diamonds, platinum, c. 1910	5000.00	5300.00
☐	**10** Flower motif, pearls, round diamonds, gold, American, c. 1885	300.00	325.00

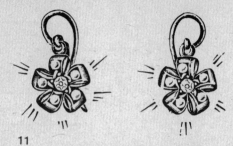

11

12

13

14

		Price Range	
☐	**11** *Flower motif, pearls, round diamonds, gold, American, c. 1895*	300.00	325.00
☐	**12** *Fly and shell motif, rubies, rose diamonds, gold, silver, fitted leather box inscribed: E. Emanuel, c. late 19th.*	1650.00	1850.00
☐	**13** *Geometric motif, 14 round diamonds, four pearls, approx. 9MM to 9.5MM, platinum, c. 1915-30*	900.00	1100.00
☐	**14** *Jade, gold, c. 20th.*	2850.00	3100.00

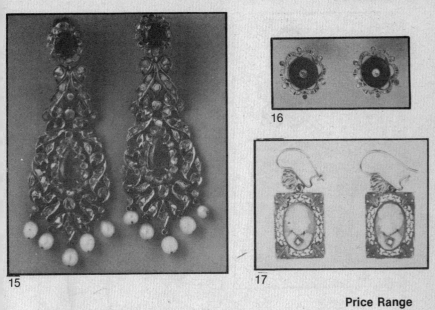

15

16

17

			Price Range	
☐	**15**	*Ribbon dangle motif, two round and two pear-shape emeralds, ten seed pearls, rose diamonds, silver, gold, c. 19th.*	1850.00	2000.00
☐	**16**	*Ribbon motif, black onyx, rose diamonds, gold, c. 19th.*	800.00	900.00
☐	**17**	*Shell cameo motif, filigree frame, diamond in necklaces, gold, c. 1920-30*	525.00	550.00

1

GEMSTONE
☐ **1** *Angel dangle motif, cabochon opals, gold, c. late 19th.* 1100.00 1300.00

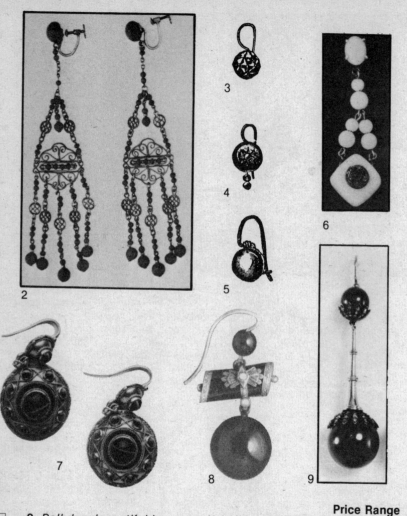

		Price Range	
☐	**2** *Ball dangle motif, blue ceramic balls, sterling silver, c. 1920*	105.00	125.00
☐	**3** *Bead motif, faceted, gold, American, c. 1895*	75.00	90.00
☐	**4** *Bead motif, pearls, gold, American, c. 1895*	95.00	125.00
☐	**5** *Bead motif, gold, American, c. 1895*	95.00	125.00
☐	**6** *Bead dangle motif, opals, round rubies in square opal, gold, c. 1890*	1550.00	1750.00
☐	**7** *Banded agate, 15K gold, English, Victorian*	450.00	550.00
☐	**8** *Black onyx ball and bar motif, seed pearls, gold, c. 1860-80*	650.00	700.00
☐	**9** *Bead dangle motif, lapis lazuli, rose diamonds, gold, c. 1810*	1850.00	2200.00

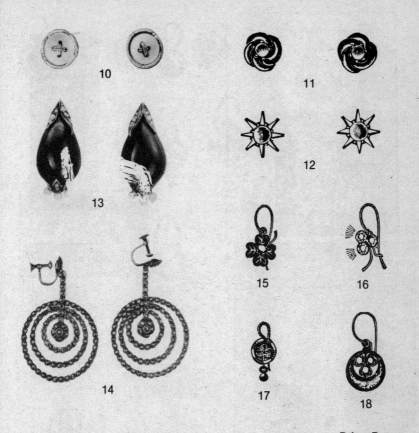

10

11

12

13

15 16

14

17

18

		Price Range	
☐	**10** Button motif, mother-of-pearl, platinum, c. 1915 ..	300.00	350.00
☐	**11** Button loveknot motif, opals, gold, American, c. 1895	135.00	160.00
☐	**12** Button star motif, opals, gold, American, c. 1895 .	110.00	125.00
☐	**13** Cabochon garnets, rose diamonds, seed pearls, silver, gold, c. 1860	325.00	450.00
☐	**14** Circle dangle motif, marcasites, sterling silver, c. 1920-30	110.00	125.00
☐	**15** Clover motif, pearls, gold, American, c. 1895	135.00	160.00
☐	**16** Clover motif, white sapphires, gold, American, c. 1895	135.00	160.00
☐	**17** Clover and bead motif, gold, American, c. 1895 ...	90.00	100.00
☐	**18** Clover and hoop motif, pearls, gold, American, c. 1895	145.00	175.00

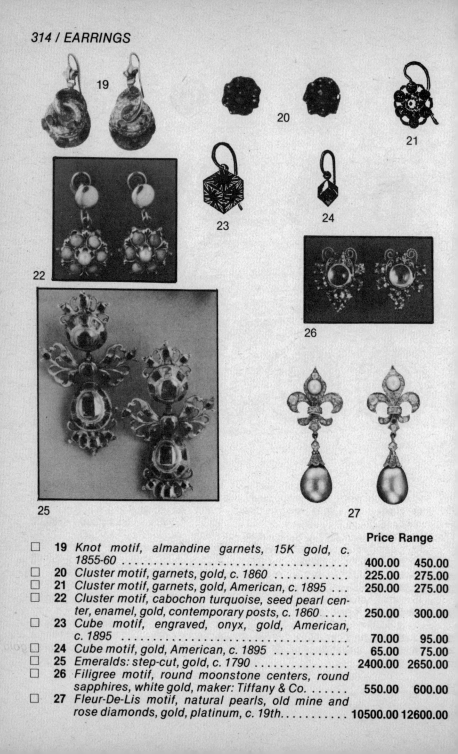

			Price Range	
☐	**19**	Knot motif, almandine garnets, 15K gold, c. 1855-60	**400.00**	**450.00**
☐	**20**	Cluster motif, garnets, gold, c. 1860	**225.00**	**275.00**
☐	**21**	Cluster motif, garnets, gold, American, c. 1895 . . .	**250.00**	**275.00**
☐	**22**	Cluster motif, cabochon turquoise, seed pearl center, enamel, gold, contemporary posts, c. 1860	**250.00**	**300.00**
☐	**23**	Cube motif, engraved, onyx, gold, American, c. 1895	**70.00**	**95.00**
☐	**24**	Cube motif, gold, American, c. 1895	**65.00**	**75.00**
☐	**25**	Emeralds: step-cut, gold, c. 1790	**2400.00**	**2650.00**
☐	**26**	Filigree motif, round moonstone centers, round sapphires, white gold, maker: Tiffany & Co.	**550.00**	**600.00**
☐	**27**	Fleur-De-Lis motif, natural pearls, old mine and rose diamonds, gold, platinum, c. 19th.	**10500.00**	**12600.00**

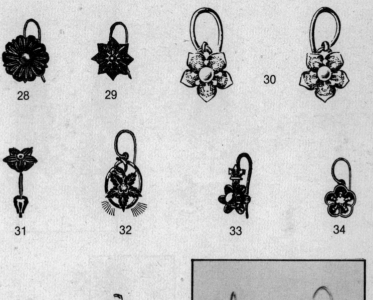

28   29   30

31   32   33   34

35   36

37

			Price	Range
☐	28	*Flower motif, onyx, gold, American, c. 1895*	100.00	125.00
☐	29	*Flower motif, onyx, gold, American, c. 1895*	100.00	125.00
☐	30	*Flower motif, onyx, gold, American, c. 1895*	100.00	125.00
☐	31	*Flower motif, pearl, gold, American, c. 1895*	200.00	225.00
☐	32	*Flower motif, rubies, gold, American, c. 1895*	150.00	175.00
☐	33	*Flower motif, pearl, gold, American, c. 1895*	135.00	160.00
☐	34	*Flower motif, pearls, gold, American, c. 1895*	100.00	125.00
☐	35	*Flower motif, rubies, gold, American, c. 1895*	135.00	160.00
☐	36	*Flower motif, coral, gold, American, c. 1895*	140.00	170.00
☐	37	*Flower motif, garnets, gold, c. 1850-60*	450.00	500.00

38

39

40

41

42

43

44

		Price Range	
☐	**38** *Flower dangle motif, pearls, gold, German, c. 1860-80*	475.00	525.00
☐	**39** *Flower dangle motif, garnets, gold, maker: G. Ehni, Stuttgart, Germany, c. 1870-80*	750.00	800.00
☐	**40** *Flower dangle motif, green malachite, engraved silver, c. 1850*	250.00	300.00
☐	**41** *Flower dangle motif, pearls, gold, German, c. 1860-80*	525.00	575.00
☐	**42** *Flower dangle motif, pearls, gold, Stuttgart, Germany, c. 1870-80*	475.00	525.00
☐	**43** *Flower dangle motif, bloodstone, carnelian, engraved silver, contemporary conversion, c. 1860* ..	275.00	325.00
☐	**44** *Genuine sea shell motif, gold, American, c. 1895* .	90.00	100.00

45

47

48

46

49

Price Range

☐ **45** *Grape cluster and tassel motif, seed pearl and gold grape cluster mounted on an oval cabochon malachite plaque, gold, contemporary conversion, c. mid 19th.* 800.00   900.00

☐ **46** *Hoop motif, seed pearls, gold, c. 1860-80* 550.00   600.00

☐ **47** *Intaglio and leaf dangle motif, gold, c. 1840-60* . . . 1550.00   1750.00

☐ **48** *Lava cameos with hardstone teardrop dangles, gold, c. 1870-80* 600.00   700.00

☐ **49** *Lava cameos, openwork frames, silver gilt, c. 1870-80* 475.00   575.00

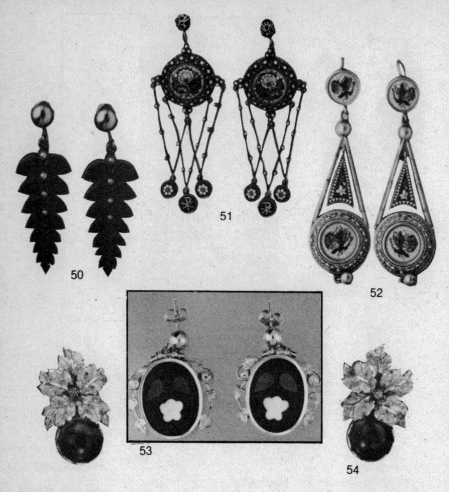

50

51

52

53

54

			Price Range	
☐	**50**	Leaf motif, black onyx, seed pearls, gold, c. 1860-80	300.00	350.00
☐	**51**	Micro-mosaic motif, gold, c. 19th.	500.00	700.00
☐	**52**	Mosaic butterfly dangle motif, gold, c. 1860	2000.00	2200.00
☐	**53**	Mosaic flower motif, bezel frame with leaf motif, gold, contemporary conversion, c. 1860-80	450.00	525.00
☐	**54**	Oak leaf motif, cabochon citrines, 18K gold, maker: M. Buccellati, Italy	1100.00	1300.00

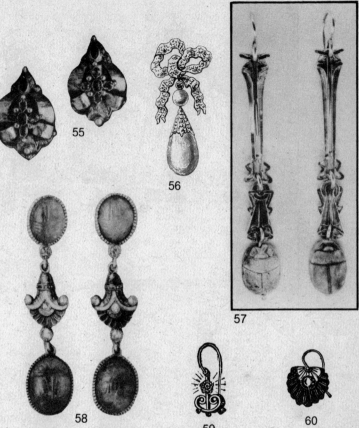

55

56

57

58

59

60

			Price Range	
☐	**55**	*Ribbon motif, two seed pearls, peridots, one red stone, gold, c. 1840*	325.00	350.00
☐	**56**	*Ribbon dangle motif, pearls, gold, German, c. 1860-80*	700.00	800.00
☐	**57**	*Scarab motif, faience scarabs, reverse: one carved hieroglyphics, one Royal cartouche of 18th Dynasty Pharaoh: Tuthmosis, translucent blue-green enamel links, gold, Art Nouveau, maker: Rene Lalique, French, c. 1890*	2000.00	2100.00
☐	**58**	*Scarab motif, four carved emerald scarabs, translucent red, blue and apple green enamel, ten round diamonds, gold, Fabergé, workmaster: Henrik Wigstrom, c. 1900, Russian*	7350.00	7850.00
☐	**59**	*Scroll motif, garnets, gold, American, c. 1895*	135.00	160.00
☐	**60**	*Sea shell motif, pearls, gold, American, c. 1895* ...	135.00	160.00

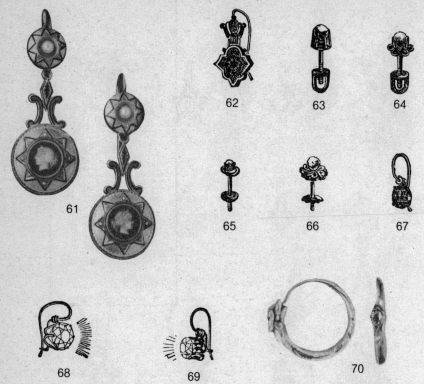

61

62

63

64

65

66

67

68

69

70

		Price Range	
☐	**61** Shell cameo and star dangle motif, seed pearl, enamel, gold, c. 1860	900.00	1100.00
☐	**62** Shield motif, garnets, gold, American, c. 1895	200.00	225.00
☐	**63** Single stone motif, pearl, gold, American, c. 1895	90.00	110.00
☐	**64** Single stone motif, moonstone, gold, American, c. 1895	90.00	110.00
☐	**65** Single stone motif, pearl, gold, American, c. 1895 .	65.00	75.00
☐	**66** Single stone motif, pearl, gold, American, c. 1895 .	75.00	90.00
☐	**67** Single stone motif, amethyst, gold, American, c. 1895	160.00	175.00
☐	**68** Single stone motif, white sapphires, gold, American, c. 1895	160.00	175.00
☐	**69** Single stone motif, white sapphires, gold, American, c. 1895	135.00	160.00
☐	**70** Snake motif, pear-shape diamond in head, gold, c. 19th.	1400.00	1550.00

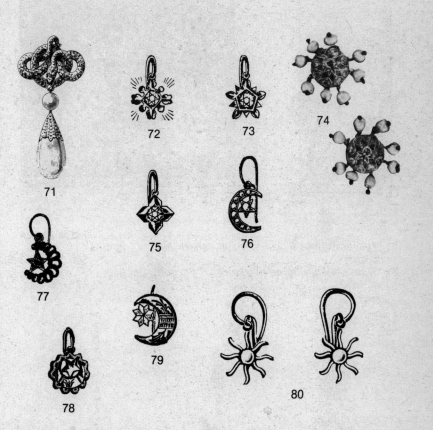

71

72

73

74

75

76

77

79

80

78

		Price Range	
☐	**71** *Snake dangle motif, pearls, gold, German, c. 1860-80*	**700.00**	**800.00**
☐	**72** *Star motif, white sapphires, gold, American, c. 1895*	**200.00**	**225.00**
☐	**73** *Star motif, emeralds, gold, American, c. 1895*	**475.00**	**600.00**
☐	**74** *Star motif, jaipur enamel, table-cut diamonds, baroque pearls, gold, Indian, c. 19th.*	**450.00**	**550.00**
☐	**75** *Star motif, rubies, gold, American, c. 1895*	**225.00**	**250.00**
☐	**76** *Star and crescent motif, pearls, gold, American, c. 1895*	**225.00**	**250.00**
☐	**77** *Star and crescent motif, turquoise, gold, American, c. 1895*	**160.00**	**175.00**
☐	**78** *Star and crescent motif, gold, American, c. 1895* .	**135.00**	**150.00**
☐	**79** *Star and crescent motif, gold, American, c. 1895* .	**125.00**	**150.00**
☐	**80** *Sunburst motif, pearls, gold, American, c. 1895* ..	**150.00**	**175.00**

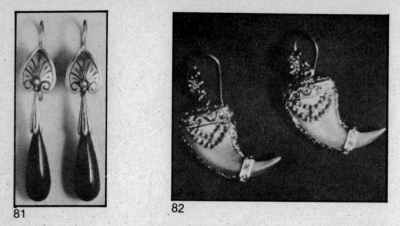

81

82

		Price Range	
☐	**81** Teardrop motif, lapis lazuli, seed pearls, gold, c. 1890	500.00	550.00
☐	**82** Tiger claws, filigree gold motif, 15K gold, English, c. 1870	475.00	600.00

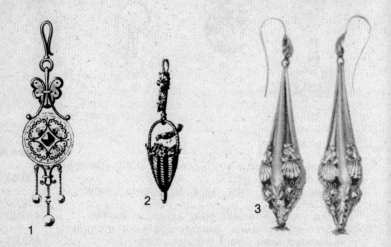

1

2

3

GOLD

☐	**1** Ball and butterfly wing dangle motif, gold, German, c. 1871	700.00	800.00
☐	**2** Bird, nest and flower motif, gold, French, c. 1860-80 .	900.00	1000.00
☐	**3** Applied shell and flower motif, 22K gold, c. 1820s	800.00	1000.00

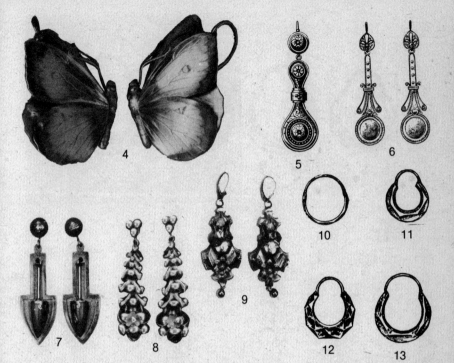

		Price Range	
☐	4	*Butterfly motif, enamel, gold, c. mid to late 19th...*	1600.00	2050.00
☐	5	*Circular dangle motif, gold, German, c. 1866 .....*	650.00	750.00
☐	6	*Circular dangle motif, gold, maker: Hugo Schaper,*		
		Berlin, Germany, c. 1871	650.00	750.00
☐	7	*Enamel, blue, American, c. 1900.................*	550.00	650.00
☐	8	*Floral motif, gold, c. 1880 ....*	375.00	400.00
☐	9	*Flower motif, 14K rose, yellow and green gold, c.*		
		1840	400.00	500.00
☐	10	*Hoop motif, 14K gold, American, c. 1894-95 ......*	55.00	65.00
☐		*Same as above but gold plated ....*	30.00	35.00
☐	11	*Hoop motif, 14K gold, American, c. 1894-95 ......*	70.00	80.00
☐		*Same as above but gold plated ....*	30.00	35.00
☐	12	*Hoop motif, 14K gold, American, c. 1894-95 ......*	90.00	110.00
☐		*Same as above but gold plated ....*	35.00	40.00
☐	13	*Hoop motif, 14K gold, American, c. 1894-95 ......*	105.00	135.00
☐		*Same as above but gold plated ....*	40.00	45.00

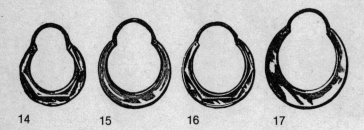

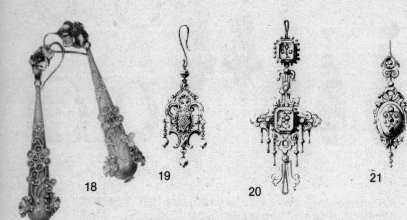

			Price Range	
☐	**14**	Hoop motif, 14K gold, American, c. 1894-95	125.00	150.00
☐		Same as above but gold plated	45.00	55.00
☐	**15**	Hoop motif, 14K gold, American, c. 1894-95	135.00	175.00
☐		Same as above but gold plated	55.00	65.00
☐	**16**	Hoop motif, 14K gold, American, c. 1894-95	150.00	175.00
☐		Same as above but gold plated	55.00	65.00
☐	**17**	Hoop motif, 14K gold, American, c. 1894-95	160.00	180.00
☐		Same as above but gold plated	60.00	70.00
☐	**18**	Floral motif, 22K gold, c. 1830s	800.00	1000.00
☐	**19**	Renaissance revival motif, pearls, gold, c.1840-60 .	700.00	800.00
☐	**20**	Renaissance revival motif, gold, c. 1840-60	700.00	800.00
☐	**21**	Ribbon dangle motif, gold, German, c. 1872	550.00	600.00

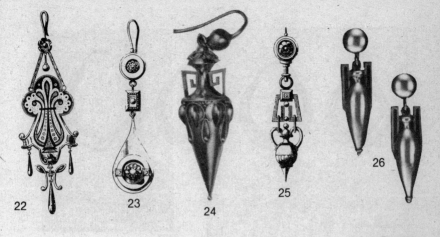

			Price Range	
☐	**22**	*Scroll teardrop dangle motif, gold, German, c. 1871*	800.00	900.00
☐	**23**	*Teardrop circle dangle motif, gold, Stuttgart, Germany, c. 1870*	475.00	525.00
☐	**24**	*Urn dangle motif, 15K gold, English, c. 1860*	400.00	500.00
☐	**25**	*Urn dangle motif, gold, Italian, c. 1840-60*	475.00	525.00
☐	**26**	*Urn motif, gold, c. 3rd quarter 19th*	450.00	500.00

1

HUMAN HAIR – GOLD
All items made from hair referred to throughout this section are of brunette human hair unless stated otherwise.

☐	**1**	*Ball motif, woven hair in beehive pattern, gold fittings, c. 1840-60*	95.00	105.00

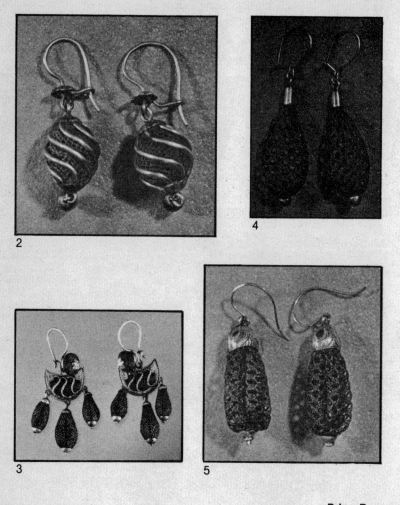

		Price Range	
☐	**2** *Cage oval motif, woven hair inside, gold fittings, c. 1870*	125.00	150.00
☐	**3** *Crescent and dangle motif, woven hair, gold fittings, c. 1870*	175.00	200.00
☐	**4** *Teardrop motif, woven hair in beehive pattern, gold fittings, contemporary earwires, c. 1840-60* ..	135.00	160.00
☐	**5** *Tube motif, woven hair in beehive pattern, gold fittings, c. 1840-60*	135.00	160.00

1

2

3

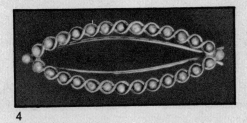

4

HAIR COMBS, HATPINS and BARRETTES

BARRETTES

			Price Range	
☐	1	*Floral motif barrette, half pearls, gold, c. 1920* ...	160.00	225.00
☐	2	*Greek key motif barrette or brooch, 200 round diamonds approx. 9.0 cts., platinum topped gold, c. 1870*	7350.00	9450.00
☐	3	*Lattice motif barrette, seed pearls, engraved, gold, c. 1925*	450.00	550.00
☐	4	*Vine motif barrette, seed pearls, gold, c. 1920*	350.00	375.00

HAIR COMBS

Price Range

☐ **1** *Axe filigree motif, tortoise hair ornament, gold plated, c. 1890-1900* 70.00   80.00

☐ **2** *Filigree wreath motif, tortoise shell hair comb, sterling silver, American, c. 1896* 160.00   185.00

☐ **3** *Filigree swirl motif, tortoise shell hair comb, sterling silver, American, c. 1896* 180.00   200.00

☐ **4** *Filigree swirl motif, tortoise shell hair comb, sterling silver, American, c. 1896* 160.00   175.00

☐ **5** *Filigree flower motif, tortoise shell hair comb, sterling silver, American, c. 1896* 180.00   200.00

6

7

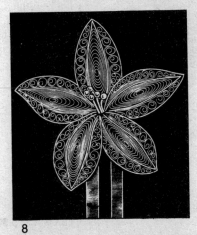

8

9

			Price Range	
☐	**6**	*Filigree leaf motif, tortoise shell hair comb, sterling silver, American, c. 1896*	180.00	200.00
☐	**7**	*Filigree axe motif, tortoise shell hair ornament, sterling silver, American, c. 1896*	150.00	175.00
☐	**8**	*Filigree flower motif, tortoise shell hair comb, sterling silver, American, c. 1896*	180.00	200.00
☐	**9**	*Flower and leaf motif, hair ornament, sterling silver, c. 1860-70*	160.00	185.00

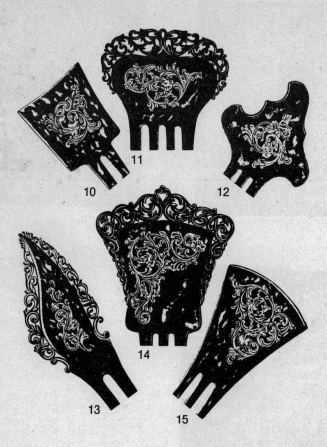

		Price Range	
☐	**10** *Flower swirl motif, tortoise shell hair comb, 14K gold, American, c. 1896*	95.00	105.00
☐	**11** *Flower swirl motif, tortoise shell hair comb, 14K gold, American, c. 1896*	110.00	145.00
☐	**12** *Flower swirl motif, tortoise shell hair comb, 14K gold, American, c. 1896*	95.00	105.00
☐	**13** *Flower swirl motif, tortoise shell hair comb, 14K gold, American, c. 1896*	105.00	125.00
☐	**14** *Flower swirl motif, tortoise shell hair comb, 14K gold, American, c. 1896*	150.00	175.00
☐	**15** *Flower swirl motif, tortoise shell hair comb, 14K gold, American, c. 1896*	105.00	125.00

COLOR PLATE #1

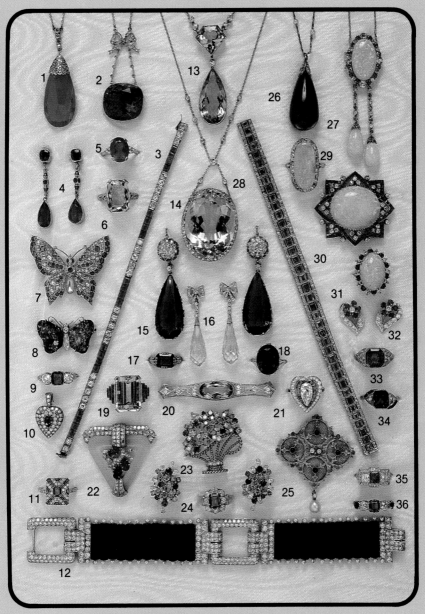

Courtesy: N. Bloom & Son (Antiques) Limited, London, England.

COLOR PLATE #2

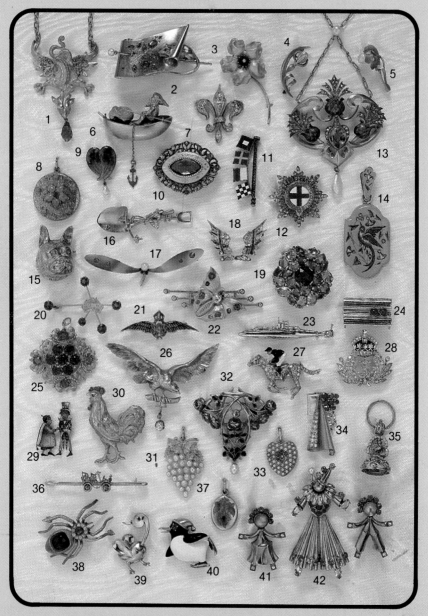

Courtesy: N. Bloom & Son (Antiques) Limited, London, England.

COLOR PLATE #5

FLUORITE

ZIRCON

TOURMALINE

TOURMALINE

GARNET (Hessonite)

GARNET (Demantoid)

PHENAKITE

OLIVINE (Peridot)

ZIRCON

SPHENE

GARNET (Spessartine)

CORUNDUM (Yellow Sapphire)

QUARTZ (Amethyst)

BERYL (Heliodor)

SPODUMENE (Kunzite)

BERYL (Aquamarine)

QUARTZ (Rock Crystal)

CHRYSOBERYL

ZIRCON

ZIRCON

SPHALERITE

TOURMALINE

APATITE

AMBLYGONITE

SPINEL

SCAPOLITE

ANDALUSITE

ZIRCON

FLUORITE

CHRYSOBERYL

SILLIMANITE (Fibrolite)

TOURMALINE

ZIRCON

Courtesy: Director, Institute of Geological Sciences, Crown Copyright reserved, London, England.

COLOR PLATE #6

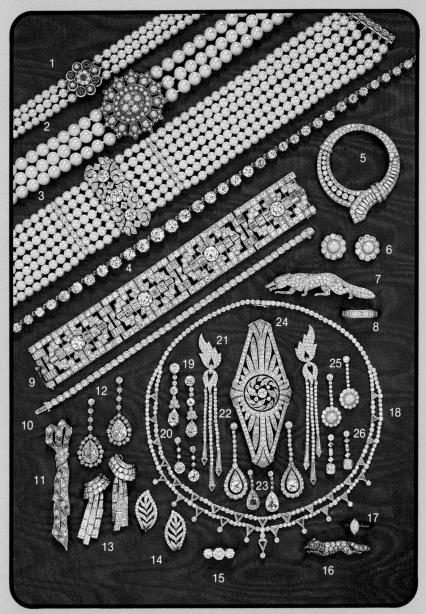

Courtesy: N. Bloom & Son (Antiques) Limited, London, England.

COLOR PLATE #7

Courtesy: N. Bloom & Son (Antiques) Limited, London, England.

COLOR PLATE #8

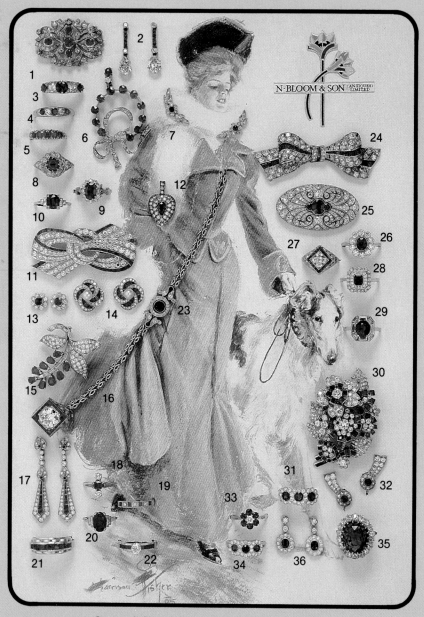

Courtesy: N. Bloom & Son (Antiques) Limited, London, England.

COLOR PLATE #1

			Price Range	
☐	1	Pendant, Mexican fire-opal, pavé diamonds, platinum ..	2000.00	2500.00
☐	2	Pendant, amethyst, diamonds, platinum, Edwardian ...	1800.00	2000.00
☐	3	Bracelet, straight-row motif, Burma rubies, diamonds, platium, c. 1930s	8000.00	10000.00
☐	4	Earrings, Mexican fire opals, enamel, 14K gold	1000.00	1200.00
☐	5	Ring, Mexican fire-opal, diamonds, platinum, 18K gold .	750.00	900.00
☐	6	Ring, aquamarine, diamonds, platinum, Edwardian	2400.00	2800.00
☐	7	Brooch, butterfly motif, rubies, pearl, sapphires, emeralds, diamonds, Victorian	4400.00	4800.00
☐	8	Brooch, butterfly motif, black opal, diamonds, gold	2500.00	2800.00
☐	9	Ring, straight-row motif, one emerald, two diamonds, 18K gold, Victorian	3500.00	3800.00
☐	10	Pendant/locket, heart motif, one emerald, pavé diamonds	1600.00	1800.00
☐	11	Ring, emeralds, diamonds, platinum, Edwardian	3500.00	3800.00
☐	12	Bracelet, diamonds, pearls, carved black onyx, platinum, Art Deco	15000.00	18000.00
☐	13	Necklace, aquamarines, diamonds, platinum, Edwardian	5000.00	6000.00
☐	14	Necklace, aquamarine approx. 81.60 cts., diamonds, platinum, Edwardian	8000.00	10000.00
☐	15	Earrings, amethyst, diamonds, gold, Victorian	2000.00	2400.00
☐	16	Earrings, aquamarine, diamonds, 14K gold	2800.00	3200.00
☐	17	Ring, amethyst, platinum, Edwardian	400.00	500.00
☐	18	Ring, amethyst, diamonds, platinum, Edwardian	600.00	800.00
☐	19	Ring, aquamarine, rubies, platinum, c. 1930-40s	2400.00	2600.00
☐	20	Bar brooch, aquamarine, diamonds, platinum, Edwardian	1500.00	1800.00
☐	21	Ring, one pear-shape diamond 1.31 cts., D color flawless with a GIA certificate, emeralds, diamonds, platinum, Edwardian	30000.00	35000.00
☐	22	Clip brooch, frosted crystal, diamonds, carved emerald, carved sapphire, carved ruby, Art Deco	6000.00	6400.00
☐	23	Brooch and earrings, emeralds, fancy-color diamonds, 18K gold, platinum	5500.00	6000.00
☐	24	Ring, emerald, diamonds, 18K gold, Victorian	1800.00	2000.00
☐	25	Brooch, mesh motif, cabochon sapphires, one pearl, rubies, diamonds, platinum, Edwardian	3000.00	3400.00
☐	26	Pendant, amethyst, diamonds, pearls, platinum, Edwardian	1800.00	2000.00
☐	27	Pendant, opals, demantoid garnets, diamonds, converts to brooch with choker fitting in original case, Edwardian	8000.00	8500.00
☐	28	Bracelet, straight-row motif, emeralds, diamonds, platinum, c. 1930s	8000.00	8500.00
☐	29	Ring, opal, diamonds, gold	2500.00	3000.00
☐	30	Brooch, star motif, one opal, rubies, diamonds, 18K gold ..	4700.00	5000.00
☐	31	Ring, one opal, rubies, diamonds, 14K gold	2000.00	2500.00
☐	32	Earrings, flower motif, rubies, diamonds, 18K gold	1300.00	1500.00
☐	33	Ring, one emerald approx. 3 cts., pavé diamonds, platinum, Art Deco	4000.00	4500.00
☐	34	Ring, one emerald approx. 2.87 cts., calibre emeralds, diamonds, platinum	12000.00	14000.00
☐	35	Ring, emerald, diamonds, platinum, c. 1920s	4000.00	4500.00
☐	36	Ring, straight-row motif, emerlds, diamonds	4500.00	5000.00

COLOR PLATE #2

☐	1	Pendant, dragon motif, rose diamonds, 18K gold, French, c. 1880	2000.00	2500.00
☐	2	Brooch, mouse motif, one sapphire, one ruby, one pearl, rose diamonds, 18K gold, English, Victorian	1600.00	2000.00

☐	3	*Brooch, flower motif, translucent enamel, 18K gold, English, Victorian*	700.00	900.00
☐	4	*Brooch, flower motif, translucent enamel, freshwater pearl, 14K gold, American, Art Nouveau*	400.00	500.00
☐	5	*Brooch, flower motif, translucent enamel, freshwater pearl, 14K gold, American, Art Nouveau*	500.00	500.00
☐	6	*Brooch, dwarf in canoe with gold nugget and anchor motif, 18K gold, English, Victorian*	800.00	1000.00
☐	7	*Brooch, fleur-de-lys motif, diamonds, 18K gold, English, Victorian*	800.00	1000.00
☐	8	*Locket, one ruby, turquoise, 18K gold, English, Victorian*	750.00	850.00
☐	9	*Brooch, wing motif, translucent enamel, one freshwater pearl, silver gilt, maker: Child & Child, English*	350.00	400.00
☐	10	*Brooch, amethyst, diamonds, enamel, 18K gold, silver, maker: Guiliano, English*	2300.00	2600.00
☐	11	*Brooch, flat motif, polychrome opaque enamel, rose diamonds, gold, English*	700.00	800.00
☐	12	*Brooch, Garter Star motif, diamonds, polychrome opaque enamel, English, Victorian*	1600.00	1800.00
☐	13	*Pendant, artichoke motif, translucent enamel, one pearl, rose diamonds, peridot, 18K gold, English, Art Nouveau*	3000.00	3500.00
☐	14	*Locket, bird of paradise motif, Limoges enamel, rose diamonds, 18K gold, English*	2000.00	2400.00
☐	15	*Brooch, pug's head motif, rose diamonds, 14K gold, American, Victorian*	600.00	650.00
☐	16	*Bar pin, gold-diggers motif, 18K gold, American, Victorian* .	400.00	500.00
☐	17	*Bar pin, mistletoe motif, rubies, one pearl, sapphires, 14K gold, American, Victorian*	650.00	750.00
☐	18	*Brooch, City of London crest motif, diamonds, rubies, English, Edwardian*	700.00	800.00
☐	19	*Brooch, citrines, diamonds, maker: Cartier, c. 1950s* ...	2000.00	2400.00
☐	20	*Brooch, Southern Cross and Australia motif, garnets, 9K gold, English, Victorian*	250.00	350.00
☐	21	*Brooch, RAF motif, rose diamonds, enamel, 14K gold, platinum, English*	300.00	350.00
☐	22	*Brooch, butterfly motif, one diamond, sapphires, rubies, 14K gold, Austrian, c. 1880s*.....................	1300.00	1500.00
☐	23	*Bar pin, submarine motif, 9K gold, English, c. 1930-40s* .	240.00	280.00
☐	24	*Brooch, park bench and heart motif, red enamel, 19K gold, c. 1940-50s*	240.00	280.00
☐	25	*Brooch, garnets, gold filigree, English, Georgian*	475.00	550.00
☐	26	*Brooch, eagle motif, one diamond, heavy cast 18K gold, French, c. 1880*	1200.00	1400.00
☐	27	*Brooch, racehorse with jockey motif, pave diamonds, enamel, platinum*	1500.00	1800.00
☐	28	*Brooch, navy cap badge motif, diamonds, garnets, platinum, English, c. 1930*	1500.00	1600.00
☐	29	*Brooch, Uncle Sam and Chinaman motif, polychrome opaque enamel, 14K gold, maker: P. Cox, American, c. 1892*	600.00	800.00
☐	30	*Brooch, cockerel motif, fancy-cut rubies, heavy cast 18K gold, French, c. 1880*	1800.00	2200.00
☐	31	*Pendant, bunch of grapes motif, natural pearls, gold, platinum, Edwardian*	700.00	900.00
☐	32	*Brooch with scarf-clip attachment, flower motif, one diamond, one pearl, enamel, heavy cast 18K gold, French, Art Nouveau*	2200.00	2600.00
☐	33	*Pendant, heart motif, demantoid garnets, half-pearls, 15K gold, English, Victorian*	1000.00	1200.00
☐	34	*Clip brooch, diamonds, rubies, 14K gold, American, c. 1940*	900.00	1100.00

Price Range

- ☐ 35 *Seal, peacock motif, 3-color gold, amethyst seal with Kett family crest and motto, English, c. 1820* **650.00 850.00**
- ☐ 36 *Bar pin, car motif, rose diamonds, one ruby, platinum, 18K gold, English, Edwardian* **700.00 900.00**
- ☐ 37 *Locket, ivy motif, enamel, 18K gold, English, Victorian* .. **250.00 300.00**
- ☐ 38 *Brooch, spider motif, one cabochon garnet, one emerald, ruby eyes, diamonds, 18K gold, English, Victorian* **1800.00 2200.00**
- ☐ 39 *Clip brooch, duck motif, heavy 18K gold, French, c. 1850s* **350.00 375.00**
- ☐ 40 *Brooch, skating penguin motif, enamel, one ruby, 18K gold, maker: Cartier, Paris, c. 1850s* **1800.00 2000.00**
- ☐ 41 *Clip brooches, boy and girl motif, moonstone, diamonds, rubies or emeralds, 18K gold, c. 1850s, pair* .. **1400.00 1600.00**
- ☐ 42 *Brooch, clown motif, pearls, emeralds, rubies, 3-color gold and base metal, c. 1950s* **1300.00 1500.00**

COLOR PLATE #3

- ☐ 1 *Maltese Cross, natural pearls, garnets, 18K gold, c. Victorian* **1000.00 1200.00**
- ☐ 2 *Bracelet, 18K gold, c. 1850* **1200.00 1400.00**
- ☐ 3 *Brooch, lizard motif, diamonds, rubies, Victorian* **3500.00 3800.00**
- ☐ 4 *Earrings, opals, diamonds, maker: Marcus, American, c. 1900* **3500.00 3800.00**
- ☐ 5 *Ring, one opal, diamonds, 18K gold* **1600.00 1800.00**
- ☐ 6 *Ring, armorial intaglio motif, 14K gold, Victorian* **450.00 500.00**
- ☐ 7 *Ring, hardstone cameo, 18K gold, Victorian* **550.00 600.00**
- ☐ 8 *Brooch, rose motif, translucent enamel, diamonds, Victorian* **5500.00 6000.00**
- ☐ 9 *Ring, opal, diamonds* **2000.00 2200.00**
- ☐ 10 *Ring, armorial motif, platinum* **650.00 750.00**
- ☐ 11 *Earrings, onyx, coral, pearl, silver, Art Deco* **1000.00 1200.00**
- ☐ 12 *Pendant/brooch, sapphires, American, Edwardian* **1700.00 2000.00**
- ☐ 13 *Brooch, Welsh dragon motif, 9K gold, inscribed: Xmas 1914* **250.00 300.00**
- ☐ 14 *Pendant, Burma ruby, diamonds* **700.00 800.00**
- ☐ 15 *Scatter pins, bee motif, enamel, rubies, diamonds, 15K gold, Victorian* **1000.00 1200.00**
- ☐ 16 *Earrings, carved jade, coral, onyx, diamonds, Art Deco* . **2800.00 3000.00**
- ☐ 17 *Brooch, Chinese motif, rose diamonds, enamel, platinum, French, Art Deco, c. 1920s* **2800.00 3000.00**
- ☐ 18 *Bar pin, rider on horse motif, enamel, rubies, diamonds, platinum, gold* **1300.00 1500.00**
- ☐ 19 *Brooch and earrings, peridot, diamonds, 18K gold, Art Nouveau, set* **2000.00 2400.00**
- ☐ 20 *Cuff Links, onyx, coral, enamel, heavy platinum, Art Deco* **700.00 800.00**
- ☐ 21 *Cuff links, green agate, onyx, platinum, 18K gold, Art Deco* **1300.00 1500.00**
- ☐ 22 *Cuff links, enamel, diamonds, platinum* **1100.00 1300.00**
- ☐ 23 *Cuff links, horsehead and stirrup motif, enamel, 18K gold* **650.00 800.00**
- ☐ 24 *Cuff links, engraved, 18K gold, Victorian* **250.00 300.00**
- ☐ 25 *Cuff links, jade, rose diamonds, pearls, platinum, 18K gold, Edwardian* **1300.00 1500.00**
- ☐ 26 *Brooch, cupid motif, mosaic, gold, Italian, c. 1860* **2400.00 2600.00**
- ☐ 27 *Ring, garnet, heavy 18K gold, c. 1873* **450.00 475.00**
- ☐ 28 *Brooch, Egyptian motif, mosaic, gold, Italian, c. 1860* ... **1000.00 1200.00**
- ☐ 29 *Seal, citrine with armorial intaglio, gold, c. 1810* **800.00 900.00**
- ☐ 30 *Pendant, opals, diamonds, pearls, enamel, 18K gold* ... **1800.00 2000.00**

			Price Range	
☐	31	Brooch, dragonfly motif, enamel, sapphires, American, Edwardian	3000.00	3500.00
☐	32	Ring, pearl, diamonds, 18K gold, Art Nouveau	750.00	850.00
☐	33	Ring, one emerald, rubies, rose diamonds, 18K gold, French, Art Nouveau	2000.00	2400.00
☐	34	Ring, hardstone cameo of The Judgment of Paris, 18K gold, French, c. 1790	2000.00	2400.00
☐	35	Pendant, Medieval Revival motif, almandine garnets, turquoise, 18K gold, c. 1850	2400.00	2800.00
☐	36	Ring, Limoges enamel, 18K gold, Victorian	250.00	350.00
☐	37	Pendant, floral wreath motif, peridot, pearls, rose diamonds, Edwardian	1200.00	1400.00
☐	38	Pendant, heart and arrow motif, cabochon garnet, rose diamonds, gold, silver, c. 1850	4000.00	4400.00
☐	39	Brooch, terrier motif, heavy 9K gold, c. 1900	225.00	250.00
☐	40	Brooch, hardstone cameo of a black person's head, rose diamonds, rubies, gold, Victorian	2600.00	3000.00
☐	41	Brooch, fox motif, heavy 18K gold, c. 1900	300.00	350.00
☐	42	Stickpin, terrier motif, heavy 18K gold, c. 1900	250.00	300.00

COLOR PLATE #4: GEMSTONE IDENTIFICATION

COLOR PLATE #5: GEMSTONE IDENTIFICATION

COLOR PLATE #6

☐	1	Choker necklace, cultured pearls, sapphires, diamonds, gold, Edwardian	3000.00	3400.00
☐	2	Choker, necklace, cultured pearls, clasp with natural pearls, diamonds, gold, Victorian	3300.00	3600.00
☐	3	Choker necklace, cultured pearls, diamonds, gold, Edwardian	14000.00	16000.00
☐	4	Necklace, graduated diamond collet set approx. 35 cts., Victorian	48000.00	52000.00
☐	5	Brooch, diamonds, platinum, maker: Van Cleef and Arpels, Art Deco	7800.00	8200.00
☐	6	Earrings, natural pearls, diamonds	4000.00	4200.00
☐	7	Brooch, fox motif, diamonds, platinum	5500.00	6000.00
☐	8	Eternity ring, baguette diamonds, platinum	2500.00	2800.00
☐	9	Bracelet, diamonds, platinum, French, Art Deco	35000.00	40000.00
☐	10	Bracelet, rope motif, diamonds, platinum, maker: J.E. Caldwell, American, c. 1920	5800.00	6200.00
☐	11	Jabot brooch, diamonds, platinum, Edwardian	2400.00	2600.00
☐	12	Earrings, diamonds approx. 4.39 cts., platinum, Edwardian	30000.00	34000.00
☐	13	Earrings, round and baguette diamonds approx. 10 cts., platinum, c. 1950	12000.00	14000.00
☐	14	Ear clips, leaf motif, diamonds, platinum	2400.00	2600.00
☐	15	Ring, straight-row motif, diamonds, center diamond is approx. 1.04 ct.	5000.00	5500.00
☐	16	Brooch, fox motif, diamonds, Victorian	1900.00	2200.00
☐	17	Ring, marquise diamond, platinum	2000.00	2400.00
☐	18	Necklace, round and triangular diamonds, platinum ...	16000.00	20000.00
☐	19	Earrings, diamonds, platinum	7500.00	8500.00
☐	20	Earrings, diamonds, platinum	3200.00	3400.00
☐	21	Earrings, round, baguette and triangular cut diamonds .	12000.00	15000.00
☐	22	Earrings, diamonds, platinum, Edwardian	7500.00	8500.00
☐	23	Earrings, round diamonds, pear-shape diamonds approx. 3.50 cts., platinum	5800.00	6200.00
☐	24	Brooch, diamonds, platinum, maker: Dreicer & Co., American, Edwardian	10000.00	12000.00
☐	25	Earrings, diamonds, pearls, platinum, Edwardian	4200.00	4500.00

			Low	High
☐	26	Earrings, square, baguette and round diamonds, platinum, Art Deco	4800.00	5200.00

COLOR PLATE #7

			Low	High
☐	1	Choker necklace, cultured pearls, ruby, rose diamonds, Victorian	2200.00	2600.00
☐	2	Choker necklace, 8.5 MM cultured pearls, diamond clasp detaches as brooch/pendant, Victorian	18000.00	20000.00
☐	3	Choker necklace, cultured pearls, clasp with natural pearls and diamonds detaches as brooch or pendant, Victorian	11000.00	13000.00
☐	4	Ring, cross-over motif, cultured pearls approx. 11 MM, baguette diamonds, platinum, c. 1950	3000.00	3200.00
☐	5	Choker necklace, cultured pearls, rubies, sapphires, 18K gold	2000.00	2400.00
☐	6	Bracelet, diamonds, platinum, c. 1920s	10000.00	12000.00
☐	7	Pendant, leopard head motif, diamonds, rubies	18000.00	2000.00
☐	8	Pendant, leaf motif, diamonds, platinum, Edwardian	2200.00	2400.00
☐	9	Bracelet, diamonds, platinum, Edwardian	4800.00	5000.00
☐	10	Brooch, lily-leaf motif, diamonds, platinum, c. 1950s	2000.00	2400.00
☐	11	Ring, diamonds, three center stones approx. 4 cts., Victorian	16000.00	18000.00
☐	12	Ring, diamonds, Edwardian	6400.00	6800.00
☐	13	Ear-clips, diamonds, platinum, c. 1950s	2100.00	2300.00
☐	14	Brooch, scroll motif, diamond, pearl, Victorian	1000.00	1200.00
☐	15	Brooch, bow motif, diamonds, platinum	10000.00	12000.00
☐	16	Earrings, leaf motif, diamonds, 18K white gold	1000.00	1200.00
☐	17	Brooch, arrow motif, diamonds, platinum, Edwardian	1000.00	1200.00
☐	18	Brooch, bow motif, diamonds, Victorian	2700.00	3000.00
☐	19	Ring, diamonds, platinum, Edwardian	1800.00	2000.00
☐	20	Brooch, cloverleaf motif, diamonds, Victorian	700.00	900.00
☐	21	Earrings, cushion-cut diamond approx. 2.25 cts., Victorian	4000.00	4200.00
☐	22	Earrings, flower basket motif, natural pearls, diamonds, emeralds, platinum, Edwardian	8000.00	10000.00
☐	23	Earrings, emeralds, diamonds, platinum, Edwardian	3000.00	3200.00
☐	24	Earrings, flower motif, emeralds, diamonds, platinum	6300.00	6600.00
☐	25	Stud earrings, emeralds, diamonds	1800.00	2000.00
☐	26	Earrings, baroque cultured pearls, diamonds	2400.00	2600.00
☐	27	Ring, cut-out motif, natural pearl, diamonds, platinum, Edwardian	2400.00	2600.00
☐	28	Earrings, South Sea cultured pearls, diamonds	3500.00	3800.00
☐	29	Charm, poodle motif, diamonds, platinum, c. 1920s	800.00	1000.00
☐	30	Earrings, Biwa pearls, diamonds, platinum, Edwardian	500.00	600.00
☐	31	Brooch, dog motif, diamonds, platinum, Edwardian	1800.00	2000.00
☐	32	Ring, ball motif, diamonds, 18K gold	1200.00	14000.00
☐	33	Ring, straight-row motif, 5 diamonds approx. 3.25 cts., 18K gold, Victorian	4700.00	5000.00
☐	34	Ring, cut-out motif, diamonds, platinum, French, c. 1910	2000.00	2200.00
☐	35	Ring, straight-row motif, diamonds, 18K gold, Victorian	1800.00	2000.00
☐	36	Ring, diamond approx. 2.83 cts.	12000.00	15000.00
☐	37	Ring, diamonds, platinum, Art Deco	3000.00	3400.00
☐	38	Brooch, poodle motif, diamonds, silver, gold, Victorian	1500.00	1800.00
☐	39	Ring, straight-row motif, diamonds approx. 3.25 cts., Georgian	2200.00	2400.00
☐	40	Ring, cluster motif, diamonds, 18K gold, platinum	700.00	900.00
☐	41	Ring, diamonds, Victorian	2000.00	2400.00
☐	42	Ring, diamond approx. 1.10 cts., platinum, Edwardian	4000.00	4500.00
☐	43	Ring, cluster motif, one diamond approx. 1.50 cts., platinum, Edwardian	4000.00	4400.00

		Price Range	
☐	44	Ring, diamond approx. 1.23 cts., platinum	4000.00	4400.00
☐	45	Ring, straight-row motif, diamonds, gold, c. 1876	800.00	1000.00
☐	46	Ring, straight-row motif, 8 diamonds, 18K gold, Victorian ..	2000.00	2400.00
☐	47	Earrings, flower motif, diamonds, 18K gold	1200.00	1400.00
☐	48	Pendant, flower motif, rose diamonds, platinum, Edwardian	3000.00	3400.00
☐	49	Clasp, diamonds, platinum, c. 1950s	1500.00	1800.00
☐	50	Charm, diamonds, ruby, sapphire, enamel, platinum, Contemporary	800.00	900.00

COLOR PLATE #8

☐	1	Brooch, Burma rubies, diamonds, Victorian	3200.00	3400.00
☐	2	Earrings, pear-shaped diamond approx. 2.59 cts., rubies	6600.00	7000.00
☐	3	Ring, straight-row motif, rubies, diamonds, 18K gold, Victorian	1500.00	1800.00
☐	4	Ring, straight-row motif, diamonds, rubies, 18K gold, Victorian	500.00	600.00
☐	5	Ring, straight-row motif, Burma rubies, 18K gold, Victorian	2400.00	2600.00
☐	6	Pendant/brooch, rubies, diamonds, Victorian	2800.00	3000.00
☐	7	Earrings, crescent motif, rubies, diamonds	650.00	800.00
☐	8	Ring, Burma ruby, diamonds, 18K gold, Victorian	3000.00	3400.00
☐	9	Ring, ruby, diamonds, 18K gold	1400.00	1600.00
☐	10	Ring, ruby, diamonds, platinum	2500.00	2800.00
☐	11	Brooch, bow motif, diamonds, Burma rubies, platinum, 18K gold, Edwardian	5500.00	6000.00
☐	12	Locket, heart motif, diamonds, ruby, Victorian	1800.00	2000.00
☐	13	Earrings, stud motif, Burma, diamonds, 18K gold, platinum, Edwardian	1500.00	1800.00
☐	14	Earrings, stud motif, Burma rubies, diamonds, natural pearls, platinum, Edwardian	4600.00	5000.00
☐	15	Brooch, Wisteria motif, Burma rubies, diamonds, platinum	4700.00	5000.00
☐	16	Ring, diamond approx. 3.13 cts., Burma rubies, platinum, Art Deco	14000.00	16000.00
☐	17	Earrings, diamonds, Burma rubies, platinum, Art Deco .	4800.00	5200.00
☐	18	Ring, ruby, diamonds, 18K gold, Edwardian	650.00	750.00
☐	19	Ring, half-hoop motif, rubies, diamonds, 18K gold	350.00	450.00
☐	20	Ring, ruby approx. 2.32 cts., diamonds, platinum	6600.00	6800.00
☐	21	Ring, Burma rubies, platinum, Art Deco	2200.00	2400.00
☐	22	Ring, diamond approx. .66 ct., rubies, 18K gold	1200.00	1400.00
☐	23	Bracelet, sapphire, diamonds, platinum, Edwardian	2700.00	3000.00
☐	24	Brooch, bow motif, diamonds, sapphires, 18K white gold ..	6000.00	8000.00
☐	25	Brooch, oval motif, sapphires, diamonds, platinum, Edwardian	7000.00	9000.00
☐	26	Ring, Ceylon sapphire, diamonds, 18K gold	2600.00	2800.00
☐	27	Ring, diamond, approx. 1.43 cts., sapphires, small diamonds, platinum	7500.00	8500.00
☐	28	Ring, sapphire, diamonds, platinum	1800.00	2000.00
☐	29	Ring, sapphire, diamonds, platinum	4200.00	4600.00
☐	30	Brooch, flower motif, diamonds, sapphires, platinum, maker: Cartier, c. 1950s	12000.00	14000.00
☐	31	Ring, triple cluster motif, sapphires, diamonds, platinum, 18K gold	2500.00	2800.00
☐	32	Earrings, Comet motif, sapphires, diamonds, platinum .	1500.00	1600.00
☐	33	Ring, sapphires, diamond, 18K gold	800.00	900.00
☐	34	Ring, triple cluster motif, sapphires, diamonds, platinum, 18K gold	1600.00	1800.00
☐	35	Ring, Ceylon sapphire, diamonds, 18K gold	10000.00	12000.00
☐	36	Earrings, sapphires, diamonds	1600.00	1800.00

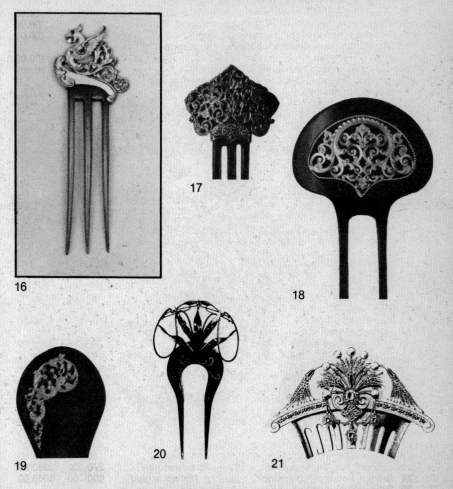

			Price Range	
☐	**16**	*Dragon motif, one diamond, one ruby, one pink sapphire, amber hair comb, gold, American, c. 1880*	600.00	650.00
☐	**17**	*Openwork motif, tortoise shell hair comb, gold, c. 1870*	450.00	475.00
☐	**18**	*Flower swirl motif, tortoise hair comb, gold, c. 1890-1900*	450.00	475.00
☐	**19**	*Flower swirl motif, tortoise hair ornament, gold, c. 1890-1900*	275.00	300.00
☐	**20**	*Flower motif, sterling silver, Art Nouveau, c. 1890*	225.00	250.00
☐	**21**	*Lotus flower motif, tortoise shell hair comb, rubies, sapphires, pearls, gold, maker: O. Weber, Hanau, Germany, c. 1860-80*	1100.00	1450.00

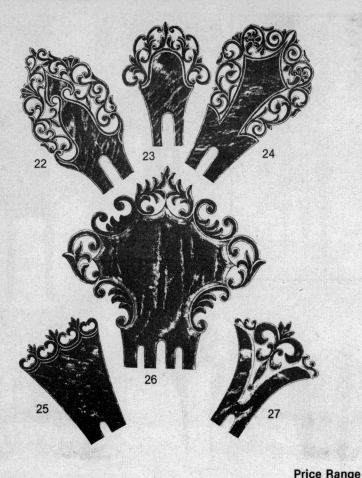

		Price Range	
☐ **22**	Openwork scroll motif, tortoise shell hair comb, American, c. 1896	90.00	100.00
☐ **23**	Openwork scroll motif, tortoise shell hair comb, American, c. 1896	75.00	90.00
☐ **24**	Openwork scroll motif, tortoise shell hair comb, American, c. 1896	90.00	100.00
☐ **25**	Openwork scroll motif, tortoise shell hair comb, American, c. 1896	75.00	90.00
☐ **26**	Openwork scroll motif, tortoise shell hair comb, American, c. 1896	125.00	150.00
☐ **27**	Openwork scroll motif, tortoise shell hair comb, American, c. 1896	75.00	90.00

28

29

30

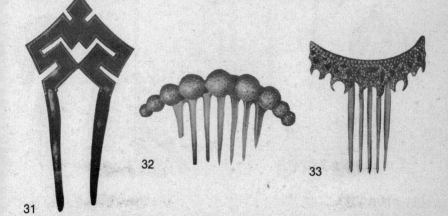
31

32

33

			Price Range	
☐	**28**	*Openwork flower motif, tortoise shell hair comb, sterling silver, American, c. 1896*	**135.00**	**160.00**
☐	**29**	*Openwork swirl motif, tortoise shell hair comb, sterling silver, American, c. 1896*	**135.00**	**160.00**
☐	**30**	*Oriental cloud motif rim, tortoise shell hair comb, seed pearls, gold, maker: Pickslay & Co., New York, c. 20th*	**300.00**	**325.00**
☐	**31**	*Geometric motif, piqué tortoise shell hair comb, gold, c. 1920-30*	**105.00**	**125.00**
☐	**32**	*Star and ball motif, blond tortoise shell hair comb, gold, c. 19th*	**105.00**	**125.00**
☐	**33**	*Cresent motif, blond tortoise shell hair comb, cut steel, c. 19th*	**135.00**	**175.00**

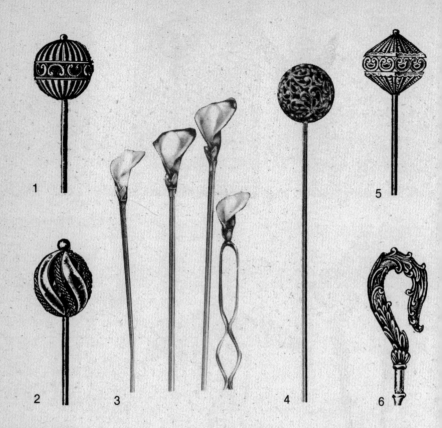

HAT PINS

			Price Range	
☐	**1**	*Ball cutout motif hatpin, 14K gold top, American, c. 1896*	75.00	90.00
☐		*Same as above but sterling silver top*	50.00	60.00
☐	**2**	*Ball cutout swirl motif hatpin, 14K gold top, American, c. 1896*	75.00	90.00
☐		*Same as above but sterling silver top*	50.00	60.00
☐	**3**	*Calla lily flower motif hatpins and hair pin, translucent white and green enamel, gold, Art Nouveau, c. 1910. Set*	550.00	650.00
☐	**4**	*Cutout sphere motif, gold top, American, c. 20th.*	110.00	175.00
☐	**5**	*Dome cutout motif hatpin, 14K gold top, American, c. 1896*	75.00	90.00
☐		*Same as above but sterling silver top*	50.00	60.00
☐	**6**	*Loop motif hatpin, 14K gold top, American, c. 1896*	60.00	80.00
☐		*Same as above but sterling silver top*	55.00	65.00

7   8

		Price Range	

7 *Shield motif hatpin, 14K gold top, American, c. 1896* **75.00 90.00**
  Same as above but sterling silver top **55.00 65.00**
8 *Snake motif, ruby head, mother-of-pearl, gold top, American* **175.00 200.00**

LOCKETS

1 *Baby locket, oval engraved, one round diamond, 14K gold, American, c. 1896* **125.00 140.00**
2 *Baby locket, oval engraved, 14K gold, American, c. 1896* **60.00 75.00**
  Same as above but gold filled **35.00 40.00**
3 *Baby locket, oval with half pearl, 14K gold, American, c. 1896* **50.00 75.00**
  Same as above but gold filled **35.00 40.00**

4   5   6   7

8   9   10

			Price Range	
☐	4	*Baby locket, square with one round diamond, 14K gold, American, c. 1896*	95.00	120.00
☐	5	*Baby locket, round engraved, one round diamond, 14K gold, American, c. 1896*	120.00	160.00
☐	6	*Baby locket, square engraved, one round diamond, 14K gold, American, c. 1896*	160.00	175.00
☐		*Same as above but gold filled and one round paste*	40.00	55.00
☐	7	*Baby locket, engraved, sterling, c. 1940*	30.00	35.00
☐	8	*Butterfly and grape vine motif, enamelled, rose diamonds, gold, c. late 19th.*...................	3300.00	3500.00
☐	9	*Enamel miniature portrait of a lady, diamonds, rubies, gold, c. 1900*	1650.00	2000.00
☐	10	*Enamel portrait of a masked lady, diamond in eye, gold, c. 1860*	650.00	750.00

11

12

13

14

15

		Price Range	
☐	**11** *Etruscan granulation frame, pearls, onyx cameo of a lady, 18K gold, American, c. 1880*	750.00	850.00
☐	**12** *Fleur-de-lys motif, pearl and diamonds in silver, opaque white and translucent green enamel, gold, c. late 19th.*	650.00	750.00
☐	**13** *Floral and geometric motif, alternating pink gold and platinum approx. 21 dwt*	500.00	600.00
☐	**14** *Floral motif, hair compartment turquoise, three color gold, c. late 19th*	700.00	950.00
☐	**15** *Floral and scenic engraved motif, 14K gold, American, c. 1896*	300.00	350.00
☐	*Same as above but gold filled*	100.00	125.00

16

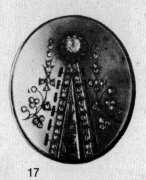

17

18

19

20

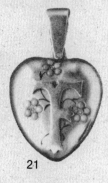

21

			Price Range	
☐	16	Flower basket motif, 57 round diamonds, three round rubies, gold, c. 19th.	3500.00	3950.00
☐	17	Flower and triangle motif, square-cut emeralds, one old mine diamond, rose diamonds, gold, c. 1860	1200.00	1450.00
☐	18	Geometric, motif, one diamond, square-cut rubies, gold, American, c. 1930	500.00	600.00
☐	19	Hair curl behind beveled glass, seed pearls and gold wire glued onto hair, gold frame, c. 1860	550.00	750.00
☐	20	Heart engraved floral, diamonds, gold	550.00	650.00
☐	21	Heart, floral and letter "F" motif, turquoise, flower rosettes, signed: JB, fitted leather box marked: John Brogden, Goldsmith, gold, c. 1860	1550.00	1750.00

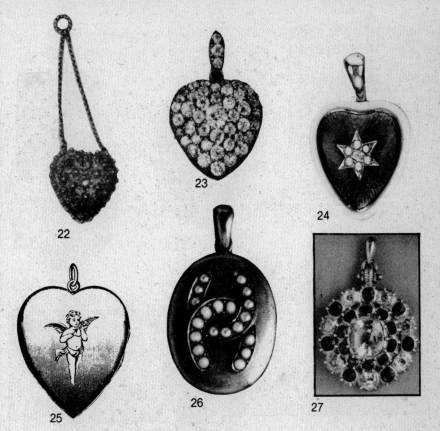

		Price Range	
☐	**22** *Heart motif, diamond, 22K gold, c. 1820*	**650.00**	**750.00**
☐	**23** *Heart motif, pave with 44 old mine diamonds approx. 3.0 cts., one old mine diamond approx. .50 ct., reverse: crystal locket, gold, c. late 19th*	**6300.00**	**7350.00**
☐	**24** *Heart motif, white enamel, blue guilloché enamel, seed pearls, one diamond, gold*	**600.00**	**700.00**
☐	**25** *Heart engraved angel motif, sterling, American, c. 1896*	**175.00**	**210.00**
☐	**26** *Horseshoe motif, pearls, turquoise, gold, c. 1870* .	**475.00**	**575.00**
☐	**27** *Indian, obverse: cushion-cut yellow sapphire in center, rubies, seven diamonds approx. 3.0 cts.; reverse: floral motif in blue, green, red and white opaque champlevé enamel, c. 19th*	**3500.00**	**3750.00**

28

30

31

29

29

Price Range

☐ **28** *Indian, obverse: rose diamond wreath with photo-*
graph portrait of Indian gentleman; reverse: Jaipur
blue, green, gold, red and white enamel of tiger,
gazelle and floral motif; gold, c. 19th. 750.00   900.00

☐ **29** *Intaglios, obverse: crest, reverse: initials, triple*
hinged frame inside, gold, c. late 19th. 900.00 1100.00

☐ **30** *Leaf motif, cabochon turquoise in center, gold,*
c. mid 19th. 1300.00 1550.00

☐ **31** *Leaf motif, sterling, English, c. late 19th.* 135.00   160.00

		Price Range	
☐	**32** Lion motif, one round diamond in mouth, emeralds in eyes, 14K gold, Art Nouveau, American, c. 1910	475.00	575.00
☐	**33** Medallion portrait of a lady and birds, 14K gold, Art Nouveau, c. 1900	475.00	575.00
☐	**34** Medallion portrait of a lady, 14K gold, Art Nouveau, c. 1890-1910	350.00	400.00
☐	**35** Medallion portrait of a lady, rose diamonds, slides to open, gold, Art Nouveau, maker: Diolot, c. 1890	2400.00	2650.00
☐	**36** Medallion repoussé portrait of a lady, diamonds, gold, Art Nouveau	500.00	600.00
☐	**37** Memorial motif, black and white enamel, gold filled, c. mid 19th.	140.00	175.00

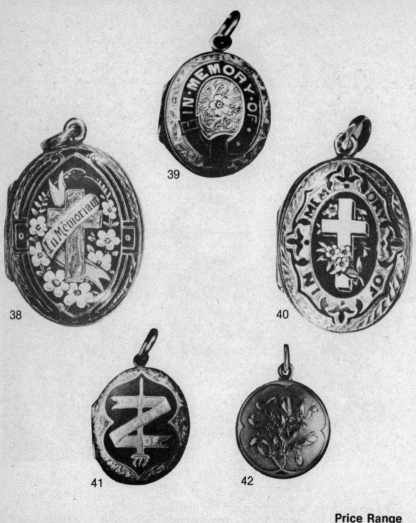

		Price Range	
☐	**38** Memorial motif, black and white enamel, gold front and back covers, gold filled locket, c. mid 19th......	175.00	225.00
☐	**39** Memorial motif, black and white enamel, gold front and back covers, gold filled locket, c. mid 19th...	150.00	175.00
☐	**40** Memorial motif, black and white enamel, gold, c. mid 19th....................................	300.00	325.00
☐	**41** Memorial motif, black and white enamel, gold filled, c. mid 19th.............................	135.00	150.00
☐	**42** Mistletoe motif, slides open, gold, c. early 20th. ..	475.00	575.00

43

44

47

46

45

			Price Range	
☐	43	*Mosaic beetle motif, 15K gold, c. 1860*	500.00	550.00
☐	44	*Octagonal wreath and ribbon motif, 14K green gold, c. 1930*	525.00	650.00
☐	45	*Open locket, seed pearl initials on woven hair, enamel, inscription around border: Forgive the wish that would have kept thee here, gold, c. 1790*	800.00	1000.00
☐	46	*Oval motif, 14K gold, c. late 19th to early 20th.*	300.00	400.00
☐	47	*Oval motif, Etruscan granulation, one seed pearl, gold, c. 1880*	1550.00	1750.00

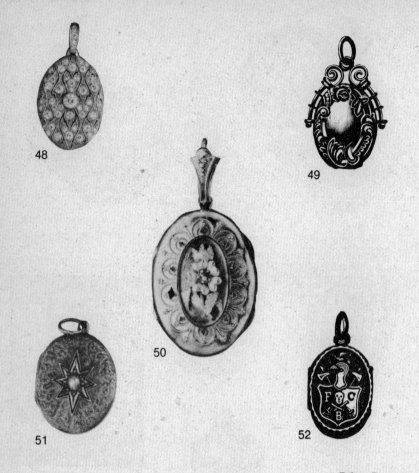

48

49

50

51

52

		Price Range	
☐	**48** Oval cutout motif, 55 round diamonds approx. 2.25 cts., platinum, signed: J.E.C. & Co., c. 1900	3750.00	3950.00
☐	**49** Oval engraved motif, 14K gold, American, c. 1896 .	300.00	350.00
☐	Same as above but gold filled	100.00	110.00
☐	**50** Oval and flower motif, green gold flower, yellow gold locket, Etruscan granulation, c. 1860	650.00	750.00
☐	**51** Oval and star motif, blue enamel, half pearl, 14K gold, c. late 19th.	475.00	525.00
☐	**52** Oval motif with Knights of Pythias insignia, enamelled, 14K gold, American, c. 1896	300.00	350.00
☐	Same as above but gold filled	100.00	110.00

53

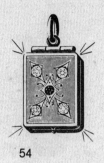

54

55

56

57

58

		Price Range	
☐	**53** Piqué, tortoise shell with gold rose, reverse: glass locket, 9K gold, maker: C & Co., Edinburgh, Scotland, c. 1947	250.00	300.00
☐	**54** Rectangular motif, one round ruby, four round diamonds, 14K gold, American, c. 1896	475.00	525.00
☐	Same as above but gold filled and glass stones	105.00	120.00
☐	**55** Rectangular motif, one round ruby, one round sapphire, two round diamonds, 14K gold, American, c. 1896	350.00	400.00
☐	Same as above but gold filled and glass stones	105.00	120.00
☐	**56** Rectangular engraved motif, 14K gold, American, c. 1896	150.00	175.00
☐	Same as above but gold filled	50.00	55.00
☐	**57** Rectangular engraved motif, one round diamond, 14K gold, American, c. 1896	375.00	425.00
☐	Same as above but gold filled and glass stone .	105.00	125.00
☐	**58** Rectangular floral motif, one round diamond, 14K gold, American, c. 1896	300.00	325.00
☐	Same as above but gold filled and glass stones	95.00	105.00

59

60

61

62

63

64

		Price Range	
☐	**59** Rectangular moon and star motif, one round emerald, seven round diamonds, 14K gold, American, c. 1896	475.00	525.00
☐	Same as above but gold filled and glass stones	105.00	125.00
☐	**60** Rectangular moon and star motif, six round diamonds, 14K gold, American, c. 1896	375.00	450.00
☐	Same as above but gold filled and glass stones	105.00	125.00
☐	**61** Round motif, interior two-sided glass hinged locket, gold, English, c. 1870	550.00	650.00
☐	**62** Round floral motif, 14K gold, American, c. 1896 ..	135.00	160.00
☐	Same as above but gold filled	40.00	50.00
☐	**63** Round floral motif, 14K gold, American, c. 1896 ..	150.00	175.00
☐	Same as above but gold filled	50.00	55.00
☐	**64** Round motif with a single initial, 14K gold, American, c. 1896	135.00	160.00
☐	Same as above but gold filled	40.00	50.00

65

67

69

66

68

70

			Price Range	
☐	**65**	*Shell motif, gold, English, c. 19th.*	325.00	375.00
☐	**66**	*Shield motif, Etruscan granulation, one old mine diamond, link chain, gold, c. 1860*	1850.00	2100.00
☐	**67**	*Shield motif, diamonds, sapphires, 14K gold, c. 19th.*...	700.00	950.00
☐	**68**	*Square motif, one round emerald, four round diamonds, 14K gold, American, c. 1896*	475.00	525.00
☐		*Same as above but gold filled and glass stone* .	105.00	125.00
☐	**69**	*Square motif with Masonic insignia, enamelled, 14K gold, American, c. 1896*	275.00	325.00
☐		*Same as above but gold filled*	95.00	105.00
☐	**70**	*Square engraved motif, one round diamond, 14K gold, American, c. 1896*......................	350.00	400.00
☐		*Same as above but gold filled and glass stone* .	105.00	125.00

71

72

73

74

75

76

				Price Range	
☐	**71**	Square engraved motif, 14K gold, American, c. 1896		**275.00**	**325.00**
☐		Same as above but gold filled		**125.00**	**140.00**
☐	**72**	Square floral motif, 14K gold, American, c. 1896 ..		**150.00**	**175.00**
☐		Same as above but gold filled		**50.00**	**55.00**
☐	**73**	Star motif, gold, c. 19th.		**375.00**	**425.00**
☐	**74**	Swirl motif, one round diamond, 14K gold, Art Nouveau, American, c. 1900		**450.00**	**550.00**
☐	**75**	Sword and leaf motif, round engraved, one round ruby, three round diamonds, 14K gold, American, c. 1896		**475.00**	**525.00**
☐		Same as above but gold filled and glass stones		**105.00**	**125.00**
☐	**76**	Wreath motif, round engraved, sterling, American, c. 1896		**75.00**	**90.00**

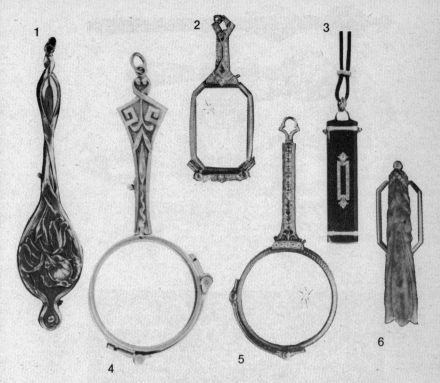

LORGNETTES

			Price Range	
☐	**1**	*Iris motif, 14K gold, Art Nouveau, American, c. 1910*	**900.00**	**1100.00**
☐	**2**	*Octagonal retractable lenses, numerous round diamonds, two trapezoid diamonds, platinum, c. 1925*	**3100.00**	**3500.00**
☐	**3**	*Rectangular retractable lenses, black and white enamel case, diamonds set in platinum, gold, c. 1925*	**950.00**	**1050.00**
☐	**4**	*Round retractable lenses, gold, Art Deco, American*	**375.00**	**450.00**
☐	**5**	*Round retractable lenses, 11 French-cut diamonds and five round diamonds approx. 1.75 cts., platinum, c. 1925*	**2400.00**	**3100.00**
☐		*Similar to above without diamonds, gold not platinum*	**650.00**	**900.00**
☐	**6**	*Octagonal retractable lenses, 15 round diamonds, leaf motif handle of carved jade, platinum, c. 1915*	**3500.00**	**4600.00**

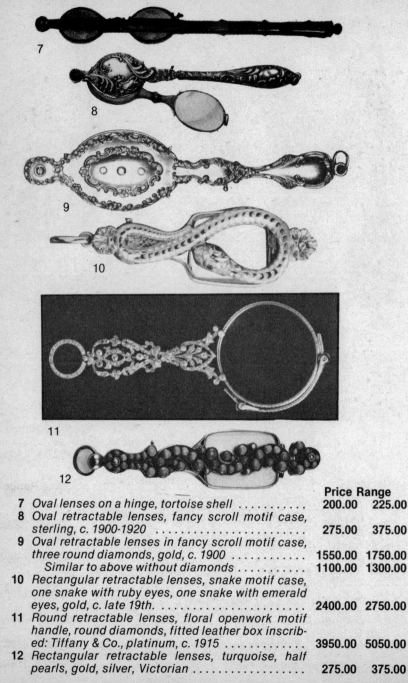

		Price Range	
☐	**7** *Oval lenses on a hinge, tortoise shell*	**200.00**	**225.00**
☐	**8** *Oval retractable lenses, fancy scroll motif case, sterling, c. 1900-1920*	**275.00**	**375.00**
☐	**9** *Oval retractable lenses in fancy scroll motif case, three round diamonds, gold, c. 1900*	**1550.00**	**1750.00**
☐	*Similar to above without diamonds*	**1100.00**	**1300.00**
☐	**10** *Rectangular retractable lenses, snake motif case, one snake with ruby eyes, one snake with emerald eyes, gold, c. late 19th.*	**2400.00**	**2750.00**
☐	**11** *Round retractable lenses, floral openwork motif handle, round diamonds, fitted leather box inscribed: Tiffany & Co., platinum, c. 1915*	**3950.00**	**5050.00**
☐	**12** *Rectangular retractable lenses, turquoise, half pearls, gold, silver, Victorian*	**275.00**	**375.00**

MINIATURES

MEMORIAL   Price Range

☐ **1** *Ivory miniature of a lady looking out to sea leaning on an anchor, painted, gold, brooch or pendant, c. 1790* 450.00   500.00

☐ **2** *Ivory miniature of a lady looking out to sea holding an anchor at gravesite, painted, gold, brooch or pendant, c. 1790* 500.00   600.00

☐ **3** *Ivory miniature of children weeping at urn, painted, gold, brooch or pendant, c. 1800* 525.00   575.00

☐ **4** *Ivory miniature of lovebirds and urn, painted, dissolved hair, inscribed: "His Hair I wear whose Friendship is Sincere," c. 1820, contemporary frame, 14K gold* 450.00   500.00

☐ **5** *Ivory miniature of two ladies and a child weeping at urn, rose gold, c. 1796* 1100.00 1550.00

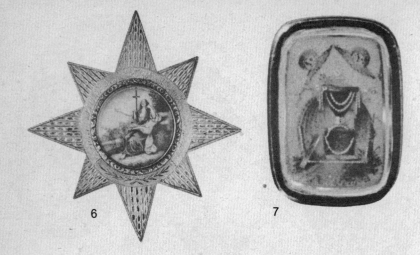

6   7

			Price Range	
☐	**6**	*Ivory miniature of religious scene, painted, star motif frame, silver, inscribed: Presented to P.G.L.M.G.E. Hawkes.June.for Meritorious services Sept. 1853," maker: MS, London, England, c. 1852*	375.00	450.00
☐	**7**	*Porcelain miniature of two angels with urn, painted, dissolved hair, gold wire, ivory cutout pieces, black enamel, gold, c. 1830*	275.00	325.00

1   2

PORTRAIT

☐	**1**	*Enamel miniature of a lady, pearls, gold, French, c. 1900*	1300.00	1450.00
☐	**2**	*Enamel miniature portrait of a Medieval warrior, nine round diamonds, American, 1.25 cts., pendant or brooch, gold, c. late 19th.*	3200.00	3500.00

3

5

6

4

7

			Price Range	
☐	3	*Enamel miniature portrait of a lady and a bunny, locket, gold, c. 1840*	900.00	1100.00
☐	4	*Enamel miniature portrait of a lady, 12 round diamonds, gold, c. 1870*	1750.00	2000.00
☐	5	*Enamel miniature portrait of a lady, 36 rose diamonds, gold, French, c. mid 19th.*	2400.00	2650.00
☐	6	*Enamel miniature portrait of a lady, round diamonds in border, 18K gold, Art Nouveau, signed: Gollay Fils & Stah, Geneve, c. 1890*	2400.00	2650.00
☐	7	*Enamel miniature portrait of a Turkish lady, rose diamonds in cloak, seed pearls, six old mine diamonds approx. .75 ct. in frame, gold, c. 1880*	1550.00	1750.00

8

9

10

11

12

			Price Range	
☐	**8**	*Ivory miniature portrait of a baby, reverse: woven hair locket, gold, English, c. 1900*	200.00	250.00
☐	**9**	*Ivory miniature portrait of a child, Swiss-cut sapphires set in silver backed gold, gold pendant, c. 1915*	1300.00	1550.00
☐	**10**	*Ivory miniature portrait of a child, black enamel frame, seed pearls, round diamonds, frame marked: BB&B (Bailey, Banks & Biddle), miniature signed: I. W. Curion Roma 1898*	600.00	700.00
☐	**11**	*Ivory miniature portrait probably of Dante, sterling, c. 1840*	500.00	550.00
☐	**12**	*Ivory miniature portrait of a gentleman, rose, green, white and yellow gold frame, miniature c. 1815-30, frame c. 1840*	700.00	950.00

			Price Range
☐	**13**	*Ivory miniature portrait of a lady by Richard Crosse, 1742-1810, 2⅝ in. high, half pearl and blue enamel ribbon frame, gold, fitted leather case, English*	27300.00 31500.00
☐	**14**	*Ivory miniature portrait of Owen Owen of Slynafon by John Bogle, 1746-1803, Scottish, 1½ in. high, half pearl border, gold, dated 1781*	1800.00 2050.00
☐	**15**	*Ivory miniature portrait of a gentleman by John Bogle, 1746-1803, 1½ in. high, pearl border, gold, fitted leather case, dated 177-*	2450.00 2700.00
☐	**16**	*Ivory miniature portrait of a child by John Bogle, 1746-1803, 2 in. high, reverse: urn motif and inscribed: Affection Weeps Heaven Rejoices, gold* .	8300.00 8700.00

17

18

19

20

Price Range

☐	**21**	Ivory miniature portrait of a lady by Gervase Spencer, 1⅝ in. high, gilt, English, dated 1759	**1750.00** **2100.00**
☐	**22**	Ivory miniature portrait of a wench by Samuel Finney, 1718/9-1798, 2 in. high, gold, English	**1300.00** **1550.00**
☐	**23**	Ivory miniature portrait of Lady Mary King Cooper by Gervase Spencer, gold, half pearl border, reverse: hair under glass, English, dated 1754	**1750.00** **2100.00**
☐	**24**	Ivory miniature portrait of a gentleman by John Downman, 1750-1824, 1¾ in. high, gold, English. One of a pair with following portrait. Pair	**2850.00** **3500.00**
☐	**25**	Ivory miniature portrait of a lady by John Downman, 1750-1824, 1¾ in. high, gold, English. One of a pair with above portrait. Pair	**2850.00** **3500.00**

26

27

28

29

30

			Price Range	
☐	**26**	*Ivory miniature portrait of a lady by Thomas Hull, 2¼ in. high, reverse: plaited hair, gold, English, c. 1775-1827*	3850.00	4000.00
☐	**27**	*Ivory miniature portrait of a gentleman by Samuel Rickards, 1735-1823, 1¼ in. high, gilt, English*	1300.00	1450.00
☐	**28**	*Ivory miniature portrait of a gentleman by R. B. de Chair, 1⅝ in. high, reverse: mother-of-pearl, gilt, English, dated 1783. One of a pair with above portrait. Pair*	1750.00	2100.00
☐	**29**	*Ivory miniature portrait of a gentleman by Peter Paillou, 2¾ in. high, reverse: plaited hair with "B" composed of seed pearls, gold, dated 1813*	1300.00	1550.00
☐	**30**	*Ivory miniature portrait of an infantry officer by Richard Bull, reverse: plaited hair with cutout "J N" and inscribed: "Born 30 June 1760", gold, dated 1787*	650.00	750.00

31

32

33

34

35

			Price Range	
☐	**31**	*Ivory miniature portrait of a gentleman by Thomas Richmond, Jr., 1802-74, 2⅜ in. high, gilt, English, dated 1822*	**700.00**	**950.00**
☐	**32**	*Ivory miniature portrait of a gentleman by William John Thomson, 1771/3-1845, 2⅜ in. high, gilt, dated 1800*	**550.00**	**750.00**
☐	**33**	*Ivory miniature portrait of a gentleman by Charles G. Dillon, 2⅞ in. high, gold, c. 1810-30*	**700.00**	**950.00**
☐	**34**	*Ivory miniature portrait of a lady by Abraham Daniel, 2 in. high, silver, c. 1806*	**1300.00**	**1650.00**
☐	**35**	*Ivory miniature portrait of a gentleman by Joseph Daniel, 1760-1803, 2¾ in. high, gold*	**1300.00**	**1650.00**

			Price Range	
☐	**36**	Ivory miniature portrait of a gentleman by J. T. Mitchell, 2⅞ in. high, gold, English, c. 1798-1830	900.00	1300.00
☐	**37**	Ivory miniature portrait of an officer by Abraham Daniel, 2¾ in. high, reverse: hair under glass, gilt, ivory cracked, c. 1806	600.00	700.00
☐	**38**	Ivory miniature portrait of a gentleman by John Barry, 2⅝ in. high, reverse: hair under glass with initials "JH," gold, c. 1784-1827	900.00	1050.00
☐	**39**	Ivory miniature portrait of an officer of the 2nd Dragoon Guards by J. Burman, 2⅝ in. high, gold, c. 1802	1300.00	1550.00
☐	**40**	Ivory miniature portrait of an officer of the 25th Bengal Native Infantry by Frederick Buck, 1771-1839/40, 2¾ in. high, reverse: plaited hair with "JW" composed of seed pearls, gold	1550.00	1750.00

41

42

43

44

45

			Price Range	
☐	**41**	Ivory miniature portrait of a lady, gold, signed: Pagan Bologna, c. 3rd quarter 19th.	450.00	500.00
☐	**42**	Ivory miniature portrait of a lady, round diamonds, seed pearls, gold, inscribed: Dec. 25, 1890	750.00	1000.00
☐	**43**	Ivory miniature of a lady, seed pearls, silver, c. 19th.	325.00	450.00
☐	**44**	Ivory miniature portrait of a mother and daughter, gold, c. 20th.	550.00	750.00
☐	**45**	Mother-of-pearl miniature portrait of a lady, seed pearls, gold, French, c. 1900	550.00	650.00

46

47

48

			Price Range	
☐	**46**	*Ivory miniature portrait of a lady, Etruscan granulation on frame, gold, c. 1860*	750.00	1000.00
☐	**47**	*Ivory miniature portrait of a lady by Kirkpatrick, pearls, gold*	725.00	850.00
☐	**48**	*Ivory miniature portrait of a lady, reverse: seed pearl and hair design, gold, English, c. late 19th...*	800.00	950.00

49

50

51

52

53

54

			Price Range	
☐	**49**	*Ivory miniature portrait of a lady, four seed pearls, c. late 19th.*	650.00	900.00
☐	**50**	*Ivory miniature portrait of a lady, pavé rose diamonds in gold frame, signed: "Henri/28 Moi/1887"*	1300.00	1550.00
☐	**51**	*Ivory miniature portrait of a lady, flower motif frame, gold, c. mid to late 19th.*	650.00	750.00
☐	**52**	*Porcelain miniature portrait of a lady, diamonds and seed pearls in frame, pendant or brooch, silver, Hungarian, c. late 19th.*	1000.00	1100.00
☐	**53**	*Porcelain miniature portrait of Empress Marie-Louise, metal frame, inscribed on reverse: "To Ella-Esther Cohen 1901"*	60.00	80.00
☐	**54**	*Vellum miniature portrait of a lady, paste, silver, signed on reverse: N. Ritter fecit Amsterdam 1774*	650.00	900.00

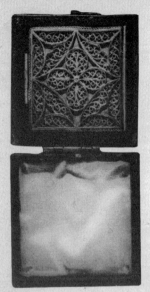

1

2

3

4

MISCELLANEOUS

		Price Range	
☐	**1** *Almanac miniature, silver filigree cover, fitted leather box, London, England, c. 1847*	475.00	500.00
☐	**2** *Bookmark, anchor, cross and heart in sterling silver, satin ribbon, 9 in. long, American, c. 1896*	75.00	90.00
☐	**3** *Box, faceted black onyx, moonstone on top and thumbpiece, rose diamonds, platinum, Art Deco, c. 1930*	2000.00	2200.00
☐	**4** *Box, blue guilloche enamel, red enamel, 18K gold, maker: Cartier*	1100.00	1300.00

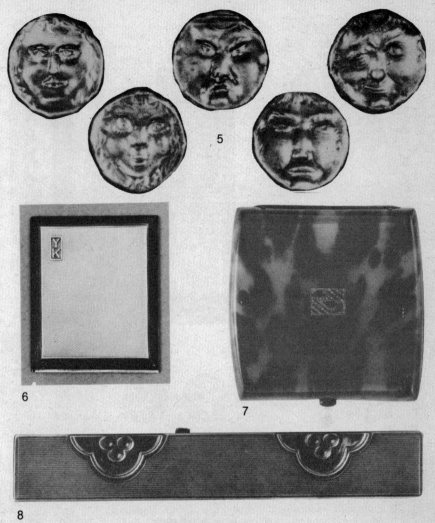

			Price Range	
☐	**5**	*Buttons, moon-face motif, silver*	150.00	200.00
☐	**6**	*Cigarette box, platinum monogram, four troy oz. of*		
		14K gold, maker: Asprey, London, c. 19th.	750.00	1000.00
☐	**7**	*Cigarette case, tortoise shell, marcasites*	375.00	450.00
☐	**8**	*Comb case, six cabochon sapphires in gold motif,*		
		sterling silver, Art Deco, c. 1935	600.00	700.00

9

11

10   12

		Price Range	
☐	**9** Compact, translucent blue enamel, engraved, cabochon sapphire thumb-piece, gold, maker: Cartier, c. 1900-20	1450.00	1650.00
☐	**10** Compact, geometric motif, one round diamond, four square sapphires, chain, gold, c. 1930	700.00	800.00
☐	**11** Diary, leather cover, finger shape, "De La Rue's Improved Condensed Diary and Engagement Book, edited by Edward Roberts, F.R.A.S., Chief Assistant at the 'Nautical Almanac' office," sterling silver holder made in Birmingham, England, registration number 320421, maker: HM, holder c. 1897, almanac c. 1899	325.00	350.00
☐	**12** Earring covers or opera caps, , black enamel, gold, c. 1850	500.00	550.00

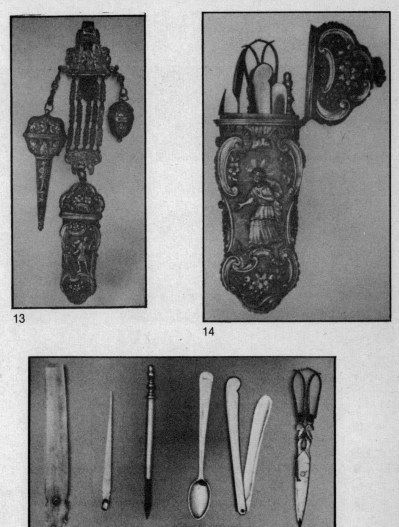

13

14

15

		Price Range	
☐	**13** *Etui with repoussé shield plaque, scissors case and thimble case, pinchbeck, c. 1780*	1750.00	1850.00
☐	**14** *Close-up of above opened etui.*	900.00	1100.00
☐	**15** *Implements from above etui consisting of strap for razor, combination ear cleaner cup and tooth-pick, pencil, snuff spoon, razor and scissors*		

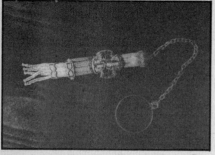

16

17

18

19

20

			Price Range	
☐	**16**	Handkerchief or dress train holder, woven mesh bracelet motif, one seed pearl, black enamel, gold, c. 1850	375.00	450.00
☐	**17**	Handkerchief or dress train holder, fan motif, gold, c. 1869	175.00	190.00
☐	**18**	Lipstick holder with ring attached to chain, spinach green nephrite, 14K gold, c. 1920	375.00	500.00
☐	**19**	Match safe, beaver motif lid, maple leaf motif container, obverse: shield for initials, reverse: Canadian crest, sterling silver, c. 1900	325.00	375.00
☐	**20**	Match safe, cigar cutter base, Art Nouveau engraved initials, sterling silver, c. 1910	200.00	250.00

		Price Range	
☐	**21** Match safe, clover motif of green marble, engraved case, silver, English, c. 1925	150.00	200.00
☐	**22** Match safe, horseshoe motif, coin silver, American, c. 1930	175.00	225.00
☐	**23** Match safe, star motif on plain case, one round diamond, 14K gold, American, c. 1920	550.00	750.00
☐	**24** Mirror sliding, diamond, opaque and translucent enamel, sterling silver, Art Nouveau	350.00	375.00
☐	**25** Minaudiere, geometric motif, three compartments with mirror and money clip, engraved, 11 round diamonds, 20 calibre sapphires, platinum corner, 18K gold, c. 1920	3100.00	3300.00
☐	**26** Minaudiere, geometric motif, engraved, champleve black and white enamel, diamond thumbpiece, gold, c. 1920-30	3300.00	3850.00

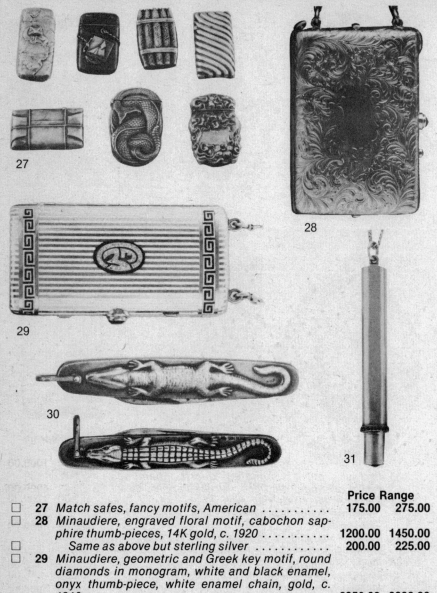

27

28

29

30

31

		Price Range	
☐	**27** *Match safes, fancy motifs, American*	175.00	275.00
☐	**28** *Minaudiere, engraved floral motif, cabochon sapphire thumb-pieces, 14K gold, c. 1920*	1200.00	1450.00
☐	*Same as above but sterling silver*	200.00	225.00
☐	**29** *Minaudiere, geometric and Greek key motif, round diamonds in monogram, white and black enamel, onyx thumb-piece, white enamel chain, gold, c. 1910*	2950.00	3300.00
☐	**30** *Pencil, rubies, curb link chain, 18K gold*	450.00	525.00
☐	**31** *Penknife, alligator motif, sterling silver, c. 1915* . .	175.00	200.00

		Price Range	
☐	**32** *Pill box, flower motif, mother-of-pearl top, colored stone flowers, rose diamond leaves, gold, c. 1900* .	950.00	1000.00
☐	**33** *Perfume bottle, nutilated quartz, diamonds, rubies, platinum, Art Deco, Cartier, Paris, c. 1930* .	3850.00	4200.00
☐	**34** *Perfume flask, carved moonstone face, purple guilloché enamel baton links with silver stars on chain, gold*	750.00	1000.00
☐	**35** *Perfume flask, faceted glass with red, blue and white designs, silver top with bust of a Negress, cabochon turquoise, rubies, c. early 19th*	650.00	900.00
☐	**36** *Perfume flask, red, blue and green guilloché enamel, gold, c. 1880*	750.00	1000.00
☐	**37** *Perfume flask, enamel, gold*	450.00	550.00

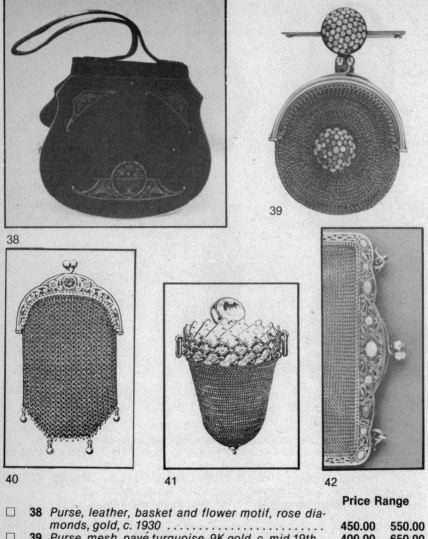

38

39

40

41

42

			Price Range	
☐	**38**	*Purse, leather, basket and flower motif, rose dia-monds, gold, c. 1930*	450.00	550.00
☐	**39**	*Purse, mesh, pavé turquoise, 9K gold, c. mid 19th.*	400.00	650.00
☐	**40**	*Purse, mesh, three round diamonds in openwork frame, 14K gold, c. 1903-04*	600.00	700.00
☐	**41**	*Purse, mesh, hinged expandable frame, 14K gold, c. 1903-04*	650.00	750.00
☐		*Same as above but sterling silver*	135.00	175.00
☐	**42**	*Purse, mesh, seven cabochon turquoise and four round diamonds in openwork ribbon motif frame, gold, Art Nouveau, maker: Black, Star and Frost, American, c. 1900*	3850.00	4400.00

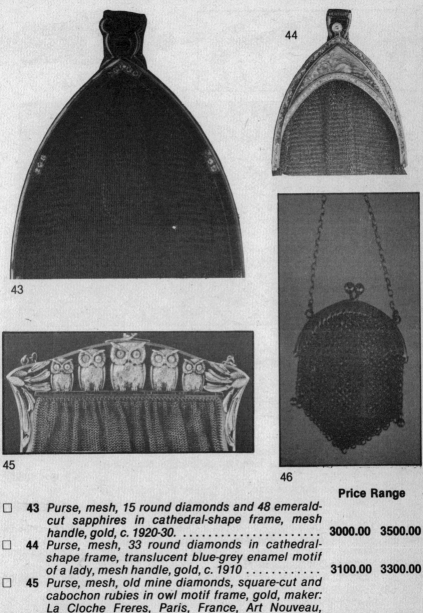

43

44

45

46

		Price Range	
☐	**43** Purse, mesh, 15 round diamonds and 48 emerald-cut sapphires in cathedral-shape frame, mesh handle, gold, c. 1920-30.	3000.00	3500.00
☐	**44** Purse, mesh, 33 round diamonds in cathedral-shape frame, translucent blue-grey enamel motif of a lady, mesh handle, gold, c. 1910	3100.00	3300.00
☐	**45** Purse, mesh, old mine diamonds, square-cut and cabochon rubies in owl motif frame, gold, maker: La Cloche Freres, Paris, France, Art Nouveau, c. 1890	25200.00	27300.00
☐	**46** Purse, mesh miniature, 9K gold, English, c. early 20th.	175.00	200.00
☐	Same as above but sterling silver	65.00	80.00

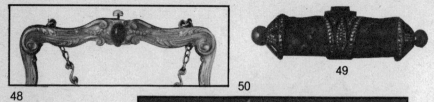

48

49

50

47

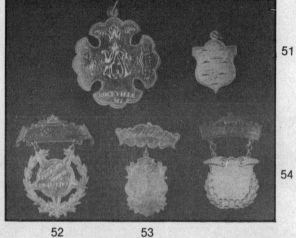

51

54

52   53

		Price Range	
☐ **47**	*Purse, mesh miniature, sterling silver, American, c. early 20th.*	**60.00**	**80.00**
☐ **48**	*Purse frame, scroll motif, moonstones, half pearls, round diamonds, orange tourmaline scarab, gold, maker: Spaulding & Co., Art Nouveau, c. 1902*	**2650.00**	**2850.00**
☐ **49**	*Purse handle, lapis lazuli, green onyx, cut steel, sterling silver, Art Deco, c. 1930*	**300.00**	**325.00**
☐ **50**	*School award, gold, pendant, Rockville, Maryland, American, c. 1900*	**95.00**	**105.00**
☐ **51**	*School award, obverse: "For regular attendance at Sunday School 1905 to 1920," reverse: "Presented to Dora E. Grimes by First Lutheran S.S. Dec. 25, 1919," gold, charm, American, c. 1920*	**50.00**	**55.00**
☐ **52**	*School award, obverse: "General Excellency, Green Street Junior High School," reverse: "Queen City Council No. 49 Jr. O.V.A.M.," gold, brooch, maker: Peters, American, c. 1900*	**100.00**	**125.00**
☐ **53**	*School award, obverse: "Blanche Schlichter, Presented by Prof. H. M. Bell May 7, 1901," gold, brooch, American, c. 1901*	**60.00**	**70.00**
☐ **54**	*School award, obverse: "C.E.L.S.S. Geo. E. Emmerich Regular Attendance 1902 1903 1904," reverse: "With approval of Miss Cora Wraver, Baltimore," gold, brooch, American, c. 1904*	**65.00**	**75.00**

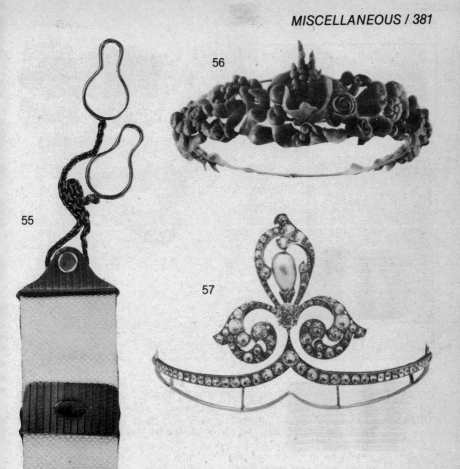

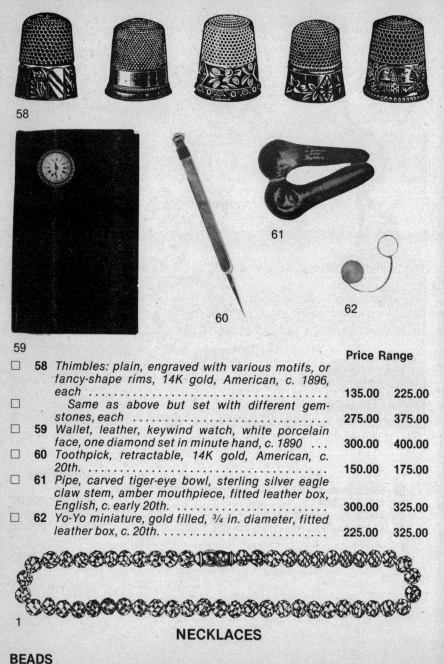

58

59

60

61

62

			Price Range	
☐	**58**	Thimbles: plain, engraved with various motifs, or fancy-shape rims, 14K gold, American, c. 1896, each	**135.00**	**225.00**
☐		Same as above but set with different gemstones, each	**275.00**	**375.00**
☐	**59**	Wallet, leather, keywind watch, white porcelain face, one diamond set in minute hand, c. 1890 . . .	**300.00**	**400.00**
☐	**60**	Toothpick, retractable, 14K gold, American, c. 20th.	**150.00**	**175.00**
☐	**61**	Pipe, carved tiger-eye bowl, sterling silver eagle claw stem, amber mouthpiece, fitted leather box, English, c. early 20th.	**300.00**	**325.00**
☐	**62**	Yo-Yo miniature, gold filled, ¾ in. diameter, fitted leather box, c. 20th.	**225.00**	**325.00**

1

NECKLACES

BEADS

☐	**1**	Amber, round faceted beads, screw clasp, c. 1896	**135.00**	**175.00**

			Price Range	
☐	**2**	*Amber, graduated oval faceted beads, screw clasp, c. 1896*	**175.00**	**200.00**
☐	**3**	*Art Deco, faceted black glass rectangles, oval faceted pastes, black metal mountings, 15 in. long, Czechoslovakian, c. 1920-30*	**55.00**	**65.00**
☐	**4**	*Art Deco, oval and round bittersweet amber colored plastic beads, 15½ in. long, c. 1920-30*	**35.00**	**45.00**
☐	**5**	*Art Deco, fancy shaped pumpkin, orange and amber colored plastic beads, 16½ in. long, c. 1920-30* .	**45.00**	**55.00**
☐	**6**	*Art Deco, round jade green ceramic beads spaced with white metal fancy links, 15½ in. long, c. 1920-30*	**45.00**	**55.00**

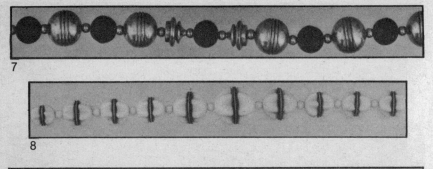

7

8

9

10

11

		Price Range	
☐	**7** *Art Deco, fancy shape aluminum and round black glass beads, 16½ in. long, c. 1920-30*	**150.00**	**175.00**
☐	**8** *Art Deco, fancy shape green and white plastic beads, 20 in. long, c. 1920-30*	**55.00**	**65.00**
☐	**9** *Art Deco, geometric motif, beige, apple green and white plastic beads, 17 in. long, c. 1920-30*	**45.00**	**55.00**
☐	**10** *Art Deco, three pendants of round pastes sandwiched between two round amber glass beads, chain of small cherry red plastic tubes, 22½ in. long, c. 1920-30*	**45.00**	**55.00**
☐	**11** *Banded black and white onyx beads, c. 19th.*	**475.00**	**525.00**

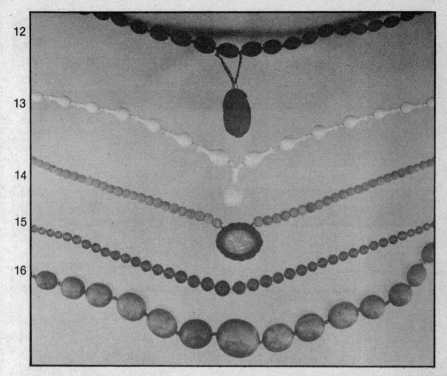

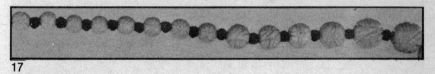

			Price Range	
☐	**12**	Carnelian beads with carved carnelian pendant, 28 in. long, c. early 20th.	**350.00**	**450.00**
☐	**13**	Ivory beads, 32 in. long, c. early 20th.	**400.00**	**500.00**
☐	**14**	Bone, carved beads and plaque, iron filigree frame, 16 in. long, German, c. 1814	**350.00**	**450.00**
☐	**15**	Amethyst, graduated faceted beads alternating with faceted crystal rondelles, 27 in. long, c. 20th. .	**225.00**	**325.00**
☐	**16**	Amber, egg-shape beads, 42 in. long, Russian, c. early 20th.	**500.00**	**600.00**
☐	**17**	Carved bone beads spaced with faceted jet beads, 25 in. long, c. early 20th.	**75.00**	**100.00**

18

19

20

21

22

23

			Price Range	
☐	18	Cherry amber oval beads, 19¾ in. long, c. early 20th.	135.00	175.00
☐	19	Coral beads, three strands, 20 in. long, interspersed with large coral beads surrounded by faceted crystal rondelles, 14K clasp, c. late 19th.	300.00	375.00
☐	20	Crystal, faceted round aqua beads, 24½ in. long, c. 1920-30	100.00	125.00
☐	21	Crystal, faceted round and rectangular clear beads, 23¾ in. long, c. 1920-30	135.00	175.00
☐	22	Crystal, faceted clear squares in sterling with fancy shape clear crystal pendant, 16¼ in. long, c. 1920-30	175.00	200.00
☐	23	Crystal, faceted round red beads alternating with clear crystal rondelles, 44 in. long, c. 1920-30	75.00	100.00

24

25

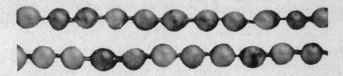

26

27

			Price Range	
☐	**24**	*Faceted beads, flower motif clasp, gold, c. 19th* ..	**750.00**	**1000.00**
☐	**25**	*Indian champlevé translucent red, green and blue enamel beads, gold, c. 19th.*	**1300.00**	**1550.00**
☐	**26**	*Jade beads spaced with carved carnelian beads, c. early 20th.*	**650.00**	**750.00**
☐	**27**	*Jade beads, 73 ranging from 6MM to 7MM, c. early 20th.*	**2200.00**	**2650.00**

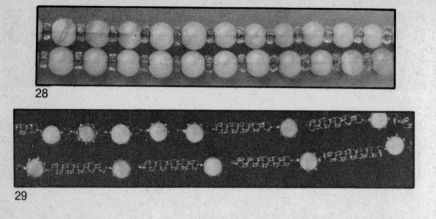

28

29

		Price Range	
☐	**28** Opal beads, 43 alternating with faceted crystal rondelles, opal bead clasp, c. 1890	1750.00	2000.00
☐	**29** Opal beads in silver, spaced with contemporary curb link chain, gold, c. 1820	1550.00	1750.00

1

CHOKERS

☐ **1** *Art Nouveau scroll links, lozenge-shape peridots, 54 old mine diamonds approx. 4.50 cts., forms two bracelets, maker: Harvey & Gore, English, c. late 19th.* 6800.00 7350.00

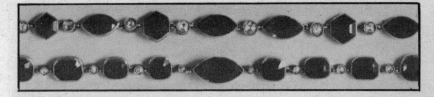

2

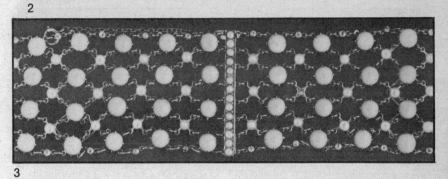

3

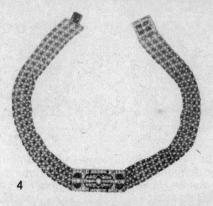

4

			Price Range	
☐	**2**	*Fire opal choker, 25 faceted marquise, emerald and hexagonal-shape fire opals alternating with rose diamonds*	3950.00	4400.00
☐	**3**	*Open mesh choker, round cabochon turquoise, button pearls, round diamonds, gold, forms two bracelets, c. 1895*	3950.00	4200.00
☐	**4**	*Seed pearl choker, 65 round diamonds in center panel, 38 round diamonds in clasp, platinum, maker: T.B. Starr, Inc.*	2850.00	3300.00

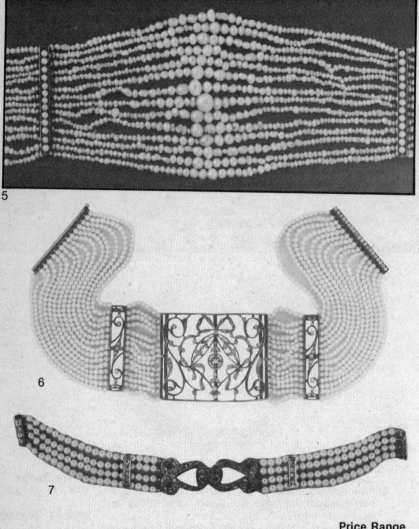

		Price Range	
☐	**5** Seed pearl choker, 14 strands, three gold bars with half pearls, c. 1900	1750.00	2000.00
☐	**6** Seed pearl choker, bow and ribbon motif, simulated diamonds	1100.00	1550.00
☐	**7** Seed pearl choker, diamonds, platinum	1200.00	1450.00

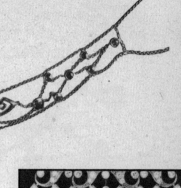

			Price Range	
☐	**8**	Sapphires, 14K gold, Art Nouveau, c. 1910	2750.00	3300.00
☐	**9**	Snake choker, snake link chain, ruby eyes, contemporary baroque pearl pendant, gold, c. 1870 . .	2000.00	2200.00
☐	**10**	Velvet ribbon choker with cut-out slide, 39 round diamonds, platinum, c. early 1870	1750.00	2000.00
☐	**11**	Velvet ribbon choker with cut-out slide and tassel, rose diamonds, one baroque pearl and 15 seed pearls, fitted leather box, platinum, English, c. 1900	2000.00	2200.00

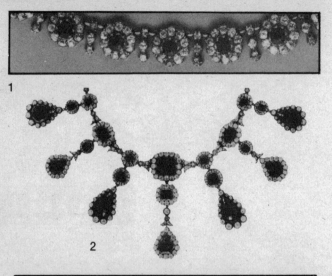

1

2

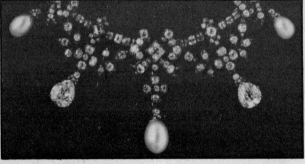

3

DIAMOND   **Price Range**

☐ **1** *Cluster motif, 24 clusters of old mine diamonds
surrounding one round blue sapphire per cluster,
three old mine diamonds between each cluster, a
total of 264 old mine diamonds approx. 14.75 cts.,
silver, gold, maker: Frazier & Haws, c. mid 19th.* ... 31500.00 35700.00

☐ **2** *Cluster motif, emeralds bordered by diamonds, c.
late 18th.* 57750.00 63000.00

☐ **3** *Flower and bow motif, seven pearl pendants, two
pear-shape diamonds approx. 5.25 cts., two
smaller pear-shape, 189 round and old mine diamonds approx. 19.50 cts., rose diamonds, silver,
gold, c. mid 19th.* 25200.00 27300.00

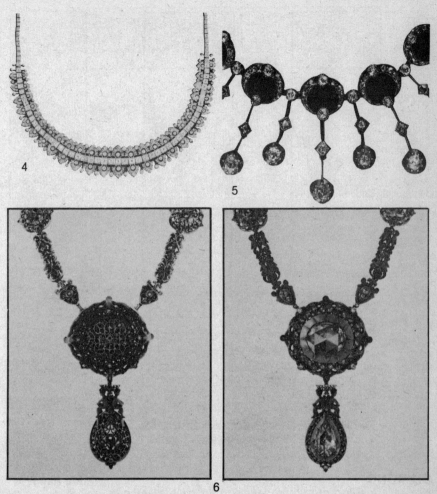

			Price Range	
☐	4	Crescent motif, rose diamonds, silver topped gold	6300.00	8400.00
☐	5	Flower motif, 92 European cut diamonds, 156 rose diamonds, total diamond weight approx. 18 cts., silver topped gold, c. mid 19th.................	10500.00	12600.00
☐	6	Renaissance motif, 21 clusters with large rose diamonds surrounded with round diamonds, translucent enamelled mermaids and angels, reverse: openwork and pierced, forms choker, brooch or pendant, 32 in. long, maker: Tiffany & Co., French, c. late 19th...........................	120500.00	136500.00

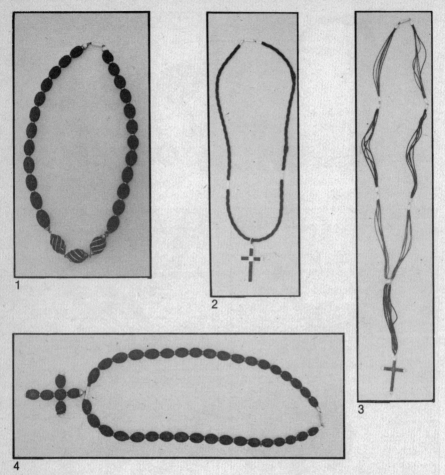

HAIR
All items made from hair referred to throughout this section are of brunette human hair unless stated otherwise.

			Price Range	
☐	**1**	*Ball motif chain, woven hair, gold fittings and barrel clasp, c. 1850-70*	**150.00**	**200.00**
☐	**2**	*Cross motif, woven and braided hair, gold fittings and barrel clasp, 17 in. long, c. 1850-70*	**175.00**	**200.00**
☐	**3**	*Cross motif, tightly woven chains of different brunette shades of hair, engraved gold fittings and barrel clasp, 22½ in. long, c. 1800-40*	**425.00**	**450.00**
☐	**4**	*Cross motif, wooden molds removed from woven hair to form ball motif chain, gold fittings and barrel clasp, 21 in. long, c. 1850-70*	**175.00**	**200.0⁰**

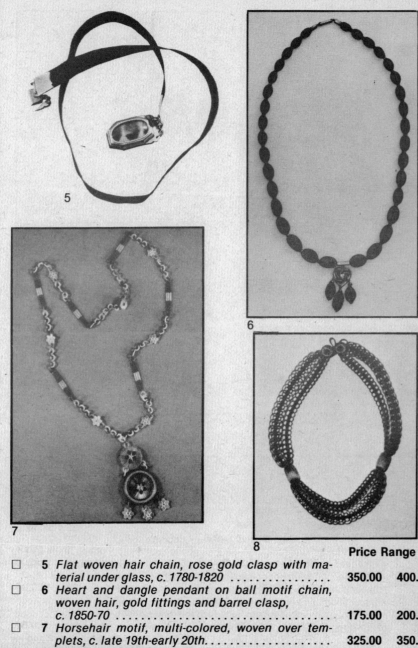

			Price Range	
☐	5	*Flat woven hair chain, rose gold clasp with material under glass, c. 1780-1820*	350.00	400.00
☐	6	*Heart and dangle pendant on ball motif chain, woven hair, gold fittings and barrel clasp, c. 1850-70*	175.00	200.00
☐	7	*Horsehair motif, multi-colored, woven over templets, c. late 19th-early 20th.*	325.00	350.00
☐	8	*Ribbon motif woven hair, two wooden bead connectors covered with hair, c. 1840-60*	200.00	225.00

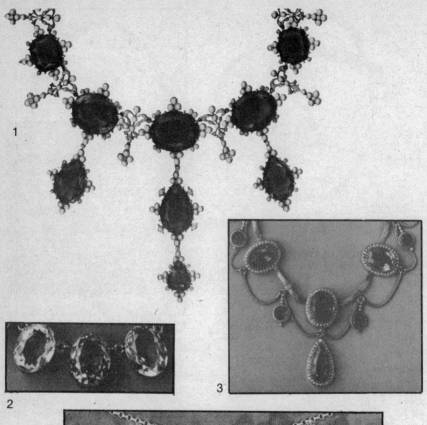

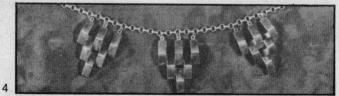

MISCELLANEOUS

Price Range

- [ ] **1** *Amethyst, half seed pearls, rose diamonds, gold, c. 3rd quarter 19th.* 6300.00 8400.00
- [ ] **2** *Amethyst necklace, oval amethysts, gold, c. 1860* 1550.00 1650.00
- [ ] **3** *Amethyst necklace, cushion-cut amethysts surrounded by seed pearls, one pear-shape amethyst surrounded by seed pearls and small round amethyst drops, foxtail chain, gold, fitted leather box inscribed: D. Sapio, Nice, France, hallmarks, c. 1830* 5250.00 5750.00
- [ ] **4** *Art Deco triple pendant necklace, 14K gold, American, c. 1930* 900.00 11000.00

			Price Range	
☐	**5**	*Bacchantes and grape cluster motif, carved coral, gold, c. 1860*	3300.00	3950.00
☐	**6**	*Bird and flower motif, 26 openwork panels in green, yellow and rose gold, maker: Tiffany, New York, c. 1875*	27300.00	29400.00
☐	**7**	*Black onyx carved rectangular links alternating with gold link chain, shield motif medallion with seed pearl buckle, c. 1880*	1200.00	1400.00

8

10

9

11

			Price Range	
☐	**8**	*Black opal, baroque pearl, gold, Art Nouveau*	**1100.00**	**1200.00**
☐	**9**	*Bow motif, round and rose diamonds, cabochon turquoise, gold*	**1100.00**	**1300.00**
☐	**10**	*Cabochon rubies, diamonds, enamel oblong beads, 18K gold, American, c. 1890*	**750.00**	**900.00**
☐	**11**	*Cabochon garnets, seed pearls, snake motif chain, gold, c. 1865*	**1100.00**	**1300.00**

13

12

14

		Price Range	
12	*Cameo of Greek Warrior, lapis lazuli, gold, marked: Bell*	650.00	750.00
13	*Cameos, coral, agates, gold, approx. 15 in., c. 19th.*	2400.00	2650.00
14	*Carnelian plaque motif, seed pearls, cabochon carnelians in square links, gold, English, c. 1830* .	3750.00	3950.00

15

16

19

18

17

20

			Price Range	
☐	**15**	*Citrine pear-shape pendants dangling from three plaques, ten fancy-cut peridots and six round diamonds in center plaque, fancy link chains spaced with baroque pearls, 18K gold, c. late 19th.*	3850.00	4300.00
☐	**16**	*Chrysoberyl alternating with pink topaz, gold, fitted case marked: Liberty & Co. Ltd., English, Victorian*	1100.00	1550.00
☐	**17**	*Coral cameos, gold, c. 1865*	2200.00	2650.00
☐	**18**	*Cross motif, old mine diamonds pavé set, green guilloché enamel, locket with glass reverse, fancy link chain*	3950.00	4400.00
☐	**19**	*Dove motif, pearls, peridot, two color, 14K gold, marked: B + W, Victorian*	600.00	700.00
☐	**20**	*Emeralds, buff-top emeralds, table-cut diamonds, baroque pearls, champleve enamelled red flowers with green and white background on the reverse of the links, gold, Indian, c. 19th.*	7050.00	8100.00
☐		*Same as above, along with similar ear pendants in fitted leather box*	7350.00	8400.00

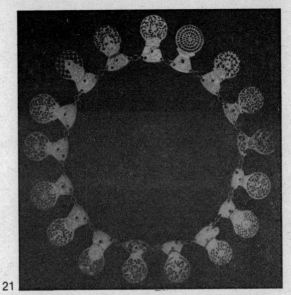

21

22

Price Range

☐ **21** *Escapement cover motif, known as watchcocks, from verge watches, c. late 18th, assembled as necklace c. late 19th, hand-engraved and pierced with animals and designs, metal, English* 425.00 525.00

☐ **22** *Festoon motif, amethyst, seed and fresh water pearls, gold, Art Nouveau* 900.00 1100.00

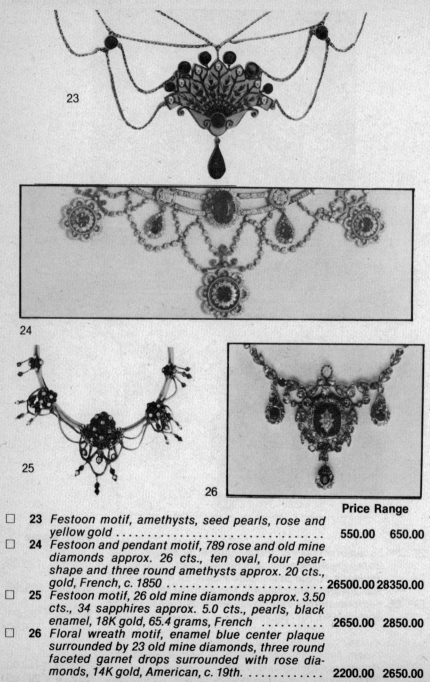

23

24

25

26

		Price Range	
☐ **23**	Festoon motif, amethysts, seed pearls, rose and yellow gold	550.00	650.00
☐ **24**	Festoon and pendant motif, 789 rose and old mine diamonds approx. 26 cts., ten oval, four pear-shape and three round amethysts approx. 20 cts., gold, French, c. 1850	26500.00	28350.00
☐ **25**	Festoon motif, 26 old mine diamonds approx. 3.50 cts., 34 sapphires approx. 5.0 cts., pearls, black enamel, 18K gold, 65.4 grams, French	2650.00	2850.00
☐ **26**	Floral wreath motif, enamel blue center plaque surrounded by 23 old mine diamonds, three round faceted garnet drops surrounded with rose diamonds, 14K gold, American, c. 19th.	2200.00	2650.00

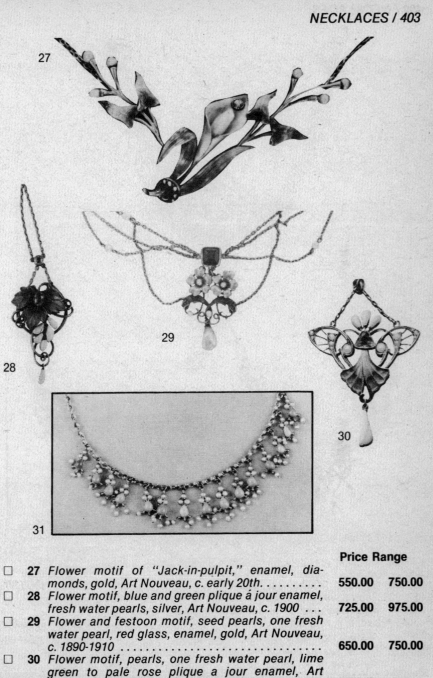

		Price Range	
☐	**27** *Flower motif of "Jack-in-pulpit," enamel, diamonds, gold, Art Nouveau, c. early 20th.*	550.00	750.00
☐	**28** *Flower motif, blue and green plique á jour enamel, fresh water pearls, silver, Art Nouveau, c. 1900* . . .	725.00	975.00
☐	**29** *Flower and festoon motif, seed pearls, one fresh water pearl, red glass, enamel, gold, Art Nouveau, c. 1890-1910*	650.00	750.00
☐	**30** *Flower motif, pearls, one fresh water pearl, lime green to pale rose plique a jour enamel, Art Nouveau, "900" silver, French*	1200.00	1450.00
☐	**31** *Fringe motif, turquoise, pearls, gold*	650.00	900.00

32

33

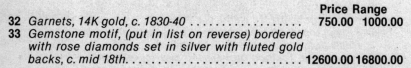

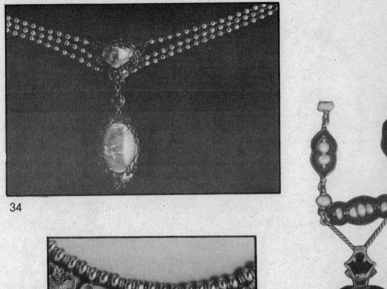

34

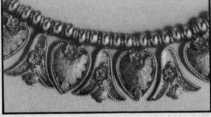

36

35

		Price Range
☐	**34** Grape cluster and vine motif, enamelled, black opals, sapphires and demantoid garnets in center pendant and necklace, gold bead chains, gold, Arts and Crafts style, signed: Tiffany & Co.,, American, c. late 19th.	44100.00 48300.00
☐	**35** Heart motif, blue enamel, five rose diamonds around one half-pearl, gold chain spaced with pearls and three blue enamel modified oval frames around pearls, c. mid 19th.	3750.00 4400.00
☐	**36** Heart and flower motif links on gold bead necklace, double-heart clasp, c. 1850	4200.00 4600.00

37

·39

38

		Price Range	
☐	**37** Ivory medallion and curved links, silver, Chinese, c. 1900-20	350.00	475.00
☐	**38** Jade, seven pierced and carved oval medallions separated by rose diamonds in oval scroll motif links, white gold, c. early 20th.	4200.00	4400.00
☐	**39** Japanese motif locket, book link chain, silver, maker: S. Bros., Birmingham, England, c. 1883 ...	450.00	500.00

40

41

42

			Price Range	
☐	**40**	*Juggling pin motif, 41 graduated juggling pin shaped pendants, gold, c. late 19th.*	1750.00	2000.00
☐	**41**	*Ladies and birds motif, carved coral, teardrop pendants, floral motif links, gold, c. 1860*	2850.00	3100.00
☐	**42**	*Lady with dragonfly wing motif, green and blue plique-a-jour wings with one calibre sapphire surrounded by rose diamonds, one Holland-rose diamond set in hair of lady, 11 calibre sapphires in tail, two baroque pearls, opaque enamelled cattails, detachable pin and chain, gold, Art Nouveau, c. late 19th.*	25200.00	29400.00

43

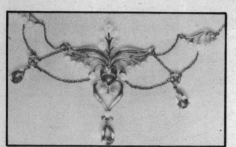

44

45

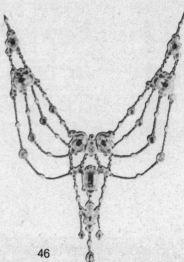

46

		Price Range	
☐	**43** *Leaf motif, oval faceted amethysts, 14K gold, American, c. 1900*	1650.00	1850.00
☐	*Same as above, along with similar bracelet and earrings*	3100.00	3750.00
☐	**44** *Leaf and heart motif, one heart-shape and one pear-shape peridot with baroque pearls set in center, two round and one pear-shape peridot with baroque pearls on either side of center, 14K gold, American, c. 1900*	975.00	1075.00
☐	**45** *Leaf and swirl motif, translucent green and yellow enamel, one oval and two round faceted peridots, one large baroque pearl suspended from center, smaller baroque pearls spaced in chain, 14K gold, Art Nouveau, American, c. 1890-1910*	750.00	975.00
☐	**46** *Leaf motif, peridots, seed pearls, citrines, green enamel, 18K gold, Art Nouveau*	2200.00	2400.00

47

48

49

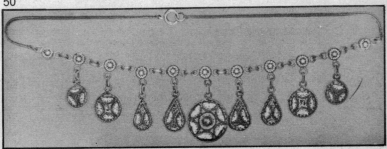

50

			Price Range	
☐	**47**	*Micro mosaic of two angels with blue enamel border and seed pearls c. 18th, scroll motif necklace with seed pearls, gold, c. 19th.*	4850.00	5300.00
☐	**48**	*Moonstones, oval cabochon moonstones in pendant and spaced in chain, round sapphires surrounding pendant and spaced in chain, white gold, signed: Tiffany & Co., American, c. early 20th.*	4400.00	4600.00
☐	**49**	*Mosaic beetle motif, silver gilt, c. early 20th.*	300.00	375.00
☐	**50**	*Mosaic motif, oval and pear-shape pendants, foxtail chain, gold-plated metal, Italian, c. mid 20th.*	200.00	350.00

51

52

Price Range

☐ **51** *Mosaic swans, flowers and classical head motif,*
18K gold, Italian, c. 1850-60 .... 27300.00 29400.00
☐ **52** *Onyx bead and plaque motif, seed pearls, gold,*
c. 1850 .... 1450.00 1550.00

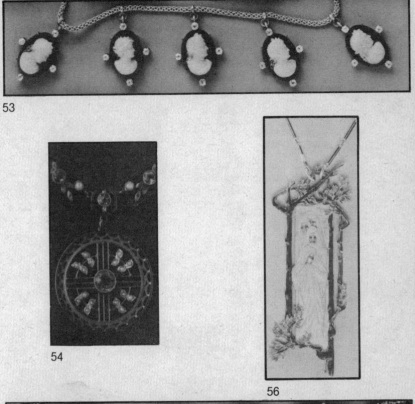

53

54

56

55

		Price Range	
☐	**53** Onyx cameos of 12 Roman Senators, 48 round diamonds approx. 2.50 cts., gold, c. 1870	6500.00	6900.00
☐	**54** Openwork flower motif, one round peridot in each link and pendant, seed pearls, gold, c. 1915	1750.00	2000.00
☐	**55** Pink topaz necklace, fancy scroll motif links, each with one oval foil-back pink topaz, c. 1810	2400.00	2650.00
☐	**56** Priestess motif, green and blue enamel, bar link chain, gold, 3¾ in. long, Art Nouveau, maker: Rene Lalique, French, c. late 19th.	38850.00	44100.00

57

59

60

58

		Price Range	
☐ **57**	Rock crystal carved discs alternating with carnelian carved discs, gold links, c. 1920	750.00	1000.00
☐ **58**	Ram's head motif, sapphires, pearls, foxtail link chain, c. 19th.	1100.00	1300.00
☐ **59**	Rosette motif, garnets, gold, c. mid 19th.	1100.00	1300.00
☐ **60**	Rosette motif, seven cabochon turquoise rosettes, gold, forms pair of bracelets, gold, c. 1840	2200.00	2400.00

61

62

63

64

65

			Price Range	
☐	**61**	Sapphires, four cabochon sapphires surrounded with seed pearls, four half-pearls in center pendant, white gold, c. 19th.	2850.00	3850.00
☐	**62**	Satsuma medallions depicting birds, flowers and butterflies, each link marked "FS," white metal, Oriental, c. 19th.	750.00	1000.00
☐	**63**	Scalloped cut-out links, painted porcelain cherub plaque, diamonds, pearl, French, c. 1870	3100.00	3300.00
☐	**64**	Scarabs made from dried green beetles, yellow metal, English, Victorian	225.00	275.00
☐	**65**	Scotch agate, various colors, 15K gold mounts, English, c. 1860	700.00	950.00

66

67

68

			Price Range	
☐	**66**	*Shell broad collar motif, whole and cut shells, brass beads, hand-knotted with silk thread, Pacific Islands, c. early 20th*	200.00	300.00
☐	**67**	*Shell motif, pink and green enamel, seed pearls, gold, Victorian*	3100.00	3300.00
☐	**68**	*Simulated sapphires, half pearls, seed pearls, silver gilt, Austro-Hungarian marks, c. 3rd quarter 19th.*	550.00	750.00

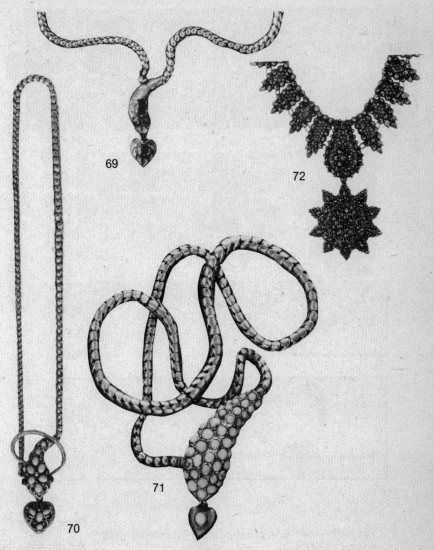

		Price Range	
☐	**69** Snake motif, oval-cut garnet in head with cabo-chon garnet eyes, square-cut garnet in heart pen-dant, scale link chain, c. 1840	1650.00	2200.00
☐	**70** Snake and heart motif, turquoise, gold, c. 1840 ...	1550.00	2000.00
☐	**71** Snake motif, pavé turquoise, rose diamond eyes, gold, c. 1840-60	1300.00	1550.00
☐	**72** Star motif, Bohemian garnets, pendant removable as brooch, c. mid-late 19th....................	1300.00	1550.00

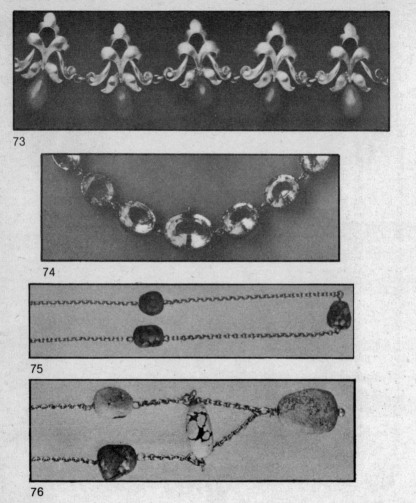

73

74

75

76

		Price Range	
☐	**73** Teardrop motif, corals suspended from fancy gold links, c. 1900	750.00	1000.00
☐	**74** Topaz, 30 graduated topaz, collet-set, gold, c. 1860	2750.00	2950.00
☐	**75** Turquoise baroque beads, 9K gold, English, c. 20th	300.00	375.00
☐	**76** Turquoise baroque beads, 18K gold, English, c. 20th	375.00	450.00

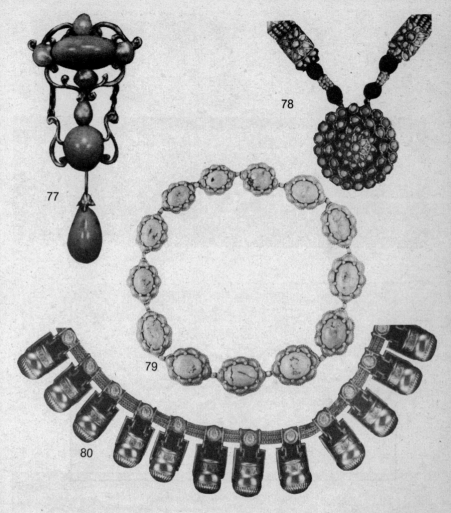

			Price Range	
☐	**77**	*Turquoise, baroque pearls, gold, Art Nouveau, c. 1900*	275.00	350.00
☐	**78**	*Turquoise in medallion pendant and in square links forming necklace, Jaipur enamelled sides and backs to square links spaced with five seed pearl chains, gold over bead frame, Indian, c. 19th.......*	3300.00	3400.00
☐	**79**	*Turquoise cabochon links set with eight diamonds, collet-set, one diamond collet-set between each link, 18K gold, signed: Nannini*	2000.00	2400.00
☐	**80**	*Urn motif, mesh chain, gold, c. 3rd quarter 19th.* ..	900.00	1100.00

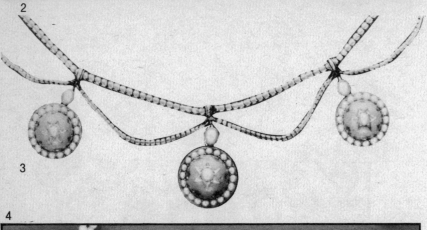

PEARLS

				Price Range	
☐	**1**	Ball motif, five strands of seed pearls, green stones, gold clasp		**750.00**	**1000.00**
☐	**2**	Crescent and flower links, seed pearls, rope twist chain, gold, c. 1850		**1000.00**	**1200.00**
☐	**3**	Dome and festoon motif, black enamel, half seed pearls, gold, c. 1850		**1100.00**	**1550.00**
☐	**4**	Emerald drop and emerald beads with button-shape pearls spaced on 2.0MM seed pearl strands, gold, c. 1920		**3100.00**	**3750.00**

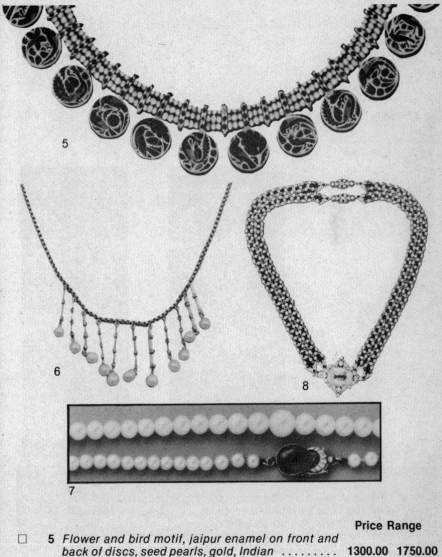

			Price Range	
☐	5	Flower and bird motif, jaipur enamel on front and back of discs, seed pearls, gold, Indian	1300.00	1750.00
☐	6	Fringe motif, rose diamonds collet-set, pearls, gold, Victorian	1100.00	1300.00
☐	7	Graduated 98 cultured pearls from 4.0MM to 8.0MM, pear-shape jade in clasp, 14K gold, c. 1930	425.00	550.00
☐	8	Lattice work motif, seed pearls, yellow sapphire, diamonds, platinum, Edwardian	3950.00	4400.00

			Price Range	
☐	**9**	*Lattice work seed pearl chain, pierced and carved jade, diamonds, platinum, Art Deco*	5900.00	6100.00
☐	**10**	*Natural pearls, turquoise, gold*	900.00	1100.00
☐	**11**	*Openwork pendant with one small round diamond and a fresh water pearl drop attached to a double link chain spaced with seed pearls, Art Nouveau motif circle, gold, c. 1900*	550.00	650.00
☐	**12**	*Ribbon motif woven seed pearl necklace, gold clasp, c. 1870*	900.00	1100.00

13

14

15

			Price Range	
☐	**13**	Single strand motif, 96 graduated natural pearls, eight old mine diamonds approx. .75 ct. set in clasp, silver topped gold, c. 19th.	2750.00	3300.00
☐	**14**	Star and flower motif, pavé seed pearls, seed pearl link chain, one pendant or brooch with detachable pin, English, 15K gold, c. 1870-80	1450.00	1650.00
☐	**15**	Tassels of seed pearls, 14 strands of seed pearls, rose diamonds, colored stones, silver	4200.00	4850.00

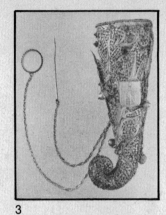
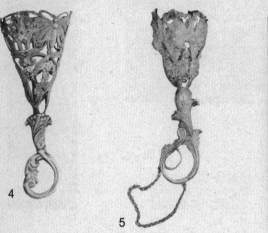

NOSEGAY HOLDERS

			Price Range	
☐	**1**	*Filigree circle motif, miniature converted to pin, silver, c. 19th.*	100.00	125.00
☐	**2**	*Filigree fish motif handle, silver, c. 19th.*	750.00	800.00
☐	**3**	*Filigree oak leaf and acorn motif, shield with crest, silver, c. 19th.*	550.00	600.00
☐	**4**	*Cutout butterfly motif, silver, c. 19th.*	325.00	375.00
☐	**5**	*Cutout grape leaf motif, silver, c. 19th.*	325.00	375.00
☐	**6**	*Cutout motif, two round amethysts, carved mother-of-pearl handle, 18K gold, c. 19th.*	1750.00	2000.00

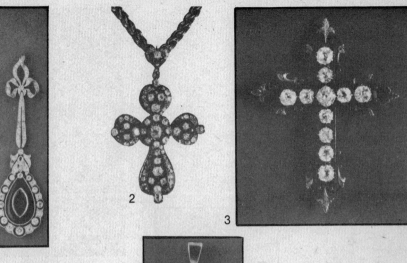

PENDANTS

DIAMOND		Price Range

☐ **1** *Black onyx center border, missing marquise-shape diamond center, round diamonds, platinum, c. 1900* 2850.00 3100.00

☐ **2** *Cross, 95 round diamonds approx. 10.0 cts., fancy link chain, gold, c. 1850* 9950.00 12050.00

☐ **3** *Cross, 11 old mine diamonds approx. 11.0 cts., gold, pendant or brooch, c. 1870* 8950.00 11000.00

☐ **4** *Cross, 11 foil-back rose diamonds, gold, c. 1840* .. 475.00 525.00

☐ **5** *Cross, one oval sapphire, 39 old mine diamonds approx. 2.0 cts., silver, gold, c. 1840* 2200.00 2400.00

☐ **6** *Cultured pearl center, openwork motif, 13 rose diamonds in leaf design, 36 round diamonds set around pearl and border, platinum, c. 1900* 1900.00 2050.00

7

8

9

10

11

			Price Range	
☐	**7**	*Double straight line drop motif, seven round diamonds approx. 1.50 cts., two simulated pearls, platinum, c. 1915*	1550.00	1750.00
☐	**8**	*Dove with laurel branch and star motif, 106 round diamonds approx. 6.0 cts., gold, c. 1860*	4950.00	5200.00
☐	**9**	*Flower motif, rose diamonds, gold, c. late 18th. ...*	475.00	525.00
☐	**10**	*Geometric motif, nine bagette diamonds, one marquise-shape diamond, 28 round diamonds, all approx. .75 ct., coral or jade beads, platinum, clip or pendant, Art Deco, c. 1930*	1900.00	2100.00
☐	**11**	*Leaf motif, old mine diamonds, silver topped gold, detachable pin fitting, English, c. 1840*	2000.00	2200.00

12

13

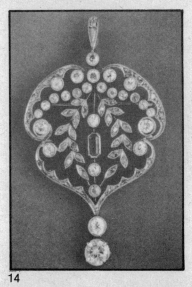

14

15

Price Range

☐ **12** *Openwork flower motif, 201 round diamonds, two marquise-shape diamonds, all approx. 3.50 cts., platinum, brooch or pendant, c. 1900* 3300.00 4400.00

☐ **13** *Openwork leaf motif, two old mine diamonds approx. 2.40 cts., 102 small old mine diamonds, gold, platinum, brooch or pendant, c. 1900* 9450.00 11550.00

☐ **14** *Openwork leaf motif, 27 round diamonds approx. 2.40 cts., one emerald-cut emerald, pendant or brooch, gold, platinum, c. 1910* 4200.00 4400.00

☐ **15** *Openwork leaf motif, four marquise-shape and 136 round diamonds approx. 3.0 cts., platinum, c. 1910* 7350.00 8400.00

16

17

18

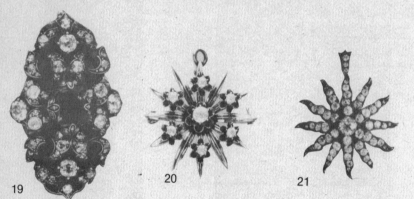

19

20

21

			Price Range	
☐	**16**	*Ribbon motif, 28 round diamonds approx. 1.10 cts., pendant or brooch, gold, c. 1900*	1650.00	1850.00
☐	**17**	*Scroll motif, 31 round diamonds, platinum, c. 1900* .	750.00	1000.00
☐	**18**	*Scroll motif, two pear-shape sapphires, two diamonds approx. .40 ct. each, 16 round diamonds, white gold backed yellow gold, 14K white gold chain*	800.00	1025.00
☐	**19**	*Shield motif, scissor-cut emerald approx. 2.75 cts. in center, four old mine diamonds approx. 3.75 cts., 30 rose diamonds, gold topped silver, c.1840* .	5800.00	6850.00
☐	**20**	*Star motif, round diamonds, brooch or pendant, 14K gold, American*	600.00	700.00
☐	**21**	*Sunburst motif, 38 round diamonds approx. 3.50 cts., gold topped silver, c. 1840*	3850.00	4300.00

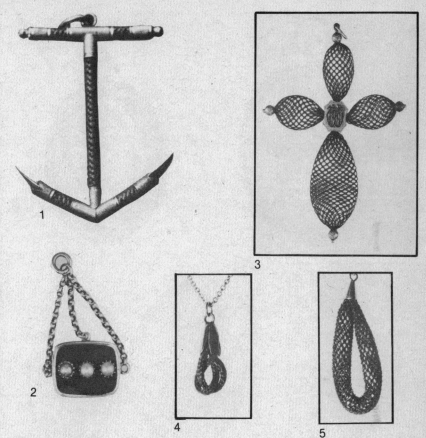

HUMAN HAIR

All items made from hair referred to throughout this section are of brunette human hair unless stated otherwise.

			Price Range	
☐	**1**	*Anchor motif, woven hair over metal tube, engraved gold fittings, c. 19th.*	**200.00**	**250.00**
☐	**2**	*Black enamel motif with three half seed pearls on obverse, reverse: black enamel "It Is The Lord 22 Sep. 1823," inside: Prince of Wales feathers of hair and gold wire, hinged glass cover and inscription: "Set not your affections on the things of this World," gold, English, c. 1823.*	**750.00**	**900.00**
☐	**3**	*Cross motif, woven hair, gold ball tips and center plaque with cobalt-blue enamel monogram, English, c. 1850-70.*	**175.00**	**200.00**
☐	**4**	*Flower motif, woven and braided hair, gold filled cap, c. 1850-70.*	**40.00**	**50.00**
☐	**5**	*Loop motif, woven hair, gold filled cap, c. 1850-70.*	**55.00**	**65.00**

			Price Range	
☐	**6**	*Miniature of doves symbolizing love and peace, branches and arrows painted with dissolved and cut and paste hair on ivory plaque, sterling silver, English, c. 1860.*	500.00	525.00
☐	**7**	*Miniature of gravesite by river with trees, cross and heart painted with dissolved hair and sepia paint on porcelain plaque, faceted black onyx frame, gold fittings, English, c. 1860-80.*	650.00	750.00
☐	**8**	*Ribbed dangle with shield motif, gold, French, c. mid 19th.*	375.00	475.00
☐	**9**	*Seed pearl border and monogram, basket weave hair under glass, pendant or brooch, leather covered boxwood box, English, c. 1790-1800.*	575.00	635.00

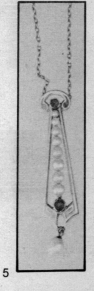

MISCELLANEOUS

			Price Range	
☐	**1**	*Agate cameo of a lion, lion is yellow with grey background, gold, c. late 17th.*	**5450.00**	**5900.00**
☐	**2**	*Amethyst: emerald-cut and marquise-shape, round diamonds, white gold, c. 1915*	**3300.00**	**3500.00**
☐	**3**	*Amethyst: cushion-cut, carved oak leaf frame, fancy link chain, gold, maker: Tiffany & Co., American, c. 1900*	**3950.00**	**4400.00**
☐	**4**	*Anchor motif, 11 seed pearls, 12 in. chain, 14K gold, American, c. 1894-95*	**135.00**	**175.00**
☐	**5**	*Bell motif, opaque white enamel, two round cornflower blue sapphires, seed pearls, gold, c. 1915* ..	**375.00**	**450.00**

			Price Range	
☐	**6**	Bell motif, round diamond, seed pearls, 14K gold, American, c. 1920	150.00	175.00
☐	**7**	Bird motif, mosaic, gold, Italian, c. 1855	250.00	350.00
☐	**8**	Bird motif, rose diamonds, one baroque pearl, silver topped gold bird, 18K white gold chain spaced with seed pearls, c. mid 19th.	525.00	625.00
☐	**9**	Black opal: one oval and one pear-shape, round diamonds, platinum, c. 1915	2650.00	3100.00
☐	**10**	Bow motif, pearls, hair compartment on reverse, 14K gold, c. 1850	700.00	950.00

13

15

			Price Range	
☐	**11**	*Cherub motif, ivory miniature, 79 seed pearls, gold* .	700.00	750.00
☐	**12**	*Chrysoprase, baroque pearls, green and peach enamel, silver, c. mid 19th.*	225.00	275.00
☐	**13**	*Circle cutout motif, two half pearls, one oval cabochon opal, one faceted Mexican opal, gold, Arts & Crafts Mvt., c. 1905*	750.00	800.00
☐	**14**	*Citizenship medal, red and white opaque enamel, silver, Eastern European, c. 1891*	350.00	400.00
☐	**15**	*Cluster motif, cabochon rubies, diamonds, reverse: opaque white enamel with translucent red and green enamel flowers, Indian, c. 19th.*	550.00	650.00

16

17

18

19

20

			Price Range	
☐	16	*Coral teardrops, pearls, 14K gold, c. 1900*	225.00	275.00
☐	17	*Crescent motif, nine rose diamonds, nine baroque pearls, reverse: red and green enamel, 20K gold, Indian, c. 19th.*	1850.00	2200.00
☐	18	*Crescent motif, plique á jour enamel, rose diamonds, seed pearls, citrine, gold, Victorian*	450.00	550.00
☐	19	*Cross, one 16 pt. diamond in center, four diamonds at 8 pts. each, 45 small diamonds, white gold front, c. late 19th.*	525.00	625.00
☐	20	*Crown motif, seed pearls, one baroque pearl, gold, c. mid 19th.*	325.00	375.00
☐	21	*Flower and ribbon motif, four seed pearls, rose diamonds, gold, c. mid 19th.*	525.00	675.00

22

23

24

25

26

27

			Price Range	
☐	**22**	Cross motif, silver, French, c. 19th.	135.00	175.00
☐	**23**	Cruciform motif, resurrection painted on vellum, pearls, white, green and red enamel, gold, c. late 16th.	2850.00	3300.00
☐	**24**	Cutout swirl motif, marcasites, sterling silver, American, c. 1920	50.00	60.00
☐	**25**	Dance card holder, Assyrian motif, silver, c. 1855-60	200.00	225.00
☐	**26**	Dance card holder, repoussé sterling silver front and back with celluloid cards inside, formerly part of a chatelaine, American, c. 1900	90.00	100.00
☐	**27**	Dancing lady motif, enamel, Etruscan granulation, gold	750.00	900.00

28

30

32

29

31

		Price Range	
☐ **28** *Dragonfly motif, pink and blue plique-à-jour wings, green enamel body, ruby eyes, old mine and rose diamonds, gold, Art Nouveau, c. 1890*	3950.00	4600.00
☐ **29** *Fire opal: cabochon, rose diamonds, silver, gold, c. mid 19th.*	2000.00	2200.00
☐ **30** *Flower motif, foil-back jargoons, rose diamonds, reverse: Jaipur enamel, Indian, c. 19th.*	1100.00	1300.00
☐ **31** *Flower motif, carved amethyst, one round diamond in center, rose diamonds, gold, c. 19th.*	1100.00	1300.00
☐ **32** *Flower motif, pearls, enamel, 14K gold, c. 1900* . . .	175.00	250.00

33

34

35

36

37

38

39

		Price Range	
☐	**33** *Flower motif, two cabochon moonstones, 11 cabochon opals, 830 silver, maker: RRCi, Copenhagen, c. early 20th.*	375.00	425.00
☐	**34** *Flower motif, pearls, pale rose and blue enamel, motto: "Guam Accipere Dare Multo Beatius," maker: Tiffany & Co., French, c. 19th.*	2950.00	3200.00
☐	**35** *Flower motif, translucent colored enamel, one round diamond, 12 in. chain, 14K gold, American, c. 1894-95*	275.00	325.00
☐	**36** *Flower motif, chrysoprase, turquoise, ruby, 2-color gold, English, early Victorian*	450.00	550.00
☐	**37** *Flower motif, seed pearls, 12 in. chain, 14K gold, American, c. 1894-95*	225.00	250.00
☐	**38** *Flower motif, 20 old mine diamonds, 16 pearls, gold, platinum, pendant or brooch, c. early 20th.*	1200.00	1450.00
☐	**39** *Flower motif, repoussé, one oval pink sapphire, four seed pearls, gold, c. 1840*	750.00	800.00

40

41

42

43

44

45

			Price Range	
☐	**40**	Flower motif, one emerald-cut amethyst approx. 20.0 cts., rose diamonds, gold, silver, c. 1860	1750.00	2000.00
☐	**41**	Flower motif, marcasites, sterling silver, American, c. 1920	75.00	90.00
☐	**42**	Flower motif, translucent pea green enamel, 930 silver, French, c. 1920	105.00	125.00
☐	**43**	Flower basket motif, faceted sardonyx, marcasites, sterling silver, American, c. 1920	90.00	110.00
☐	**44**	Flower motif, carved amethyst, one round diamond in each, gold, c. 20th. Pair	900.00	1000.00
☐	**45**	Flower motif, pearls, fresh water pearls, green enamel leaves, pink enamel flower, "900" silver, Art Nouveau, c. 1900	325.00	450.00

		Price Range	
☐	**46** Fringe motif, pearls, emerald, ruby and black beads, enamel, gold cap, Mogul	500.00	600.00
☐	**47** Hardstone cameo of a lady, half seed pearl border, gold, pendant or brooch, c. 1880	1650.00	1850.00
☐	**48** Heart motif, one seed pearl, 12 in. chain, 14K gold, American, c. 1894-95	90.00	110.00
☐	**49** Heart motif, green and blue translucent enamel, rose diamonds, silver, gold, c. 19th.............	750.00	950.00
☐	**50** Heart motif, pavé seed pearls, gold, c. late 19th. ..	300.00	325.00
☐	**51** Heart motif, one pear-shape table-cut diamond in center, rose diamonds, gold, c. 1860	1550.00	1650.00
☐	**52** Heart motif, heart-shape moonstone, rose diamonds, silver topped gold, c. 1870	550.00	575.00
☐	**53** Heart and star motif, garnet, turquoise and pearl in heart, one garnet in each star, 12 in. chain, 14K gold, American, c. 1894-95	300.00	325.00

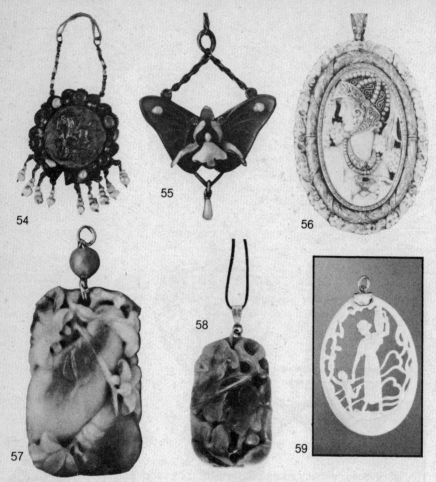

54

55

56

57

58

59

		Price Range	
☐	**54** Horseman with griffin motif, emeralds, pearls, fresh water pearls, blue and green enamel, silver, c. 19th......................................	475.00	575.00
☐	**55** Iris flower and wings motif, green and pink plique-à-jour enamel, two seed pearls, one wing pearl, chain spaced with seed pearls, silver gilt, Art Nouveau, c. 1910	1200.00	1450.00
☐	**56** Ivory cameo of a warrior, chased gold helmet and frame, opaque blue champlevé enamel, seed pearls, diamonds, rubies, Gothic Revival, c. 1860 .	6500.00	6700.00
☐	**57** Jade, carved, gold fitting	650.00	750.00
☐	**58** Jade, carved green jade, gold	1650.00	1850.00
☐	**59** Lady and child motif, cutout ivory, gold, c. 1925 ..	95.00	125.00

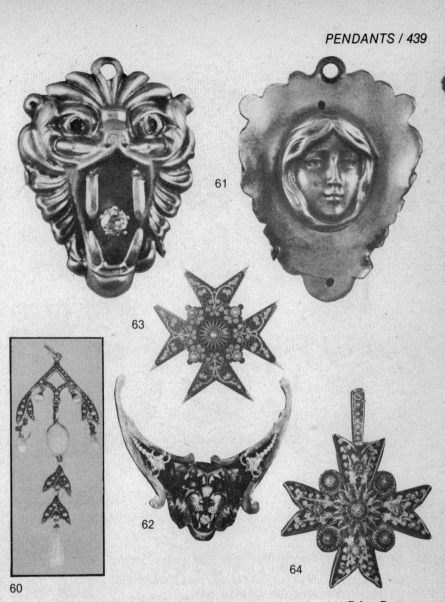

65

68

67

66

69

70

			Price Range	
☐	**65**	Medalion motif, obverse: warrior with griffin, reverse: a lady, gold, Art Nouveau, maker: RL, c. 1900	1100.00	1300.00
☐	**66**	Mermaid motif, carved lava, c. 1840	450.00	550.00
☐	**67**	Micro-mosaic of Swan, silver gilt, c. 1840	250.00	350.00
☐	**68**	Mirror, repoussé lady and flower motif, sterling silver, Art Nouveau, American, c. 1900	135.00	175.00
☐	**69**	Mirror, scenic motif on both sides, slides with mirror interior, sterling silver, artist: B. Wicker, French, c. 19th.................................	400.00	450.00
☐	**70**	Monkey motif, carved ivory, "See no evil, Hear no evil, Speak no evil," sterling silver reverse, c. 19th.	425.00	525.00

71

72

73

74

75

76

		Price Range	
☐	**71** Moonstone intaglio of mythological scene, two diamonds, pearls, gold, platinum	1300.00	1550.00
☐	**72** Moonstones, one cushion-cut sapphire approx. 7.50 cts., round sapphires, filigree, white gold, maker: Tiffany & Co., American, c. late 19th.	1550.00	1750.00
☐	**73** Mosaic motif of a lady, Etruscan granulation, gold, pendant or brooch, c. mid 19th.............	1550.00	1750.00
☐	**74** Mosaic scarab motif, Etruscan, granulation, 15K gold, English, c. 1865	600.00	650.00
☐	**75** Mosaic bulla pendant, dove and religious motif, pendant and locket, foxtail chain, gold, Italian, c. 1870	2400.00	3300.00
☐	**76** Mosaic birds of paradise motif, 18K gold, c. 1870 .	650.00	750.00

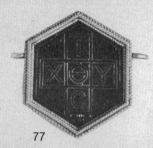

77

78

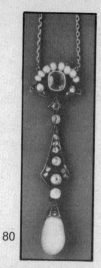

80

79

82

81

			Price Range	
☐	**77**	*Mosaic religious motif, silver cloisonné wire, gold, maker: Castellani, Italian, c. 1860*	**2750.00**	**3300.00**
☐	**78**	*Nymph with dove, cranberry glass, signed: R. Lalique*	**625.00**	**750.00**
☐	**79**	*Openwork motif, coral, pearls, gold, silver, c. 1850* .	**1450.00**	**1650.00**
☐	**80**	*Openwork motif, one faceted emerald, pearls, rose and round diamonds, gold, c. mid 19th.*	**1300.00**	**1550.00**
☐	**81**	*Oval center of frosted crystal, marcasites, sterling silver, American, c. 1920*	**80.00**	**110.00**
☐	**82**	*Oval flower motif, cabochon black and white banded agate, seed pearls, gold, c. 1850*	**900.00**	**1100.00**

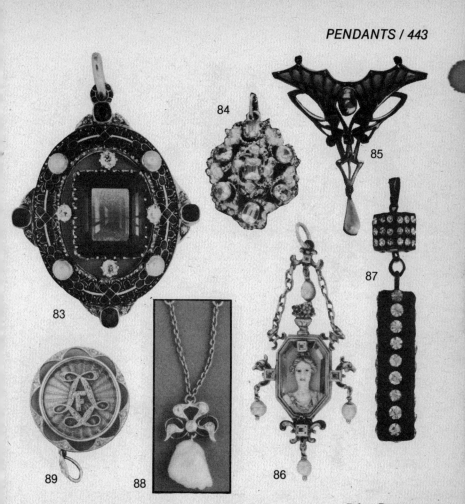

		Price Range	
☐	83 Oval motif, tourmaline approx. 10 cts., four diamonds approx. 60 pts., pearls, rubies, blue, green, red and white champlevé enamel, engraved: 1846 & 1896 Lady Tupper, Hon. Sir Charles	2000.00	2200.00
☐	84 Peridots, gold, c. early 19th.	450.00	550.00
☐	85 Plique à jour enamel, fresh water pearl, sterling, c. 1890	1100.00	1550.00
☐	86 Portrait miniature of Roman lady, rock crystal, table cut diamonds, pearls, white enamel, gold, c. 19th..	3950.00	4400.00
☐	87 Rectangular motif, black plastic cube and rectangle, pastes, silver chain, Art Deco, American	175.00	225.00
☐	88 Ribbon motif, five round diamonds, one baroque pearl, gold, c. late 19th.	475.00	575.00
☐	89 Round motif, translucent blue guilloché enamel, rose diamonds, gold, silver, c. 1900	750.00	900.00

			Price Range	
☐	**90**	Ruby teardrop, rose diamonds in cap, gold	1000.00	1200.00
☐	**91**	Sardonyx cameo of a lady, pearls, Etruscan granulation, gold, pendant or brooch, c. 1820	750.00	1000.00
☐	**92**	Scarab motif, carved ruby body, six square cut sapphires, one round sapphire, carved sapphire leaves, one fancy-cut emerald, rose diamonds, silver, gold, gold chain, c. 1840-60	3300.00	3850.00
☐	**93**	Scroll motif, cabochon opals, gold, c. 1900	700.00	950.00
☐	**94**	Scroll motif, red, blue and green enamel, oval cabochon garnet, pearls, c. 3rd quarter 19th.	2000.00	2200.00
☐	**95**	Seed pearl motif, strung with white horsehair on mother-of-pearl templets, ten diamonds, silver, fitted leather box inscribed: "Read & Son, London," c. 1880	475.00	525.00
☐	**96**	Shell cameo in center, carved tortoise shell frame	375.00	450.00

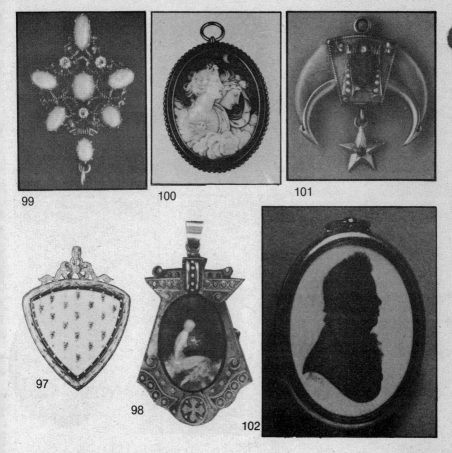

			Price Range	
☐	97	Shield motif, guilloché cream, red and blue enamel, rose diamonds, gold, c. 1900	3200.00	3500.00
☐	98	Shield motif locket, hardstone cameo, gold	500.00	600.00
☐	99	Shield openwork motif, opaque black and white enamel, seven oval cabochon opals, three old mine diamonds, silver, gold, c. 1840	1550.00	1750.00
☐	100	Shell cameo of two ladies, beaded frame, gold, c. 19th..	750.00	1000.00
☐	101	Shriner's motif, two tiger claws, carved tiger's eye portrait, seed pearls, one garnet, one round diamond, 14K gold, American, c. 20th.	375.00	400.00
☐	102	Silhouette of a gentleman, gold paint trim on shoulders and hair, gold frame, signed: Miers, c. mid 18th.	1550.00	1750.00

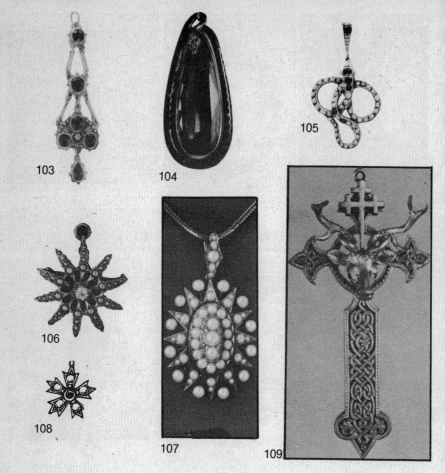

		Price Range	
☐ **103**	*Simulated sapphires, gold, Victorian*	250.00	325.00
☐ **104**	*Snake motif, green and black enamel, ruby eyes, four diamonds in head, one pear-shape amethyst, gold, c. 1890*	2000.00	2200.00
☐ **105**	*Snake motif, turquoise, round and cushion-cut rubies, gold, Georgian, c. 1830*	450.00	550.00
☐ **106**	*Snowflake motif, one round diamond, seed pearls, 14K gold, c. mid 19th*	375.00	475.00
☐ **107**	*Snowflake motif, pearls, four rose diamonds, gold, c. 1890*	1550.00	1750.00
☐ **108**	*Snowflake motif, one turquoise, five seed pearls, 12 in. chain, 14K gold, American, c. 1894-95*	160.00	200.00
☐ **109**	*St. Huberts' cross motif, opaque blue enamel, silver gilt, c. 19th.*	425.00	500.00

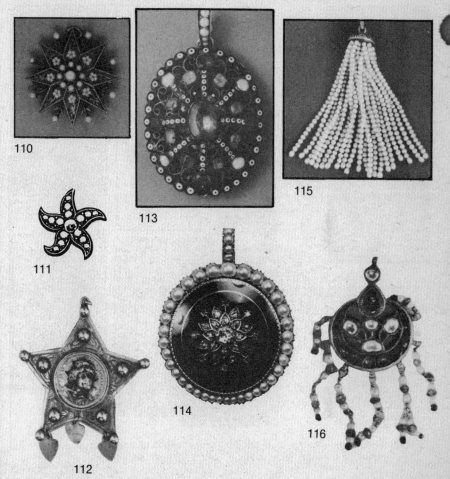

110

113

115

111

112

114

116

		Price Range	
☐ **110**	*Star motif, filigree, seed pearls, gold, c. 19th*	500.00	550.00
☐ **111**	*Star motif, seed pearls, 12 in. chain, 14K gold, American, c. 1894-95*	200.00	225.00
☐ **112**	*Star coin motif, 14K gold, American, c. 1920*	475.00	500.00
☐ **113**	*Star oval motif, opaque black and white enamel, one oval amethyst in center, other gemstones, silver gilt, Hungarian, c. 1860*	900.00	950.00
☐ **114**	*Sunburst motif of diamonds, half pearls, blue enamel, gold, c. 19th*	900.00	1000.00
☐ **115**	*Tassel motif, seed pearls, diamonds in cap, 14K white gold, c. 1920*	750.00	800.00
☐ **116**	*Tassel motif, seed pearls, table-cut diamonds foil-backed, enamel on reverse, Moghul-style*	350.00	400.00

		Price Range	
☐ **117**	*Tassel motif, one oval cabochon garnet, one seed pearl, Etruscan granulation, gold, fitted leather box, c. 1850*	750.00	900.00
☐ **118**	*Tiger claw and arrow motif, engraved, 15K gold, English, c. 1870*	385.00	400.00
☐ **119**	*Tourmaline: one oval and one pear-shape, seed pearls, 15K gold, English, c. early 20th.*	550.00	600.00
☐ **120**	*Turquoise, gold, Arts & Crafts MVT., maker: Murrle Bennett, English, c. 1910*	900.00	1050.00
☐ **121**	*Twisted rope motif, oval cabochon garnet, rose diamonds, gold, Victorian*	700.00	900.00
☐ **122**	*Wreath motif, eight emerald-cut emeralds, eight seed pearls, two oval cabochon opals, gold pendant or brooch, c. 1900*	2000.00	2200.00
☐ **123**	*Wreath motif, one oval sapphire, one baroque pearl, diamonds, gold, silver, c. 19th.*	3950.00	4200.00
☐ **124**	*Wreath and bow motif, one emerald-cut emerald, round emeralds, rose diamonds, gold, silver, c. 1860*	650.00	750.00

125

		Price Range	

☐ **125** *Wreath motif, opaque green enamel, nine seed pearls, 12 in. chain, 14K gold, American, c. 1896 ..* **225.00 250.00**

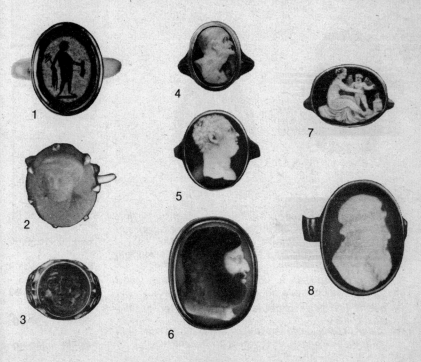

RINGS

CAMEO and INTAGLIO

☐ 1 *Ancient Roman intaglio, setting c. 18th.* 2850.00 2950.00
☐ 2 *Coral cameo of a lady, 14K gold, c. 1930* 175.00 225.00
☐ 3 *Emerald cameo of a gentleman, gold, c. early 20th.*. 4400.00 4950.00
☐ 4 *Hardstone cameo after a drawing by Leonardo da Vinci, gold* 375.00 500.00
☐ 5 *Hardstone cameo of a man, 14K gold* 450.00 550.00
☐ 6 *Hardstone cameo of Hercules, 14K gold* 550.00 650.00
☐ 7 *Hardstone cameo of Venus and Amor, gold* 500.00 600.00
☐ 8 *Onyx cameo of a gentleman, 14K gold* 450.00 550.00

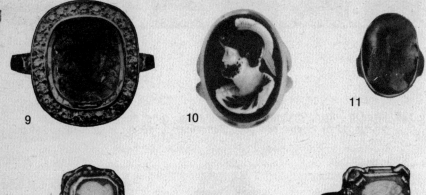

			Price Range	
☐	9	Sapphire cameo approx. 6.06 cts., diamonds, gold	5250.00	6300.00
☐	10	Sardonyx cameo of a Greek warrior, remounted in 22K gold ring, cameo c. early 19th..............	1550.00	1650.00
☐	11	Sardonyx cameo of a warrior, 10K gold, American, c. 20th..	625.00	700.00
☐	12	Shell cameo of a lady, diamond, swivels with black onyx on reverse, white gold, American	175.00	200.00
☐	13	Shell cameo of a lady and dog in garden, 14K gold, c. 1910	325.00	450.00
☐	14	Shell cameo of a lady, diamond, swivels with black onyx on reverse, white gold, American	250.00	275.00

CHILD'S – BAND

			Price Range	
☐	1	*"Baby" band, 14K gold, American, c. 1894-95*	105.00	125.00
☐	2	*Fancy engraved band, 14K gold, American, c. 1894-95*	70.00	80.00
☐	3	*Fancy engraved band, 14K gold, American, c. 1894-95*	90.00	100.00
☐	4	*Fancy engraved band, 14K gold, American, c. 1894-95*	70.00	80.00
☐	5	*Fancy engraved band, 14K gold, American, c. 1894-95*	90.00	100.00
☐	6	*Plain band, 14K gold, American, c. 1894-95*	65.00	75.00

CHILD'S – GEMSTONE

			Price Range	
☐	1	*Cabochon garnet, 14K gold, American, c. 1896* ...	125.00	150.00
☐	2	*Garnet, eight seed pearls, 14K gold, American, c. 1896*	100.00	125.00
☐	3	*Garnets, one seed pearl, 14K gold, American, c. 1896*	100.00	125.00
☐	4	*Garnets, two seed pearls, 14K gold, American, c. 1894-95*	105.00	130.00
☐	5	*Garnets, one seed pearl, 14K gold, American, c. 1894-95*	90.00	110.00
☐	6	*Garnets, 14K gold, American, c. 1894-95*	125.00	150.00
☐	7	*Garnets, two seed pearls, 14K gold, American, c. 1894-95*	110.00	135.00
☐	8	*Moonstone, 14K gold, American, c. 1896*	80.00	105.00

9

10

11

12

13

14

15

16

17

18

19

20

21

			Price Range	
☐	9	Opal, 14K gold, American, c. 1896	100.00	125.00
☐	10	Rose diamond, 14K gold, American, c. 1896	90.00	110.00
☐	11	Ruby, one seed pearl, 14K gold, American, c. 1896	110.00	135.00
☐	12	Ruby, 14K gold, American, c. 1896	95.00	125.00
☐	13	Rubies, one seed pearl, 14K gold, American, c. 1896	125.00	150.00
☐	14	Rubies, one seed pearl, 14K gold, American, c. 1896	115.00	150.00
☐	15	Seed pearl, two rubies, 14K gold, American, c. 1896	115.00	155.00
☐	16	Seed pearl, 14K gold, American, c. 1896	75.00	90.00
☐	17	Seed pearl, two turquoise, 14K gold, American, c. 1896	90.00	110.00
☐	18	Seed pearl, two turquoise, 14K gold, American, c. 1896	110.00	135.00
☐	19	Seed pearl, 14K gold, American, c. 1896	70.00	90.00
☐	20	Seed pearl, turquoise, 14K gold, American, c. 1896 .	75.00	100.00
☐	21	Seed pearl, two turquoise, 14K gold, American, c. 1896	90.00	110.00

22   23   24   25

26   27   28   29

			Price Range	
☐	22	*Seed pearls, two almondine garnets, 14K gold, American, c. 1896*	125.00	150.00
☐	23	*Turquoise, 14K gold, American, c. 1896*	75.00	100.00
☐	24	*Turquoise, two seed pearls, 14K gold, American, c. 1896*	100.00	125.00
☐	25	*Turquoise, one seed pearl, 14K gold, American, c. 1896*	110.00	135.00
☐	26	*Turquoise, one seed pearl, 14K gold, American, c. 1896*	100.00	125.00
☐	27	*Turquoise, 14K gold, American, c. 1896*	90.00	100.00
☐	28	*Turquoise, 14K gold, American, c. 1896*	90.00	110.00
☐	29	*Turquoise, one seed pearl, 14K gold, American, c. 1894-95*	100.00	110.00

1   2   3   4

GENTLEMENS'

☐	1	*Band motif, coin silver, American, c. 1894-95*	65.00	75.00
☐	2	*Carbuncle, engraved shank, 14K gold, American, c. 1896*	450.00	525.00
☐	3	*Carbuncle, 14K gold, American, c. 1896*	375.00	450.00
☐	4	*Clasped hands motif, coin silver, American, c. 1894-95*	135.00	165.00

5

6

7

8

9

10

11

12

13

		Price Range	
☐	**5** Flower and bird motif, translucent enamel, one diamond, gold, Indian, c. 19th.	500.00	600.00
☐	**6** Heart motif, coin silver, American, c. 1894-95	135.00	160.00
☐	**7** Initial motif, gold initial with diamonds on polished black onyx, engraved shank, American, c. 1895	400.00	500.00
☐	Same as above but without diamonds	300.00	400.00
☐	**8** Knights of Pythias motif, polished black onyx, engraved shank, 14K gold, American, c. 1896	135.00	175.00
☐	**9** Masonic motif, polished black onyx, engraved shank, 14K gold, American, c. 1896	135.00	175.00
☐	**10** Similar to above but with diamonds in insignia . . .	325.00	425.00
☐	**11** Mermaid motif, one round diamond, 14K gold, Art Nouveau, American, c. 1895	475.00	525.00
☐	**12** Modern Woodmen motif, polished black onyx, engraved shank, 14K gold, American, c. 1896	135.00	175.00
☐	**13** Odd Fellows motif, polished black onyx, engraved shank, 14K gold, American, c. 1896	135.00	175.00

14

15

16

17

18

19

20

21

			Price Range	
☐	14	*"Repeal 18th Amendment" motif, sterling silver, American, c. 1930*	**175.00**	**225.00**
☐	15	*Sardonyx cameo of a lady, 14K gold, American, c. 1896*	**275.00**	**325.00**
☐	16	*Sardonyx cameo of a lady, engraved shank, 14K gold, American, c. 1896*	**375.00**	**425.00**
☐	17	*Sardonyx cameo, 14K gold, American, c. 1896*	**150.00**	**200.00**
☐	18	*Shield initial plaque motif, coin silver, American, c. 1894-95*	**140.00**	**175.00**
☐	19	*Shield initial plaque motif, coin silver, American, c. 1894-95*	**150.00**	**185.00**
☐	20	*Single stone motif, one old mine diamond approx. .22 ct., gold, English, c. 1894*	**575.00**	**650.00**
☐	21	*Skull and crossbones motif, coin silver, American, c. 1894-95*	**135.00**	**175.00**

			Price Range	
☐	**22**	Straight row motif, three round diamonds, gold, c. 1890	750.00	950.00
☐	**23**	Straight row motif, center row of rubies, two rows and center rose diamonds, gold, c. late 19th.	2650.00	2850.00
☐	**24**	Square initial plaque motif, coin silver, American, c. 1894-95	95.00	135.00
☐	**25**	Tiger eye cameo, 14K gold, American, c. 1896	200.00	275.00
☐	**26**	Tiger eye intaglio, engraved shank, 14K gold, American, c. 1894-95	200.00	275.00

HUMAN HAIR

All items made from hair referred to throughout this section are of brunette human hair unless stated otherwise.

☐	**1**	Cabochon garnet, white enamel band: "Vivit Post. Funera Virtus. M. W. OBT 13 APR 1729 AET 28," gold, c. 1729	750.00	900.00
☐	**2**	Cluster motif, six cabochon angel skin coral, one seed pearl, reverse: hair locket, c. 1860	175.00	200.00
☐	**3**	Coffin motif, hair under crystal, black enamel band: "I. Saxton. OB. 26 Aug. 1720. AET46," gold, c. 1720	1750.00	2000.00

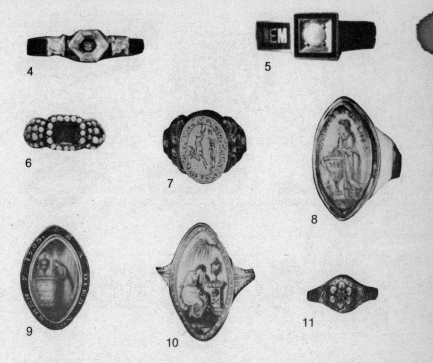

4

5

6

7

8

9

10

11

			Price Range	
☐	**4**	*Diamonds: one hexagonal-shape and two fancy-shape diamonds, black enamel band: "Sr. F. Leicester, Bart. OB 30 JUNE 1742, AET 68," gold, c. 1742*	**1550.00**	**1750.00**
☐	**5**	*Geometric motif, one half pearl in center, black and white enamel, Roman block script "IN MEMORY OF," gold, c. 1880-90*	**200.00**	**225.00**
☐	**6**	*Hair under glass in center, pavé turquoise, gold, Victorian*	**550.00**	**650.00**
☐	**7**	*Hidden compartment motif, chased and engraved, top plaque with hidden hinge, gold, c. 1830-40*	**450.00**	**500.00**
☐	**8**	*Lady and urn motif, sepia paint on ivory, c. 1790*	**500.00**	**550.00**
☐	**9**	*Lady and urn motif, sepia paint and dissolved hair, black and white enamel border: "S A Died November 7 1793," gold, c. 1793*	**600.00**	**650.00**
☐	**10**	*Lady sitting weeping by urn with skull and crossbone motif, sepia painted on ivory, gold, inscribed inside: "Ann Allan ob 16 Oct. 1785 AE 68," English, c. 1785*	**525.00**	**575.00**
☐	**11**	*Locket on inside shank, enamel on shank "In Memory Of," seed pearls, one diamond, 18K gold, English, Victorian*	**225.00**	**335.00**

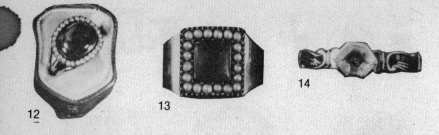

		Price Range	
☐	**12** Locket oval motif, hair under glass, seed pearl border, gold, c. 1870, ...	300.00	325.00
☐	**13** Locket square motif, hair under glass, seed pearl border, gold, inscribed inside: "A memory of Mother," gold, c. 1906	200.00	225.00
☐	**14** Locket with hexagonal crystal motif, portrait under crystal, black enamel scroll band: "A. Cooper, OB 21 APR 1741 AET 46," gold, c. 1741	1550.00	1750.00
☐	**15** Locket with hexagonal crystal motif, portrait under crystal, black enamel scroll band: "Rich D. Tucker, OB 9 APR 1748. AET 72," gold, c. 1748	1550.00	1750.00
☐	**16** Opals, black enamel, woven hair hidden between outer and inner shank, gold, c. late 19th.	475.00	525.00
☐	**17** Plaque motif, black enamel, "Tho Lost To Sight To Memory Dear," chased, gold, c. 1820	375.00	450.00
☐	**18** Sandwich motif of inner band, woven hair and outer etched band with "MAMIE" cutout, gold, c. 1880	225.00	275.00

19

20

21

22

23

24

25

		Price Range	
☐	**19** Sandwich motif on inner band, woven hair and outer black and white enamel squares with letters spelling "REGARD," gold, c. 1860	275.00	300.00
☐	**20** Sandwich motif of inner band with raised edges holding woven hair, shield for monogram covers joining of hair, gold, c. 1860	175.00	200.00
☐	**21** Sandwich motif of inner band with raised edges holding woven hair, heart for monogram covers joining of hair, gold, c. 1860	175.00	200.00
☐	**22** Sandwich motif of inner band with raised edges holding woven hair, heart, cross and anchor covers joining of hair, gold, maker: H. H. & S., c. 1860 .	200.00	250.00
☐	**23** Sandwich ring of inner band, woven hair and outer engraved and cutout band, gold, c. 1880	175.00	225.00
☐	**24** Sandwich ring of inner band, woven hair and outer engraved and cutout band, third middle band slides to cover openings, gold, c. 1880	575.00	650.00
☐	**25** Sheaf-of-wheat motif, stalk of strands of hair, wheat grains of dissolved hair, gold, c. 1800	550.00	625.00

26

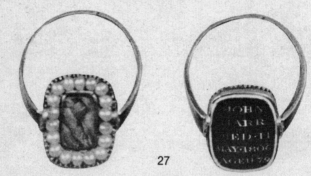

27

28

29

30

		Price Range	
☐	**26** *Skull and crossbone motif, yellow paint on white porcelain, black enamel band, gold, c. 1820*	1650.00	2000.00
☐	**27** *Swivel motif, obverse: blond hair locket with seed pearl border, reverse: black and white enamel inscribed: "John Harr died 11 May 1806 aged 79," gold, c. 1806*	750.00	900.00
☐	**28** *Urn and angel motif, sepia paint and dissolved hair on ivory, gold, c. 1820*	275.00	300.00
☐	**29** *Urn and weeping willow motif, sepia paint on ivory, gold, c. 1790*	500.00	550.00
☐	**30** *Urn and weeping willow motif, sepia paint on ivory, enamel shank, c. 1774*	700.00	950.00

31

32

		Price Range	

☐ **31** *Urn motif, shield locket in center, black and white enamel, white enamel signifies dealth of infant or young child, gold, c. 1790* **375.00 425.00**

☐ **32** *Urn motif, sepia paint and dissolved hair on ivory, gold, c. 1790* **450.00 500.00**

1

2

3

4

5

LADIES – DIAMOND

☐ **1** *Art Deco motif, one round diamond approx. .50 ct., six baguette diamonds, 20 round diamonds, platinum, c. 1930* **2400.00 2850.00**

☐ **2** *Art Deco motif, one round diamond approx. 1.90 cts., six baguette diamonds, round diamonds, platinum, c. 1930* **7550.00 9150.00**

☐ **3** *Art Deco motif, one round diamond approx. .50 ct., one round diamond approx. .25 ct., 16 round diamonds approx. .32 ct., 14K white gold, c. 1935* **2200.00 2650.00**

☐ **4** *Belt motif, three old mine diamonds, 18K gold, c. 1860* **750.00 900.00**

☐ **5** *Belt motif, two diamond chips, English, maker: W. W. Ld., 9K gold* **225.00 275.00**

6

7

8

9

10

11

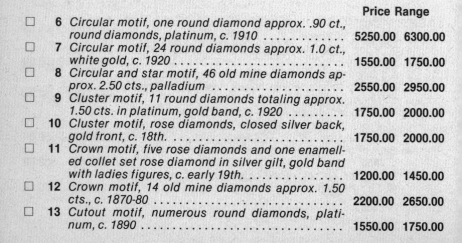

12

13

		Price Range	
☐	**6** *Circular motif, one round diamond approx. .90 ct., round diamonds, platinum, c. 1910*	**5250.00**	**6300.00**
☐	**7** *Circular motif, 24 round diamonds approx. 1.0 ct., white gold, c. 1920*	**1550.00**	**1750.00**
☐	**8** *Circular and star motif, 46 old mine diamonds approx. 2.50 cts., palladium*	**2550.00**	**2950.00**
☐	**9** *Cluster motif, 11 round diamonds totaling approx. 1.50 cts. in platinum, gold band, c. 1920*	**1750.00**	**2000.00**
☐	**10** *Cluster motif, rose diamonds, closed silver back, gold front, c. 18th.*	**1750.00**	**2000.00**
☐	**11** *Crown motif, five rose diamonds and one enamelled collet set rose diamond in silver gilt, gold band with ladies figures, c. early 19th.*	**1200.00**	**1450.00**
☐	**12** *Crown motif, 14 old mine diamonds approx. 1.50 cts., c. 1870-80*	**2200.00**	**2650.00**
☐	**13** *Cutout motif, numerous round diamonds, platinum, c. 1890*	**1550.00**	**1750.00**

14

15

16

17

18

19

20

		Price Range	
☐	**14** *Cutout oval motif, round diamonds approx. 1.75 cts., platinum, c. 1910*	**1900.00**	**2200.00**
☐	**15** *Cutout oval motif, 74 round diamonds approx. 1.50 cts., one round diamond approx. 1.10 cts., platinum, c. 1920*	**7350.00**	**9450.00**
☐	**16** *Diamond-shape motif, nine pave rose diamonds, 14K gold, c. 1870*	**450.00**	**550.00**
☐	**17** *Domed mount motif, one old mine diamond approx. 1.35 cts., round diamonds, platinum, c. 1910*	**3950.00**	**5050.00**
☐	**18** *Double cluster motif, 14 old mine diamonds approx. .70 ct. in clusters, six rose diamonds in band, 14K gold, c. 1880*	**1450.00**	**1650.00**
☐	**19** *Flower motif, rose diamonds, simulated diamond center, silver flower, contemporary gold shank, flower c. 1840*	**550.00**	**650.00**
☐	**20** *Flower motif, one round diamond approx. 1.67 cts., round diamonds, platinum, c. 1900*	**5250.00**	**6300.00**

21

22

23

24

25

26

27

		Price Range	
☐	**21** Geometric motif, one round diamond approx. .90 ct., round diamonds, platinum, c. 1920	2850.00	3500.00
☐	**22** Geometric cutout motif, one round diamond approx. 1.20 cts., round diamond, platinum, c. 1910 .	5250.00	6300.00
☐	**23** Horseshoe motif, seven diamonds totaling approx. .15 ct., 14K gold, c. 1880	300.00	425.00
☐	**24** Marquis motif, 15 old mine diamonds, 18K gold, c. 1850	1100.00	1300.00
☐	**25** Marquise openwork motif, round diamonds, one square-shape diamond, two marquise-shape diamonds, calibre cabochon emeralds, platinum, c. 1920	1750.00	2000.00
☐	**26** Marquise openwork motif, marquise-shape diamond approx. .15 ct., 20 round diamonds, platinum, c. 1925	2000.00	2750.00
☐	**27** Octagonal motif, one round diamond approx. .30 ct., 24 round diamond approx. 1.68 cts., pave, 18K white gold, c. 1940	3100.00	3300.00

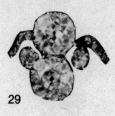

28

29

30

31

32

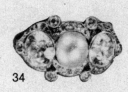

34

33

Price Range

☐ **28** *Open band motif, two round diamonds approx.
1.60 cts., 10 old mine and two rose diamonds,
gold, c. 1870* 3500.00 4100.00

☐ **29** *Open band motif, one old mine diamond approx.
2.75 cts., one old mine diamond approx. 3.0 cts.,
small old mine diamonds, silver, gold,
c. 1875* 7350.00 8900.00

☐ **30** *Openwork motif, 26 round and marquise diamonds
approx. 1.30 cts., calibre emeralds, white gold,
c. 1920* 2650.00 3100.00

☐ **31** *Openwork motif, one round fancy yellow diamond
approx. 1.0 cts. in center, round diamonds,
platinum, c. 1900* 4400.00 4950.00

☐ **32** *Openwork motif, round diamonds, four calibre
sapphires, platinum, c. 1900* 750.00 1000.00

☐ **33** *Openwork motif, 27 round diamonds, c. 1900* 2650.00 3100.00

☐ **34** *Openwork motif, round diamonds, grey pearl approx. 6.3MM in center, c. 1890* 1650.00 2200.00

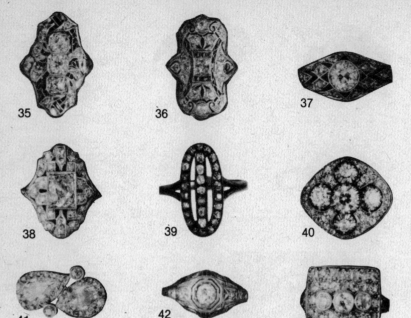

			Price Range	
☐	**35**	*Openwork motif, 13 round diamonds approx. 1.50 cts., platinum, c. 1910*	1550.00	2000.00
☐	**36**	*Openwork motif, 21 round diamonds approx. 1.50 cts., six square sapphires, platinum, c. 1915*	1750.00	2200.00
☐	**37**	*Openwork motif, one round diamond approx. .75 ct. in center, small rose diamonds, platinum, c. 1910*	1750.00	2000.00
☐	**38**	*Openwork geometric motif, 26 diamonds approx. .45 ct., one oval diamond approx. 1.15 cts., platinum, c. 1930*	2850.00	3300.00
☐	**39**	*Oval motif, 29 rose diamonds, c. 1865*	750.00	900.00
☐	**40**	*Oval motif, old mine diamonds, white gold, c. 1890*	4400.00	5250.00
☐	**41**	*Pear-shape motif, two pear-shape diamonds approx. 2.50 cts., two old mine diamonds, rose diamonds, gold topped silver, c. 1860*	5250.00	6300.00
☐	**42**	*Pierced motif, round diamonds, calibre sapphires, platinum, c. 1920*	550.00	650.00
☐	**43**	*Rectangular motif, pave round diamonds, engraved gallery, platinum, c. 1910*	2200.00	2650.00

44

45

46

47

48

49

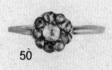
50

51

52

			Price Range	
☐	44	Rectangular motif, two round diamonds approx. 1.40 cts., six round diamonds, platinum, c. 1910 ..	2850.00	3300.00
☐	45	Renaissance motif, five table cut diamonds, black and white champleve enamel, silver, gold, c. 17th..	1550.00	1750.00
☐	46	Rose cut diamonds, white gold	325.00	450.00
☐	47	Rose diamonds, platinum topped gold	375.00	500.00
☐	48	Rose diamonds, silver topped gold, English	450.00	600.00
☐	49	Rosette motif, 21 round diamonds approx. 2.25 cts., gold, c. late 19th.	2000.00	2200.00
☐	50	Rosette motif, rose diamonds, gold, c. 1860	450.00	550.00
☐	51	Rosette motif, 12 old mine diamonds approx. 8.0 cts., 13 old mine and rose diamonds, c. mid 19th. .	7350.00	9450.00
☐	52	Rosette motif, nine old mine diamonds approx. 1.75 cts., gold, c. 1870	2000.00	2750.00

53

54

55

56

57

58

59

60

			Price Range	
☐	53	*Rosette motif, one old mine diamond approx. .90 ct. in center, old mine diamonds, platinum, c. 1910*	2400.00	2850.00
☐	54	*Rosette motif, seven old mine diamonds approx. 3.0 cts., engraved shank, c. 1880*	2850.00	3950.00
☐	55	*Rosette motif, seven old mine diamonds, white gold, c. 1880*	1550.00	1750.00
☐	56	*Ruby approx. 1.50 cts., two old mine diamonds, ten round diamonds, three cushion rubies, c. late 19th.*	2650.00	3100.00
☐	57	*Shield motif, one marquise-shape diamond approx. .50 ct., round diamonds, square emeralds, platinum, c. 1925*	2650.00	2850.00
☐	58	*Shield openwork motif, 13 round diamonds approx. 2.25 cts., platinum, c. 1910*	2400.00	3500.00
☐	59	*Shield motif, translucent blue enamel, old mine diamonds, c. late 18th.*	4400.00	4600.00
☐	60	*Single stone motif, one round diamond approx. 1.30 cts., small round diamonds on shank, platinum, c. 1915*	3300.00	3500.00

61

62

63

64

65

66

67

			Price Range	
☐	**61**	Single stone motif, one round diamond approx. 1.75 cts., small round diamonds on shank, platinum, c. 1910	12600.00	4700.00
☐	**62**	Single stone motif, one old mine diamond approx. 1.0 ct., gold, c. 1860	1100.00	1300.00
☐	**63**	Single stone motif, one round diamond approx. 2.50 cts., sapphires on shank, platinum, c. 1920 ..	8400.00	12600.00
☐	**64**	Single stone motif, one round diamond approx. 1.20 cts., four French-cut sapphires, white gold, c. 1890	1750.00	2100.00
☐	**65**	Single stone motif, one round diamond approx. 1.20 cts., round diamonds, c. 1928	1750.00	2100.00
☐	**66**	Single stone motif, one round diamond approx. 1.10 cts., six round diamonds, platinum, c. 1910 ..	4850.00	5650.00
☐	**67**	Single stone motif, one round diamond approx. 1.10 cts., six round diamonds, platinum, c. 1920 ..	3750.00	4200.00

68

70

69

71

72

73

72

75

74

			Price Range	
☐	**68**	Single stone motif, one round diamond approx. 1.0 ct., 14K gold, American, c. 1895	1350.00	2050.00
☐	**69**	Same as above except diamond approx. 1.0 ct. . . .	1350.00	2050.00
☐	**70**	Same as above except diamond approx. .50 ct. . . .	800.00	1100.00
☐	**71**	Same as above except diamond approx. .35 ct. . . .	500.00	700.00
☐	**72**	Same as above except diamond approx. .30 ct. . . .	375.00	450.00
☐	**73**	Same as above except diamond approx. .25 ct. . . .	300.00	375.00
☐	**74**	Same as above except diamond approx. .35 ct. . . .	500.00	700.00
☐	**75**	Same as above except diamond approx. .25 ct. . . .	300.00	375.00

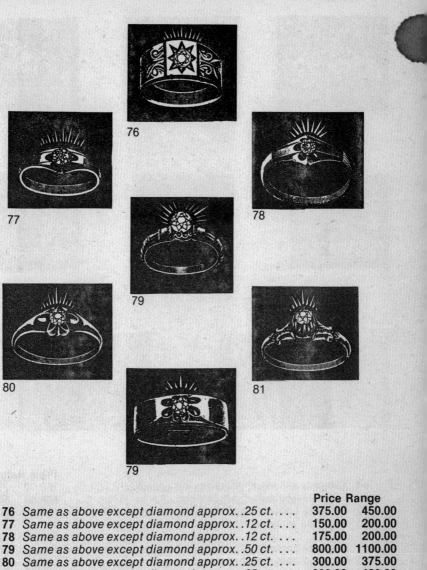

76

77

78

79

80

81

79

			Price Range	
☐	**76**	*Same as above except diamond approx. .25 ct. ...*	375.00	450.00
☐	**77**	*Same as above except diamond approx. .12 ct. ...*	150.00	200.00
☐	**78**	*Same as above except diamond approx. .12 ct. ...*	175.00	200.00
☐	**79**	*Same as above except diamond approx. .50 ct. ...*	800.00	1100.00
☐	**80**	*Same as above except diamond approx. .25 ct. ...*	300.00	375.00
☐	**81**	*Same as above except diamond approx. .25 ct. ...*	300.00	400.00
☐	**82**	*Same as above except diamond approx. .12 ct. ...*	175.00	250.00

83

84

85

86

87

88

89

90

			Price Range	
☐	83	Same as above except diamond approx. .12 ct. . . .	150.00	200.00
☐	84	Same as above except diamond approx. .34 ct. . . .	450.00	500.00
☐	85	Same as above except diamond approx. .12 ct. . . .	150.00	200.00
☐	86	Same as above except each diamond approx. .12 ct.	400.00	475.00
☐	87	Same as above except diamond approx. .12 ct. . . .	185.00	250.00
☐	88	Same as above except diamond approx. .12 ct. . . .	175.00	200.00
☐	89	Same as above except diamond approx. .12 ct. . . .	150.00	200.00
☐	90	Same as above except diamond approx. .06 ct. . . .	150.00	200.00

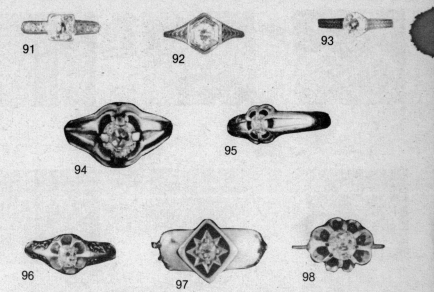

			Price Range	
☐	**91**	Single stone motif, one round diamond approx. .80 ct., eight round diamonds in band, 14K gold, c. 1915	1300.00	1750.00
☐	**92**	Single stone motif, one round diamond approx. .40 ct., platinum, c. 1925	750.00	900.00
☐	**93**	Single stone motif, one round diamond approx. .60 ct., platinum, c. 1910	1000.00	1200.00
☐	**94**	Single stone motif, one cushion-cut diamond approx. .35 ct., 18K gold, c. late 19th.	450.00	650.00
☐	**95**	Single stone motif, one cushion-cut diamond approx. .15 ct., 14K gold, c. late 19th.	300.00	350.00
☐	**96**	Single stone motif, one cushion-cut diamond approx. .20 ct., 14K gold, c. late 19th.	550.00	650.00
☐	**97**	Single stone motif, one round diamond approx. .15 ct., bead set in star on wide band, English, 15K gold, c. 1875	375.00	450.00
☐	**98**	Single stone motif, one round diamond approx. .30 ct., 14K gold, c. late 19th.	475.00	575.00

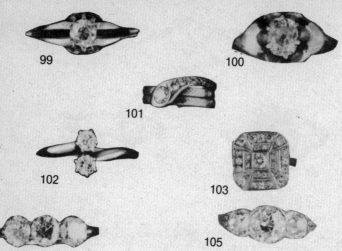

			Price Range	
☐	**99**	*Single stone motif, one round diamond approx. .25 ct., 14K gold, c. 1915*	450.00	550.00
☐	**100**	*Single stone motif, one round diamond approx. .40 ct., 14K gold, c. 1870.*	650.00	750.00
☐	**101**	*Snake motif, etched, round diamonds, gold, c. late 19th.*	750.00	900.00
☐	**102**	*Split band motif, two round diamonds approx. .20 ct. each, 14K gold, c. 1900.*	450.00	550.00
☐	**103**	*Square motif, round diamonds, gold, platinum, c. 1920*	1750.00	2000.00
☐	**104**	*Straight row motif, three round diamonds approx. 2.0 cts., platinum, c. 1920*	4700.00	5750.00
☐	**105**	*Straight row motif, one round diamond approx. 1.50 cts., two round diamonds approx. 1.60 cts., small round diamonds on shank, platinum, c. 1920*	6800.00	8900.00
☐	**106**	*Straight row motif, round diamonds, gold, English*	375.00	450.00
☐	**107**	*Straight row motif, three round diamonds approx. 3.50 cts., white gold, c. 1890*	7350.00	9450.00

108

109

110

111

112

113

114

115

116

117

		Price Range	
☐ **108**	Straight row motif, three round diamonds approx. .90 ct., c. 1900	**750.00**	**900.00**
☐ **109**	Straight row motif, three round diamonds approx. .45 ct., gold, c. 1930	**550.00**	**650.00**
☐ **110**	Straight row motif, three round diamonds approx. 1.0 ct., round diamonds, platinum, c. 1910	**900.00**	**1100.00**
☐ **111**	Straight row motif, five old mine diamonds total-ing approx. .25 ct., 18K gold, c. 1880	**550.00**	**650.00**
☐ **112**	Straight row motif, five old mine diamonds total-ing approx. .18 ct., 14K gold, c. 1860	**450.00**	**550.00**
☐ **113**	Straight row motif, four round diamonds totaling approx. .20 ct., 14K white gold, c. 1930	**325.00**	**450.00**
☐ **114**	Straight row motif, seven rose and old mine dia-monds totaling approx. .70 ct., collet set, yellow gold shank, inscribed: "N. Biichner 1747"	**1450.00**	**1650.00**
☐ **115**	Straight row motif, three round diamonds approx. 1.25 cts., 14K gold, c. 1925	**1650.00**	**1850.00**
☐ **116**	Star motif, 21 round diamonds approx. .75 ct., 14K white gold, c. mid 20th.	**750.00**	**900.00**
☐ **117**	Triangular motif, 11 old mine diamonds approx. 1.20 cts., platinum, c. 1910	**1750.00**	**2000.00**

LADIES – DIAMOND and GEMSTONE

Price Range

☐ **1** *Almandine garnets, two pearls, 14K gold, American, c. 1896* 150.00 175.00

☐ **2** *Almandine garnet, 14K gold, American, c. 1896* ... 200.00 250.00

☐ **3** *Almandine garnets, six rose diamonds, 14K gold, American, c. 1896* 375.00 450.00

☐ **4** *Almandine garnet, one olivine, one pearl, 14K gold, American, c. 1896* 275.00 325.00

☐ **5** *Almandine garnet, cabochon, 14K gold* 300.00 350.00

☐ **6** *Amethyst, rose diamonds, silver topped 18K gold, c. 1850* 550.00 650.00

☐ **7** *Amethyst, 14K gold, approx. c. 1896* 250.00 300.00

☐ **8** *Amethysts, six pearls, 14K gold, American, c. 1896* 275.00 325.00

☐ **9** *Amethyst, 12 pearls, 14K gold, American, c. 1895* . 700.00 800.00

☐ **10** *Amethyst, 14K gold, American, c. 1895* 175.00 225.00

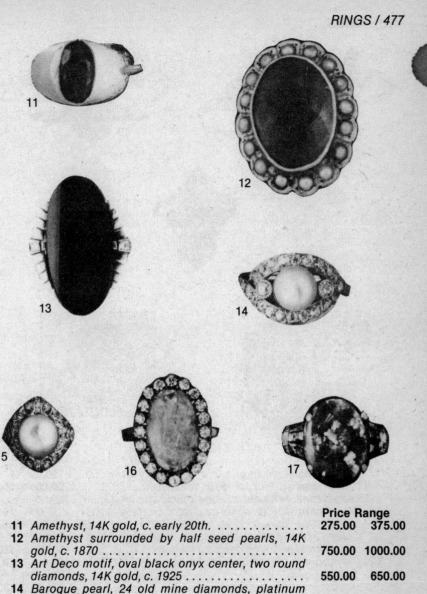

		Price Range	
☐	**11** Amethyst, 14K gold, c. early 20th.	275.00	375.00
☐	**12** Amethyst surrounded by half seed pearls, 14K gold, c. 1870	750.00	1000.00
☐	**13** Art Deco motif, oval black onyx center, two round diamonds, 14K gold, c. 1925	550.00	650.00
☐	**14** Baroque pearl, 24 old mine diamonds, platinum topped gold, c. 1890	1650.00	1850.00
☐	**15** Baroque pearl, 80 round diamonds approx. 1.60 cts., platinum, c. 1900	1850.00	2100.00
☐	**16** Black opal, 20 old mine diamonds approx. 1.50 cts., gold topped silver, c. 1890	3500.00	3950.00
☐	**17** Black opal, baguette and rose diamonds, white gold, c. 1910	3850.00	4950.00

18

19

20

21

22

			Price Range	
☐	**18**	*Black opal, eight baguette and round yellow diamonds approx. 1. ct., c. 1910*	4200.00	5300.00
☐	**19**	*Bloodstone, 14K gold, c. early 20th.*	150.00	200.00
☐	**20**	*Blue zircon, 10K three color gold mounting, c. 1920*	200.00	300.00
☐	**21**	*Carved amethyst quartz, seed pearl border, carved leaf motif shank, 14K gold, c. late 19th.*	450.00	550.00
☐	**22**	*Chrysoberyl, 18K white and yellow gold, c. 1880* ..	450.00	550.00

23

24

25

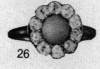
26

27

28

29

30

31

			Price Range	
☐	23	Citrene: rose cut, 14K gold, c. late 19th.	135.00	150.00
☐	24	Cluster motif, oval cabochon center garnet, rose garnet border, 14K gold, c. 1880	450.00	550.00
☐	25	Cluster motif, one ruby approx. .20 ct. in center surrounded by eight old mine diamonds approx. .48 ct., stones in platinum, 14K gold shank, c. early 20th.	1200.00	1450.00
☐	26	Cluster motif, cabochon turquoise in center surrounded by ten old mine diamonds, gold, c. 1870 .	1000.00	1300.00
☐	27	Cluster motif, one round ruby in center, eight old mine diamonds approx. 1.20 cts., 14K gold, c. late 19th.	1650.00	1850.00
☐	28	Coral, gold, c. 1910	225.00	275.00
☐	29	Crisscross motif, pink coral, seed pearls, gold, c. 1840	375.00	450.00
☐	30	Cross motif, one pear-shape sapphire, two old mine diamonds, one round sapphire and one round ruby surrounded by old mine diamonds, silver, gold, c. 1840	750.00	1000.00
☐	31	Crystal, ruby, 10K white and rose gold, c. 1925 . . .	225.00	325.00

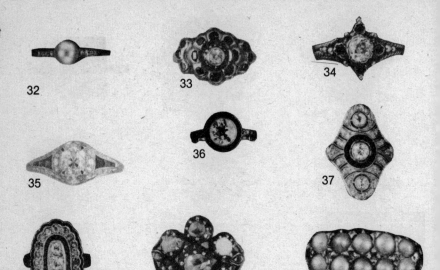

		Price Range	
☐	**32** *Cultured pearl, diamonds, platinum, maker: Tiffany & Co., American*	350.00	450.00
☐	**33** *Diamond, emeralds, gold, c. 1850*	650.00	900.00
☐	**34** *Diamond, four round rubies, gold, c. 1800*	1850.00	2200.00
☐	**35** *Diamond: old mine approx. 1.30 cts., round diamonds, six calibre French-cut sapphires, platinum, c. 1925*	5050.00	5300.00
☐	**36** *Diamond: one round approx. 1.50 cts., six round diamonds, calibre-cut emeralds, all in platinum, gold band, c. 1925*	6300.00	7350.00
☐	**37** *Diamonds: 31 round approx. .65 ct., calibre sapphires, white gold, c. 1925*	2200.00	2400.00
☐	**38** *Diamonds: 23 old mine approx. 1.50 cts., calibre rubies, platinum, gold, c. 1910*	3300.00	4400.00
☐	**39** *Diamonds: seven Holland rose, silver topped gold, c. 1840*	1100.00	1300.00
☐	**40** *Double straight row of ten half-seed pearls, 18K gold, London, England, c. 1895*	225.00	275.00

41

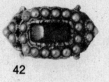
42

43

44

45

46

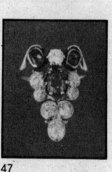
47

48

49

50

			Price Range	
☐	41	Emeralds, diamonds, gold, c. 1790	750.00	900.00
☐	42	Emerald, half-seed pearls, gold, c. 1860	750.00	900.00
☐	43	Emerald: emerald-cut, rose diamonds, gold, platinum, c. 1880	1550.00	2000.00
☐	44	Emerald: intaglio emerald-cut, five old mine diamonds, 18K gold	2200.00	2650.00
☐	45	Emerald: step-cut, one round diamond, rose diamonds, gold, silver, c. 1900	750.00	1000.00
☐	46	Emerald: emerald-cut, 14 round diamonds, 18K gold, c. 1910	1850.00	2200.00
☐	47	Emeralds: one emerald-cut and two step-cut, seven old European-cut and one round diamond, gold, platinum, c. 1910	3850.00	4400.00
☐	48	Emeralds: one emerald-cut approx. .50 ct. and 12 calibre emeralds, round diamonds approx. 1.0 ct., platinum, c. 1920	3750.00	4200.00
☐	49	Emeralds: square-cut in center, round diamonds, black enamelled edges, platinum, c. 1900	4850.00	5300.00
☐	50	Emerald: oval faceted, rose diamonds, silver topped gold, c. 1870	2100.00	2400.00

51

52

53

54

55

56

57

58

59

60

			Price Range	
☐	**51**	*Emerald: emerald-cut approx. 1.70 cts., nine round diamonds approx. .75 ct., 14K gold, c. mid 20th....*	4400.00	5250.00
☐	**52**	*Emerald: emerald-cut approx. 1.35 cts., 14 round diamonds approx. .75 ct., platinum and 18K white gold, c. mid 20th.*	3500.00	4200.00
☐	**53**	*Emerald, one ruby, five pearls, 14K gold, American, c. 1896*	175.00	225.00
☐	**54**	*Emerald, one ruby, 14K gold, American, c. 1896*	165.00	200.00
☐	**55**	*Emeralds, 14K gold, American, c. 1896*	225.00	275.00
☐	**56**	*Emerald, 12 rose diamonds, 14K gold, American, c. 1896*	450.00	550.00
☐	**57**	*Emerald, four rose diamonds, 14K gold, American, c. 1896*	350.00	400.00
☐	**58**	*Emeralds, 20 pearls, 14K gold, American, c. 1895*	325.00	400.00
☐	**59**	*Emeralds, five diamonds, 14K gold, American, c. 1895*	650.00	750.00
☐	**60**	*Emeralds, two rubies, six pearls, 14K gold, American, c. 1895*	375.00	400.00

61

62

63

64

66

65

67

69

68

			Price Range	
☐	**61**	*Emeralds, three rubies, 13 pearls, 14K gold, American, c. 1895*	375.00	400.00
☐	**62**	*Emeralds, three rubies, 13 pearls, 14K gold, American, c. 1895*	375.00	450.00
☐	**63**	*Emerald, two pearls, 14K gold, American, c. 1895* .	200.00	225.00
☐	**64**	*Emeralds, six pearls, 14K gold, American, c. 1895* .	325.00	375.00
☐	**65**	*Emerald, 14K gold, American, c. 1895*	1300.00	1550.00
☐		*Same as above but garnet*	450.00	500.00
☐	**66**	*Emeralds, two pearls, 14K gold, American, c. 1895* .	225.00	275.00
☐	**67**	*Emerald center, two half seed pearls, English, 15K gold, c. 1890*	250.00	300.00
☐	**68**	*Emerald: emerald-cut approx. 1.0 ct., rose diamonds in silver, gold shank, c. 1860*	5750.00	6300.00
☐	**69**	*Emerald: emerald-cut, rose diamonds, platinum, gold, c. 1880-1900*	3300.00	3850.00

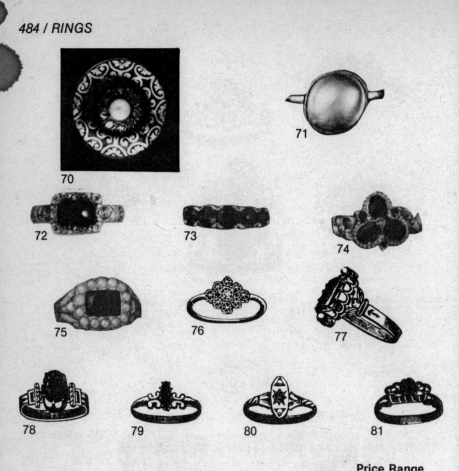

			Price Range	
☐	**70**	Flower motif, center cluster of one cultured pearl and rose diamonds, champleve blue enamel, 14K gold, c. early 20th.	550.00	575.00
☐	**71**	Fresh water pearl, earring converted to ring, 14K gold, c. early 20th.	65.00	125.00
☐	**72**	Garnet: rectangular, gold, c. 1865	450.00	650.00
☐	**73**	Garnets, gold, c. 1860	325.00	450.00
☐	**74**	Garnets: three oval faceted, three faceted emeralds, gold, c. 1830	550.00	650.00
☐	**75**	Garnet: square faceted, half seed pearls, English, c. 1840	400.00	525.00
☐	**76**	Garnets, 14K gold, American, c. 1896	175.00	225.00
☐	**77**	Garnet, pearls, 14K gold, American, c. 1895	200.00	235.00
☐	**78**	Garnet, 14K gold, American, c. 1895	375.00	450.00
☐	**79**	Garnet, 14K gold, American, c. 1895	150.00	175.00
☐	**80**	Garnet, two pearls, 14K gold, American, c. 1895 ..	150.00	175.00
☐	**81**	Garnet, pearls, 14K gold, American, c. 1895	275.00	335.00

82

83

84

85

86

87

88

89

90

		Price Range	
☐	82	Garnet, 22K gold, Oriental, c. late 19th.	225.00	275.00
☐	83	Garnet, cabochon foil-backed, gold, c. 1820	800.00	950.00
☐	84	Garnets, seed pearls, gold, c. 1830	400.00	450.00
☐	85	Green sapphire: oval-cut, rose diamonds and seed pearls set in silver topped gold, gold shank, c. 1920	750.00	1000.00
☐	86	Half pearls, gold, c. mid 19th.	475.00	500.00
☐	87	Jade cabochon, calibre sapphires, 18K gold, Art Deco	700.00	800.00
☐	88	Jade: oblong cabochon, 22K gold, c. 1860	1300.00	1550.00
☐	89	Jade, two triangular-shape diamonds, 20 round diamonds, platinum, c. 1925	2750.00	3300.00
☐	90	Jade, gold, c. 1930	1450.00	1650.00

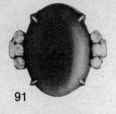

91

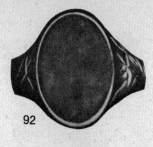

92

93

94

95

96

97

			Price Range	
☐	91	Jade, six round diamonds, 14K gold, c. mid 20th...	1650.00	1850.00
☐	92	Jade, sculptured shank, 14K gold, c. early 20th....	1200.00	1450.00
☐	93	Loveknot motif with three small turquoise, 14K gold, c. late 19th.	300.00	325.00
☐	94	Marquise motif, oval cabochon banded agate in center surrounded by seed pearls, cabochon banded agate along shank, 14K gold, c. 1850	325.00	450.00
☐	95	Marquise motif, rose diamonds in silver, blue enamel background, gold shank, c. 1840	1200.00	1450.00
☐	96	Openwork motif, emeralds, ruby, sapphires and diamonds, gold, c. 1750	1200.00	1450.00
☐	97	Marquise motif, three round sapphires, 20 round diamonds, 14K gold, c. 1860	1450.00	1650.00

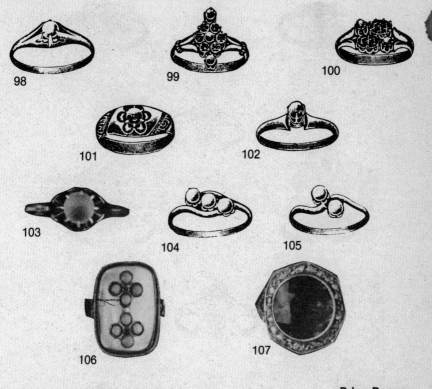

		Price Range	
☐	**98** Moonstone, 14K gold, American, c. 1896	110.00	150.00
☐	**99** Moonstones, six garnets, 14K gold, American, c. 1895	235.00	300.00
☐	**100** Moonstones, two rubies, 14K gold, American, c. 1895	225.00	275.00
☐	**101** Moonstone, 14K gold, American, c. 1895	125.00	150.00
☐	**102** Moonstone, 14K gold, American, c. 1895	125.00	150.00
☐	**103** Moonstone, 14K gold, c. early 20th.	125.00	150.00
☐	**104** Moonstones, 14K gold, American, c. 1896	175.00	200.00
☐	**105** Moonstones, 14K gold, American, c. 1896	150.00	185.00
☐	**106** Mother-of-pearl, eight cabochon turquoise, gold, c. 1915	350.00	400.00
☐	**107** Octagonal motif, one round tourmaline surrounded by rose diamonds, gold, platinum, c. 1890	1550.00	1750.00

108

109

110

111

112

113

114

115

		Price Range	
☐ **108**	*Olivines, two almondine garnets, 14K gold, American, c. 1896*	**175.00**	**200.00**
☐ **109**	*Olivines, four pearls, 14K gold, American, c. 1896*	**150.00**	**175.00**
☐ **110**	*Olivine, two pearls, 14K gold, American, c. 1896*	**150.00**	**175.00**
☐ **111**	*Olivine, four rose diamonds, 14K gold, American, c. 1896*	**325.00**	**400.00**
☐ **112**	*Olivines, six pearls, 14K gold, American, c. 1896*	**175.00**	**200.00**
☐ **113**	*Olivines, seven pearls, 14K gold, American, c. 1896*	**200.00**	**250.00**
☐ **114**	*Olivines, 14 pearls, 14K gold, American, c. 1895*	**250.00**	**300.00**
☐ **115**	*Olivines, moonstone in center, 14K gold, American, c. 1895*	**200.00**	**250.00**

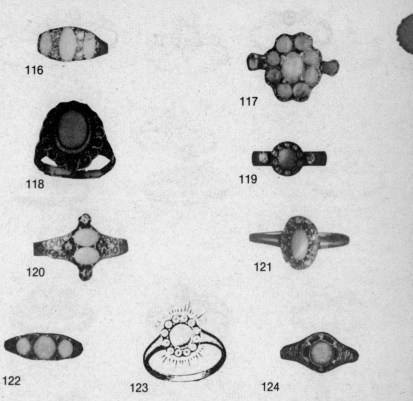

		Price Range	
☐ **116**	Opals, six round diamonds, gold, c. 1860.........	425.00	525.00
☐ **117**	Opals, gold, c. 1880	375.00	500.00
☐ **118**	Opal, rose diamonds, 18K gold, c. 1890	425.00	600.00
☐ **119**	Opal, rose diamonds, gold, c. 1870	550.00	650.00
☐ **120**	Opals, four rose diamonds, gold, c. 1860	375.00	500.00
☐ **121**	Opal, rose diamonds, gold, c. 1870	375.00	500.00
☐ **122**	Opals, rose diamonds, 18K gold	325.00	375.00
☐ **123**	Opal, 12 rose diamonds, 14K gold, American, c. 1896	375.00	450.00
☐ **124**	Opal, simulated, 18K gold	135.00	175.00

125

126

127

128

129

130

131

132

133

134

135

136

			Price Range	
☐	125	Opal, 14K gold, American, c. 1896	175.00	224.00
☐	126	Opals, 14K gold, American, c. 1896	175.00	225.00
☐	127	Opal, 18K gold, American, c. 1896	125.00	150.00
☐	128	Opals, five pearls, 14K gold, American, c. 1896 ...	175.00	225.00
☐	129	Opal, two sapphires, 14K gold, American, c. 1895 .	200.00	250.00
☐	130	Opal, ruby, emerald, 14K gold, American, c. 1895 .	350.00	400.00
☐	131	Opal, two rubies, 14K gold, American, c. 1895	325.00	375.00
☐	132	Opals, 14K gold, American, c. 1895	275.00	325.00
☐	133	Opals, 14K gold, American, c. 1895	325.00	375.00
☐	134	Opals, 14K gold, American, c. 1895	150.00	175.00
☐	135	Opal, 14K gold, American, c. 1895	125.00	150.00
☐	136	Opal, 14K gold, American, c. 1895	135.00	160.00

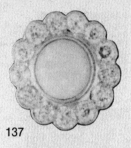

137

138

139

140

141

142

		Price Range	
☐ **137**	*Opal center approx. 2.0 cts. and 13 old mine diamonds approx. 1.30 cts. in platinum, 14K gold shank, c. 1890*	1750.00	2200.00
☐ **138**	*Opal approx. .75 ct., maker: H W ld., 18K gold, c. early 20th.*	175.00	225.00
☐ **139**	*Opal, 14K gold, c. early 20th.*	135.00	175.00
☐ **140**	*Opal, 22K gold, c. early 20th.*	200.00	275.00
☐ **141**	*Opal doublet in center, 16 old mine diamonds, silver, gold, c. late 19th.*	900.00	1000.00
☐ **142**	*Cross over motif, one oriental pearl approx. 22MM, one old mine diamond approx. .35 ct., eight rose diamonds, all diamonds in platinum, 14K gold shank, c. 1870*	750.00	1000.00

143

144

145

146

147

148

149

150

151

		Price Range	
☐ **143**	Openwork motif, one oval sapphire in center, rose and mine cut diamonds, silver topped gold, c. 1890	900.00	1000.00
☐ **144**	Openwork floral motif, ruby, emerald and cabochon sapphire in silver, gold shank, c. 1750	550.00	650.00
☐ **145**	Heart and crown motif, emerald in heart, rose diamonds in crown, gold, c. 1840	550.00	650.00
☐ **146**	Pear-shape cluster with opal center, border of 14 rose diamonds approx. .30 ct., 14K gold, c. mid 19th.	750.00	900.00
☐ **147**	Pearls, gold, c. 1860	450.00	550.00
☐ **148**	Pearl, four Holland rose diamonds, four rose diamonds, gold, silver, c. 1750	1650.00	1850.00
☐ **149**	Pearls: natural, round diamonds, gold, platinum, c. 1900	1200.00	1450.00
☐ **150**	Pearls, 12 rose diamonds, gold, c. 1880	550.00	650.00
☐ **151**	Pearls, diamond center, gold, c. 1860	375.00	500.00

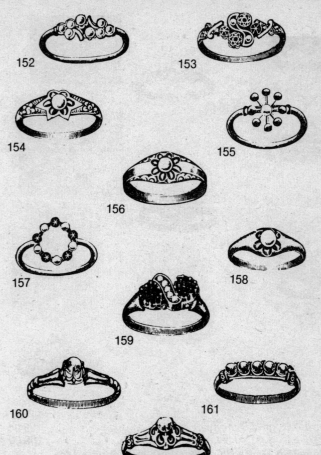

			Price Range	
☐	**152**	*Pearls, 14K gold, American, c. 1896*	**150.00**	**175.00**
☐	**153**	*Pearls, two rubies, two emeralds, 14K gold, American, c. 1896*	**250.00**	**300.00**
☐	**154**	*Pearl, 14K gold, American, c. 1896*	**150.00**	**175.00**
☐	**155**	*Pearl, eight turquoise, 14K gold, American, c. 1896*	**200.00**	**250.00**
☐	**156**	*Pearls, Garnets, 14K gold, American, c. 1896*	**135.00**	**160.00**
☐	**157**	*Pearl, 14K gold, American, c. 1896*	**105.00**	**125.00**
☐	**158**	*Pearls, two heart rubies, 14K gold, American, 1895*	**375.00**	**450.00**
☐	**159**	*Pearl, 14K gold, American, c. 1895*	**135.00**	**160.00**
☐	**160**	*Pearls, 14K gold, American, c. 1895*	**150.00**	**200.00**
☐	**161**	*Pearl, 14K gold, American, c. 1895*	**135.00**	**160.00**
☐	**162**	*Pearl, 14K gold, American, c. 1895*	**150.00**	**175.00**

163

164

166

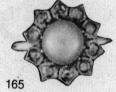

165

167

169

168

170

171

			Price Range	
☐	163	*Pearl, 14K gold, American, c. 1895*	125.00	150.00
☐	164	*Pearl, 14K gold, American, c. 1895*	105.00	125.00
☐	165	*Pearl approx. 5.7MM, rose diamond border, 14K gold*	325.00	450.00
☐	166	*Pink sapphires, rose diamonds, gold, c. 1860*	1650.00	1850.00
☐	167	*Pink topaz, one olivine in center, 14K gold, American, c. 1895*	300.00	350.00
☐	168	*Pink topaz, pearl in center, 14K gold, American, c. 1895*	225.00	275.00
☐	169	*Pink topaz, pearl in center, 14K gold, American, c. 1895*	225.00	275.00
☐	170	*Pink topaz, olivine in center, 14K gold, American, c. 1895*	225.00	285.00
☐	171	*Pink topaz, one pearl, 14K gold, American, c. 1895* .	175.00	225.00

172

173

174

175

176

177

178

		Price Range	
☐ **172**	Pink tourmaline, gold balls replaced original round diamonds, 14K gold, c. mid 20th...........	325.00	385.00
☐ **173**	"Regard" motif, different colored gem stones, gold, c. early 19th.	300.00	350.00
☐ **174**	Ruby: round, old mine diamonds, c. 1920	800.00	950.00
☐ **175**	Ruby: round approx. 1.25 cts., old mine diamonds, platinum, c. 1925	2750.00	3300.00
☐ **176**	Ruby, old mine diamonds, gold, c. 1850	1200.00	1450.00
☐ **177**	Ruby: oval, old mine and round diamonds, gold topped platinum, c. 1880	3850.00	4400.00
☐ **178**	Ruby: oval approx. .90 ct., 27 old European-cut diamonds, gold, silver, c. 1870	3300.00	4400.00

179

180

181

182

183

184

185

186

			Price Range	
☐	**179**	Ruby, ten round diamonds, 14K gold, c. 1870	750.00	1000.00
☐	**180**	Ruby: oval approx. 1.0 ct., rose diamonds, silver topped platinum, c. 1850	3750.00	3950.00
☐	**181**	Rubies: one oval approx. 1.0 ct., calibre rubies, 14 round diamonds, platinum, c. 1920	4100.00	4400.00
☐	**182**	Rubies: six square-cut, 23 round diamonds approx. 1.0 ct., platinum, French, Art Deco, c. 1925 . .	2200.00	2400.00
☐	**183**	Ruby: oval cabochon approx. 9.75 cts., 32 round diamonds approx. .75 ct., platinum, c. 1910	3500.00	4200.00
☐	**184**	Rubies, seven pearls, 14K gold, American, c. 1896 .	175.00	225.00
☐	**185**	Ruby, two diamonds, 18K gold, English, Victorian	500.00	600.00
☐	**186**	Rubies, three pearls, 14K gold, American, c. 1896 .	150.00	175.00

187

188

189

190

189

191

192

193

194

195

			Price Range	
☐	**187**	*Ruby, 14K gold, American, c. 1896*	175.00	200.00
☐	**188**	*Rubies, 14K gold, American, c. 1896*	185.00	225.00
☐	**189**	*Ruby, four pearls, 14K gold, American, c. 1896* ...	175.00	200.00
☐	**190**	*Ruby, four pearls, 14K gold, American, c. 1896* ...	175.00	200.00
☐	**191**	*Ruby, two pearls, 14K gold, American, c. 1896*	180.00	225.00
☐	**192**	*Rubies, six pearls, 14K gold, American, c. 1896* ...	150.00	175.00
☐	**193**	*Rubies, six pearls, 14K gold, American, c. 1896* ...	200.00	250.00
☐	**194**	*Rubies, 14K gold, American, c. 1896*	225.00	275.00
☐	**195**	*Ruby, four pearls, 14K gold, American, c. 1896* ...	175.00	200.00

196

197

198

199

200

201

202

203

			Price Range	
☐	196	Rubies, 18 rose diamonds, 14K gold, American, c. 1896	375.00	425.00
☐	197	Ruby, two rose diamonds, 14K gold, American, c. 1896	475.00	550.00
☐	198	Rubies, nine pearls, 14K gold, American, c. 1896 ..	400.00	475.00
☐	199	Ruby, six pearls, 14K gold, American, c. 1896	185.00	225.00
☐	200	Ruby, eight pearls, 14K gold, American, c. 1896 ..	175.00	200.00
☐	201	Rubies, six pearls, 14K gold, American, c. 1896 ...	300.00	350.00
☐	202	Rubies, eight pearls, 14K gold, American, c. 1896 .	225.00	300.00
☐	203	Ruby, ten pearls, 14K gold, American, c. 1895	250.00	325.00

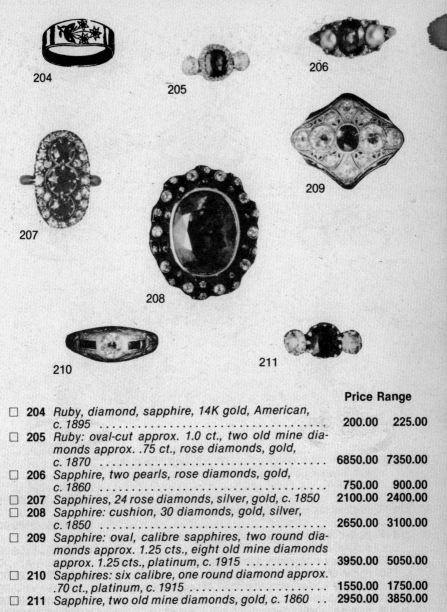

204

205

206

207

209

208

210

211

		Price Range	
☐ 204	Ruby, diamond, sapphire, 14K gold, American, c. 1895	200.00	225.00
☐ 205	Ruby: oval-cut approx. 1.0 ct., two old mine diamonds approx. .75 ct., rose diamonds, gold, c. 1870	6850.00	7350.00
☐ 206	Sapphire, two pearls, rose diamonds, gold, c. 1860	750.00	900.00
☐ 207	Sapphires, 24 rose diamonds, silver, gold, c. 1850	2100.00	2400.00
☐ 208	Sapphire: cushion, 30 diamonds, gold, silver, c. 1850	2650.00	3100.00
☐ 209	Sapphire: oval, calibre sapphires, two round diamonds approx. 1.25 cts., eight old mine diamonds approx. 1.25 cts., platinum, c. 1915	3950.00	5050.00
☐ 210	Sapphires: six calibre, one round diamond approx. .70 ct., platinum, c. 1915	1550.00	1750.00
☐ 211	Sapphire, two old mine diamonds, gold, c. 1860 ..	2950.00	3850.00

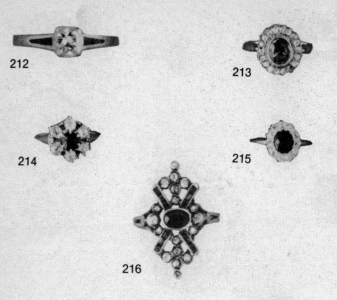

			Price Range	
☐	**212**	Sapphires: four calibre French-cut, one round diamond approx. .60 ct., platinum, signed: Tiffany & Co., c. 1940	2750.00	3300.00
☐	**213**	Sapphire, 18 rose diamonds, 14K gold, c. 1880 . . .	650.00	850.00
☐	**214**	Sapphire, six old mine diamonds, 14K gold, c. 1870	750.00	1000.00
☐	**215**	Sapphire: oval approx. .90 ct., old mine diamonds, 14K gold, c. 1900	1200.00	1450.00
☐	**216**	Sapphires: one oval and 12 square, diamonds, gold, silver, c. 1880	2300.00	2750.00
☐	**217**	Sapphire: square approx. 2.70 cts., 58 round diamonds, platinum, c. 1890-1900	3950.00	4600.00
☐	**218**	Sapphires, round diamonds, platinum, c. 1930 . . .	2750.00	3300.00

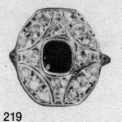

219

220

221

222

223

224

225

			Price Range	
☐	**219**	Sapphire: French-cut, 16 round diamonds, c. 1925 .	750.00	1000.00
☐	**220**	Sapphire: cabochon, three rose diamonds, 14K gold, c. 1890-1900	450.00	550.00
☐	**221**	Sapphires: square-cut, two rose diamonds, silver, c. 1900	350.00	475.00
☐	**222**	Sapphire, pearls, gold, c. 1860	525.00	575.00
☐	**223**	Sapphire: oval cabochon, 54 round diamonds approx. 1.50 cts., platinum, signed: J. E. C. & Co., c. early 20th.	15750.00	16800.00
☐	**224**	Sapphire, 28 old mine diamonds, gold, c. 1890 . . .	1750.00	2000.00
☐	**225**	Sapphire: oval approx. 3.25 cts., 48 round diamonds approx. 1.50 cts., platinum, c. 1925	21000.00	23100.00

226

227

228

229

230

231

232

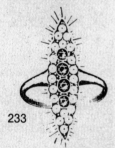

233

			Price Range	
☐	226	Sapphire, four pearls, 14K gold, American, c. 1896 .	175.00	200.00
☐	227	Sapphire, four pearls, 14K gold, American, c. 1896 ..	135.00	150.00
☐	228	Sapphire, 14K gold, American, c. 1896	150.00	200.00
☐	229	Sapphires, 14K gold, American, c. 1896	200.00	250.00
☐	230	Sapphires, two pearls, 14K gold, American, c. 1896	200.00	225.00
☐	231	Sapphire, two pearls, 14K gold, American, c. 1896	150.00	200.00
☐	232	Sapphire, 12 rose diamonds, 14K gold, American, c. 1896	400.00	450.00
☐	233	Sapphires, 22 rose diamonds, 14K gold, American, c. 1896	500.00	550.00

235

234

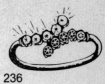

236

238

237

239

240

		Price Range	
☐ **234**	Sapphire, 14 rose diamonds, 14K gold, American, c. 1896	400.00	450.00
☐ **235**	Sapphire, 16 rose diamonds, 14K gold, American, c. 1896	650.00	750.00
☐ **236**	Sapphires, five rose diamonds, 14K gold, American, c. 1896	375.00	450.00
☐ **237**	Sapphire, six pearls, 14K gold, American, c. 1895 .	225.00	275.00
☐ **238**	Sapphires, four pearls, 14K gold, American, c. 1895	250.00	285.00
☐ **239**	Sapphires, two pearls, 14K gold, American, c. 1895	175.00	225.00
☐ **240**	Sapphires, five pearls, 14K gold, American, c. 1895	225.00	300.00

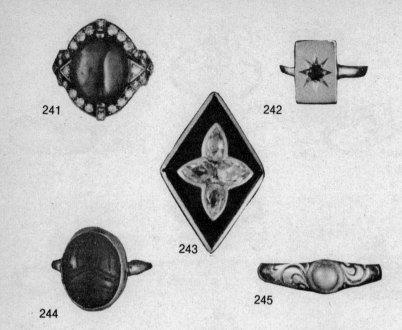

		Price Range	
☐ 241	Sapphire: cabochon, round diamonds, silver topped gold, c. 1925	3950.00	4200.00
☐ 242	Sapphire, 9K gold, English, c. 20th.	225.00	275.00
☐ 243	Sardonyx plaque with four pear-shape diamonds approx. .80 ct., 14K gold, American, c. 1930-40 ...	1450.00	1750.00
☐ 244	Scarab, sardonyx, 14K gold, c. mid 19th.	225.00	275.00
☐ 245	Seed pearl, engraved band, gold, c. 1880	150.00	200.00
☐ 246	Seed pearl pave set, garnet in center, 14K gold, c. late 19th.	135.00	175.00
☐ 247	Seed pearls, calibre turquoise, gold, c. 1850	175.00	200.00

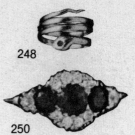

248

249

250

251

252

253

254

		Price Range	
☐ **248**	*Snake motif, one diamond, gold, c. 20th*	**325.00**	**350.00**
☐ **249**	*Snake motif, two round diamonds, 14K gold, American, c. 1915*	**375.00**	**450.00**
☐ **250**	*Straight row motif, three round sapphires approx. .40 ct., ten old mine diamonds approx. .18 ct., 18K gold, Chester, England, c. 1896*	**1750.00**	**2400.00**
☐ **251**	*Straight row motif, two garnets, three rose diamonds, collet-set, gold, c. 1850*	**1200.00**	**1450.00**
☐ **252**	*Straight row motif, five cabochon turquoise, rose diamonds, gold, c. 1850*	**900.00**	**1100.00**
☐ **253**	*Straight row motif, three round rubies, two old mine diamonds, small rose diamonds, 18K gold, c. 1870*	**2000.00**	**2200.00**
☐ **254**	*Straight row motif, one round diamond approx. 1.70 cts. in center, two round sapphires, two round diamonds approx. .90 ct., gold, c. 1880*	**6300.00**	**6850.00**

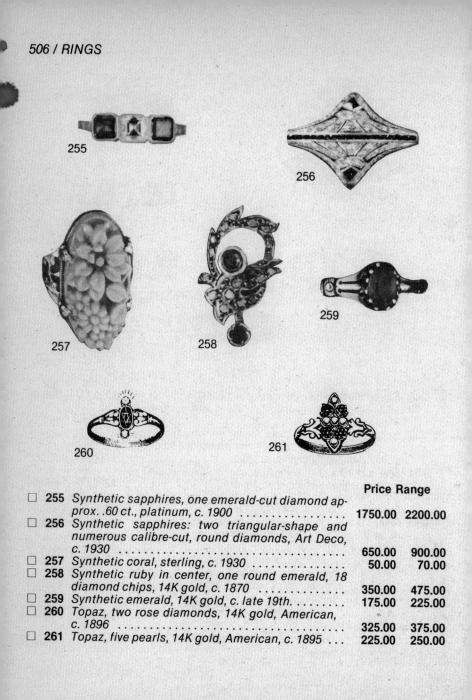

255

256

257

258

259

260

261

			Price Range	
☐	**255**	*Synthetic sapphires, one emerald-cut diamond approx. .60 ct., platinum, c. 1900*	**1750.00**	**2200.00**
☐	**256**	*Synthetic sapphires: two triangular-shape and numerous calibre-cut, round diamonds, Art Deco, c. 1930*	**650.00**	**900.00**
☐	**257**	*Synthetic coral, sterling, c. 1930*	**50.00**	**70.00**
☐	**258**	*Synthetic ruby in center, one round emerald, 18 diamond chips, 14K gold, c. 1870*	**350.00**	**475.00**
☐	**259**	*Synthetic emerald, 14K gold, c. late 19th.*	**175.00**	**225.00**
☐	**260**	*Topaz, two rose diamonds, 14K gold, American, c. 1896*	**325.00**	**375.00**
☐	**261**	*Topaz, five pearls, 14K gold, American, c. 1895* ...	**225.00**	**250.00**

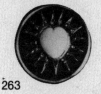

262

263

264

265

266

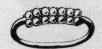

267

268

269

271

270

			Price Range	
☐	262	Triple band motif, one round sapphire, one round diamond, one round ruby, each stone approx. .25 ct., 14K gold, American, c. 1930-40	1100.00	1550.00
☐	263	Turquoise heart, 16 rose diamonds, gold, c. 1870 .	450.00	650.00
☐	264	Turquoise: calibre, pearl, gold, c. 1840	350.00	500.00
☐	265	Turquoise: pear-shape, diamonds, gold, c. 1860 . .	475.00	600.00
☐	266	Turquoise, gold, c. 1850	450.00	550.00
☐	267	Turquoise, 16 pearls, 14K gold, American, c. 1896 .	150.00	200.00
☐	268	Turquoise, four pearls, 14K gold, American, c. 1896	150.00	200.00
☐	269	Turquoise, seven pearls, 14K gold, American, c. 1896	225.00	275.00
☐	270	Turquoise, eight pearls, 14K gold, American, c. 1895	225.00	275.00
☐	271	Turquoise, three pearls, 14K gold, American, c. 1895	225.00	275.00

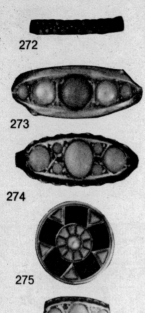

272

277

278

279

280

281

275

276

			Price Range	
☐	272	Turquoise pavé set band, 14K gold, c. 1870	275.00	375.00
☐	273	Turquoise, two half pearls, 9K gold, Birmingham, England, c. early 20th..........................	200.00	225.00
☐	274	Turquoise, four round corals, maker: C L, 9K gold, Chester, England, c. 1928	200.00	225.00
☐	275	Turquoise: calibre and triangular-cut, seed pearl center, champlevé black enamel, 15K gold, c. late 19th...............................	650.00	750.00
☐	276	Turquoise: cabochon, four rose diamonds, 15K gold, English, c. 1910	275.00	300.00
☐	277	Turquoise: cabochon, seed pearls, 18K gold, Birmingham, English, c. 1887 ...·...............	275.00	310.00
☐	278	Turquoise: cabochon, four rose diamonds, 18K gold, Birmingham, England, c. 1910	250.00	300.00
☐	279	Turquoise: cabochon, engraved shank, 18K gold inscribed: "Geo. Wood ob. 12 Mar. 1843 at 65," London, England, c. 1817	275.00	325.00
☐	280	Turquoise: cabochon, eight rose diamonds, 18K gold, English, c. 1880	375.00	450.00
☐	281	Turquoise: cabochon, 18K gold, maker: J. S., Birmingham, England, c. 1898	200.00	275.00

282   283   284

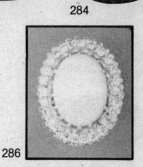

285   286

Price Range

☐	**282**	Turquoise: cabochon, two pearls, 9K gold, Birmingham, England, c. 1900	150.00 200.00
☐	**283**	Turquoise: cabochon, two rose diamonds, 18K gold, maker: JR, London, England, c. 1900	325.00 375.00
☐	**284**	Turquoise: cabochon, four small cabochon coral, 9K gold, maker: C. L., Chester, England, c. 1928 ..	200.00 250.00
☐	**285**	Turquoise, pearls, diamonds, blue enamel, gold, c. 1870	450.00 500.00
☐	**286**	White Opal: cabochon, 28 round diamonds approx. 1.50 cts., white gold, c. 1925	2100.00 2650.00

1

2

LADIES – MISCELLANEOUS

☐	**1**	Belt motif, maker: W. W., London, England, 22K gold, c. 1904	450.00 475.00
☐	**2**	Enamel angel, gold, c. 1870	475.00 575.00

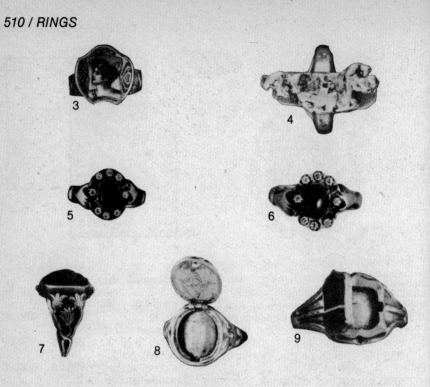

			Price Range	
☐	**3**	*Enamel face of Ceres, the goddess of agriculture in Roman mythology, gold, c. 1890*	550.00	650.00
☐	**4**	*Gold nugget on 14K gold band, c. 1890*	450.00	550.00
☐	**5**	*Hands holding an oval center of a cabochon garnet and eight diamonds, gold, c. 1880*	650.00	750.00
☐	**6**	*Hands holding cabochon garnet surrounded by diamonds, modified gimmal ring, gold, c. 1850* ...	750.00	1000.00
☐	**7**	*Hardstone scarab, lotus leaf motif on shank, 18K gold, maker: Tiffany & Co., American*	750.00	1000.00
☐	**8**	*Hidden compartment, shell cameo of gentleman in cover, gold, c. 1820*	450.00	550.00
☐	**9**	*Hidden compartment, onyx shield in cover, gold, c. 1860*	325.00	450.00

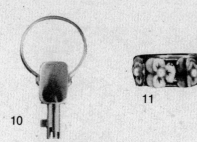

10

11

12

13

14

15

16

17

			Price Range	
☐	10	Key to jewelry box hinged to fit under plain rectangular plaque for monogram, gold, English, c. 1880	550.00	650.00
☐	11	Pansy motif, polychrome enamel, seed pearls, gold	500.00	600.00
☐	12	Sculptured childs face, two baroque pearls, two round rubies, Art Nouveau, c. 1890-1910	750.00	900.00
☐	13	Snake, five round diamonds, gold	750.00	900.00
☐	14	Snake, ruby in head, diamond eyes, gold, c. 1840 .	375.00	450.00
☐	15	Snake, natural fancy color diamond approx. 1.0 ct. in head, rose diamond eyes, gold, c. 1860	3750.00	4200.00
☐	16	Snakes, opal and amethyst in heads, maker: A. C. Co., Birmingham, England, 9K gold	375.00	500.00
☐	17	Sphinx carved from garnet, inlaid with gold and two rose diamonds, border of rose diamonds in silver, 18K gold band, c. 1870	6300.00	7350.00

18

19

			Price Range	
☐	**18**	Vinaigrette ring, silver, maker: H.W.D., London, England, c. 1869	550.00	650.00
☐	**19**	Vinaigrette ring, swivels, carnelian on reverse, gold, c. late 18th	650.00	750.00

1

2

WATCH

☐	**1**	Watch ring, rose diamonds, enamel dial, steel hands, white gold case, maker: Nomos, c. 1920 ..	1750.00	1800.00
☐	**2**	Watch ring, round and fancy-cut diamonds, enamel dial, steel hands, platinum case, c. 1925	6900.00	7900.00
☐	**3**	Watch ring, oval Art Deco motif, polychrome enamels, white enamel dial, steel hands, 18K gold case, c. 1930	1900.00	2200.00

1

WEDDING BAND

Price Range

☐ **1** *Fancy cutout and shaped motif, engraved and chased, 14K gold, American, c. 1896* **275.00   450.00**

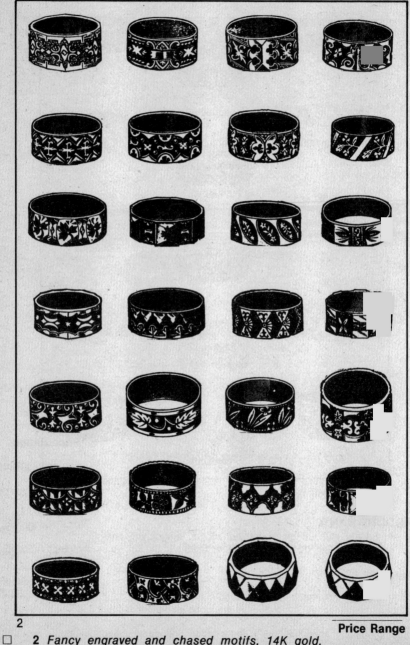

	Price Range	
2 Fancy engraved and chased motifs, 14K gold, American, c. 1894-95, each	**225.00**	**325.00**

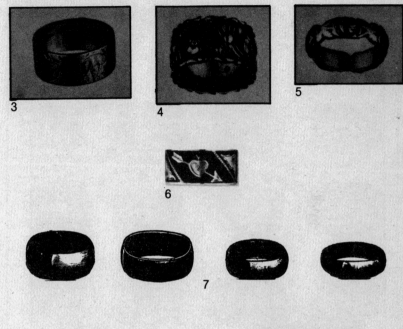

		Price Range	
☐	**3** *Bird and flower motif, rose and green 14K gold, c. 20th*	250.00	275.00
☐	**4** *Flower motif, round rubies, yellow, rose and green 14K gold, c. 20th.*	400.00	450.00
☐	**5** *Flower motif, white, yellow, rose and green 14K gold, c. 20th.*	350.00	400.00
☐	**6** *Heart and arrow motif, black enamel, gold, c. 1900 .*	375.00	450.00
☐	**7** *Polished rounded motif, 14K gold, American, c. 1894-95*	125.00	175.00
☐	**8** *Rose diamond, chased 14K gold, American, c. 1896*	300.00	325.00
☐	**9** *Round diamonds, calibre rubies, platinum, c. 1915 .*	1000.00	1100.00

Photograph of a young woman taken by Sweet in Springfield, Illinois. She is wearing a brooch in a half-moon and star motif at the neckline. The knife-edge brooch is set with six faceted gemstones.

1

2

3

4

5

6

7

SCARF RINGS and STICKPINS

		SCARF RINGS	Price Range	
☐	1	*Arrow motif, garnets, gold, c. 1900-10*	300.00	325.00
☐	2	*Belt motif, three old mine diamonds, gold,*		
		c. 1900-10	275.00	300.00
☐	3	*Belt motif, engraved leaves, sterling silver, c. 1890* .	125.00	175.00
☐	4	*Belt motif, sterling, maker: S.J.R., London, En-*		
		gland, c. 1957	125.00	165.00
☐	5	*Belt motif, black enamel, half seed pearls, rose*		
		diamonds, gold, c. 1890-1900	300.00	325.00
☐	6	*Belt motif, tortoise shell, silver, c. 1890-1910*	125.00	175.00
☐	7	*Cluster motif, pearls, gold, c. 1900-10*	250.00	300.00

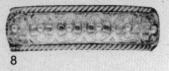

8

9

10

11

13

12

14

			Price Range	
☐	**8**	*Etruscan granulation and rope motif, gold, c. 1900-10*	185.00	225.00
☐	**9**	*Etruscan granulation and rope motif, 15K gold, maker: A & W, English, c. 19th.*	275.00	300.00
☐	**10**	*Flower motif, gold, c. late 19th.*	800.00	900.00
☐	**11**	*Flower motif, green, rose and yellow gold, c. 1900-10*	185.00	225.00
☐	**12**	*Flower motif, one cushion cut diamond approx. .15 ct., gold, registration mark of February 13, 1878*	400.00	450.00
☐	**13**	*Flower motif, six seed pearls, four turquoise, gold, c. 1900-10*	225.00	275.00
☐	**14**	*Flower motif, 20K gold, maker: HS, English, c. 19th.*	350.00	475.00

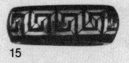

15

16

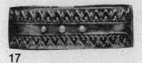

17

18

19

20

21

			Price Range	
☐	**15**	*Greek key motif, piqué: tortoise shell inlaid with gold, c. late 19th.*	185.00	225.00
☐	**16**	*Grill motif, five seed pearls, gold, c. 1900-10*	250.00	300.00
☐	**17**	*Heart border motif, three seed pearls, gold, c. 1900-10*	175.00	225.00
☐	**18**	*Horseshoe and riding crop motif, engraved sterling silver, c. 1900-10*	135.00	150.00
☐	**19**	*Lily-of-the-valley flower motif, champlevé black enamel, seed pearls, gold, c. 1870*	250.00	275.00
☐	**20**	*Locket motif, hair in basketweave pattern, engraved gold, c. 1880*	275.00	300.00
☐	**21**	*Loveknot motif, gold, c. 1900-10*	275.00	300.00

22

23

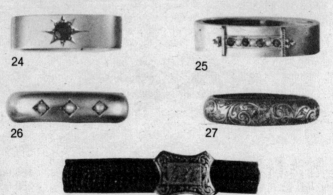

24   25

26   27

28

			Price Range	
☐	22	*Single stone motif, opal, gold, c. 1900-10*	225.00	250.00
☐	23	*Snake motif, ruby eyes, seven baroque pearls, two wing pearls, gold, c. 1880*	375.00	425.00
☐	24	*Star motif, one faceted garnet, 9K gold, English, c. 1900-10*	225.00	250.00
☐	25	*Straight line motif, four garnets, three seed pearls, Etruscan granulation, 9K gold, English, c. 1900-10*	350.00	400.00
☐	26	*Straight line motif, three half seed pearls, gold, c. 1900-10*	225.00	250.00
☐	27	*Swirl motif, engraved, 15K gold, English, c. 19th. . .*	175.00	200.00
☐	28	*Woven hair motif, gold shield for initials, c. 1840-60*	135.00	175.00

STICKPINS – ANIMALS and BUGS

			Price Range	
☐	**1**	*Alligator, one seed pearl, 14K gold, American, c. 1896*	135.00	160.00
☐	**2**	*Bird, reverse painting under crystal, gold, c. 19th.* .	135.00	160.00
☐	**3**	*Bird, reverse painting under crystal, gold, c. 19th.* .	135.00	160.00
☐	**4**	*Beetle, gold, c. 1870*	115.00	175.00
☐	**5**	*Bird, rose diamonds, silver, gold, c. 1860*	250.00	275.00
☐	**6**	*Bird, rose diamonds in body, ruby in eye, gold, c. early 20th*	135.00	160.00

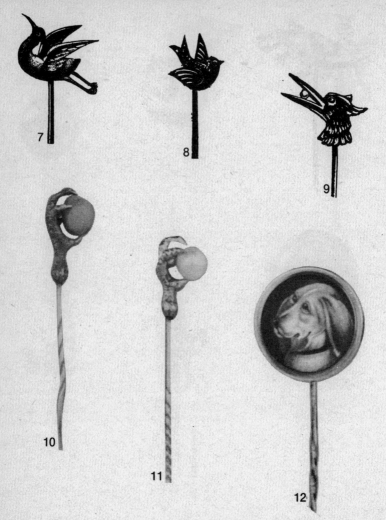

			Price Range	
☐	**7**	Bird, 14K rose and yellow gold, American, c. 1894-95	125.00	140.00
☐	**8**	Bird, sterling silver, American, c. 1894-95	50.00	60.00
☐	**9**	Bird head, one seed pearl, 14K green gold, American, c. 1894-95	150.00	175.00
☐	**10**	Bird claw, button-shape coral, gold, c. 1880	165.00	200.00
☐	**11**	Bird claw, pearl, gold, c. 1880	165.00	200.00
☐	**12**	Bloodhound painted on ivory, gold, English, c. 1865	350.00	400.00

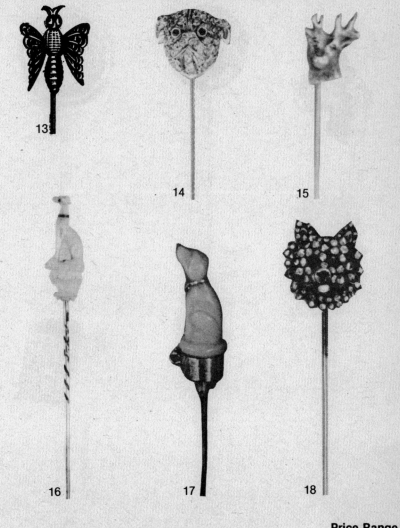

			Price Range	
☐	**13**	*Bug, sterling silver, American, c. 1896*	**55.00**	**65.00**
☐	**14**	*Bulldog head, pavé diamonds, ruby eyes, silver topped gold, c. 19th.*	**500.00**	**600.00**
☐	**15**	*Deer head, rose diamond eyes, gold, c. early 20th..*	**135.00**	**170.00**
☐	**16**	*Dog, carved coral, gold, c. 19th*	**175.00**	**200.00**
☐	**17**	*Dog, carved ivory, gold, c. 19th*	**175.00**	**200.00**
☐	**18**	*Dog head, Husky, pavé rose diamonds, emerald eyes, pink enamel tongue, silver topped gold, c. 19th.*	**600.00**	**700.00**

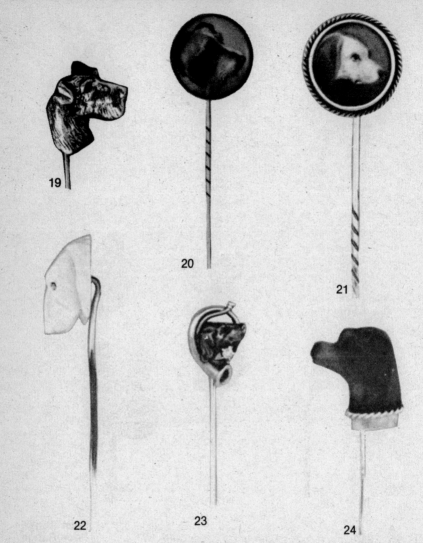

			Price Range	
☐	**19**	Dog head, gold, c. 20th	95.00	115.00
☐	**20**	Dog head, painted on porcelain, gold, Victorian ..	275.00	300.00
☐	**21**	Dog's head painted on porcelain, gold, c. 1865....	300.00	350.00
☐	**22**	Dog head, carved ivory, yellow metal pin, c. 20th ..	70.00	90.00
☐	**23**	Dog head with horn, translucent brown and gold enamel, one round diamond, gold, c. 1920	275.00	325.00
☐	**24**	Dog head, carved amethyst, gold, c. 1915	650.00	750.00

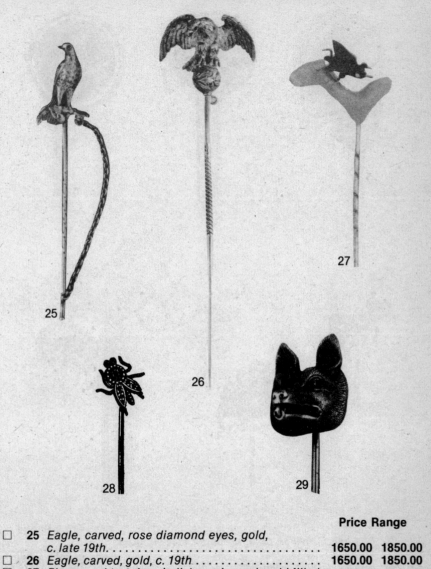

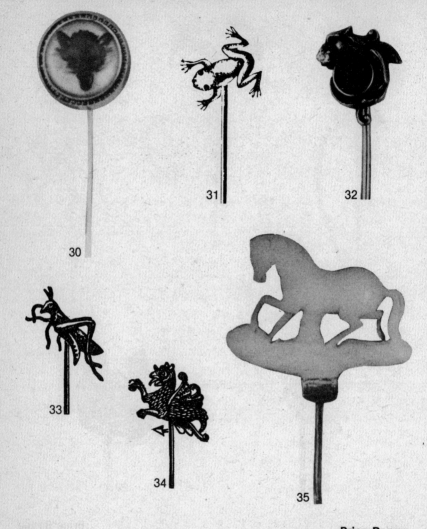

			Price Range	
☐	**30**	Fox head, reverse painting under crystal, gold, c. 19th..	375.00	400.00
☐	**31**	Frog, 14K gold, American, c. 1896	150.00	175.00
☐	**32**	Gargoyle, one round diamond, one round cabochon jade, gold, c. 1900	225.00	250.00
☐	**33**	Grasshopper, 14K gold, American, c. 1894-95.....	105.00	125.00
☐	**34**	Griffin, 14K gold, American, c. 1894-95	135.00	150.00
☐		Same as above but gold filled................	40.00	45.00
☐	**35**	Horse, carved ivory, gold, c. 19th ......:........	200.00	225.00

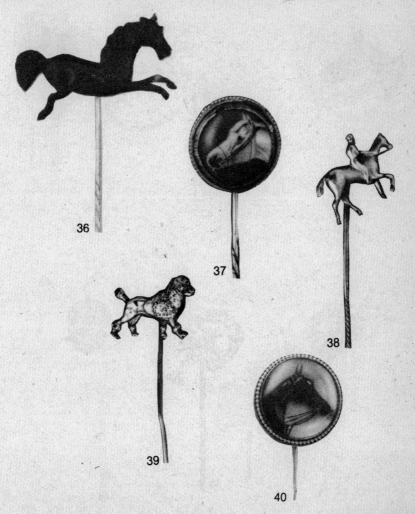

			Price Range	
☐	**36**	*Horse, carved tortoise shell, gold pin, c. 1850*	375.00	450.00
☐	**37**	*Horse head painted on porcelain, gold, c. 19th*	225.00	250.00
☐	**38**	*Horse and rider, gold, c. 19th*	250.00	275.00
☐	**39**	*Poodle, gold, c. 20th*	185.00	225.00
☐	**40**	*Horse, reverse painting under crystal, c. 1880*	275.00	325.00

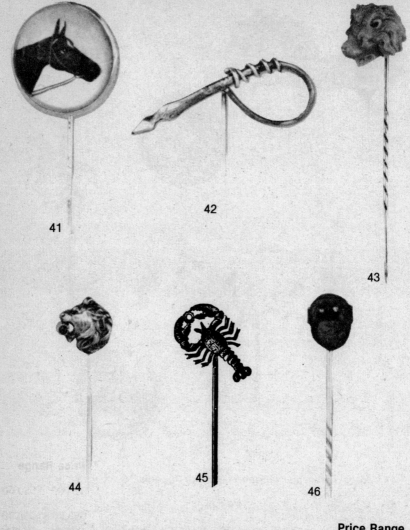

			Price Range	
☐	**41**	Horse head, reverse painting under crystal gold, c. 19th..	300.00	350.00
☐	**42**	Horse hoof with whip, gold, c. 1890	200.00	225.00
☐	**43**	Lion head, carved coral, gold, c. 1860	200.00	225.00
☐	**44**	Lion head, one garnet in mouth, gold, c. 20th	160.00	200.00
☐	**45**	Lobster, one seed pearl, 14K gold, American, c. 1896	160.00	200.00
☐	**46**	Monkey head, carved labradorite, diamond eyes, gold, c. 19th...................................	450.00	550.00

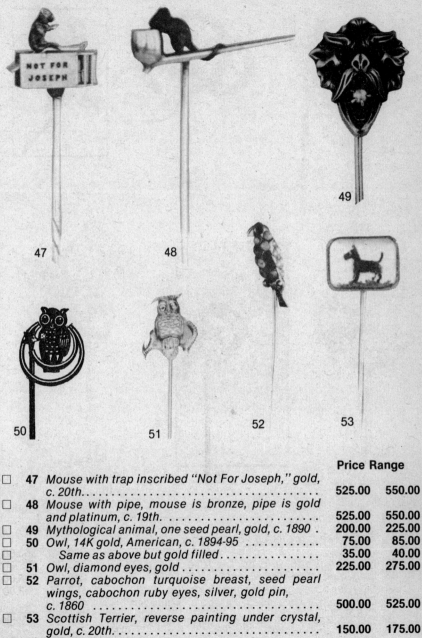

			Price Range	
☐	**47**	*Mouse with trap inscribed "Not For Joseph," gold, c. 20th.*	**525.00**	**550.00**
☐	**48**	*Mouse with pipe, mouse is bronze, pipe is gold and platinum, c. 19th.*	**525.00**	**550.00**
☐	**49**	*Mythological animal, one seed pearl, gold, c. 1890*	**200.00**	**225.00**
☐	**50**	*Owl, 14K gold, American, c. 1894-95*	**75.00**	**85.00**
☐		*Same as above but gold filled*	**35.00**	**40.00**
☐	**51**	*Owl, diamond eyes, gold*	**225.00**	**275.00**
☐	**52**	*Parrot, cabochon turquoise breast, seed pearl wings, cabochon ruby eyes, silver, gold pin, c. 1860*	**500.00**	**525.00**
☐	**53**	*Scottish Terrier, reverse painting under crystal, gold, c. 20th.*	**150.00**	**175.00**

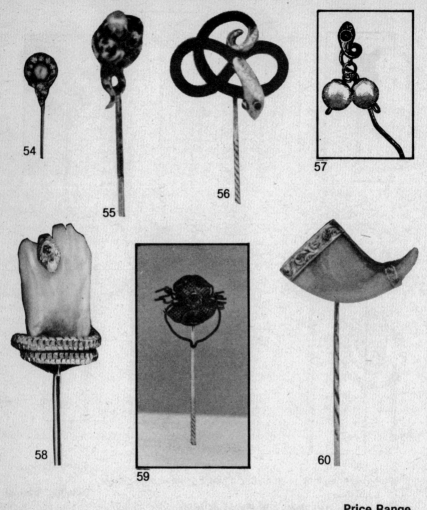

		Price Range	
☐	**54** Snake, one pearl, diamonds, platinum, gold pin, c. 20th.	625.00	650.00
☐	**55** Snake, cobalt-blue enamel, one pearl, gold, c. 1860	300.00	325.00
☐	**56** Snake, woven hair body, ruby eyes, gold, c. mid 19th.	325.00	375.00
☐	**57** Snake, one round emerald in head, two moonstone balls, 14K gold, American, c. 1894-95	175.00	200.00
☐	**58** Snake, fresh water pearl, one diamond, 14K gold..	325.00	450.00
☐	**59** Spider, silver, c. 19th	65.00	75.00
☐	**60** Tiger claw, engraved mountings, gold, c. 1870	300.00	325.00

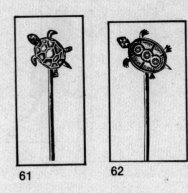

61   62   63   64

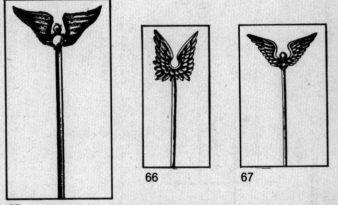

65   66   67

		Price Range	
☐	**61** Turtle, 14K gold, American, c. 1896	110.00	125.00
☐	**62** Turtle, five cabochon turquoise, 14K gold, American, c. 1896	150.00	175.00
☐	**63** Wing, one seed pearl, 14K gold, American, c. 1896 .	75.00	90.00
☐	**64** Wing and wishbone, one round ruby, 14K gold, American, c. 1896	175.00	200.00
☐	**65** Wings, one seed pearl, 14K gold, American, c. 1896	100.00	110.00
☐	**66** Wings, 14K gold, American, c. 1896	125.00	135.00
☐	Same as above but gold filled.	45.00	50.00
☐	**67** Wings, one cabochon turquoise, 14K gold, American, c. 1896	125.00	135.00

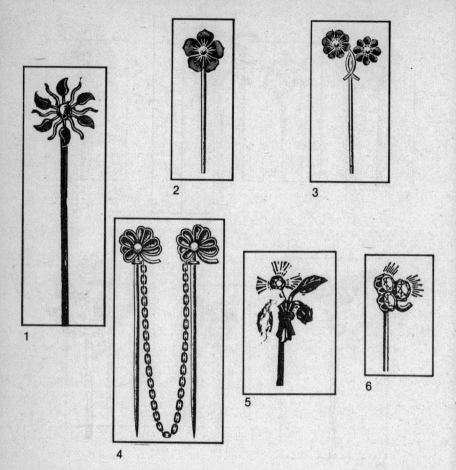

STICKPINS - FLOWERS

Price Range

☐ **1** *Black enamel, one seed pearl, 14K gold, American, c. 1898* **110.00** **135.00**
☐ **2** *Black onyx, 14K gold, American, c. 1896* **65.00** **85.00**
☐ **3** *Black onyx, 14K gold, American, c. 1896* **90.00** **110.00**
☐ **4** *Chain connected pair, two seed pearls, 14K gold, American, c. 1894-95* **200.00** **225.00**
☐ **5** *Diamond: one round, 14K gold, American, c. 1894-95* **135.00** **160.00**
☐ **6** *Diamonds: three round, 14K gold, American, c. 1894-95* **250.00** **300.00**

		Price Range	
☐ **7**	*Enamel flower in pink, gold and white, one round diamond, gold, c. 19th*	300.00	325.00
☐ **8**	*Enamel flower on leaf, 14K gold, American, c. 1894-95*	75.00	100.00
☐ **9**	*Enameled leaf, one seed pearl, 14K gold, American, c. 1896*	75.00	100.00
☐ **10**	*Fan motif flower, engraved, seed pearl, gold, c. 20th.*	125.00	175.00
☐ **11**	*Fresh water pearl flower, seed pearls in leaves, gold, c. 20th.*	75.00	100.00
☐ **12**	*Garnet, 14K gold, American, c. 1894-95*	65.00	90.00

		Price Range	
☐	**13** *Gold flower, one round diamond, c. 20th*	125.00	175.00
☐	**14** *Hardstone cameo of a flower, buckle motif frame, gold, English, c. 19th.*	225.00	250.00
☐	**15** *Ivory cameo of a bouquet of flowers, rose gold, c. 19th.*	225.00	250.00
☐	**16** *Ivory carving of a flower, one round garnet, yellow metal, c. 19th*	135.00	150.00
☐	**17** *Ivy leaves, one seed pearl, 14K gold, American, c. 1896*	80.00	110.00

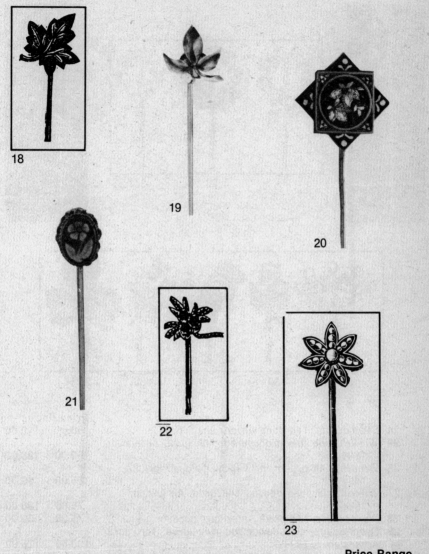

		Price Range	
☐	**18** *Leaf, sterling silver, American, c. 1894-95*	45.00	50.00
☐	**19** *Leaf motif, enamel, round diamond, gold, American, c. early 20th.*	175.00	200.00
☐	**20** *Mosaic, gold, French, c. 19th*	250.00	300.00
☐	**21** *Onyx cameo of a flower, gold, c. 20th*	110.00	125.00
☐	**22** *Ruby, emerald, sapphire, 14K gold, American, c. 1894-95*	150.00	175.00
☐	**23** *Seed pearls, 14K gold, American, c. 1896*	105.00	125.00

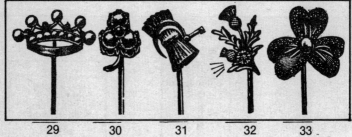

		Price Range	
☐	24 *Seed pearls, 14K gold, American, c. 1896*	90.00	110.00
☐	25 *Wreath, one round diamond, 14K gold, American, c. 1894-95*	100.00	125.00
☐	26 *Wreath, 14K green and yellow gold, American, c. 1894-95*	65.00	90.00
☐	27 *Wreath, six seed pearls, 14K gold, American, c. 1894-95*	75.00	100.00
☐	28 *Seed pearls, 14K gold, American, c. 1896*	75.00	100.00
☐	29 *Seed pearls, one cabochon turquoise, 14K gold, American, c. 1894-95*	100.00	125.00
☐	30 *Seed pearls, one cabochon turquoise, 14K gold, American, c. 1894-95*	90.00	110.00
☐	31 *Sheaf of wheat and sickle motif, 14K gold, American, c. 1894-95*	90.00	110.00
☐	32 *Thistle, one round diamond, 14K gold, American, c. 1894-95*	135.00	160.00
☐	33 *Three-leaf clover, sterling silver, American, c. 1894-95*	45.00	55.00

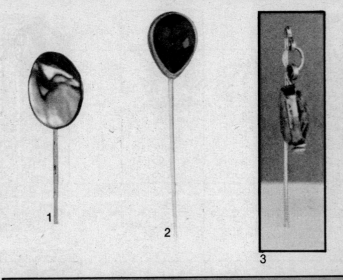

STICKPINS – GEMSTONE

			Price Range	
☐	**1**	*Abalone, sterling silver, American, c. 20th*	45.00	65.00
☐	**2**	*Almondine garnet: pear-shape, gold, c. 20th*	200.00	225.00
☐	**3**	*Ancient scarab, gold, converted to stick pin,*		
		c. 20th	175.00	200.00
☐	**4**	*Amethyst, 14 old mine diamonds approx. .70 ct.,*		
		gold, c. 19th.	750.00	800.00
☐	**5**	*Monkey, one round diamond, 18K gold, c. 20th*	325.00	375.00
☐	**6**	*Bow motif, blue and white enamel, one round dia-*		
		mond, gold, c. 20th	175.00	200.00
☐	**7**	*Crystal carved petals, one round diamond, gold,*		
		c. 20th.	250.00	275.00

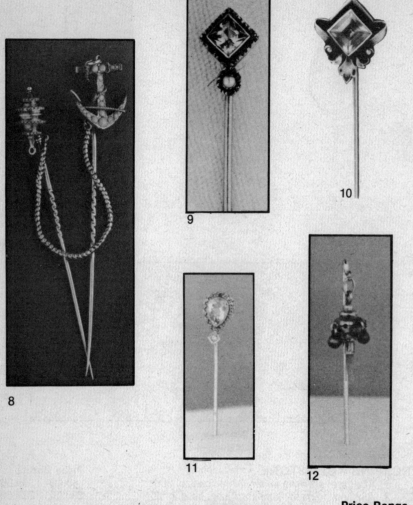

8

9

10

11

12

		Price Range	
☐	**8** Anchor and buoy motif, cabochon turquoise, connecting chain, gold, c. 1830. Pair	750.00	800.00
☐	**9** Aquamarine: square-cut, one seed pearl, 14K gold, c. 20th.....................................	200.00	225.00
☐	**10** Aquamarine, Art Nouveau, gold, c. 1880	150.00	175.00
☐	**11** Aquamarine: one pear-shape, one round diamond, 14K white gold, American, c. 1930	250.00	275.00
☐	**12** Baby rattle, coral, silver bells, gold, contemporary pin, c. 19th.	550.00	650.00

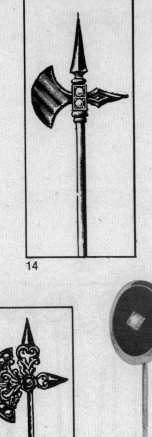

14

13

15

16

17

			Price Range	
☐	**13**	*Battle ax motif, sterling silver, American, c. 1894-95*	**50.00**	**60.00**
☐	**14**	*Battle ax motif, two seed pearls, 14K gold, American, c. 1896*	**105.00**	**125.00**
☐	**15**	*Battle ax motif, blue enamel, 14K gold, American, c. 1896*	**95.00**	**115.00**
☐	**16**	*Battle ax motif, ten seed pearls, one cabochon turquoise, 14K gold, American, c. 1894-95*	**150.00**	**185.00**
☐	**17**	*Black onyx, one round diamond, 14K gold, American, c. 20th.*	**110.00**	**125.00**

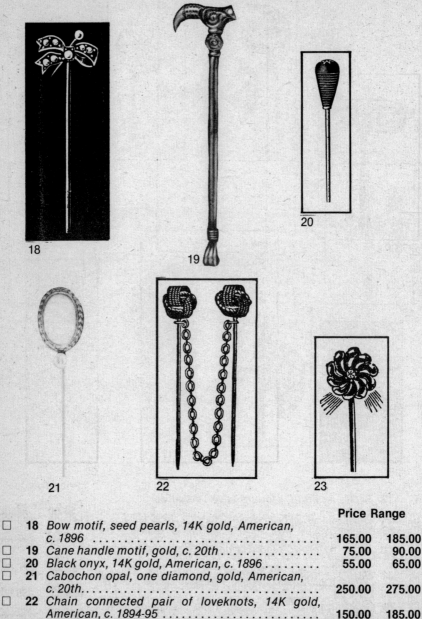

18

19

20

21

22

23

		Price Range	
☐	**18** *Bow motif, seed pearls, 14K gold, American, c. 1896*	165.00	185.00
☐	**19** *Cane handle motif, gold, c. 20th*	75.00	90.00
☐	**20** *Black onyx, 14K gold, American, c. 1896*	55.00	65.00
☐	**21** *Cabochon opal, one diamond, gold, American, c. 20th*...	250.00	275.00
☐	**22** *Chain connected pair of loveknots, 14K gold, American, c. 1894-95*	150.00	185.00
☐	**23** *Diamond: one round, 14K gold, American, c. 1894-95*	105.00	125.00

25

26

27

24

28

29

30

			Price Range	
☐	24	*Cornet motif, 14K gold, American, c. 1894-95*	**125.00**	**135.00**
☐	25	*Crescent and star motif, five seed pearls, one round diamond, 14K gold, American, c. 1894-95* . . .	**135.00**	**175.00**
☐	26	*Crescent and star motif, five seed pearls, one cabochon turquoise, 14K gold, American, c. 1894-95*	**95.00**	**125.00**
☐	27	*Crown motif, seed pearls, 14K gold, American, c. 1894-95*	**105.00**	**135.00**
☐	28	*Cruciform motif, one pearl, rose diamonds, gold, French, c. 1830*	**250.00**	**275.00**
☐	29	*Dagger motif, coral handle, gold, c. 19th*	**125.00**	**150.00**
☐	30	*Diamond: one round, gold, c. 1860*	**175.00**	**200.00**

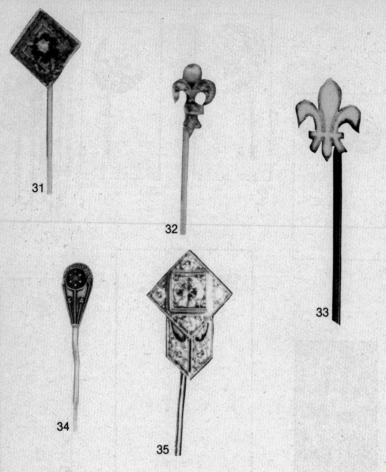

			Price Range	
☐	**31**	*Filigree motif, one round diamond, 14K gold, American, c. 1920*	150.00	175.00
☐	**32**	*Fleur-de-lys motif, diamonds, one pearl, platinum, 14K gold, American, c. 1915*	525.00	575.00
☐	**33**	*Fleur-de-lys, white enamel, gold, c. 20th*	75.00	110.00
☐	**34**	*Garnet: one round, Etruscan granulation, gold, c. 1860.*	125.00	150.00
☐	**35**	*Geometric motif, one round diamond approx. .45 ct., six round diamonds approx. .25 ct., platinum, c. 1920.*	750.00	1000.00

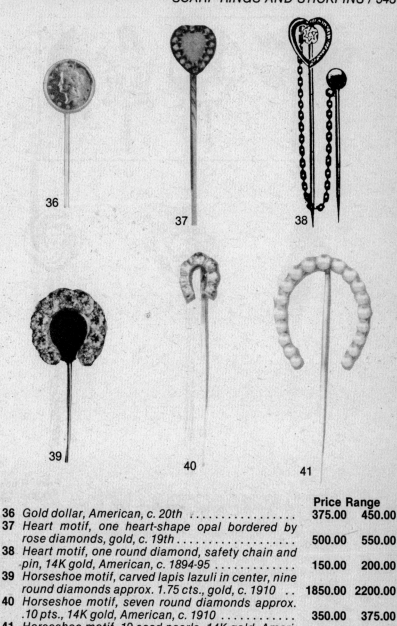

		Price Range	
☐	**36** Gold dollar, American, c. 20th	375.00	450.00
☐	**37** Heart motif, one heart-shape opal bordered by rose diamonds, gold, c. 19th	500.00	550.00
☐	**38** Heart motif, one round diamond, safety chain and pin, 14K gold, American, c. 1894-95	150.00	200.00
☐	**39** Horseshoe motif, carved lapis lazuli in center, nine round diamonds approx. 1.75 cts., gold, c. 1910 ..	1850.00	2200.00
☐	**40** Horseshoe motif, seven round diamonds approx. .10 pts., 14K gold, American, c. 1910	350.00	375.00
☐	**41** Horseshoe motif, 19 seed pearls, 14K gold, American, c. 1880	300.00	325.00

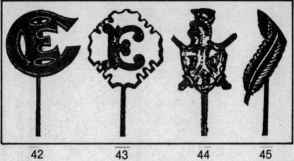

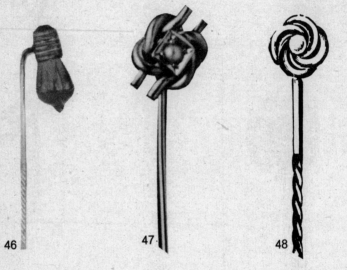

		Price Range	
☐	**42** *Initial motif, sterling silver, American, c. 1894-95* ..	30.00	35.00
☐	**43** *Initial motif, carved mother-of-pearl, 14K gold, American, c. 1894-95*	40.00	50.00
☐	**44** *Knights of Pythias insignia, 14K gold, American, c. 1894-95*	55.00	75.00
☐	**45** *Leaf motif, 14K gold, American, c. 1894-95*	50.00	65.00
☐	*Same as above but gold filled*	25.00	30.00
☐	*Same as above but sterling silver*	30.00	35.00
☐	**46** *Lightbulb motif, glass, yellow metal, American, c. 20th.*	65.00	95.00
☐	**47** *Loveknot motif, one seed pearl, 14K gold, American, c. 20th.*	65.00	85.00
☐	**48** *Loveknot motif, one seed pearl, 14K gold, American, c. 1896*	50.00	65.00

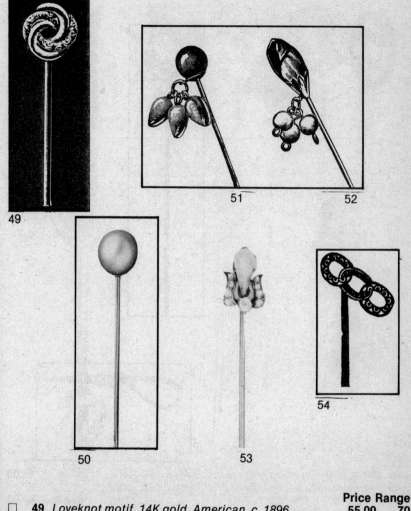

			Price Range	
☐	**49**	*Loveknot motif, 14K gold, American, c. 1896*	**55.00**	**70.00**
☐	**50**	*Natural pearl: approx. 6MM x 7MM, gold, maker:*		
		Spaulding & Co., c. 20th.	**300.00**	**325.00**
☐	**51**	*Moonstone ball, three genuine sea shells, 14K*		
		gold, American, c, 1894-95	**60.00**	**80.00**
☐	**52**	*Moonstone balls, one genuine sea shell, 14K gold,*		
		American, c. 1894-95	**60.00**	**80.00**
☐	**53**	*Moonstone: pear-shape, round and rose dia-*		
		monds, gold, American, c. early 20th.	**200.00**	**250.00**
☐	**54**	*Odd Fellows insignia, 14K gold, American,*		
		c. 1894-95	**55.00**	**75.00**
☐		*Same as above but gold filled*	**30.00**	**35.00**

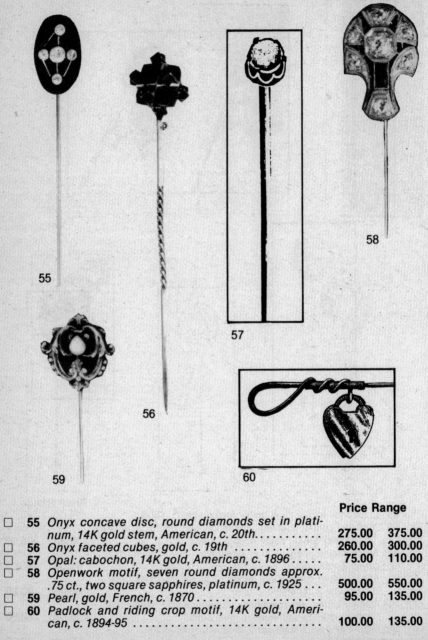

			Price Range	
☐	**55**	*Onyx concave disc, round diamonds set in plati-num, 14K gold stem, American, c. 20th.*	275.00	375.00
☐	**56**	*Onyx faceted cubes, gold, c. 19th*	260.00	300.00
☐	**57**	*Opal: cabochon, 14K gold, American, c. 1896*	75.00	110.00
☐	**58**	*Openwork motif, seven round diamonds approx. .75 ct., two square sapphires, platinum, c. 1925*	500.00	550.00
☐	**59**	*Pearl, gold, French, c. 1870*	95.00	135.00
☐	**60**	*Padlock and riding crop motif, 14K gold, Ameri-can, c. 1894-95*	100.00	135.00

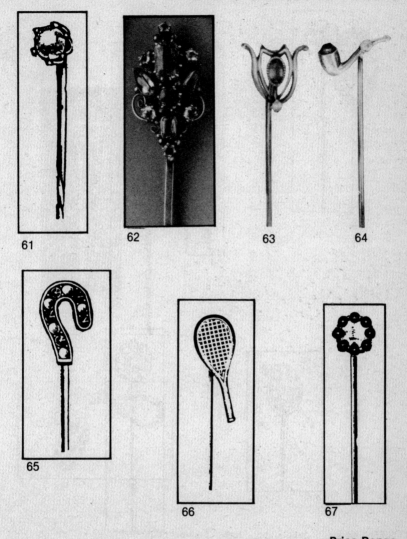

61 62 63 64

65 66 67

		Price Range	
☐	**61** *Pearl, 14K gold, American, c. 1894-95*	55.00	75.00
☐	**62** *Pink tourmaline, silver, c. 19th*	350.00	375.00
☐	**63** *Pink tourmaline, diamond, gold, c. 1925*	135.00	150.00
☐	**64** *Pipe motif, diamond, simulated ruby, American,*		
	c. 20th.	175.00	200.00
☐	**65** *Question mark motif, five seed pearls, five round*		
	rubies, 14K gold, American, c. 1896	150.00	225.00
☐	**66** *Racket motif, 14K gold, American, c. 1896*	65.00	85.00
☐	**67** *Rubies: eight round, 14K gold, American, c. 1896* . .	150.00	175.00

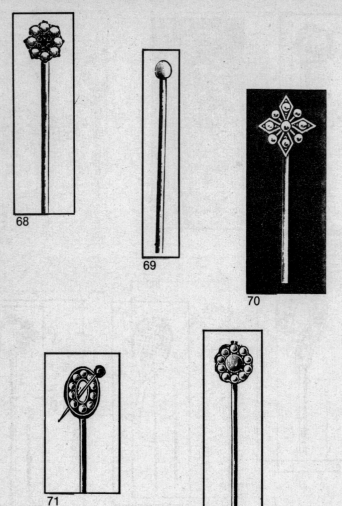

		Price Range	
☐	**68** *Seed pearls, one round ruby, 14K gold, American,* *c. 1896*	90.00	110.00
☐	**69** *Seed pearl, 14K gold, American, c. 1896*	55.00	75.00
☐	**70** *Seed pearls, 14K gold, American, c. 1896*	75.00	100.00
☐	**71** *Seed pearls, 14K gold, American, c. 1896*	75.00	100.00
☐	**72** *Seed pearls, one cabochon turquoise, 14K gold,* *American, c. 1896*	75.00	100.00

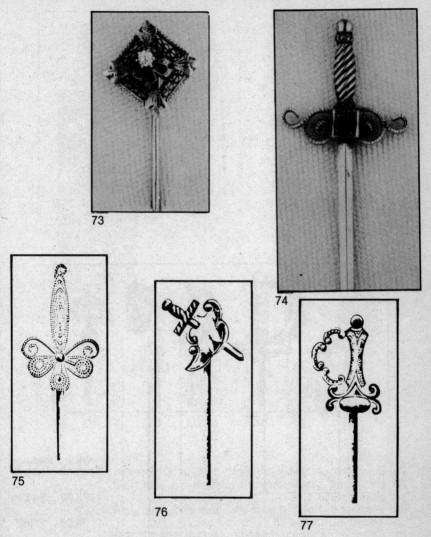

		Price Range	
☐	**73** *Square filigree motif, one round diamond, green and yellow gold, c. 1920*	**135.00**	**160.00**
☐	**74** *Sword motif, opaque enamel, one garnet, gold, c. 1900*	**150.00**	**175.00**
☐	**75** *Sword motif, filigree, 14K gold, American, c. 1896* .	**60.00**	**80.00**
☐	*Same as above but sterling silver*	**45.00**	**50.00**
☐	**76** *Sword with initial plaque motif, 14K gold, American, c. 1896*	**135.00**	**160.00**
☐	**77** *Sword motif, 14K gold, American, c. 1896*	**125.00**	**150.00**

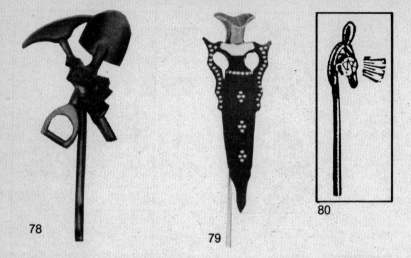

78
79
80

81   82   83   84   85

			Price Range	
☐	78	South Africa gold rush motif, 15K gold, Victorian	145.00	185.00
☐	79	Urn motif, piqué: tortoise shell inlaid with gold, gold, c. 1860	275.00	300.00
☐.	80	Wishbone motif, one round diamond, 14K gold, American, c. 1894-95	90.00	110.00
☐	81	Sword motif, enamel handle, two seed pearls, 14K gold, American, c. 1894-95	150.00	175.00
☐	82	Sword motif, five seed pearls, 14K gold, American, c. 1894-95	135.00	150.00
☐	83	Sword motif, one seed pearl, 14K gold, American, c. 1894-95	90.00	110.00
☐	84	Topaz, 14K gold, American, c. 1894-95	75.00	100.00
☐	85	Umbrella motif, one round ruby, 14K gold, American, c. 1894-95	95.00	125.00

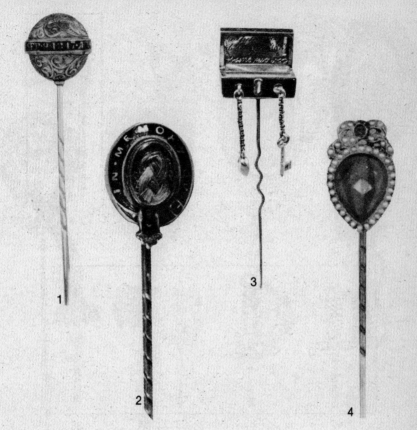

STICK PINS · HUMAN HAIR and MEMORIAL
All items made from hair referred to throughout this section are of brunette human hair unless stated otherwise.

Price Range

☐ **1** *Ball motif, chased, black enamel band inscribed: "E. D. Davenport Sep. 9, 1847 at 69.," hinge on enamel band with lock of hair under glass inside, gold, English, 1817.* 425.00 500.00

☐ **2** *Belt motif, black enamel "In Memory Of," basket weave hair under glass, gold, English, c. late 19th.* . 200.00 225.00

☐ **3** *Casket motif, bloodstone top, bottom and sides, heart and key on chains, stalk of hair wrapped with gold wire inside, inscribed: "Chapel Curig Ob. 1813 Absent not Lost," gold, English, c. 1813.* 1750.00 2000.00

☐ **4** *Heart and bow motif, hair under crystal, seed pearls, one ruby, gold, English, c. 1800.* 375.00 450.00

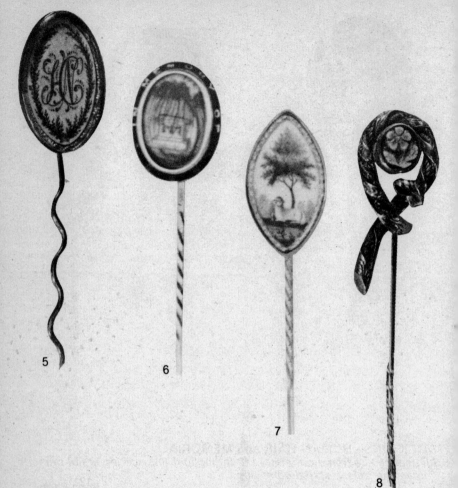

			Price Range	
☐	**5**	*Miniature on ivory of initials "NH" and wreath with dissolved hair under glass, gold, English, c. 1790. .*	**325.00**	**400.00**
☐	**6**	*Miniature on ivory of gravesite with dissolved hair and sepia paint under glass, black enamel frame "In Memory Of," gold, c. mid 19th. . . . .*	**325.00**	**400.00**
☐	**7**	*Miniature of ivory of lamb and tree with sepia paint under glass, signifying the death of a child, gold, c. 1790. . . . .*	**450.00**	**500.00**
☐	**8**	*Onyx cameo of a flower, tubular frame filled with woven hair, gold, c. 1860. . . . .*	**200.00**	**225.00**

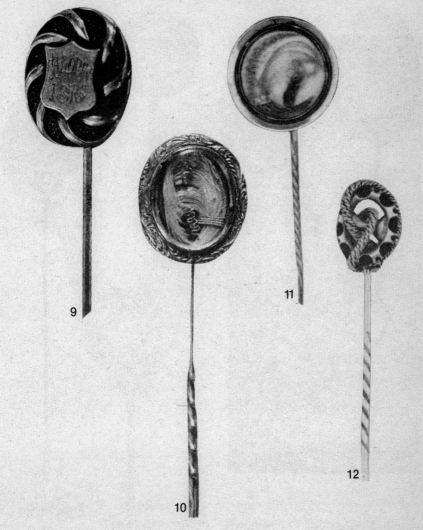

			Price Range	
☐	**9**	Oval motif with shield, woven hair inside oval, gold, c. 1875.	150.00	175.00
☐	**10**	Prince of Wales feather motif of white hair and gold thread under glass, chased frame, gold, English, c. 1870.	200.00	225.00
☐	**11**	Prince of Wales feather motif of hair with half pearls and gold wire under glass, gold, English, c. 1870.	150.00	175.00
☐	**12**	Rope motif, twisted and hollow filled with woven hair, gold, c. 1860.	175.00	200.00

13

14

15

16

		Price Range	
☐	**13** *Round motif, lock of hair under glass, safety chain, gold, c. 1880. . . . .*	110.00	135.00
☐	**14** *Round motif, black enamel "In Memory Of," lock of hair under glass, chased bezel, gold, c. 19th. . . .*	110.00	150.00
☐	**15** *Scalloped edge motif, basket weave hair under glass, gold, c. 1880. . . . .*	105.00	135.00
☐	**16** *Seed pearl in center, cobalt-blue enamel, reverse: miniature locket with lock of hair, gold, c. 1880. . . .*	250.00	300.00

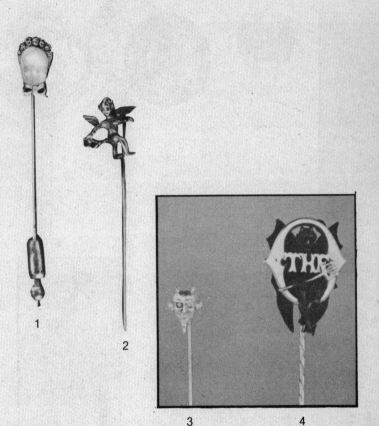

1

2

3   4

STICKPINS – PEOPLE and FIGURES

			Price Range	
☐	1	*Baby face motif, carved moonstone, rose diamonds in silver bonnet, gold bow.*	**550.00**	**650.00**
☐	2	*Cupid, gold, c. 20th*	**275.00**	**300.00**
☐	3	*Devil head, rose diamond eyes, 14K gold, American, c. 20th*	**200.00**	**225.00**
☐	4	*Devil with wings, gold, silver, c. 19th*	**475.00**	**525.00**

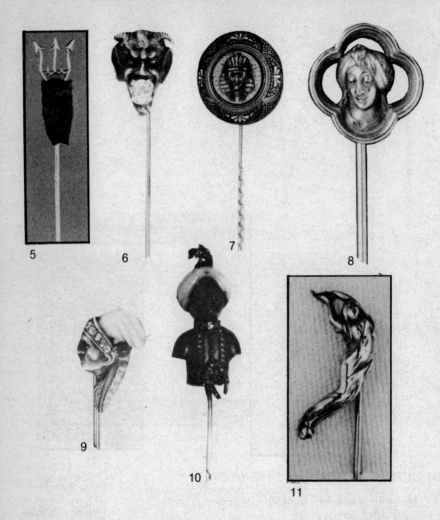

			Price Range	
☐	5	Devil head with horns, carved tiger eye, gold, c. 20th.	200.00	275.00
☐	6	Devil head, round diamond, gold.	325.00	375.00
☐	7	Egyptian mosaic motif, gold, c. 1860	600.00	650.00
☐	8	Gold carving of a lady, maker: Weise, c. 1870	1550.00	1750.00
☐	9	Indian chief motif, mother-of-pearl headdress, diamonds, gold.	300.00	325.00
☐	10	Indian Maharajah motif, gemset, gold, c. 18th.	2000.00	2200.00
☐	11	Lady, gold, Art Nouveau, c. 1910	175.00	200.00

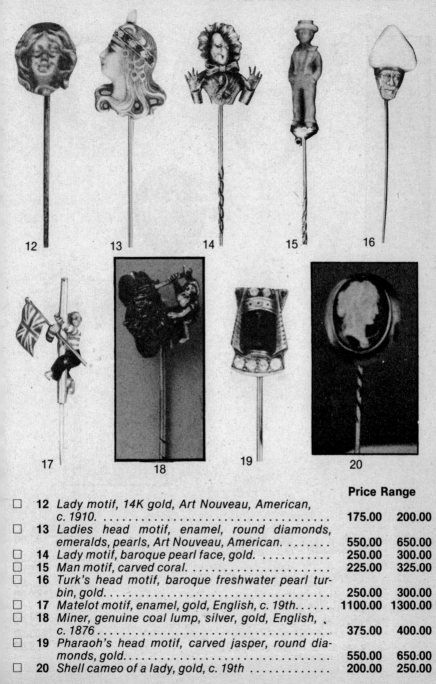

		Price Range	
☐	**12** Lady motif, 14K gold, Art Nouveau, American, c. 1910.	175.00	200.00
☐	**13** Ladies head motif, enamel, round diamonds, emeralds, pearls, Art Nouveau, American.	550.00	650.00
☐	**14** Lady motif, baroque pearl face, gold.	250.00	300.00
☐	**15** Man motif, carved coral.	225.00	325.00
☐	**16** Turk's head motif, baroque freshwater pearl turbin, gold.	250.00	300.00
☐	**17** Matelot motif, enamel, gold, English, c. 19th.	1100.00	1300.00
☐	**18** Miner, genuine coal lump, silver, gold, English, c. 1876.	375.00	400.00
☐	**19** Pharaoh's head motif, carved jasper, round diamonds, gold.	550.00	650.00
☐	**20** Shell cameo of a lady, gold, c. 19th	200.00	250.00

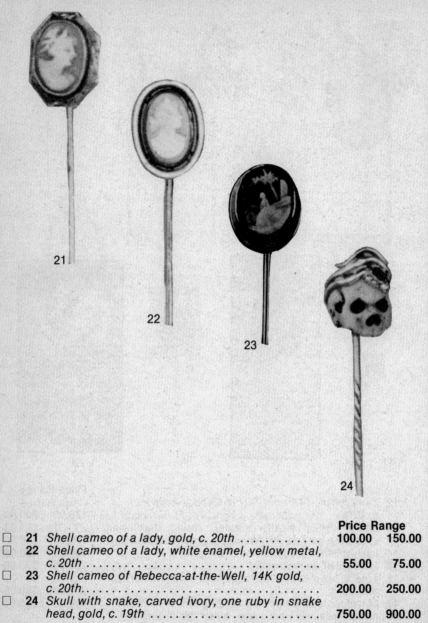

		Price Range	
☐	**21** *Shell cameo of a lady, gold, c. 20th*	100.00	150.00
☐	**22** *Shell cameo of a lady, white enamel, yellow metal, c. 20th*	55.00	75.00
☐	**23** *Shell cameo of Rebecca-at-the-Well, 14K gold, c. 20th*	200.00	250.00
☐	**24** *Skull with snake, carved ivory, one ruby in snake head, gold, c. 19th*	750.00	900.00

25

26

27

		Price Range	
☐	**25** *Skull with hinged mask, emerald eyes, silver, gold, c. late 18th*	**1200.00**	**1450.00**
☐	**26** *Winged foot, one round diamond, 14K gold, American, c. 20th*	**400.00**	**425.00**
☐	**27** *Witch's mask, diamond eyes, heart-cut amethyst, gold.*	**275.00**	**375.00**

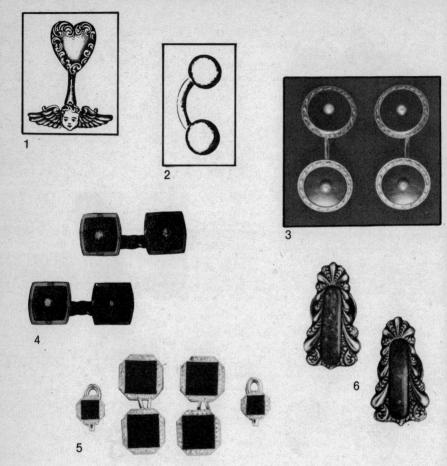

STUDS and BUTTONS, CUFF LINKS

CUFF LINKS			Price Range	
☐	**1**	*Angel and heart motif, 14K gold, American, c. 1896.*	175.00	200.00
☐		*Same as above but sterling silver*	125.00	135.00
☐	**2**	*Ball motif, 14K gold, American, c. 1896*	75.00	100.00
☐	**3**	*Black onyx, four seed pearls, platinum top, gold, maker: Tiffany & Co., c. 1920.*	275.00	300.00
☐	**4**	*Black onyx, four round diamonds, gold, c. 1920*	650.00	700.00
☐	**5**	*Black onyx, rose diamonds, white gold, cuff links and two studs, c. 1930*	650.00	700.00
☐	**6**	*Cabochon oblong opals, chased, gold, c: 1900*	525.00	650.00

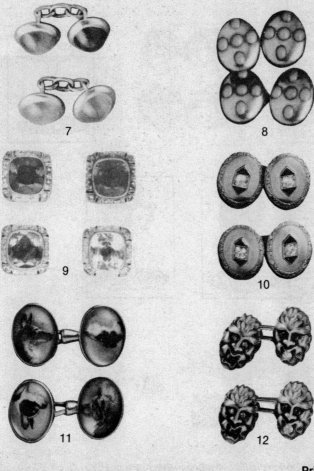

7

8

9

10

11

12

			Price Range	
☐	**7**	Cabochon pink and blue star sapphires, gold, c. 1900.	700.00	750.00
☐	**8**	Cabochon turquoise, gold, c. 1840	375.00	450.00
☐	**9**	Citrines, rose diamonds, gold, c. 1915	500.00	525.00
☐	**10**	Diamonds: four round, eight fancy-cut sapphires, platinum top, 14K gold, American, c. 1910	725.00	750.00
☐	**11**	Dog motif, reverse painting under crystal, gold, c. 1870.	650.00	750.00
☐	**12**	Face motif, one with diamonds in eyes and ruby in mouth, one with emeralds in eyes and diamond in mouth, gold, c. 1890.	2400.00	2650.00

13

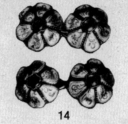

14

15

16

17

18

		Price Range	
☐	**13** *Fancy-shape motif, 14K gold, American, c. 1896* ..	90.00	110.00
☐	*Same as above but sterling silver*	45.00	55.00
☐	**14** *Flower motif, four cabochon garnets, gold, c. 1820* .	375.00	400.00
☐	**15** *Flower motif, 14K gold, American, c. 1896*	90.00	110.00
☐	*Same as above but sterling silver*	45.00	55.00
☐	**16** *Flower motif, 14K gold, American, c. 1896*	135.00	150.00
☐	*Same as above but sterling silver*	50.00	55.00
☐	**17** *Flower motif, 14K gold, American, c. 1896*	175.00	200.00
☐	*Same as above but sterling silver*	125.00	135.00
☐	**18** *Lady hand enameled motif with quill pen and envelope, one round ruby, gold, c. late 19th*	500.00	550.00

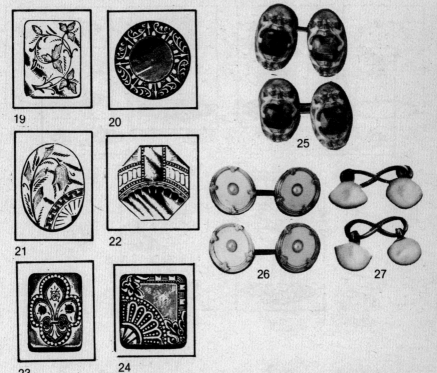

			Price Range	
☐	**19**	Lever sleeve button, rectangular flower motif, 14K gold, American, c. 1896	55.00	65.00
☐		Same as above but gold filled	30.00	35.00
☐	**20**	Lever sleeve button, round engraved motif, 14K gold, American, c. 1896	55.00	65.00
☐		Same as above but gold filled	30.00	35.00
☐	**21**	Lever sleeve button, oval flower motif, 14K gold, American, c. 1896...........................	55.00	65.00
☐		Same as above but gold filled	30.00	35.00
☐	**22**	Lever sleeve button, octagonal engraved, 14K gold, American, c. 1896	55.00	65.00
☐		Same as above but gold filled	30.00	35.00
☐	**23**	Lever sleeve button, one round diamond, sapphire and ruby, 14k gold, American, c. 1896	100.00	125.00
☐	**24**	Lever sleeve button, square chased motif, mother-of-pearl center, 14K gold, American, c. 1896	65.00	75.00
☐		Same as above but gold filled	30.00	35.00
☐	**25**	Moonface double motif, topaz, gold, c. 1900	1550.00	1750.00
☐	**26**	Mother-of-pearl, four half seed pearls, platinum top, 14K gold, c. 1915	200.00	250.00
☐	**27**	Natural baroque pearls, gold, maker: Tiffany & Co., c. 1920	525.00	550.00

28   29   30   31

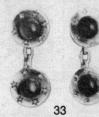

32

33

34

35

		Price Range	
☐	**28** Oval beaded edge motif, round diamonds, 14K gold, American, c. 1896	175.00	200.00
☐	**29** Oval chased motif, 14K gold, American, c. 1896 . . .	100.00	125.00
☐	Same as above but sterling silver	50.00	55.00
☐	**30** Oval chased motif, 14K gold, American, c. 1896 . . .	100.00	125.00
☐	Same as above but sterling silver	60.00	65.00
☐	**31** Oval motif, 14K gold, American, c. 1896	75.00	100.00
☐	Same as above but sterling silver	40.00	45.00
☐	**32** Rose diamonds, black enamel, 14K gold, American, c. 1930	550.00	600.00
☐	**33** Star motif, cabochon sardonyx, rose diamonds, gold, c. 1875	375.00	450.00
☐	**34** Tourmaline: square-cut, black enamel, gold, c. 1935.	500.00	550.00
☐	**35** White enamel, four round diamonds, 14K gold, American, c. 1920	300.00	325.00

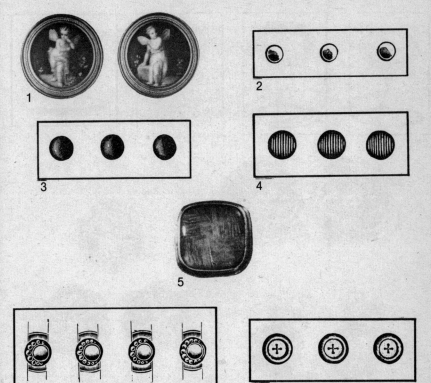

STUDS and BUTTONS

			Price Range	
☐	**1** *Angel motif, painted porcelain, gold, buttons, French, c. 1870*		600.00	625.00
☐	**2** *Ball motif, 14K gold, American, c. 1896*		70.00	80.00
☐	*Same as above but gold filled*		30.00	35.00
☐	*Same as above but sterling silver*		40.00	45.00
☐	**3** *Ball motif, black onyx, 14K gold, American, c. 1896.*		40.00	50.00
☐	**4** *Ball motif, ribbed, 14K gold, American, c. 1896.*		70.00	80.00
☐	*Same as above but gold filled*		30.00	35.00
☐	*Same as above but sterling silver*		40.00	50.00
☐	**5** *Basket weave hair under glass, gold, c. early 20th*		40.00	45.00
☐	**6** *Beaded motif, 14K gold, American, c. 1896*		70.00	80.00
☐	*Same as above but gold filled*		35.00	40.00
☐	*Same as above but sterling silver*		50.00	55.00
☐	**7** *Button motif, mother-of-pearl, 14K gold, American, c. 1896*		90.00	100.00

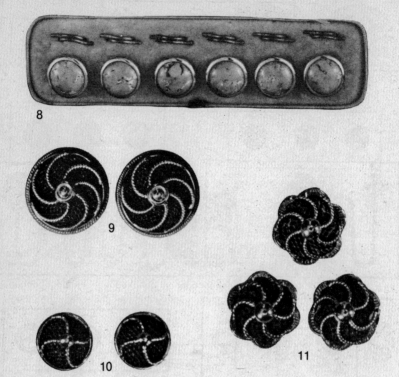

			Price Range	
☐	**8**	*Cabochon turquoise, gold covers, fitted box, English, c. 1930*	**275.00**	**325.00**
☐	**9**	*Cartwheel motif, woven hair under swirls, gold, c. 1860.*	**135.00**	**150.00**
☐	**10**	*Cartwheel motif, woven hair under swirls, gold, c. 1860.*	**110.00**	**135.00**
☐	**11**	*Cartwheel scalloped edge motif, woven hair under swirls, gold, c. 1860*	**150.00**	**175.00**

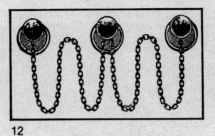

12

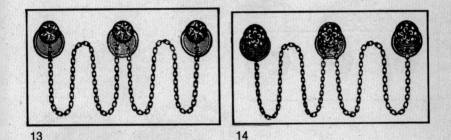

13   14

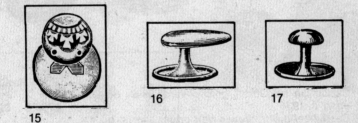

15   16   17

				Price Range	
☐	**12**	*Chain connected button set, plain, 14K gold, American, c. 1894-95*		**60.00**	**70.00**
☐	**13**	*Chain connected button set, cabochon turquoise, 14K gold, American, c. 1894-95*		**110.00**	**125.00**
☐	**14**	*Chain connected button set, chased, 14K gold, American, c. 1894-95*		**90.00**	**110.00**
☐	**15**	*Collar button, engraved, 14K gold, American, c. 1896.*		**40.00**	**45.00**
☐		*Same as above but gold filled*		**20.00**	**25.00**
☐	**16**	*Collar button, oblong, 14K gold, American, c. 1896.*		**35.00**	**40.00**
☐		*Same as above but gold filled*		**20.00**	**25.00**
☐	**17**	*Collar button, round, 14K gold, American, c. 1896* .		**35.00**	**40.00**
☐		*Same as above but gold filled*		**20.00**	**25.00**

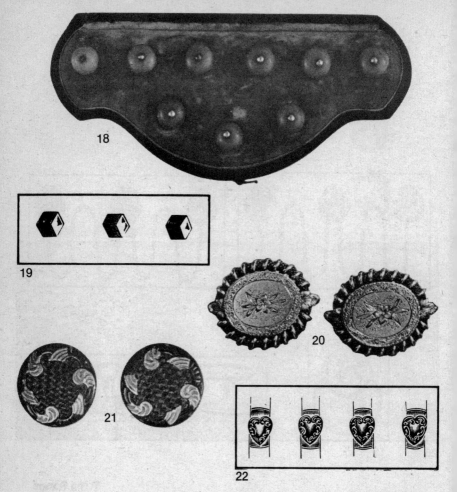

			Price Range	
☐	**18**	*Coral beads, gold, fitted leather box, English, c. late 19th.*	400.00	450.00
☐	**19**	*Cube motif, 14K gold, American, c. 1896*	75.00	90.00
☐		*Same as above but gold filled*	30.00	35.00
☐		*Same as above but sterling silver*	40.00	45.00
☐	**20**	*Flower motif, woven hair under gold loops, gold, c. 1870.*	110.00	135.00
☐	**21**	*Hair woven under white and brown enamel metal frame, buttons, c. mid to late 19th*	60.00	70.00
☐	**22**	*Heart motif, chased, 14K gold, American, c. 1896* .	90.00	110.00
☐		*Same as above but gold filled*	40.00	45.00
☐		*Same as above but sterling silver*	50.00	55.00

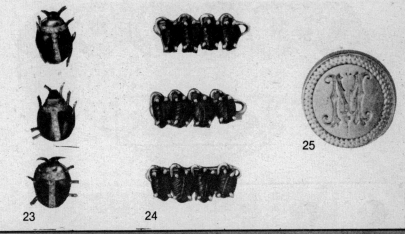

23   24   25

26

			Price Range	
☐	**23**	Lady-bug motif, translucent purple, yellow and red enamel, seed pearls, gold, fitted leather box, c. 1870.	650.00	700.00
☐	**24**	Leaf motif, carved sapphires, white gold, c. 1900. .	700.00	750.00
☐	**25**	Lovetoken, engraved gold dollar, American, c. late 19th	175.00	225.00
☐	**26**	Mosaic face motif, gold, fitted leather box inscribed: Tiffany & Co., studs and cuff links, c. 1880.	6300.00	6850.00

27

28

29

30

		Price Range	
☐	**27** Mother-of-pearl, cabochon sapphires, platinum top, gold, fitted leather box, maker: Tiffany & Co., buttons, c. 1915	750.00	775.00
☐	**28** Pearls, 14K gold, American, c. 1896	70.00	80.00
☐	**29** Plain, 9K gold, fitted leather box, English, c. 1920	200.00	225.00
☐	**30** Ribbon motif, turquoise-blue enamel, rose diamonds, converted to brooch and earclips, silver topped gold buttons, c. 1750	1750.00	2000.00

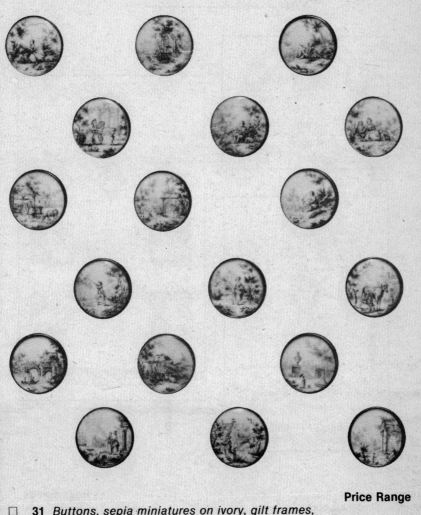

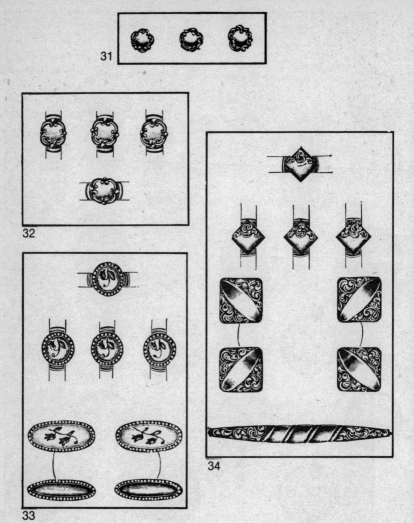

31

32

33

34

		Price Range	
☐	**32** *Scroll plaque motif, 14K gold, American, c. 1896* ..	**70.00**	**80.00**
☐	*Same as above but gold filled*	**35.00**	**40.00**
☐	*Same as above but sterling silver*	**50.00**	**55.00**
☐	**33** *Waist set, chased, sterling silver, American,*		
	c. 1896	**55.00**	**65.00**
☐	**34** *Waist set, enameled lily-of-the-valley motif,*		
	beaded edges, sterling silver, American, c. 1896 ..	**100.00**	**125.00**
☐	**35** *Waist set, square motif, chased, sterling silver,*		
	American, c. 1896	**135.00**	**150.00**

Photograph of three children taken at Pittman's Photo Studio in Springfield, Illinois. The child on the right is wearing a narrow stiff bangle bracelet. The child in the center is wearing a small rectangular baby pin near the neck. The child on the left is wearing a book chain necklace and a bar pin.

1

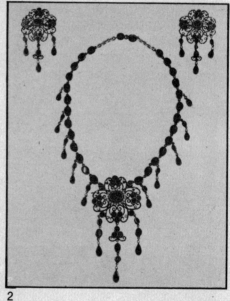

2

SUITES

		Price Range	
☐	1 Agates, rectangular cabochon, gold frames, necklace, brooch, pendant, two pairs of earrings, fitted leather box inscribed: G. M. Jarvis, c. 1815.	4850.00	5450.00
☐	2 Almandine garnets, black and white enamel, seed pearls, silver, necklace and earrings, fitted leather box, Hungarian, c. 1840.	2400.00	2850.00

			Price Range	
☐	**3**	Amethyst cameo of warriors, gold, necklace, bracelet and earrings, c. 1850	5250.00	5450.00
☐	**4**	Amethyst centered in scroll plaque with double simple link chain, gold, bracelet and necklace, c. early 20th.	2200.00	2650.00

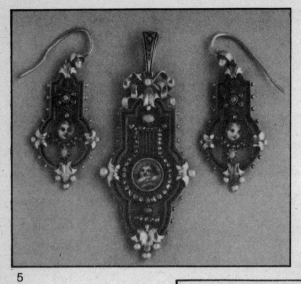

5

6

			Price Range	
☐	**5**	Angel and ribbon motif, black enamel, rose diamonds, turquoise, seed pearls, gold, pendant and earrings, fitted leather box, c. 1860	9450.00	10500.00
☐	**6**	Ball and moon motif, woven hair, gold, brooch and earrings, c. 1850-70	450.00	500.00

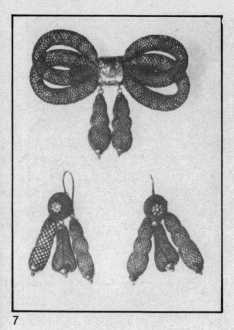

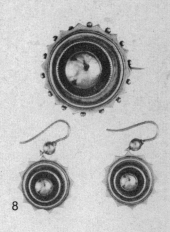

8

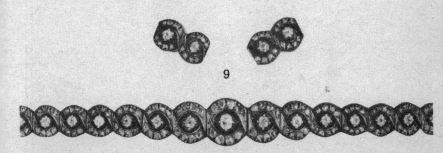

9

			Price Range	
☐	**7**	Bow and pendant motif, woven hair, gold, brooch and earrings, c. 1840-60	250.00	325.00
☐	**8**	Circle motif with scalloped edges, silver, brooch and earrings, English, c. 1880	325.00	375.00
☐	**9**	Circular motif, old mine diamond centers, rose diamond borders, silver topped gold, bracelet and earrings, c. 1860	5450.00	6500.00

10

Price Range

☐ **10** *Citrines, faceted ovals, rose, yellow and green gold floral motif mounting, necklace with pendant, brooch, bracelet, earrings, former owner: Empress Eugenia of France, wife to Napoleon III, fitted leather box, c. 1830.* **14700.00 16800.00**

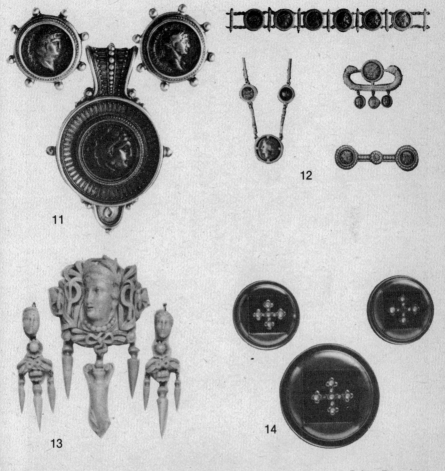

11

12

13

14

		Price Range	
☐	**11** *Coin motif, Etruscan gold granulation mounts, ancient Greek silver drachma of Alexander the Great, reverse: Zeus with an eagle in center of pendant; ancient Roman silver denarius of Emperor Nero and one of Trajan in center of each button, signed: Pierret, Roma, Italian, c. 1870.*	**5750.00**	**6850.00**
☐	**12** *Coin motif, classical revival with Greek and Roman coins, necklace, bracelet, two brooches, gold mounts, c. 1875.*	**7350.00**	**8400.00**
☐	**13** *Coral carved female heads, gold, c. mid 19th.*	**1050.00**	**1350.00**
☐	**14** *Cross motif, pearls, black enamel, gold, brooch and buttons, French, c. 1850*	**550.00**	**650.00**

15

☐ **15** *Coral, gold, necklace, brooch, earrings, bracelet, c. 1860.* **1100.00 1300.00**

16

17

Price Range

☐ **16** *Emeralds: 14 emerald-cut and two pear-shape emeralds, 60 old mine diamonds, cannetille, oval link chain, gold, necklace with detachable cross and earrings, c. 1830.* **17850.00 21000.00**

☐ **17** *Rubies: pear-shape and oval rubies, cannetille, gold, necklace and earrings, c. 1830* **15750.00 16800.00**

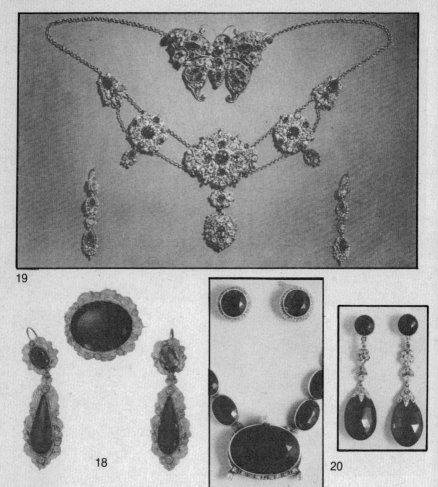

19

18

20

		Price Range	
☐ **18**	Amethyst pastes, cannetille, 22K gold work, c. 1830s	800.00	1000.00
☐ **19**	Filigree motif, amethysts, diamonds, 18K gold, necklace, earrings, butterfly brooch or pendant, English, c. 1820-40.	22000.00	24000.00
☐ **20**	Fire opals, oval and faceted, necklace with detachable brooch with three round diamonds and rose diamonds, stud earrings with rose diamonds, pendant earrings with a small emerald in each and rose diamonds, fitted leather box, c. 1890.	12600.00	14700.00

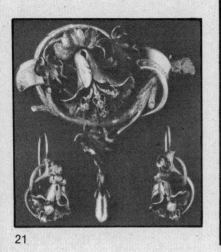

21

23

22

Price Range

☐ **21** *Floral motif, translucent green and red enamel,
old mine diamonds, gold, brooch and earrings,
c. 1840.* **1750.00 2000.00**

☐ **22** *Floral motif, brooch set with one cushion-cut tourmaline, three step-cut emeralds, pink tourmalines
and rose diamonds, silver topped gold; earrings
set with pink tourmalines and rose diamonds, sil-
ver topped gold, c. mid 19th.* **3500.00 3750.00**

☐ **23** *Flower motif, blue enamel, rose diamonds, silver,
gold, necklace, bracelet and earrings, c. 1800.* **16800.00 18900.00**

24

25

26

			Price Range	
☐	**24**	*Flower motif, carved black onyx, seed pearls, gold, pin and earrings, fitted box, English, c. 1870*	**625.00**	**750.00**
☐	**25**	*Flower motif, foilback pink topaz, gold, necklace, earring, bracelet and brooch, c. mid 19th*	**5450.00**	**5650.00**
☐	**26**	*Flower and leaf motif, woven horsehair, dyed red, gold, brooch and earrings, c. 19th*	**225.00**	**275.00**

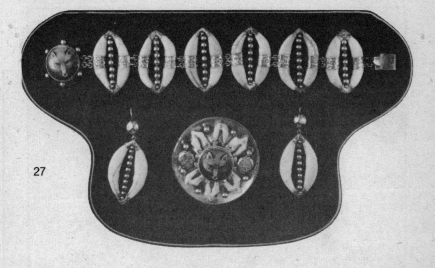

27

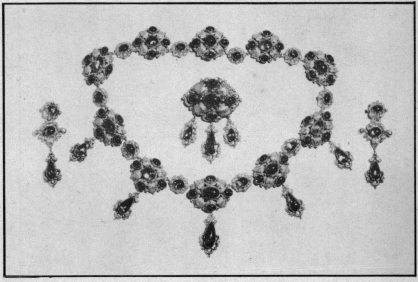

28

		Price Range	
☐	**27** Fox motif, enamelled fox head on pin and bracelet clasp, fox teeth, silver gilt, bracelet, brooch and earrings, fitted leather box, c. 1870	750.00	1000.00
☐	**28** Garnets, cabochon, gold, necklace, earrings and brooch, English, c. 1840	16800.00	18900.00

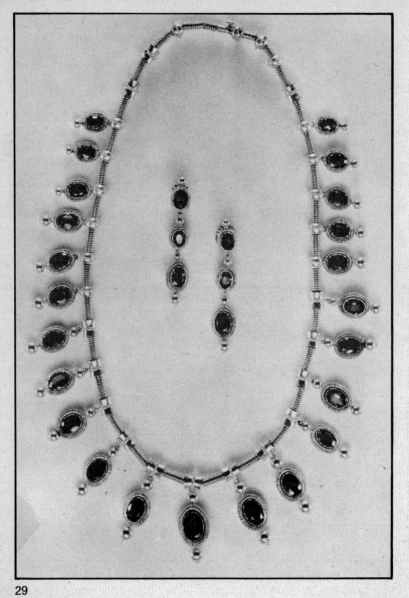

29

Price Range

☐ **29** *Garnets, faceted oval-cut, Castellani style, 18K
gold, necklace and earrings, c. mid 19th* **7350.00 9450.00**

30

Price Range

31

32

		Price Range	
☐	**31** Greek goddess, tiger and angel motif on painted porcelain plaques, Etruscan gold granulation frames with gold ball pendants, brooch and earrings, c. 1850.	3950.00	4400.00
☐	**32** Horseshoe and whip motif, black enamel, seed pearls, three colored gold, brooch and converted earrings, c. 1870.	750.00	1000.00

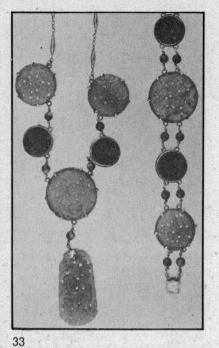

33

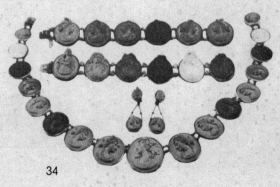

35

34

		Price Range	
☐	**33** *Jade and carnelian plaques, pierced and carved, 14K gold, bracelet and necklace, c. early 20th*	**5100.00**	**5900.00**
☐	**34** *Lava cameos, gold filled, necklace, earrings, two bracelets convert to choker, Victorian.*	**450.00**	**650.00**
☐	**35** *Lava carved angels, gold, c. 1860.*	**1300.00**	**1750.00**

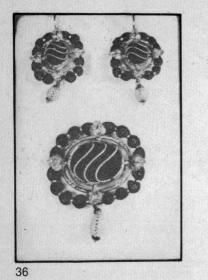

36

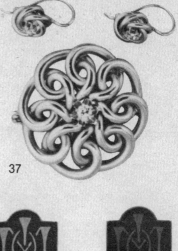

37

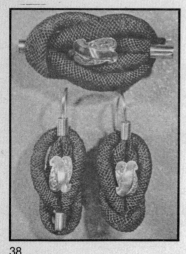

38

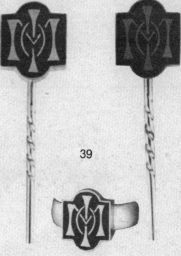

39

			Price Range	
☐	**36**	*Leaf motif, woven hair, white hair pendants, gold, brooch and earrings, c. 1850-70*	550.00	650.00
☐	**37**	*Loveknot motif, round diamonds, diamond is 15 pts., 14K gold, American.*	500.00	600.00
☐	**38**	*Loveknot motif, woven hair, plaques for initials, gold, brooch and earrings, c. 1840-60.*	275.00	375.00
☐	**39**	*Memorial shields in black and white enamel signifying "In Memory Of," hair locket behind each shield, 18K gold, ring and two detachable stick pins, Birmingham, England, c. 1884.*	750.00	950.00

40

41

                                                   Price Range

☐ **40** *Micro-mosaic bird motif, woven mesh chain, detailed Etruscan granulation on reverse of bangle bracelet, high karat gold, bangle bracelet, necklace with detachable pendant, earrings, fitted cased, Italian, c. 1840-60.* **16800.00 18900.00**

☐ **41** *Micro-mosaic, 18K gold, Victorian.* **2000.00 2400.00**

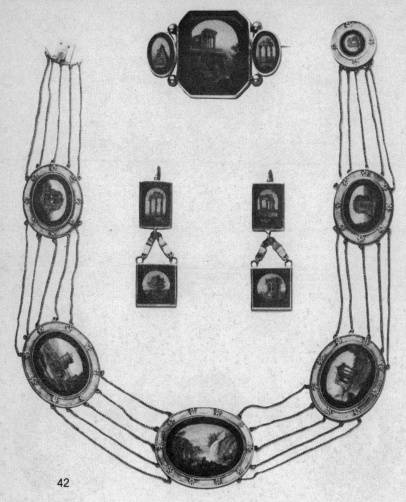

42

43

44

45

46

		Price Range	
☐	**44** *Mosaic flower motif, bangle bracelet, brooch, earrings, fitted case, gold, c. 1850.*	4950.00	6800.00
☐	**45** *Mosaic Gothic revival motif, birds and flowers, Etruscan granulation, gold, brooch and earrings, c. 1870.*	3750.00	4200.00
☐	**46** *Mosaic motif of angels, gold, brooch and earrings, c. 1860*	2400.00	2850.00

Price Range

☐ **47** *Mosaic bird and cross motif, gold, brooch and ear-*
   rings, c. 1840-50 .... **2400.00 2850.00**
☐ **48** *Mosaic bird motif, gold necklace with foxtail*
   chain ends and detachable pendant, earrings,
   c. 1840-50. .... **12600.00 14700.00**

49

50

51

52

		Price Range	
☐	**49** Mosaic Egyptian motif, pendant or brooch with detachable loop and earrings, gold, fitted leather box, c. 1870.	5450.00	5900.00
☐	**50** Mosaic Egyptian motif, Etruscan granulation, gold, brooch or pendant and earrings, c. 1870	3750.00	4200.00
☐	**51** Onyx circle motif, seed pearls, rose diamonds, gold, brooch and converted earrings, c. 1870	750.00	900.00
☐	**52** Onyx, gold, case marked: Bigelow, Kennard & Co., c. 1875.	450.00	550.00

53

54

55

			Price Range	
☐	**53**	*Onyx, seed pearls, 14K gold, c. 1860.*	**650.00**	**900.00**
☐	**54**	*Onyx teardrop motif, black enamel, gold, American, c. 1880.*	**450.00**	**550.00**
☐	**55**	*Oval cabochon garnet brooch with rose diamond border, silver topped gold; teardrop garnet earrings with rose diamond caps, silver topped gold, c. 1860.*	**4850.00**	**5300.00**

56

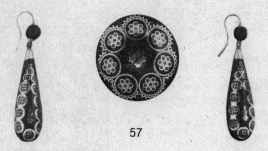

57

		Price Range	
☐	**56** Pink topaz, foil-back, seed pearls, fitted case marked: Carrington & Co., gold, necklace, brooch, earrings, Georgian, c. 1820.	2400.00	2650.00
☐	**57** Piqué: tortoise inlaid with gold and silver, c. 1860. .	325.00	375.00

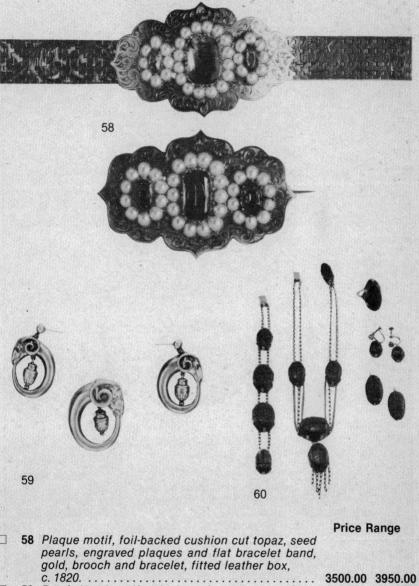

58

59

60

		Price Range	
☐	58	*Plaque motif, foil-backed cushion cut topaz, seed pearls, engraved plaques and flat bracelet band, gold, brooch and bracelet, fitted leather box, c. 1820.*	3500.00 3950.00
☐	59	*Ram's Head motif, gold, brooch, earrings, c. 1860.*	1100.00 1650.00
☐	60	*Scarab motif, carved lapis lazuli, 18K gold, bracelet, necklace, ring, two pair earrings, Egyptian Revival, c. 1925.*	1300.00 1450.00

61

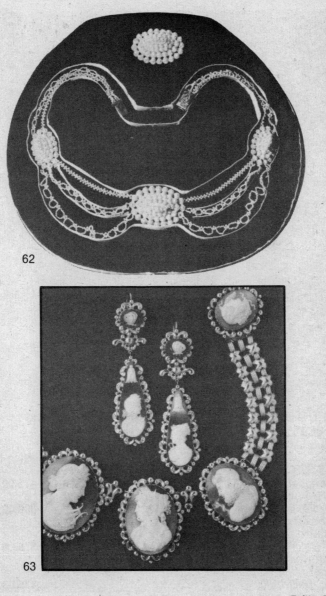

62

63

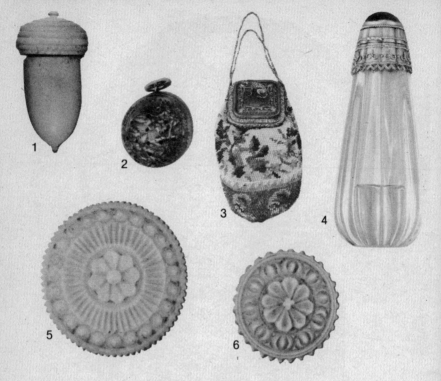

VINAIGRETTES

VINAIGRETTES, NUTMEG GRATERS, SNUFF BOXES and SCENT BOTTLES

NOTE: *Items are vinaigrettes unless states otherwise.*

			Price Range	
☐	1	*Acorn motif, grill under top which unscrews, ivory, English, c. 1800*	175.00	225.00
☐	2	*Ball with leaf motif, holes evenly spaced, 15K gold, English, c. 1870*	300.00	350.00
☐	3	*Beaded purse, frame is yellow metal, silver plated, mirror and vinaigrette in lid, six in. long, marked: "Galendrer 1846," French, c. 1846*	375.00	425.00
☐	4	*Bowed crystal motif, Star of David pierced grill under lid, gold plated inside, sterling silver, French, c. 1880-1900.*	175.00	200.00
☐	5	*Carved round box motif, unscrews with grill inside, ivory, English, c. 1840*	175.00	225.00
☐	6	*Carved round box motif, unscrews with grill inside, ivory, English, c. 1840*	135.00	150.00

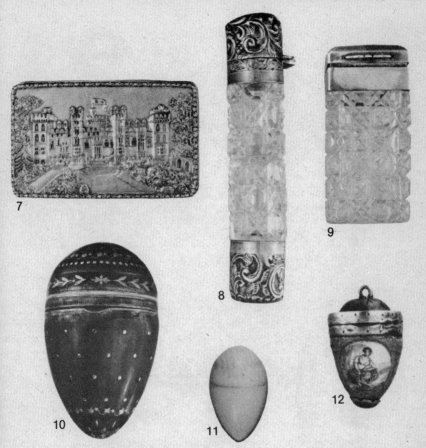

			Price Range	
☐	**7**	Castle motif, sterling silver gold plated, maker: Nathaniel Mills, Birmingham, England, c. 1838 . . .	750.00	900.00
☐	**8**	Cut glass motif double scent bottle, repousse, sterling silver, one end on hinge and one end screws, maker: DJE, Birmingham, England, c. 1890.	200.00	225.00
☐	**9**	Cut glass motif, star pierced grill under lid, gold plated inside, sterling silver, American, c. 1880-1900.	150.00	175.00
☐	**10**	Egg motif, purple, gold and white opaque and translucent enamel, silver, French, c. 19th	1000.00	1300.00
☐	**11**	Egg motif, unscrews with grill inside, ivory, English, c. 1800.	175.00	225.00
☐	**12**	Enamel motif of a lady, silver, French, c. 19th	750.00	900.00

		Price Range	
☐	**17** Horn motif, faceted citrine in lid, finger ring, sterling silver, Scottish, c. 19th	650.00	800.00
☐	**18** Knight in Armor motif, sterling silver inlaid with gold, cabochon ruby thumbpiece to open hinged helmet, gold pierced grill under helmet, c. 19th ...	3300.00	3500.00
☐	**19** Lily-of-the-valley flower motif, sterling silver, patent number 1948, American, c. 1893	300.00	350.00
☐	**20** Locket motif, cutout flower grill, chased edge, gold, American, c. 1850-65	525.00	750.00
☐	**21** Octagonal motif, Greek key, leaf and monogram engraved, gold plated inside, sterling silver, maker: M. Linwood, Birmingham, England, c. 1800	375.00	450.00

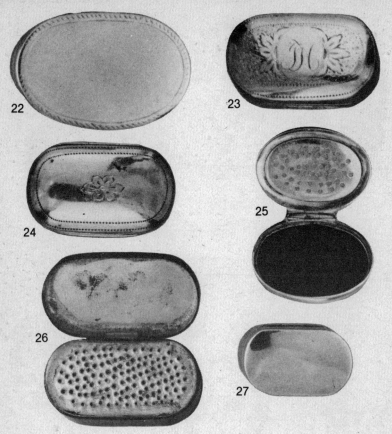

		Price Range	
☐	**22** *Oval motif, engraved edge, gold plated inside, sterling silver, English, c. 1790*	425.00	475.00
☐	**23** *Oval motif, engraved, hand-punched grill, sterling silver, maker: Joseph Willmore, Birmingham, England, c. 1809.*	500.00	550.00
☐	**24** *Oval motif, gold plated inside, sterling silver, maker: Joseph Willmore, Birmingham, England, c. 1793.*	425.00	500.00
☐	**25** *Oval motif, cut glass bottom, faceted black glass top, sterling silver gold plated grill and frame, English, c. 1880-1900*	275.00	350.00
☐	**26** *Oval motif nutmeg grater, black and maroon painted tin, opens both ends, American, c. 1750-1800.*	275.00	325.00
☐	**27** *Oval motif nutmeg grater, blue tin grill, sterling silver case, maker: J W, Birmingham, England, c. 1806.*	350.00	400.00

			Price Range	
☐	**28**	Oval motif nutmeg grater, engraved, opens both ends, gold plated inside, sterling silver, maker: Muirhead & Arthur, Glasgow, Scotland, c. 1881 ...	325.00	350.00
☐	**29**	Oval motif nutmeg grater, sterling silver, maker: CR (thought to be mark by C. Reily before he became partner with E. Storer), opens both ends, London, England, c. 1824.	500.00	550.00
☐	**30**	Oval crystal motif, faceted top, grill and frame are silver gilt, c. 19th	350.00	425.00
☐	**31**	Oval fish scale motif, swan cutout grill, gold plated inside, sterling silver, maker: John Shaw, Birmingham, England, c. 1810	500.00	550.00
☐	**32**	Oval scalloped edge motif, leaf and monogram engraved, sterling silver, maker: George Unite, Birmingham, England, c. 1890.	375.00	425.00

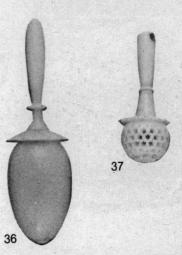

			Price Range	
☐	**33**	*Oval scalloped edge motif, engraved, sterling silver gold plated, English, c. mid 19th*	425.00	450.00
☐	**34**	*Purse motif, engraved, gold plated inside, sterling silver, maker: John Bettridge, Birmingham, England, c. 1834*	425.00	500.00
☐	**35**	*Purse motif, engraved, gold plated inside, sterling silver, maker: UP, Birmingham, England, c. 1817...*	500.00	525.00
☐	**36**	*Rattle motif, handle unscrews, holes in bottom, ivory, English, c. 1800*	200.00	250.00
☐	**37**	*Rattle motif, handle unscrews, star-shape holes, ivory, English, c. 1800*	200.00	250.00

38

41

39

40

42

			Price Range	
☐	**38**	Rectangular motif, engraved, sterling silver, maker: J. T., Birmingham, England, c. 1844	375.00	425.00
☐	**39**	Rectangular motif, geometric engraved, unusually thin, gold plated inside, sterling silver, maker: Lea & Clark, Birmingham, England, c. 1813-14	375.00	425.00
☐	**40**	Rectangular motif, gold plated inside, sterling silver, maker: I D, London, England, c. 1808	425.00	500.00
☐	**41**	Rectangular motif, engraved top and edges, gold plated inside, sterling silver, scroll cutout grill, Birmingham, England, c. 1811	425.00	525.00
☐	**42**	Rectangular motif snuff box, engraved, sterling silver, maker: Cocks & Bethridge, Birmingham, England, c. 1812	375.00	425.00

43

44

45

46

47

Price Range

☐ **43** Rectangular motif, engraved, cutout vine grill, un- usually spaced grill hinge, gold plated inside, ster- ling silver, maker: WS, Birmingham, England, c. 1831. . . . . 475.00 525.00

☐ **44** Rectangular bird and flower motif, colored opaque and translucent enamels, reverse is identical, gold, French, c. 19th. 1750.00 2000.00

☐ **45** Rectangular fish scale motif, gold plated inside, sterling silver, maker: Thomas Shaw, Birmingham, England, c. 1822 . . . . 375.00 450.00

☐ **46** Rectangular flower motif, engraved, sterling sil- ver, maker: Wheeler & Shaw, Birmingham, En- gland, c. 1840. . . . . 375.00 425.00

☐ **47** Rectangular flower motif, engraved, sterling sil- ver, maker: Taylor, London, England, c. 1812 . . . . . 400.00 475.00

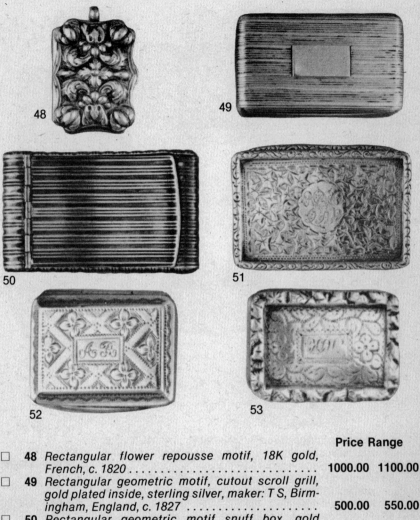

			Price Range	
☐	**48**	Rectangular flower repousse motif, 18K gold, French, c. 1820	1000.00	1100.00
☐	**49**	Rectangular geometric motif, cutout scroll grill, gold plated inside, sterling silver, maker: T S, Birmingham, England, c. 1827	500.00	550.00
☐	**50**	Rectangular geometric motif snuff box, gold plated inside, sterling silver, maker: Samuel Pemberton, Birmingham, England, c. 1807	525.00	575.00
☐	**51**	Rectangular leaf motif, engraved, cutout flower grill, gold plated inside, sterling silver, maker: S & B, Birmingham, England, c. 1903	375.00	450.00
☐	**52**	Rectangular raised lid motif, engraved, gold plated inside, sterling silver, maker: John Lawrence & Co., Birmingham, England, c. 1825	375.00	475.00
☐	**53**	Rectangular repousse edge motif, gold plated inside, sterling silver, maker: Thos. Naubold, Birmingham, England, c. 1824	450.00	475.00

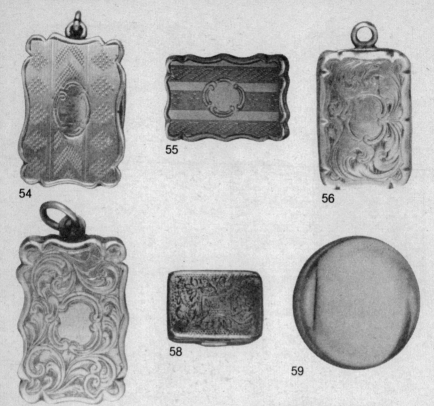

		Price Range	
☐	**54** *Rectangular scallop edge motif, engraved, gold plated inside, sterling silver, maker: N & C, Birmingham, England, c. 1859*	**375.00**	**450.00**
☐	**55** *Rectangular scalloped motif, engraved, gold plated inside, sterling silver, maker: F M, Birmingham, England, c. 1855*	**400.00**	**425.00**
☐	**56** *Rectangular scalloped edge motif, engraved, gold plated inside, sterling silver, maker: JF, Birmingham, England, c. 1858*	**400.00**	**425.00**
☐	**57** *Rectangular scalloped edge motif, engraved, flower cutout grill, gold plated inside, sterling silver, maker: Nathaniel Mills, Birmingham, England, c. 1853*	**400.00**	**475.00**
☐	**58** *Rectangular thumbnail motif, engraved, gold plated inside, sterling silver, maker: T N, Birmingham, England, c. 1830*	**275.00**	**475.00**
☐	**59** *Round box motif, unscrews with grill inside, ivory, English, c. 1800*	**225.00**	**250.00**

		Price Range	
☐	**60** *Ruby glass scent bottle, gold plated inside, sterling silver, vinaigrette with scroll cutout grill in base, maker: S. Mordan & Co., London, England, c. 1868.*	**250.00**	**325.00**
☐	**61** *Scroll motif, sterling silver, American, c. 1900*	**225.00**	**250.00**
☐	**62** *Shell motif, gold plated inside, sterling silver, c. 1840-60*	**500.00**	**550.00**
☐	**63** *Shoe motif, 800 silver, French or Dutch, c. 19th* . . .	**375.00**	**475.00**
☐	**64** *Square modified motif, banded agate top and bottom, yellow metal sides, French, c. 1820-30*	**350.00**	**400.00**

			Price Range	
☐	**65**	*Stuffed genuine ferret snuff box, engraved flowers on rear lid, silver plated, Scottish, c. early 19th*	800.00	900.00
☐	**66**	*Tiger claw motif, engraved, 15K gold, English, c. 1870*	950.00	1100.00
☐	**67**	*Urn motif nutmeg grater, sterling silver, top lifts and front opens with hinge at base, English, c. 1790-1825.*	650.00	750.00
☐	**68**	*Walnut box motif, genuine shell, silver interior fittings, two cobalt blue glass scent bottles, English, c. 1860-1900.*	450.00	475.00

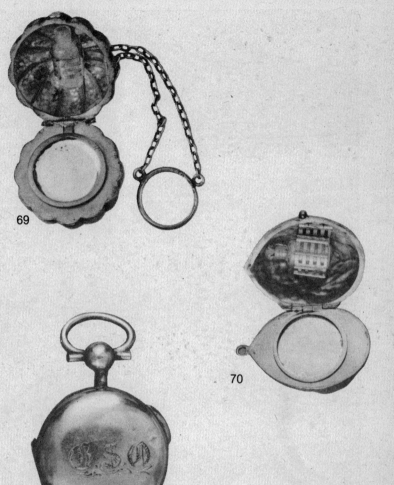

			Price Range	
☐	**69**	*Walnut box motif, one glass scent bottle, finger chain, silver plated yellow metal, English, c. 1860-1900*	225.00	250.00
☐	**70**	*Walnut box motif, one glass scent bottle and picture locket behind mirror, yellow metal, English, c. 1860-1900*	225.00	250.00
☐	**71**	*Watch, motif, monogram, sterling silver, Norwegian, c. 1900.*	325.00	350.00

Photograph taken in Newport, Pennsylvania by Lenney of a young woman wearing a bar pin with black enamel and a stick pin on her blouse.

1

2

3

4

WATCHES

GENTLEMEN'S · POCKET

The movements of all of the watches in this chapter are of average qual
unless noted otherwise. Disregard all trade names located on t
photographs.

			Price Range	
☐	**1**	Bicycle with rider motif, engraved, HC, 14K gold, American, c. 1896	600.00	800.
☐		*Same as above but gold filled*	175.00	200.
☐	**2**	Bird and flower applied motif, three color gold, en- graved, HC, 18K gold, American, c. 1900	1800.00	2000.
☐	**3**	Calendar watch, dial marked "J. Balmer Niclet St. Imier," dust cover marked "Improved Calendar No. 1552," OF, gold, Swiss, c.1900	500.00	600.00
☐	**4**	Castle engraved motif, HC, 14K gold, American, c. 1896.	500.00	600.00
☐		*Same as above but gold filled*	150.00	175.00

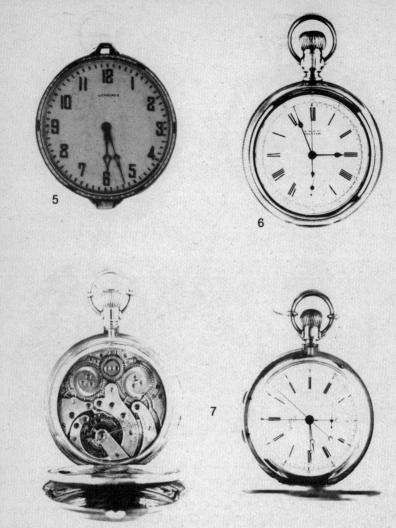

5

6

7

			Price Range	
☐	**5**	*Enamel case, black and white enamel border, brushed grey dial, black Arabic numerals, blue steeled hands, maker: Longines, OF, gold, Swiss, c. 1930.*	400.00	500.00
☐	**6**	*Chronograph, 17 jewel, plain case, white porcelain dial, OF, 16 size, gold filled, maker: Waltham, c. 1900.*	175.00	200.00
☐	**7**	*Chronograph: jump quarter split second with no return to zero, 31 jewel, stem wound, lever set, white porcelain dial, HC, 18K, maker, J. Higuenin* .	3800.00	4000.00

Price Range

- [ ] **8** *Engine turned motif, patented bow setting mechanism, highest grade movement number 10792, HC, 18K gold, 42MM, maker: Jules Jurgensen, Copenhagen, with original certificate, c. 1867.....* **2200.00 2400.00**
- [ ] **9** *Coin motif, Piaget watch housed in a 50 pesos Mexican coin, 18K gold, Swiss, c. 20th............* **1800.00 2200.00**
- [ ] **10** *Enamel case, cobalt blue enamel, portrait of a woman with a rose diamond necklace on reverse, white enamel dial, Roman numerals, keywind, HC, movement No. 91595, maker: Jules Mathey, Locle, gold, Swiss, c. 19th...........................* **1200.00 1400.00**
- [ ] **11** *Figural shell motif, opaque black enamel, seed pearls, enamel dial, steel hands, verge escapement, HC, gold, maker: Toutlemonde à Paris, France, c. 1785. ....* **8500.00 10500.00**

		Price Range	
☐	**12** Figural shoe motif, opaque colored enamel, white enamel dial, steel hands, verge escapement, opens to reveal watch, gold, inscribed: "Souvenir d' Amitie," Geneva, c. 1800.	6500.00	8500.00
☐	**13** Flower motif engraved case, engraved gold dial with three color gold applied floral wreath, movement stamped "Jos. Sewill, 61 South Castle St., Liverpool, Number 22294," OF, 18K gold, English, c. 1880.	475.00	500.00
☐	**14** Flower motif three color gold dial, Roman numerals, engine turned case, embossed rim, cylinder jeweled movement, OF, maker: L. Mathey, Locle, gold, Swiss, c. 19th.	500.00	700.00
☐	**15** Flower motif with engraved lake scene, HC, 14K gold, American, c. 1896.	500.00	700.00

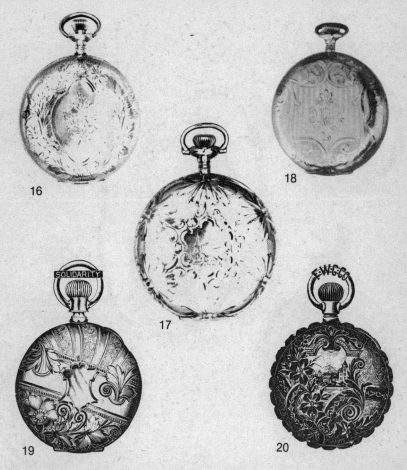

16

18

17

19

20

			Price Range	
☐	**16**	*Flower engraved motif, 7 jewel, white porcelain dial, HC, 16 size, 14K gold, maker: Waltham, c. 1900.*	480.00	580.00
☐	**17**	*Flower engraved motif, 7 jewel, white porcelain dial, HC, 23 size, 14K gold, maker: Elgin, c. 1900* . .	520.00	620.00
☐	**18**	*Flower engraved motif, 17 jewel, case number 742015, movement number 21828106, HC, 14K gold, maker: Elgin, c. 1918.*	520.00	620.00
☐	**19**	*Flower and initial shield motif, engraved, HC, 14K gold, American, c. 1896*	520.00	620.00
☐		*Same as above but gold filled*	160.00	200.00
☐	**20**	*Flower and scalloped edge motif with engraved lake scene, HC, 14K gold, American, c. 1896*	750.00	850.00
☐		*Same as above but gold filled*	200.00	240.00

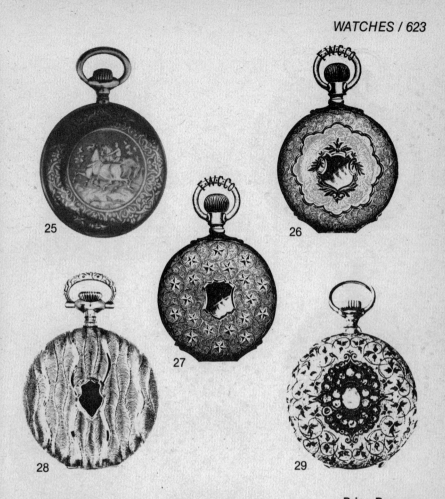

25

26

27

28

29

		Price Range	
☐	**25** Horse motif, horse and rider of inlaid gold, neillo enamel, 15 jewels, case number 2965, HC, sterling silver, c. 1900.	450.00	475.00
☐	**26** Initial shield with peacock engraving, HC, 14K gold, American, c. 1896	450.00	550.00
☐	Same as above but gold filled.	150.00	175.00
☐	**27** Initial shield and star motif, peacock engraving, HC, 14K gold, American, c. 1896.	550.00	650.00
☐	Same as above but gold filled.	150.00	200.00
☐	**28** Initial shield motif with deep wavy engraving, 21 jewel, model 993, white porcelain dial, HC, 14K gold, 16 size, maker: Hamilton, c. 1900.	650.00	850.00
☐	**29** Leaf motif, opaque black enamel, rose diamonds, silver-plated lever movement, ruby endstones, compensation balance, HC, 18K gold, maker: Ch. Suchy & Fils, c. 1880.	2800.00	3400.00

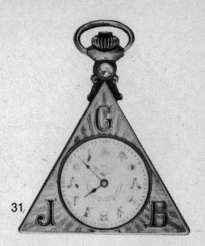

			Price Range	
☐	**30**	*Lion engraved motif, HC, 14K gold, American, c. 1896.*	600.00	800.00
☐		*Same as above but gold filled*	175.00	200.00
☐	**31**	*Masonic motif, 17 jewel, high grade movement, white porcelain dial, OF, silver, maker: Alpina, Swiss, c. 1900.*	800.00	1000.00
☐	**32**	*Miniature enamel of an angel and a putti, pink basse taille enamel background, engraved case, HC, 18K gold, Swiss, c. 19th.*	1200.00	1400.00
☐	**33**	*Miniature enamel of a putti, engraved case, front cover cutout, HC, maker: Adophe Huguenin, gold, Swiss, c. 19th.*	1200.00	1800.00

		Price Range	

☐ **34** *Octagonal motif, 108 round diamonds approx. 2.0 cts., OF, platinum, maker: Waltham, American, c. 1915.* **2000.00 2200.00**

☐ **35** *Open back motif, 23 jewel, highest quality railroad grade movement, OF, gold filled, maker: E. Howard Watch Co., Boston, U.S.A., c. 1910-20.* **350.00 450.00**

☐ **36** *Plain motif, white enamel dial, Roman numerals, rose diamond hands, maker: Paul Hri. Matthey, HC, 18K gold, Swiss, c. 19th.* **800.00 1000.00**

☐ **37** *Plain motif, HC, 14K gold, American, c. 1896* **450.00 500.00**

☐ *Same as above but gold filled* **150.00 200.00**

			Price Range	
☐	**38**	Plain motif with initial shield, HC, 14K gold approx. c. 1896....................................	450.00	500.00
☐		Same as above but gold filled................	125.00	150.00
☐	**39**	Plain motif, OF, polished dial, raised Arabic numerals, 18 jewel movement, retailed by A. B Greswald & Co., New Orleans, Louisiana, maker: Patek Philippe & Co., movement No. 182861, platinum, Swiss, c. 1925.	1000.00	1400.00
☐	**40**	Repeater: minute with chronograph, star motif, rose diamonds, glazed movement with lever escapement, enamel dial, gilt hands, HC, 5.8CM, inscribed: Invicta Chronographe, Geneva, c. 1900. ...	6000.00	8000.00
☐	**41**	Repeater: minute with chronograph, horse, dog and crescent motif, rose diamonds, glazed movement with lever escapement, enamel dial, gilt hands, HC, 6CM, 18K gold, Liege, c. 1906........	6000.00	8000.00
☐	**42**	Repeater: minute with split second chronograph, 21 jewel, high grade movement, white porcelain face, OF, 14K gold, maker: Patek, Philippe & Co., Geneva, Switzerland, c. 1900.	7000.00	9000.00

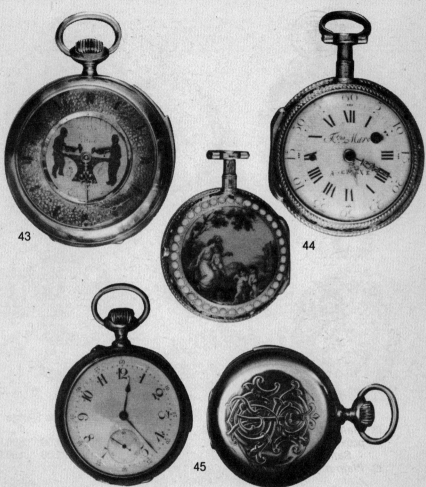

			Price Range	
☐	**43**	*Repeater: quarter hour, Jaquemar, standard better grade movement, gold hands, OF, gold, maker: Vacheron, Swiss, c. 1900. . . . .*	3800.00	4200.00
☐	**44**	*Repeater: quarter hour, verge movement, three color gold, miniature enamel of lady and angels, white enamel dot border, OF, gold, Geneva, Switzerland, c. 1794. . . . .*	4400.00	5400.00
☐	**45**	*Repeater: minute with chronometer, dust cover engraved "Frtiz Piquet & Bachmann, Geneve, Number 9997, Chronometer . . . Repetition heures quarts et minutes - 31 Rubis," OF, 18K gold, Swiss, c. 1900. . . . .*	2800.00	3200.00

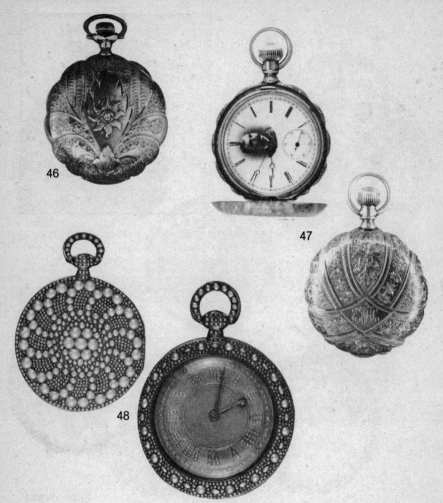

			Price Range	
☐	**46**	*Scalloped edge with applied three color gold flower motif, one round diamond, case number 6366717, movement number 15174777, 15 jewels, HC, 15K gold, maker: Waltham, American, c. 1892.*	1500.00	1800.00
☐	**47**	*Scalloped edge with photo on dial, engine turned and engraved case, white enamel dial, Roman numerals, maker: Elgin National Watch Co., movement No. 3792051, HC, gold, American, c. 1889-1900.*	650.00	850.00
☐	**48**	*Seed pearls pavé, high grade lever movement, fusee, jeweled, OF, gold, English, c. 1830-60.*	14000.00	16000.00

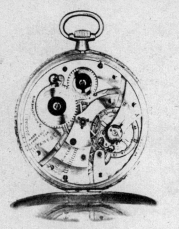

49

50

51

52

			Price Range	
☐	**49**	Skeleton motif, New England skeleton duplex escapement, seven jewel, OF, 16 size, silveroid, c. early 20th.	300.00	325.00
☐	**50**	Square opaque enamel watch, rose diamonds, white porcelain face, OF, matching oval plaque chatelaine top, two slides, seal and key, fox-tail chain, gold, c. 1850.	5400.00	5800.00
☐		Same as above but chain only	700.00	900.00
☐	**51**	Stag and scalloped edged motif, engraved, HC, 14K gold, American, c. 1896.	650.00	850.00
☐		Same as above but gold filled.	175.00	200.00
☐	**52**	Stop watch mechanism under back cover manufactured by H. A. Lugrin, movement by Waltham no. 1,010,474, OF, 18K gold, American, c. 1879. . . .	1800.00	2000.00

			Price Range	
☐	**53**	Time zone motif for three time zones, 18 jewel, adjusted eight, OF, 12 size, 18K gold, maker: unsigned Ekegrin, c. 1900........................	900.00	1200.00
☐	**54**	Train and flower engraved motif, HC, 14K gold, American, c. 1896.	650.00	850.00
☐		Same as above but gold filled.................	175.00	200.00

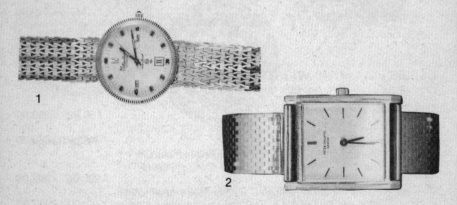

GENTLEMEN'S · WRISTWATCHES

☐	**1**	Round motif, calendar, dial marked "Automatique Seashark," marker: Lucién Piccard, No. 47093, 14K gold dial, 18K gold flattened wishbone link bracelet, 88.7 grams, Swiss, c. 20th	1200.00	1500.00
☐	**2**	Rectangular motif, maker: Patek Philippe, 18K gold, Swiss, c. 20th	1300.00	1500.00

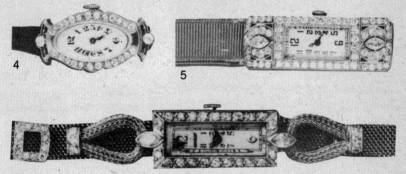

LADIES - DIAMOND WRISTWATCHES   Price Range

☐ **1** *Cushion-shape geometric motif, 32 round diamonds approx. .50 ct., two calibre French-cut black onyx, platinum, Art Deco, c. 1920* 850.00   1200.00

☐ **2** *Octagonal geometric motif, diamonds, sapphires, platinum, c. 1930.* 1200.00   1400.00

☐ **3** *Oval geometric motif, round diamonds, calibre and round sapphires, platinum, Art Deco, signed: Tiffany & Co., c. 1920.* 2400.00   2600.00

☐ **4** *Oval geometric motif, round diamonds, gold, maker: Patek Philippe, c. 1920* 1800.00   2000.00

☐ **5** *Rectangular geometric motif, 66 round and two marquise-shape diamonds approx. 2.25 cts., fancy-shape cabochon black onyx, platinum, Art Deco, c. 1920.* 1800.00   2000.00

☐ **6** *Rectangular geometric motif, two marquise-shape diamonds and round diamonds approx. .70 ct., platinum, Art Deco, maker: Nicolet, c. 1910* 1000.00   1200.00

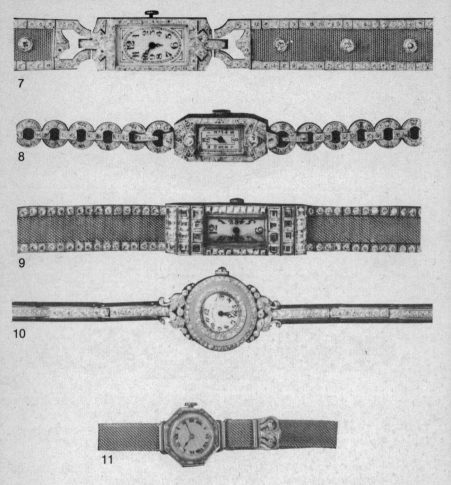

			Price Range	
☐	**7**	Rectangular geometric motif, four French-cut diamonds, and round diamonds approx. 5.25 cts., platinum, Art Deco, c. 1910.	4200.00	4600.00
☐	**8**	Rectangular geometric motif, diamonds, 14K gold, Art Deco, c. 1930	1500.00	1700.00
☐	**9**	Rectangular geometric motif, 29 square-cut diamonds approx. 5.25 cts., 112 round diamonds approx. 2.75 cts., 18 French-cut diamonds, platinum, Art Deco, c. 1925.	8000.00	9000.00
☐	**10**	Round flower motif, 125 round diamonds approx. 3.0 cts., platinum, movement: Meylan, signed: Tiffany & Co., c. 1915.	3500.00	4000.00
☐	**11**	Round geometric motif, maker: Rolex, 18K gold, Swiss, c. 1930.	850.00	1200.00

12

13

14

15

		Price Range	
☐	**12** *Round geometric motif, four round diamonds, 24 rose diamonds, platinum, maker: Agassiz, c. 1920. .*	1500.00	1700.00
☐	**13** *Square geometric motif, 64 round diamonds approx. 1.26 cts., 20 baguette diamonds approx. 1.06 cts., 14K white gold, maker: Hamilton, 22 jewels, Art Deco, c. 1930. . . . .*	3200.00	3400.00
☐	**14** *Square geometric motif, six rubies, six diamonds, maker: National, gold, American, Art Deco, c. 1935*	375.00	425.00
☐	**15** *Flower motif with rose diamonds, engraved case, HC, keywind movement, maker: American Waltham Watch Company, gold, American, c. 19th. . . .*	650.00	850.00

LADIES - PENDANT.   **Price Range**

☐ **1** *Angel motif, chased, OF, 14K gold, Art Nouveau,*
   with Jack-in-the-Pulpit flower motif brooch with
   watch loop, one fresh water pearl, 14K gold, Art
   Nouveau, c. 1895. .... **1000.00 1400.00**
☐   *Same as above but watch brooch only* **160.00   180.00**
☐ **2** *Angel motif, cobalt blue and pink enamel, mvt. no.*
   117876, retailed by: Shreve, Crump & Low, maker:
   Patek Philippe, gold, Swiss, c. 19th. **2700.00 3000.00**
☐ **3** *Art Deco motif, blue and green enamel, white*
   matte dial, Arabic numeral, 18K gold, Swiss,
   c. 1930. .... **1200.00 1400.00**
☐ **4** *Art Deco motif, blue enamel case with black*
   enamel border, marcasites in case and watch
   brooch, round dial, marked "L. Eight Mayer,
   Lucerne," silver, Swiss, c. 1920. ....   **250.00   300.00**
☐   *Same as above but watch brooch only.* **60.00   80.00**

			Price Range	
☐	5	*Ball motif, rose diamonds in platinum flowers, blue enamel, blue enamel silver link chain, OF, c. 1900.*	2600.00	2800.00
☐	6	*Bird engraved motif, fancy-shape case number 489754, HC, 14K gold, movement maker: Lady Newport, c. 1900.*	650.00	750.00
☐	7	*Bird and flower motif, engraved, HC, 14K gold, American, c. 1896.*	450.00	550.00
☐	8	*Bird and flower motif, five rose diamonds, HC, 12K gold, c. late 19th.*	500.00	600.00
☐	9	*Bird and twig motif, one round ruby in eye, nine round emeralds, 27 round diamonds, HC, 14K gold, American, c. 1896.*	1600.00	1800.00

10   11   13   12   14

Price Range

☐ **10** *Chain and watch, watch is guilloché dove grey enamel with rose diamonds in platinum and cabochon sapphire in crown, chain is fetter and three links spaced with guilloché dove grey enamel baton links, OF, gold, maker: Bailey, Banks and Biddle Co., American, c. 1910.* 1700.00 1900.00

☐ **11** *Chain and watch, watch is guilloché blue green enamel with cabochon sapphire in crown, chain is fetter and three links spaced with four guilloché blue green enamel baton links, OF, gold, maker: Black, Starr and Frost, American, c. 1910.* 850.00 1000.00

☐ **12** *Chain and watch, watch is guilloché blue enamel with cabochon sapphire in crown, chain is alternating trace links with fancy shape guilloché blue enamel links, OF, gold, maker: Tiffany & Co., American, c. 1880.* 1700.00 1900.00

☐ **13** *Chain and watch, watch is guilloché blue and white enamel with seven rose diamonds, chain is alternating curb links with baton guilloché blue and white enamel links, OF, gold, c. 1880.* 1800.00 2000.00

☐ **14** *Chain and watch, watch is guilloché blue enamel with one round diamond, chain is rectangular thin links spaced with baton guilloché blue enamel links with seed pearl terminals, OF, gold, maker: Marcus and Co., American, c. 1900.* 2200.00 2400.00

15

16

17

18

		Price Range	
☐	**15** Chain and watch, watch is guilloché green enamel with diamonds in platinum, white enamel dial, chain is trace links spaced with guilloché green enamel baton links and seed pearls, OF, 18K gold, Swiss, c. 1880.	2400.00	2600.00
☐	**16** Chain and watch, watch is guilloché blue enamel with a white gold rosette with diamond chips and one round diamond on reverse case, white enamel dial, chain is fetter and three links spaced with blue enamel oval links, OF, Longines, gold, Swiss, c. 1920.	1500.00	1700.00
☐	**17** Crescent and star motif, six round diamonds, HC, 14K gold, American, c. 1896	850.00	950.00
☐	**18** Diamond geometric motif, one round diamond approx. .70 ct., 167 round and eight baguette diamonds approx. 5.0 cts., OF, platinum, maker: Huguenin, c. 1925.	4400.00	4800.00

<table>
<tr><td></td><td></td><td></td><td>Price Range</td><td></td></tr>
</table>

			Price Range	
☐	19	Diamond motif, two round diamonds approx. 2.20 cts., 32 round diamonds, OF, gold, platinum, maker: Tiffany & Co., with rose diamond and fancy-cut black onyx bow motif brooch with watch loop, gold, platinum, c. 1900.	7800.00	8400.00
☐	20	Engraved edge motif, HC, 14K gold, American, c. 1896	475.00	575.00
☐		Same as above but OF and gold filled	125.00	150.00
☐	21	Fleur-de-lys rose diamond motif, translucent blue enamel, HC, 14K gold, with fleur-de-lys diamond motif brooch with watch loop, 14K gold, c. early 20th.	2400.00	2600.00
☐		Same as above but watch brooch only	675.00	775.00
☐	22	Flower motif, repoussé blue and lavender enamel, five diamonds, white porcelain dial with blue Arabic numbers, retailed by "Schumann's Sons, New York," with flower motif brooch, 18K gold, Art Nouveau, Swiss, c. 1890-1910.	2200.00	2600.00
☐		Same as above but watch brooch only.	325.00	375.00

			Price Range	
☐	**23**	Flower basket motif, chased, OF, 18K gold, with flower motif brooch with watch loop, 18K gold, c. 1860.	1500.00	1700.00
☐		Same as above but watch brooch only	225.00	275.00
☐	**24**	Flower engraved motif, HC, 14K gold, American, c. 1896.	550.00	650.00
☐		Same as above but OF and gold filled	100.00	125.00
☐		Same as above but gold filled.	150.00	200.00
☐	**25**	Flower motif, one border of rose diamonds, two rows of rubies, ruby thumb piece, white porcelain dial, Roman numerals, "West End Watch Co.," with diamond and platinum brooch with watch loop, 18K gold, Art Deco, Swiss, c. 1935.	750.00	950.00
☐		Same as above but watch brooch only.	200.00	225.00
☐	**26**	Flower motif, two round rubies, ten round emeralds, 14 round diamonds, HC, 14K gold, American, c. 1896.	1700.00	2000.00

		Price Range	
☐	**27** Flower motif, chased, OF, 18K gold, two round diamonds, lever escapement, 19 jewel, white porcelain face, Art Nouveau, Swiss, with carved flower motif brooch with watch loop, 18K gold, Art Nouveau, c. 1890.	2200.00	2400.00
☐	*Same as above but watch brooch only*	250.00	300.00
☐	**28** Flower motif, guilloche translucent cobalt blue and black enamel, rose diamonds, keywind, HC, 18K gold, maker: Patek, c. 1860, with cobalt blue enamel brooch with watch loop, rose diamonds, 14K gold.	2000.00	2400.00
☐	*Same as above but watch brooch only*	340.00	380.00
☐	**29** Flower motif, chased, OF, 14K gold, with peacock motif translucent enamel brooch with watch loop, 14K gold, Art Nouveau, c. 1900.	4000.00	4200.00
☐	*Same as above but watch brooch only*	3400.00	3600.00

			Price Range	
☐	**30**	Flower motif, guilloché blue enamel, gold and silver wire overlaid, seven rose diamonds, OF, gold, maker: Schumann's Sons, New York, c. early 20th. .	1400.00	1600.00
☐	**31**	Flower motif in gold and silver, guilloché green enamel face and rear cover, OF, silver gilt, Swiss, with wreath motif brooch with watch loop, gold, c. 1880.	440.00	480.00
☐		Same as above but watch brooch only	100.00	125.00
☐	**32**	Flower motif, multi-colored enamel, OF, 18K gold, maker: Henri Capt, c. late 19th	1500.00	1700.00
☐	**33**	Flower diamond motif, guilloché lavender enamel, OF, gold, c. 1900.	1700.00	1900.00
☐	**34**	Flower lily-of-the-valley motif, six round diamonds, HC, 14K gold, American, c. 1896	850.00	1000.00

35

36

37

39

38

			Price Range	
☐	**35**	*Flower and wreath motif, engraved and engine turned case, bar movement by Henry Beguelin, HC, 18K gold, Swiss, c. 1880.*	475.00	575.00
☐	**36**	*Flower with peacock engraved motif, HC, 14K gold, American, c. 1896*	550.00	650.00
☐		*Same as above but gold filled.*	175.00	200.00
☐	**37**	*Flower and scalloped edge motif, guilloché translucent blue enamel, rose diamonds, OF, gold, maker: R. F., with guilloché translucent blue enamel fleur-de-lys motif brooch with watch loop, c. 1880.*	1300.00	1500.00
☐	**38**	*Flower wreath of opaque black enamel, engraved mountain scene, case number 14210, HC, 14K rose gold, maker: H. Montandon, Locle, Switzerland, c. 1900.*	800.00	1000.00
☐	**39**	*Garland motif, OF, gold, c. late 19th*	425.00	450.00

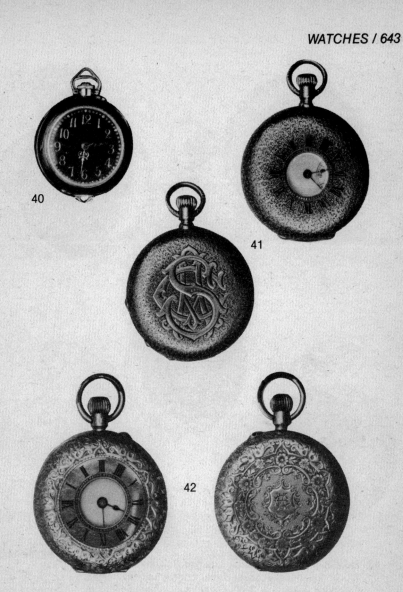

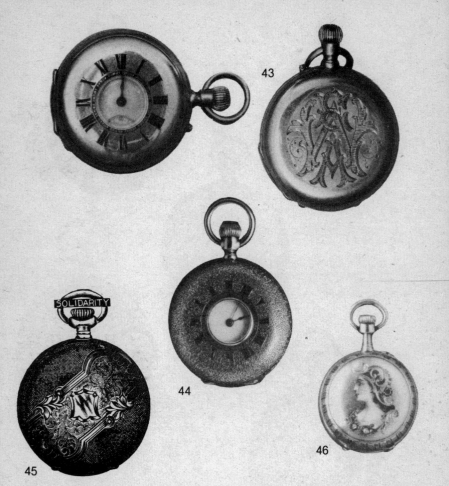

43

44

45

46

			Price Range	
☐	**43**	*Half-hunter motif, black enamel Roman numerals, white enamel dial, dust cover engraved "Howard & Co. New York No. 3595 Geneve E. Legrand Fabricant," gold, Swiss, c. 1900.*	550.00	650.00
☐	**44**	*Half-hunter motif, black enamel Roman numerals, white enamel dial, 18K gold, c. late 19th*	500.00	600.00
☐	**45**	*Initial shield engraved motif, HC, 14K gold, American, c. 1896.*	475.00	575.00
☐		*Same as above but OF and gold filled*	100.00	125.00
☐		*Same as above but gold filled.*	150.00	175.00
☐	**46**	*Miniature champlevé enamel of a lady, white enamel dial, three rose diamonds, OF, gold, marked: SG, c. mid 19th.*	850.00	1000.00

			Price Range	
☐	**47**	Key wind watch, white enamel dial, Roman numerals, black enamel on case reverse, OF, 18K gold, Swiss, c. 19th....................................	350.00	450.00
☐	**48**	Miniature enamel of a lady with a gold enamel wreath and guilloche translucent red enamel background, seed pearl border, OF, silver, with matching guilloché translucent red enamel bow motif brooch with watch loop, silver, c. early 20th.	990.00	1000.00
☐		Same as above but watch brooch only	120.00	140.00
☐	**49**	Miniature enamel of a lady, guilloché translucent green enamel, HC, gold, with Art Nouveau motif brooch with watch loop, one round peridot, gold, c. 1880.	1500.00	1700.00
☐		Same as above but watch brooch only	260.00	280.00

			Price Range	
☐	**50**	Miniature enamel of an angel, guilloche green enamel, rose diamonds, OF, 14K gold, with guilloché green enamel fleur-de-lys motif brooch with watch loop, nine rose diamonds, 14K gold, c. 1895.	2500.00	2700.00
☐		Same as above but watch brooch only	360.00	380.00
☐	**51**	Miniature enamel of a lady and lamb on one side and miniature enamel of lovers on other side, seed pearl border, HC, gold, case is French, medium grade cylinder movement is Swiss, c. 1860.	3400.00	3800.00
☐	**52**	Miniature enamel of a swan and tiger lily flower, rose diamonds, three seed pearls, OF, gold, Swiss, c. 1900.	1500.00	1600.00
☐	**53**	Miniature engraved head of a lady, opaque black enamel, keywind, patent lever movement number 20567, 15 jewels, HC, 14K gold, maker: James Tissot, c. 1860.	850.00	1000.00

54

55

56

57

58

		Price Range	
☐	**54** Oval round and rose diamond motif center, guilloche translucent steel grey and opaque white enamel, rose diamond bow, OF, gold, maker: Tiffany & Co., matching brooch with watch loop, gold, c. early 20th.	1600.00	1800.00
☐	**55** Plain motif, HC, 14K gold, American, c. 1896	400.00	450.00
☐	**56** Purse watch, black enamel, opening and closing the sliding case winds the watch, face marked "Chronometer, Movado," silver, Swiss, c. 1930. . . .	325.00	425.00
☐	**57** Purse watch, black enamel, case slides open, maker: Movado, silver, Swiss, c. 1930.	325.00	425.00
☐	**58** Ribbed edge motif, HC, 14K gold, American, c. 1896.	450.00	550.00
☐	Same as above but OF and gold filled	150.00	175.00

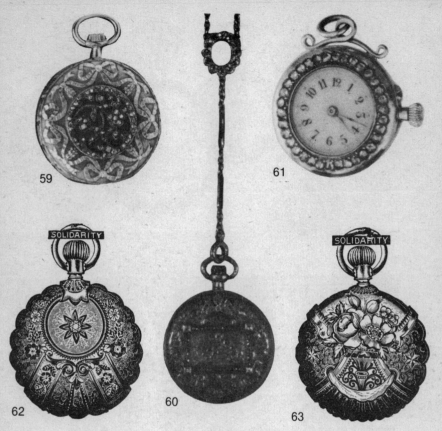

59

61

62

60

63

			Price Range	
☐	**59**	*Ribbon wreath and flower motif, rose diamonds, translucent green enamel, OF, gold, maker: Tiffany & Co., c. 1880.*	2500.00	2800.00
☐	**60**	*Ribbon wreath and flower motif, pale green basse taille enamel, rose diamonds, OF, Arabic numerals, sapphire thumbpiece, chain is fetter and five links spaced with pale green enamel baton links and centered on a diamond circle, Tiffany & Company, 18K gold, Swiss, c. late 19th.*	3000.00	3200.00
☐	**61**	*Rose diamond border, white porcelain face, case number 13051, OF, 14K gold, c. 1900*	500.00	600.00
☐	**62**	*Scalloped edge motif, three color gold applied flowers, one round diamond, HC, 14K gold, American, c. 1896.*	1600.00	1800.00
☐	**63**	*Scalloped edge and engraved flower motif, HC, 14K gold, American, c. 1896*	650.00	850.00
☐		*Same as above but gold filled.*	175.00	200.00

64

65

66

67

68

			Price Range	
☐	64	*Seed pearls pavé, HC, 18K gold, c. 1900*	2400.00	2800.00
☐	65	*Star motif, rose diamonds, seed pearl border, OF, 18K gold, French, c. 1870*	1000.00	1200.00
☐	66	*Star motif, one round diamond, HC, 14K gold, American, c. 1896.*	750.00	950.00
☐	67	*Teardrop motif, OF, enamel dial, rose diamonds, dust cover marked "LaForge Besancox," gold, Swiss, Art Nouveau, c. 19th.*	2200.00	2400.00
☐	68	*Travel watch, cabochon sapphire, blue enamel, white porcelaine dial, 15 jewel Swiss movement, maker: Cartier, French.*	3800.00	4000.00

INDEX

The index is designed to assist in the location of specific motifs of jewelry as well as locating periods, materials, jewelers, etc. The index does not include the different cuts of stones, the location of silver, gold or platinum jewelry or a designation of American vs. English jewelry, due to the fact that these items appear on almost every page. It should also be noted that specific periods of jewelry, such as Arts and Crafts Mvt., Art Nouveau, Victorian, Edwardian, etc., are only listed with a few examples to indicate the more prominent examples listed in the book. All pearls which are identified in the text are to be considered cultured pearls unless stated otherwise.

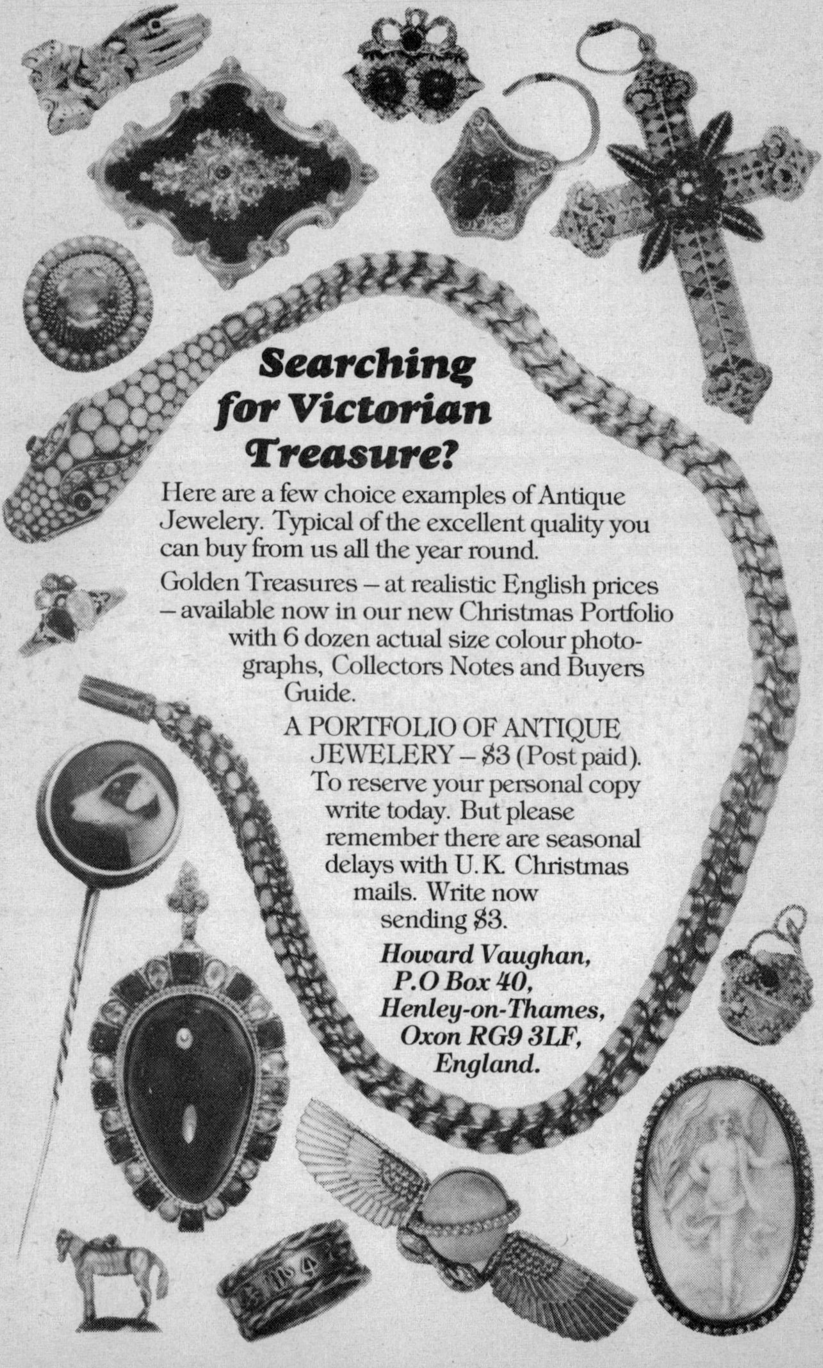

Searching for Victorian Treasure?

Here are a few choice examples of Antique Jewelery. Typical of the excellent quality you can buy from us all the year round.

Golden Treasures — at realistic English prices — available now in our new Christmas Portfolio with 6 dozen actual size colour photographs, Collectors Notes and Buyers Guide.

A PORTFOLIO OF ANTIQUE JEWELERY — $3 (Post paid). To reserve your personal copy write today. But please remember there are seasonal delays with U.K. Christmas mails. Write now sending $3.

Howard Vaughan,
P.O Box 40,
Henley-on-Thames,
Oxon RG9 3LF,
England.

Please send me the following price guides. I would like the most current edition of the books listed below.

THE OFFICIAL PRICE GUIDES TO:

☐ 465-8	American Silver & Silver Plate 4th Ed.	10.95
☐ 482-8	Antique Clocks 3rd Ed.	10.95
☐ 283-3	Antique & Modern Dolls 3rd Ed.	10.95
☐ 287-6	Antique & Modern Firearms 6th Ed.	11.95
☐ 271-X	Antiques & Other Collectibles 6th Ed.	9.95
☐ 289-2	Antique Jewelry 5th Ed.	11.95
☐ 270-1	Beer Cans & Collectibles, 3rd Ed.	11.95
☐ 262-0	Bottles Old & New 9th Ed.	10.95
☐ 255-8	Carnival Glass 1st Ed.	10.95
☐ 453-4	Collectible Cameras 2nd Ed.	10.95
☐ 277-9	Collectibles of the Third Reich 2nd Ed.	10.95
☐ 454-2	Collectible Toys 2nd Ed.	9.95
☐ 490-9	Collector Cars 6th Ed.	11.95
☐ 267-1	Collector Handguns 3rd Ed.	11.95
☐ 459-3	Collector Knives 7th Ed.	10.95
☐ 266-3	Collector Plates 4th Ed.	11.95
☐ 476-3	Collector Prints 6th Ed.	11.95
☐ 489-5	Comic Books & Collectibles 8th Ed.	9.95
☐ 433-X	Depression Glass 1st Ed.	9.95
☐ 472-0	Glassware 2nd Ed.	10.95
☐ 492-5	Hummel Figurines & Plates 5th Ed.	9.95
☐ 451-8	Kitchen Collectibles 2nd Ed.	10.95
☐ 460-7	Military Collectibles 4th Ed.	10.95
☐ 268-X	Music Collectibles 5th Ed.	11.95
☐ 491-7	Old Books & Autographs 6th Ed.	10.95
☐ 452-6	Oriental Collectibles 2nd Ed.	11.95
☐ 461-5	Paper Collectibles 4th Ed.	10.95
☐ 276-0	Pottery & Porcelain 5th Ed.	11.95
☐ 263-9	Radio, T.V. & Movie Memorabilia 2nd Ed.	11.95
☐ 288-4	Records 7th Ed.	7.95
☐ 485-2	Royal Doulton 4th Ed.	10.95
☐ 418-6	Science Fiction & Fantasy Collectibles 1st Ed.	10.95
☐ 477-1	Wicker 3rd Ed.	10.95

THE OFFICIAL:

☐ 445-3	Collector's Journal 1st Ed.	4.95
☐ 413-5	Identification Guide to Glassware 1st Ed.	9.95
☐ 448-8	Identification Guide to Gunmarks 2nd Ed.	9.95
☐ 412-7	Identification Guide to Pottery & Porcelain 1st Ed.	9.95
☐ 415-1	Identification Guide to Victorian Furniture 1st Ed.	9.95

THE OFFICIAL (POCKET SIZE) PRICE GUIDES TO:

☐ 473-9	Antiques & Flea Markets 3rd Ed.	3.95
☐ 442-9	Antique Jewelry 2nd Ed.	3.95
☐ 264-7	Baseball Cards 5th Ed.	4.95
☐ 488-7	Bottles 2nd Ed.	4.95
☐ 468-2	Cars & Trucks 2nd Ed.	4.95
☐ 260-4	Collectible Americana 1st Ed.	4.95
☐ 294-9	Collectible Records 3rd Ed.	4.95
☐ 469-0	Collector Guns 2nd Ed.	4.95
☐ 474-7	Comic Books 3rd Ed.	3.95
☐ 486-0	Dolls 3rd Ed.	4.95
☐ 292-2	Football Cards 5th Ed.	4.95
☐ 258-2	Glassware 2nd Ed.	4.95
☐ 487-9	Hummels 3rd Ed.	4.95
☐ 441-0	Military Collectibles 2nd Ed.	3.95
☐ 480-1	Paperbacks & Magazines 3rd Ed.	4.95
☐ 443-7	Pocket Knives 2nd Ed.	3.95
☐ 479-8	Scouting Collectibles 3rd Ed.	4.95
☐ 439-9	Sports Collectibles 2nd Ed.	3.95
☐ 494-1	Star Trek/Star Wars Collectibles 3rd Ed.	3.95
☐ 493-3	Toys 3rd Ed.	4.95

THE OFFICIAL BLACKBOOK PRICE GUIDES TO:

☐ 284-1	U.S. Coins 24th Ed.	3.95
☐ 286-8	U.S. Paper Money 18th Ed.	3.95
☐ 285-X	U.S. Postage Stamps 8th Ed.	3.95

THE OFFICIAL INVESTORS GUIDE TO BUYING & SELLING:

☐ 496-8	Gold, Silver and Diamonds 2nd Ed.	9.95
☐ 497-6	Gold Coins 2nd Ed.	9.95
☐ 498-4	Silver Coins 2nd Ed.	9.95
	TOTAL	

SEE REVERSE SIDE FOR ORDERING INSTRUCTIONS

FOR IMMEDIATE DELIVERY

VISA & MASTER CARD CUSTOMERS
ORDER TOLL FREE!
1-800-638-6460

This number is for orders only, it is not tied into the customer service or business office. Customers not using charge cards must use mail for ordering since payment is required with the order — sorry no C.O.D.'s.

OR SEND ORDERS TO ▍ ▍ ▍ ▍ ▍ ▍

THE HOUSE OF COLLECTIBLES, *PO BOX 149,*
WESTMINSTER, MD 21157   (301) 583-6959

——— POSTAGE & HANDLING RATE CHART———

TOTAL ORDER/POSTAGE	TOTAL ORDER/POSTAGE	
0 to $10.00 - **$1.25**	$20.01 to $30.00 - **$2.00**	$50.01 & Over -
$10.01 to $20.00 - **$1.60**	$30.01 to $40.00 - **$2.75**	**Add 10% of your total order**
	$40.01 to $50.00 - **$3.50**	(Ex. $75.00 x .10 = $7.50)

Total from columns on reverse side. Quantity_____ $ _____

☐ Check or money order enclosed $_____ (include postage and handling)

☐ Please charge $_____ to my: ☐ MASTERCARD ☐ VISA

Charge Card Customers Not Using Our Toll Free Number Please Fill Out The Information Below.

Account No. (All Digits) _____ Expiration Date _____

Signature_____

NAME (please print) _____ PHONE _____

ADDRESS _____ APT. # _____ ⑩

CITY _____ STATE _____ ZIP _____